Doctor Not Afraid

**ALSO BY
WINIFRED KELLERSBERGER VASS**

The Bantu Speaking Heritage of the United States
The African Heritage of American English
  with Joseph E. Holloway
The Lapsley Saga
  with Lachlan C. Vass III
Thirty-one Banana Leaves

IN THE BANTU VERNACULAR, TSHILUBA,
of Zaire, Africa

Geographie Muinayi
Anu Mu Nsumuinu
Bakaji, Tambulayi!
Mukanda Wetu Wa Nzambi
Nzubu Wa Kusambakena

Doctor Not Afraid

E.R. Kellersberger, M.D.

Winifred Kellersberger Vass

PROVIDENCE HOUSE PUBLISHERS
Franklin, Tennessee

First edition 1986
Second edition 1999

Printed in the United States of America

03   02   01   00   99   1   2   3   4   5

Library of Congress Catalog Card Number: 99-67574

ISBN: 1-57736-170-9

Cover design by Gary Bozeman

PROVIDENCE HOUSE PUBLISHERS
238 Seaboard Lane • Franklin, Tennessee 37067
800-321-5692
www.providencehouse.com

FOR

my husband

THE REVEREND LACHLAN CUMMING VASS III

with special love

for so uncomplainingly taking

a back seat to a book

Contents

Acknowledgments

With grateful heart I acknowledge my indebtedness to the following:

To Helen Schroeter Sundstrom, for her scholarly works on the Kellersberger family.

To Esther Richter Weaver, for information on the pioneer days of the Fuchs and Kellersberger families.

To Irma Goeth Guenther, for permission to use portions of her translation from the German of *Memoirs of a Texas Pioneer Grandmother*, by Ottilie Fuchs Goeth, Eugene Kellersberger's great aunt.

To the Bible Society of Geneva, Switzerland, for procuring from the authorities of the City of Baden, Switzerland, a photocopy of Page 159 of the *Baden State Book of Heraldry* (*Wappenbuch der Stadt Baden*), showing the Kellersberger coat-of-arms with description and family history.

To the authorities of the City of Baden, Switzerland, for their kind permission to use the reproduction of the Kellersberger coat-of-arms without limitation.

To Ursula V. Brown of Zurich, Switzerland, for her beautiful, hand-drawn reproduction of the Kellersberger coat-of-arms.

To Annie Kellersberger Schnelle, for sharing her childhood in delightful letters and conversations.

To Hubert. J. Schnelle, for permission to use his mother's book, *Yesterdays.*

To Mrs. Leslie McKay, Whitis Academy student, for insight into the contribution made by Miss Mollie Whitis and her school to her student, Eugene.

To the Moravian Archives in Winston-Salem, North Carolina, for information on Bishop Edward Rondthaler.

To the Library and Museum of the Moravian Historical Society of Nazareth, Pennsylvania, for the *Transactions of the Moravian Historical Society,* Volume X.

To William B. Ruggles, Editor Emeritus of *The Dallas Morning News,* Colonel, USAR (Retired) and Major General, Texas National Guard, for lively reminiscences of his boyhood days as next door neighbor to the Bosché family.

To Dewitt Reddick, Dean of the University of Texas College of Communication, for documenting the membership and activities of the Bosché family in the Highland Presbyterian Church of Austin, later called the University Presbyterian Church.

To Dr. Walter Shepard, for his architectural description of the Bosché home at 1402 West Avenue, Austin, Texas.

To Dr. and Mrs. Lloyd A. Doggett of Austin, for so graciously permitting exploration of the Bosché home, which they have so beautifully restored.

To B. Conn Anderson, Colonel, USA, Retired, for his recollections of the years he lived in the Bosché home as a University of Texas student.

To Philip Bosché Brown, for permission to use Winifred Bosché Brown's Washington College scrapbook and diary, and for help with naval terminology.

To Miss Edleen Begg, for sharing her memories and memorabilia of the Bosché family.

To Wilora Stockwell, for research done at The University of Texas Undergraduate Academic Center.

To Adolph G. Schlossstein for Dr. Kellersberger's Washington University School of Medicine academic record and copies of his articles contributed to the alumni publications.

To the Washington University Library, St. Louis, Missouri, for information on the history of the Washington University School of Medicine.

To Dr. Irene Koeneke of Halstead, Kansas, for insight into the contributions of Dr. Arthur Hertzler to Dr. Kellersberger's medical training.

To Dr. Paul Brand, Carville, Louisiana, for help with information pertaining to Hansen's Disease and its treatment.

To the American Leprosy Missions, Inc., for making their files and records available for research.

To Ruth D. See, Historical Foundation of the Presbyterian and Reformed Churches, Montreat, North Carolina, for information on Dr. Wylie Hamilton Forsythe.

To Martha Reid Bedinger, for permission to quote from *Light in Darkness*.

To Mrs. Boyd Stephenson and Bosque County Attorney, David Christian, for the original *Charge to the Jury*, given at the Bosché Trial.

To Attorney George Anderson, of Clifton, Texas, for answering many long-unanswered questions about the Bosché Trial at Meridian, Texas, in 1924.

To Brigitte Strubin of Basel, Switzerland, for translating into English all of Dr. Kellersberger's German letters to his parents.

To Stanton Ehrlich, for the *4th Annual Report of the Board of Commissioners of the Central Park*, filed in the museum library of the New York Historical Society, containing the November 23, 1860, report by Getulius Kellersberger to the Committee of Investigation of Central Park.

To all who read the manuscript in preparation and made practical suggestions, my grateful thanks: Helen Sundstrom, Julia Lake Kellersberger, my daughters, Edna Stucky, Julia Lake Dudley, Elizabeth Wilkerson, and Winifred Rutenbar; my nieces, Joyanne Burger and Rachel Venechanos; and friends, Virginia Pruitt, Mary Lou Tipton, Jack Stambaugh, the Charles Schechners, the Jack Tredrays, John Robert Stockwell, and Dr. William Stringfellow.

Dr. Eugene Kellersberger

Foreword

THE DIARIES OF DR. NOT AFRAID

There they stand—fifty of them ranged on the shelves—fifty worn journal-diaries covering the years 1916 to 1966.

Actually, there are fifty and a fraction, for there is also one small precursor of the mature records that would be kept in later years. It was discovered at the bottom of an old cedar chest, buried under a pile of crocheted doilies of another era, smelling of dried lavender. It is a slim, black *Memorandum* booklet in which Eugene Roland Kellersberger made entries from 1904 to 1906, while a student at the Whitis Academy in Austin, Texas.

The keen, enthusiastic observer is already evident in its miniature pages. The teenager records graphically the rousing visit of President "Teddy" Roosevelt to Austin. He describes the silent school holiday following the death of old Mrs. Whitis. He writes with pride of Austin's progress in paving Congress Avenue with brick, and tells of happy school outings at Barton Springs. He delights in fishing and swimming with his friends in the Pedernales River and camping in old Indian caves, with grinding stones and pottery still scattered about.

The youth conveys the same succinct savor of life that, in later diaries the mature man would display in describing a fearfully stormy, seventeen-day crossing of the North Atlantic on the venerable *Saxonia*, the physical sensations of being carried through the African forest in a hammock by two powerful

Baluba runners in answer to an emergency medical call, or his pride in the removal of an eighty-five-pound tumor. He would some day write with this same school-boy excitement of being a personal guest of King Farouk, as an official State Department delegate to the First World Leprosy Congress, held in Cairo, Egypt, in 1938, and of riding a diminutive Tibetan pony over precipitous Himalayan trails, to visit one of the most remote leprosariums in the world.

Dr. Kellersberger often quoted Mark Twain's saying: "The man who keeps a diary is either a great man or a fool." Then he would laughingly remark: "I am one of the 'fools' who keeps a diary!"

Who was this remarkable doctor, whose patients gave him the Tshiluba language name of *Bukitu*? The dictionary of this Bantu dialect gives the meaning of this word as: "bravery, courage, fortitude, boldness, valor." His leprosy patients marvelled: "He is NOT AFRAID TO TOUCH US!" Therefore his name—DR. NOT AFRAID.

The daily records that he kept tell his unique story.

[1]

A Heritage of Integrity

Cradled in the bend of the Limmat River, the quaint old Swiss town of Baden, a few miles northwest of Zurich, is well over a thousand years old. Its famous hot sulfur baths, called by Caesar's cohorts *Aquae Helvetiae* were enjoyed in ancient Roman times. Tacitus, writing during Nero's reign, described the location of the town and its appearance.

From the Middle Ages until the beginning of the fifteenth century, Baden was a fortress, the main residence of the princes of Hapsburg. *Schloss Stein,* their castle overlooking the city and the Limmat Valley, was destroyed first in 1415 and again in 1712.

The *Swiss Genealogical Almanach* affirms the Kellersbergers to be one of the ancient reigning families of the Old Swiss Confederacy, formed in the thirteenth century by the joining together of a group of Alpine States. A Kellersberger from Baden, Canton of Aargau, was Undersecretary and Officer of the Swiss State in 1391. Another held this same high office in 1600. Church records referring to the family, for the most part Roman Catholic, date from 1653.

The *Almanach* relates how the Alpine Ibex came to be on the family crest. A member of the family, living in medieval

1

Baden, in the bend of the Limmat River,
Canton of Aargau, Switzerland, 1840.

times, accompanied by his St. Bernard dog, scaled the heights inhabited by these nimble springbucks, in order to rescue three noble wayfarers, lost attempting to reach a high mountain pass in a snowstorm. In recognition of a proud family tradition of bold initiative and coolheaded courage, this symbol of daring agility on the steep mountain slopes became an integral part of the family coat-of-arms. The stained glass windows of the *Kapuziner Kirche* originally displayed the various emblems of the leading families of the old city. The church itself no longer stands, but the rare windows are all carefully preserved, set in the thick stone walls of the former bailiff's castle, which today houses the Baden Museum. The window depicting the Kellersberger crest may be seen among them. A picture of Dr. Eugene Kellersberger's grandfather, Julius Getulius Kellersberger, an honored city father, is the first thing visitors see on entering the foyer of the Museum.

THE SWISS ENGINEER

Julius Getulius Kellersberger was a robust, stocky five feet three inches tall, a man as sturdy of profession and character as he was of stature. He was born in Baden on February 9, 1821, the youngest of four sons, and was generally called by his middle name. He was well educated in the engineering and military sciences. From 1844 to 1849 he was director of iron works in Weiner-Neustadt, Austria, where he continued studies to improve his skills in surveying and construction.

On October 3, 1848, at the age of twenty-eight, he sailed from Hamburg, Germany, on the brig, *Hamburg*. Also aboard for this trans-Atlantic voyage was a Miss Carolina Bauch, a gifted pianist from Meklenburg-Schwerin, North Germany, who was taking her piano with her to pursue a musical career. She was accompanied by her widowed mother, a sister and a fifty-eight-year-old servant. The two latter members of her party died of cholera en route and were buried at sea.

By the time the ship docked at Galveston on December 15, Getulius and Carolina were engaged to be married. It was in the Johannes Romberg home in Black Jack Springs, Texas, that Getulius and his bride were wedded on January 16, 1850. The newlyweds left almost immediately for New York, where it is believed that the Swiss engineer was employed for a short time by the City of New York, as a surveyor for the Central Park project, begun in 1848. San Francisco, California, was his ultimate destination, however, for he wished to join his brother, Rudolf, serving as the Swiss Consul in that city.

The voyage of the bark *Steinwarder* from New York around Cape Horn to California lasted 277 days. Of this experience Getulius wrote: "By virtue of sheer boredom, I studied navigation and in a short time became useful to the captain. I looked after the logs, observations and calculations, which I enjoyed very much, without realizing that this would stand me in good stead later."

Three months were spent in the harbor of Valparaiso, Chile, repairing damage done to the vessel while rounding the icy, storm-ridden tip of South America. But that sojourn proved to be unexpectedly pleasant! One of the local wealthy estate-owners, on learning that Mrs. Kellersberger was an accomplished concert pianist, provided luxurious, free living quarters for the young couple in his *hacienda*. The one proviso was that Carolina play the piano every evening during and after dinner, for the enjoyment of their music-loving host, his family, and guests.

While in Valparaiso, Carolina was given an English *Bible* by a representative of the New York Bible Society. Recorded on the Family Record Page, between the Old and New Testaments, are the following entries in Getulius' handwriting, exactly as spelled:

> The 7th January, 1851, was born our little boy on bord the bark *Steinwarder* from Hamburg, in the North Pacific Ocean, under 23".24' latitude and 127.35 longitude. We gave him the name of Rudolf in honor of my brother.

> The Allmighty took away our little Rudolf the 29th Sept., 1851 after one week illness occasioned by teething. He was then old 8 months and 22 days. He lays in the grave 1375 in the cemetery in San Francisco.

> The first September 1854 was born a little girl in the City of Oakland, County of Alameda. We intend to give her the name of Emma.

> The 14th April 1856 was born a little boy in the City of San Francisco. We intend to give him the name of Julius Rudolf.

This last entry records the birth of Dr. Eugene Kellersberger's father, Julius. His baptismal certificate, dated May 15, 1857, is signed by the pastor of the First German Evangelical Church of San Francisco, the Reverend Adolf Kahn, with Getulius' brother, Rudolf, serving as godfather. It also bears the signature of Antoinette Rohn neé Kellersberger of Baden, Aargau, Switzerland, a sister who had joined her brother at the Swiss consulate in San Francisco.

After James Marshall caught the glitter of gold in the tailrace of Sutter's Mill in the Sierra foothills, and the 1000-ton paddlewheeler, *California*, entered the bay on February 28, 1849, bringing the first load of "49'ers," it seemed as if the whole world began to funnel through the Golden Gate into California! For Getulius, gold was not the attraction, but rather the full use of his profession as an engineer, surveyor and city-planner in a raw, new land bursting into civic and urban organization.

His first major employment was with the city of Oakland. The office of City Engineer was created for him by city ordinance on April 30, 1853. His recent experience in New York in city planning and the laying out of Central Park now stood him in good stead. His original map of Oakland, dated May 4, 1852, is preserved under glass in the mayor's office of that city.

On September 3, 1855, Getulius Kellersberger was appointed a United States deputy surveyor, working under Colonel Jack Hayes, the United States Surveyor General for California. His first contract, part of the establishment of the primary grid of the United States Land Office, covered about one hundred miles, and was for "extending the Humbolt Meridian from the point of its termination . . . north to or near the State Line; also, to extend the second standard line north . . . from said meridian West to the Pacific Ocean and East as far as it can be extended for accuracy."

This particular contract was a small one, disdained by other surveyors because of the extremely rugged terrain involved, the high degree of accuracy required, and the rapidity with which the task had to be completed — by February 1, 1856! Getulius wryly expressed his feelings about this first government contract by writing in his memoirs:* "We poor Swiss, who had no uncle sitting in Congress and no brother-in-law in the Senate, had to survey those lands which the Americans did not desire to do. But the position was a dignified one!"

A second, much larger government contract for extending the third standard north, the Mount Diablo Meridian, west to the Pacific Ocean was completed on September 30, 1856. It required ten times the number of surveys necessary for the first Humboldt project, for it covered a thousand miles. By the close of the same year, Getulius had also completed

---

* All quotes from the memoirs, translated from the original Swiss-German by Helen Sundstrom, are used with her permission.

maps for the *ranchos* of Vincente and Domingo Peralta, covering 16,970.68 acres.

He was closely involved in the actions and decisions of
the Vigilantes Committee during the years that he resided in
San Francisco. In his memoirs he recollected: "There were
neither police nor tribunals, and we had to defend ourselves
and our property as best we could . . . The Vigilantes Committee wrought a mighty and powerful influence for good in
the saga of California, because the Committee always knew
how to find the right and just middle ground between the excited mob and the corrupt official."

Carolina Kellersberger supported herself and her children during the long months that Getulius was away on his
surveying trips by giving piano lessons. The year 1856, however, brought an abrupt change in their lives. With the inauguration of President Buchanan and the triumph of the
"spoils system," not only Surveyor General Hays, but Deputy
Surveyor Kellersberger, lost his job. But a man of his professional calibre never lacked for work opportunities. He quickly
signed a three-year contract (1857–1860) with the Swiss company of Jecker, Torre and Company of Mexico City, to make
a preliminary survey for the construction of a railway across
the Isthmus of Tehuantepec to Vera Cruz.

Leaving his wife and three children in care of his brother,
Rudolf, he boarded a small sailing vessel for the Cape of San
Lucas, the southernmost tip of Baja California. High malarial
fevers delayed him for several days, before he could attempt
the overland journey of 800 miles to Tehuantepec. His party
traveled on horseback for twenty-four days, averaging thirty
to thirty-five miles a day. Arriving at Tehuantepec two
months later than scheduled, he was delighted to find his job
still awaiting him. The chief of the projected survey was none
other than Dr. August Sonntag, the Danish astronomer who
had accompanied Dr. Elisha Kent Kane on his Artic Expedi-
tions in 1850 and 1853 in search of the survivors of the Franklin Expedition.

Getulius' brother, Rudolf, mysteriously disappeared in
1858 and was never seen nor heard of again. He was a close
friend of his Swiss compatriot, Colonel Sutter, owner of Sut-

ter's Mill, where the first gold in California was discovered and had, himself, become involved in gold mining operations. His disappearance, labeled a possible suicide, was first noted in the September 11, 1858, issue of the *Daily Alta California*. Again, on October 1 of that year, this newspaper carried an article referring to his disappearance, this time denying the suicide report. The family always suspected foul play, for all the deeds to his mining concessions vanished at the same time.

Because of Rudolf's unexplained disappearance and her husband's extended absence in Mexico, Carolina decided to return to Texas with her children. Using the money from the sale of her piano, she paid the fare of $200 for the overland stagecoach journey from San Francisco to San Antonio, Texas. This six-week-long traverse of desert, mountain and Indian-infested territories was made in 1858 on one of the very first passages supervised by the Butterfield Coach Line. Safely arrived back in Texas, Carolina joined her mother, then living in LaGrange. The 1860 Census of Fayette County lists the Kellersbergers as residing there with members of the Bauch family.

There is a report in the New York Archives, written in 1860 by Getulius Kellersberger, evaluating the drainage system developed for Central Park. From this report it is surmised that, after the completion of his Mexican engineering contract, he may have been temporarily employed again by the City of New York.

On January 28, 1861, Texas seceded from the Union. Getulius took ship immediately from New York, entering Galveston Harbor on the very last vessel to arrive there before it was blockaded by a fleet of Yankee ships, anchored four miles out to sea. He enlisted at once in the Confederate Army as an engineer officer with the rank of captain. In February 1862, he received promotion to Major of Artillery, assigned to engineer duty. Recommendations by Major General Magruder for promotion and appointments, dated June 8, 1863, list him as lieutenant colonel.

As Confederate Chief Engineer for East Texas, Lieutenant Colonel Kellersberger was responsible for the construction of some twenty different coastal forts built between the Brazos and Sabine rivers, as well as for the defense of Austin.

When the city of Galveston was safely secured from Union hands, Getulius moved his family from Fayette County to be with him, as he continued his work with the Confederate Army. His two youngest daughters, Bertha and Mina, were both born in Galveston during the Civil War years.

General Lee's surrender to Grant at Appomattox, Virginia, on April 9, 1865, was followed by General Johnson's surrender to Sherman in North Carolina on April 26th. On May 4th, the Confederate forces of Alabama and Mississippi conceded. Finally, with Edmund Kirby Smith's surrender at Shreveport, Louisiana, of the Trans-Mississippi Confederate Troops, of which Getulius was a part, the Civil War came to a close.

As soon as possible, Getulius sent his entire family back to Switzerland, to obtain the best possible education, and also to spare them the bitter experiences of the reconstruction years that he knew lay ahead. He himself, after an honorable discharge from the Confederate Army, turned his face once again south toward Mexico. He accepted the position of surveyor-engineer with the railroad company then in process of constructing the line connecting Vera Cruz with Mexico City. He took passage from Galveston to New Orleans and from there, went to Vera Cruz on a small Italian sailboat. It was on this voyage that his previous navigational experience, gained on his Cape Horn journey, came in handy:

> As we reached the high sea, the captain placed two sextants on deck and asked the pilot to make a complete and thorough comparison of the instruments, in order that the sun's height might be calculated at noon and the latitude determined. The young pilot had undoubtedly never held such instruments in his hands; perspiration dropped from his face. He attempted to imitate the manipulations made by the captain, but without success. The captain, an uncultured Italian, was completely beside himself with anger and declared that we must turn back and that he would hire a pilot in New Orleans from the government.
>
> We passengers protested vigorously, for in this return

lay much more danger than continuing on our journey. I offered to take over the matter of the ship's calculations. The captain, however, did not believe that I could qualify. I took the sextant in hand and asked him to do likewise and determine the sun's height. He did so and we both arrived at the same angle.*

The result of this happy experience was that, on arriving at Vera Cruz, his entire passage money was refunded, amounting to one hundred francs in gold!

Work on the Mexican railroad, carried on during the revolution against Maximillian, was difficult and dangerous. The fact that Getulius very carefully scratched out the word "IMPERIAL" on the old "Imperial Mexican Railroad" locomotive used by the surveying party, actually saved his life. Only after Queretaro was vanquished, Maximillian dead, and Diaz had taken over, partially restoring order, was the Swiss engineer reimbursed in part for his salary.

Content with this, he returned to Switzerland where he was immediately employed by his native city of Baden to construct across the Limmat River the very first steel bridge in Europe. This bridge, still in use, was completed in 1871. He also served as city tax collector and was quite active in civic affairs. He is known to have throttled till blue in the face a Baden citizen caught cheating on his taxes! He had a tremendous gift for story-telling and could entertain his family and friends with tales of true-life adventures by the hour.

Julius, Dr. Kellersberger's father, was well prepared for business enterprise by an excellent education received in Switzerland. A picture of this solemn Swiss schoolboy shows him in his cadet's uniform, posing with his gun. He was nine years old when he arrived, fresh from his California and Texas background. He and his boyhood companion, Eugen Jeuch, loved nothing better than playing among the ruins of the old Hapsburg Castle. They crawled into dank dungeons where prisoners once languished and explored with schoolboy daring the maze of secret underground passages beneath the castle

---

* Translated from the original Swiss-German by Helen Sundstrom. Used by permission.

walls. Often they raced up the precipitous 500-yard-long stone stairway leading to the tiny gem of a medieval chapel dedicated to St. Nicholas, that crowns the ancient fortress at its summit. There the boys would rest a bit, letting the cool, alpine winds blow on their faces, looking out over the magnificent valley. In the distance they could see the old Cistercian Cloister of Wettingen, where Julius knew that his Kellersberger kin had ruled as high church fathers, seated in the famous "Bishop's Chair."

For three years, ages fifteen, sixteen, and seventeen inclusive, Eugene's father served an apprenticeship in the large Wegmann Factory on the banks of the Limmat. A letter of hearty recommendation given to him on September 4, 1875, written in flowing German script, has been preserved:

> We testify with pleasure that he worked for us as an apprentice for three years (September 1872–1875) in our bureau and all this time his morals and conduct were to our satisfaction. He was dutiful, responsible, prompt, diligent, and always willing. In this case we can recommend him unreservedly for any commerical or business house, the very best recommendation! We wish him in the future the best of luck and blessing with all our heart!
>
>   Wegmann and Company   BADEN

The young apprentice was also an excellent gymnast, like his father. The many medals that he won in various competitions throughout Europe are a treasured family possession.

Returning to the United States in 1877, Eugene's father worked for a year with a wholesale shipping company in Galveston, and then for three years with a firm in Schulenberg, Texas.

With his purchase in 1884 of the Cypress Mill facilities, Eugene's father became the central figure in a community that he served most effectively in many different capacities until his move to Fort Worth in 1911. He was store-owner, postmaster, gristmill, sawmill and cotton gin operator, local "doctor" and "dentist," called upon in many an emergency when those professionals were not available! Village barber, lodge leader of the German ethnic group called "The Sons of

Hermann," director of sharpshooter activities of the *Schuetsen Verein*, master of ceremonies of many an *Oktoberfest*, Julius Kellersberger, like his father, became a local figure dearly loved and appreciated by young and old alike.

THE GERMAN PASTOR

Eugene Kellersberger's maternal great-grandfather was the Reverend Adolf Fuchs of Guestrow, Germany, a sensitive and articulate Lutheran minister who had studied at the universities of Jena, Halle and Goettingen. Himself the son of a minister, the superintendent of the Guestrow Diocese, he was completely at home in classical Greek, Latin and Hebrew, as he also was in current French, English or his native German. Endowed with a beautiful voice, he was an accomplished violinist, as well as a gifted pianist and composer.

His farewell sermon preached to his congregation in Koelzow, Mecklenburg, Germany, on the eve of his departure for America rings with the idealism and dreams that uprooted him from his fatherland. The text of his final sermon was from the twelfth chapter of Genesis, Jehovah's words to Abraham: *Go from your country and from your kindred and your father's house to the land that I will show you. And I will make of you a great nation and I will bless you.*

As real as was the call to Abraham, so real did Adolf Fuchs feel was God's call to him to remove his family from the over-population, economic distress, corruption and military restrictions of the Germany of that era. Above all, he longed for complete freedom from the political fetters that bound his speech in the pulpit. His final words to his saddened flock were:

> Although I have never presented anything to you as being my own opinion unless it truly was; yes, even though I never lied to you, there were thousands and thousands of times when I had to remain silent concerning my inner convictions for reasons of prudence, for your sake as well as for my own. This is what I can no longer bear! . . . "And do you hope," I believe you will say, "that God will bless you there with freedom of belief, conscience and worship of

God, the most precious of assets, as well as with material
things? That, like Abraham, you even hope that God will
make you into a great nation, not only of large numbers of a
nation highly spiritual, intellectual, a religious and right-
eous people?" Yes! I do truly hope this! And did I not hope
this . . ., I could not honestly leave my Fatherland!

One of the fallen heroes of the Battle of San Jacinto in far
away Texas- was the German naturalist and author, Ferdi-
nand Lueders, assigned to do research for the Smithsonian Institute of Washington, D.C. The Republic of Texas, through
General Sam Houston, out of gratitude for Lueders' military
service and the sacrifice of his life, presented his heirs living in
Germany with "a league of land" (4,428.4 acres) in the large
Fisher-Miller Grant which lay between the Colorado and the
Llano rivers. Lueders' brother, the mayor of the city of Marlowe, Germany, had no intention of emigrating to Texas. In
1844 he presented the deed to this property to his beloved and
respected friend and pastor, the Reverend Adolf Fuchs.

On November 13, 1845, Pastor Fuchs with his wife, seven
children and two nephews, sailed from Bremen on the two-
masted sailing vessel, *Gerhard Hermann*. This was the fourth
shipload of some seven thousand German immigrants transported directly to Texas under the guidance of Prince Carl of
Solms-Braunfels and his Society of Noblemen, the *Adelsverein*.
The passenger list names Pastor Fuchs, his wife, Luise Ruem-
ker Fuchs, their children Luise, Ulrika (who was later to be
Eugene Kellersberger's grandmother), Conrad, Ottilie, Wilhelm, Adolfina and Hermann, as well as two young nephews,
Heinrich Fuchs and Ludwig Franke.

The children were kept well during the eight-week long
voyage by a dietary supplement of dried peaches that the parents had brought aboard. English classes, begun many
months before, were an important part of their daily shipboard schedule. The smell of dried peaches was closely associated for the rest of their lives with the queasy feeling of seasickness and the disparate conjugation of English verbs.

The stormy winter crossing finally ended at Galveston,
Texas, on January 10, 1846. While the ship was still on the
high seas, Texas had ceased to be an independent republic

and had become the twenty-eighth state to join the Union, with an estimated population of some one hundred and fifty thousand proud citizens.

Indianola on the Texas gulf coast was the usual point from which the German settlers started inland. Since an epidemic of fever was raging there, the family proceeded to Houston on a small sternwheeler called the *Laura M.* Ottilie Fuchs, in later years vividly described in her book, *Memoirs of a Texas Pioneer Grandmother,* the valiant struggle of the plucky little paddlewheeler through the dense, coastwise vegetation of Buffalo Bayou. The youthful members of the party enjoyed the novelty of watching the vigorous hacking and chopping with *machetes* that was necessary in order to force a passageway through the undergrowth.

Even more exciting was their father's purchase in Houston of the large wagon and five yoke of oxen that transported the family inland to Austin County. Enthusiastic nature-lover that he was, Father Fuchs noted in his journal the keen delight of his young charges in relishing food prepared over an open campfire. He also recorded the amazement of the entire family at the unexpected beauty of their new homeland. The leisurely pace of their cross-country journey, set by the patiently-plodding oxen, gave them hours in which to revel in the ever-unfolding vistas of flower-carpeted Texas in early spring.

Ascertaining that his land grant lay in a remote region of Texas still occupied and controlled by Indians, Pastor Fuchs decided to bide his time in a more populous area of the state. He bought a small farm near Cat Spring in the summer of 1846 and with the help of his sons, constructed a sturdy, two-room log cabin. A friendly neighbor, Mrs. Kleburg, will always be remembered for her cheerful and willing assistance to Mrs. Fuchs and her daughters, in sharing her knowledge of the ways of turning a rough pioneer shelter into a comfortable home. The first Christmas celebrated in their new surroundings was indeed a strange one. Ottilie recalled that the large cedar limb her father nailed to a stump had as its only decorations yellow wax candles and small molasses cookie figures baked by the two older girls.

During those early, difficult years of their family venture, when ready money was so scarce, the sale of one of Adolf's old Meerschaum pipes for about thirty dollars provided needed cash for some emergency. The sheer drudgery of hard, physical labor, the lack of certain foods and household items that they had taken quite for granted in the old country, and the loneliness and isolation of pioneer life were all forgotten in the evenings when parents and children gathered on the front porch for family worship and song. Their favorite pastime of making up songs and harmonizing together as a family always brought the most trying day to a cheerful close.

Better suited by temperament and training to pedagogy and the pulpit than the plow, Pastor Fuchs left the heavier tasks of his new pioneer life to his sons and nephews and devoted his attention to education and the arts. On October 29, 1849, four years after Texas had adopted its state constitution, he presented to the Texas legislature a petition for a state-supported school at Cat Spring. His speech to that assembly, preserved in the Archives of the Texas State Library, expresses his firm conviction that "English schools are undeniably the best way to Americanize the German population of Texas and to make good citizens of them."

The Reverend Fuchs was one of the first members of the faculty of Baylor Female College in Independence, Texas. He also had numerous music pupils in the homes of the wealthy plantation owners up and down the Brazos River. His daughter, Ottilie, recollected that whenever cash was scarce at home, her father provided for his family by "taking a tuning trip." He was always a welcome guest in any home where he cared to stop: "When Fuchs, the craftsman, had finished tuning the piano, then 'Mr. Fox,' the artist, sat down to play. The appreciation of his music meant a great deal more to him than any money he earned."

Often he sang the rousing Texas songs with verses written by Hoffman von Fallersleben, that he and his friend Kleburg had translated into English. One of his favorite renditions was "The Star of Texas," especially composed as a musical farewell when he left Germany, and dedicated to him by Fallersleben in memory of their shared boyhood delight in the novels of James Fenimore Cooper.

In 1853 the Lueders land grant was finally cleared for occupancy with the assistance of the surveyor, De Cordova, who received a third of the 4,428.4 acres in payment for his services. Pastor Fuchs sold two tracts of 600 acres each for a very low price. He retained one tract of 1000 acres on the Clear Fork of the Brazos River, where the town of Lueders is located in Jones County, north of Abilene, today. He also retained a section of 602 acres along the south bank of the Colorado River. It was to this Burnet County acreage that he moved his family in 1853. Among the possessions transported by wagon to the new homesite was a piano, the first in all that area.

Two members were lost from the family circle during the eight-year waiting period at Cat Spring, one by death and one by marriage. Louise, the oldest daughter, died at the age of seventeen. Ulrika, Eugene Kellersberger's grandmother, who had left Germany at the age of thirteen, was married to a young Bavarian craftsman. He was Carl Andreas Matern, born in Baden, in the German Schwarzwald.

Eugene's grandparents met at a Fourth of July picnic celebration held in Bellville for all the surrounding communities. Standing amidst the crowd, talking beside the smoking pits of mouth-watering Texas-style barbecue in preparation, the handsome forester and the minister's daughter both knew that they had discovered the lifetime partner they had been searching for. Carl had made the trans-Atlantic crossing on the *Johann Dethardt*, landing at Galveston on September 16, 1844.

A skilled carpenter and wood-carver, he was one of the original twenty-five men especially selected by Prince Carl of Solms-Braunfels to proceed directly inland from the coast in advance of the settlers moving in more slowly with their wagons and possessions. This party of twenty-five, under the leadership of Jean Jacques von Coll and Nicholas Zink, travelled from Lavaca Bay up the east bank of the Guadalupe River, crossing at the Old Nacogdoches Road Crossing on Good Friday, March 21, 1845. They were delegated to secure the 1,265 acres adjoining Comal Springs that the Count had purchased from the heirs of the Spanish Governor Veramendi on March 15th of that year. Carl constructed the very first log cabin at New Braunfels, erected completely without nails, the first of one hundred cabins finished before the onset of winter. He was assigned Lot Number 83, containing nine and one-half acres Bavarian measurement, in the New Braunfels settlement, which property he was forced to exchange that first winter for a desperately-needed coat.

He was a charter member of the German Protestant Congregation of New Braunfels. His signature, "Andreas Matern," may be seen today proudly entered on the church register in April 1845, immediately following that of his pastor, the Reverend Cachand-Ervendberg, employed by Prince Carl to minister to the spiritual needs of the pioneer community. The first service was held in a group of elm trees that later sheltered the first schoolhouse.

Carl Matern and Ulrika Fuchs were married by her father in Cat Spring in 1853. Even though the young couple lived for some time only seven miles up the Colorado from the Fuchs home, the two families seldom saw each other. A dramatic episode in the life of the Carl Materns has been preserved for later generations in a yellowed sheaf of papers entitled "Seeds of Freedom." There is no indication of the identity of the author, who so carefully bound the seven pages, sewing them together by hand with old-fashioned "sand-silk," embroidery thread on a spool:

> Ulrika was not to be deprived of occasional visits to her mother. Her problem was to find a means of transportation for herself and her three children. She made two large saddlebags, tied one to each side of the saddle, placed a child in each and carried the third in front of her. One chill October morning, while Carl was away as he often was, herding his sheep, she wrapped her children warmly and set out to visit her mother. She rode along the banks of the river, watching the sunlight filter through the trees. Raising her voice in song, she listened with delight to the echo coming back to her from the canyon walls. Ulrika sang louder and louder, lost in the beauty of her own voice. Carl, happening to come home and finding her gone, set out to follow her horse's footprints. Only a short distance from their home, he saw by the hoofprints of many horses that she was being followed. He realized that it was Indians and rushed on, not knowing the fate of his wife and children. But Ulrika had

ridden safely all the way to her parents' home, oblivious of the danger. The Indians, because of her beautiful singing, knew she belonged to the Great Spirit. They followed her to within a short distance of her destination, then turned and rode away.

By 1867, Carl, working together with his brother-in-law, Wilhelm Fuchs, had constructed a sturdy, ingeniously-designed water-powered sawmill on Cypress Creek in Blanco County. This is where he died of typhoid fever at the age of forty-eight, leaving Ulrika with seven children, and pregnant with the eighth.

For a while after his death she continued to live with her children on the homestead. Sheep brought from Germany in 1840 had been crossed successfully with Mexican stock, producing a hardy breed well suited to the dry Texas hill country. With the help of seven-year-old Adolf and his little brother Ivo, Ulrika bravely assumed the task of caring for her husband's large flock, which grazed on the open range of the wild, unfenced country. She had to be constantly on guard against predatory wolves and marauding Indians.

One dark night Ulrika was sure there were Indians surrounding her home, for she heard "too many owls hooting and too many wolves howling." Putting on her husband's clothes, donning his worn old hat and taking his gun in hand, she stood boldly in the open doorway, clearly outlined against the fire-lit room, in brave demonstration of the fact that a "man" was in the house! "Even the Indians had respect for such courage," relates the unknown family historian. "They departed, leaving only a menacing arrow in the flank of her horse as evidence of their original intentions."

As a result of this experience, her parents begged Ulrika even more urgently to bring her family to live with them in Llano County. Already the Fuchs homeplace was serving as a mail-stop between Burnet and Fredericksburg. It was called "Tiger Mill" for a large mountain lion that the Fuchs sons had killed early in the settlement of their grant.

Eugene's mother, Helene Matern, was eight years old when Ulrika moved to Tiger Mill. This was a tremendously significant event for the American-born grandchildren of the

Reverend Adolf Fuchs, for it brought the new generation into close, daily contact with their living German forebears. Grandmother Fuchs was equally important in passing on a rich, intellectual heritage. She, too, was well educated and, like her husband, came from a long line of Lutheran ministers.

In the rough and open Texas hill country of that era there were no schools or churches. The only direct contact with the outside world was the once-a-year journey to Austin, made by the ox-drawn wagon loaded with wool. All the Matern children received from their grandparents the equivalent of the best of secondary school educations. In each was instilled a strong and simple Christian faith, supported by a spirit of reverence and a clear concept of responsible morality. A carefully structured work schedule for the extended family of three generations provided time for the daily tasks of isolated pioneer living necessary for keeping all housed, clothed and fed. Special hours were set aside in which the children were required to practice writing and to read both German and English classics aloud as well as silently. All were taught to read and write music, to sing together in harmony and to play the piano, an item of furniture as essential to the Fuchs home as the kitchen range, the scrubbing board or the laundry tub!

Family, social and local community life gravitated quite naturally around the benign figures of the bearded patriarch and his wife. Deeply respected and much loved by his little flock, Pastor Fuchs took great pride in baptizing each of his children and grandchildren as they came along. To each he gave some little memento of the special occasions, such as the ring he gave to his daughter, Ulrika, on the day of her baptism. He was respected, not only by the members of his own immediate family, but by others as well. Ottilie recalled in her *Memoirs of a Texas Pioneer Grandmother*, that even during the worst turmoil of the Civil War, when the life of every Unionist was in danger, as were the lives of his sons, her father "calmly conducted himself as usual and was not molested, although he made little secret of his loyalty to the Union." The Christian principles of firm and loving nonviolence and active peace were basic to the deep, practical faith that held the family together.

On July 10, 1879, Adolf and Luise Fuchs celebrated their Golden Wedding Anniversary with pageantry, speech and song, surrounded by kith and kin from all over Texas. For Helene Matern this celebration was particularly significant. A young Swiss merchant named Julius Rudolf Kellersberger, came all the way from Galveston on horseback to join in the festivities honoring the old couple. He was a relative of sorts, for his sister, Emma, had married the Fuchs' youngest son, Benno, and his first cousin, Luise Romberg, had married their son, Wilhelm!

Helene had beautiful, reddish, naturally curly hair and a graceful, erect carriage. Her various suitors from the surrounding hill country communities, without exception, called her their "Rose of the Hills." Grave and reserved in manner, she was yet remarkably quick and efficient in performing her many daily tasks of cooking, sewing and caring for her brothers and sisters. From her grandparents she absorbed the gentle refinement, high idealism and firm faith that their lives so well demonstrated. From them and her courageous, widowed mother she inherited a sage wisdom far beyond her years, that made her the kind of woman to whom others always turned for comfort and advice. Her intense desire always to better herself was evident in her lifelong effort to bring her mastery of English up to the standard of her native German.

On the day that the Fuchs Golden Wedding Anniversary celebration came to a close, a group of guests who had traveled to Tiger Mill on horseback were gathered with their mounts around the front porch of the log house to bid the venerable pair and their large household a final farewell. When the last goodbye had been said, Julius, deliciously and acutely aware of Helene's queenly presence, took an energetic leap to mount his horse in a daring and gallant manner. His take off, under the impetus of the gaze of that one particular pair of eyes, was so much more exuberant than he intended that he sailed straight over his horse's back and landed in an ignominious, disarranged heap on the ground on the other side. The crowd of well-wishers roared with delighted laughter at his discomfiture — all but one! Julius, panting and red-faced, brushing the dirt from his clothes, looked up to see that alone

among all the gleeful gathering, the beautiful Helene stood
unsmiling. Her level gaze was fixed on him in sympathy and
understanding of his embarrassment. He looked directly into
those grave, kind eyes and announced in a firm, loud voice
"I'll be back!" And come back he did, to court and marry
Helene Matern.

They were married on March 31, 1882, in a quiet ceremony conducted by Grandfather Adolf Fuchs. Their honeymoon trip was simply a buggyride of a few hours, from the
family homestead at Tiger Mill, to Cypress Mill, where Julius
was employed by Helene's Uncle Wilhelm. The house in
which they lived as bride and groom was the three-room cypress board cottage fashioned from some of the very first
planks made by Carl Matern in his sawmill. It consisted of a
central, open hallway with one room on either side. Since the
larger room on the north had a large stone fireplace and one
window, it served as the living and cooking area. The smaller
room across the breezeway served as the bedroom. Much
laughter and loud talk issued from that central passageway on
Saturday afternoons, when it became a barbershop where Julius gave haircuts for five cents, adding the luxury of a shave
for the royal sum of a dime!

For seventeen years that original cypress-board cottage
served as the home of Clem Kelly, the Kellersberger's hired
hand from nearby Johnson City. He often gave the children
shivers by telling them how he was wakened at night by the
sound of rattlesnakes crawling beneath the loose floorboards.
The little house served successively as a washhouse and storage place for stacks of homemade lye soap, extra cots and
quilts, as well as bridles, ropes, saddles and saddle blankets. It
was also where Julius made and stored his famous wild grape
wine! In its final years this much-loved family landmark was
the stable for the saddle horse.

When Getulius and Carolina Kellersberger returned
from Switzerland in their old age to make their home with
their only son, Julius, a larger house became a necessity. A
seven-roomed wooden frame house, which had become the accepted style of home for Texas German-American families,
was constructed right beside the original cabin. Painted white,

with green shutters, surrounded by a white picket fence with a gate, Dr. Eugene Kellersberger's Cypress Mill birthplace appears today much as it did when he was born. The seven-room house is L-shaped, having an inside veranda extending along the south side. This protected porch, shaded by grapevines, serves as a delightful outdoor dining area throughout all but the coldest months of the year. It faces an underground cistern over which is built an attractive, white-latticed summerhouse, giving the enclosure with its old-fashioned flowerbeds the atmosphere of a cool, secluded patio.

[2]

The Texas Hill Country Boyhood

THE BIRTHPLACE

Julius Kellersberger, Eugene's father, received his post-master's certificate from Postmaster General Timothy Howe on April 18, 1882. In 1884 he purchased the Cypress Mill and General Store from his wife's Uncle Wilhelm Fuchs, who together with her father, Carl Matern, had been responsible for its original development.

The Kellersberger homestead covered approximately three hundred acres, with Cypress Creek dividing the property fairly equally into two halves.

Eugene's sister, Annie, in her book *Yesterdays*, described three very unusual features of their Cypress Mill home:

> Our underground cistern was known all over the country for its excellent taste and coolness. It was grandfather Getulius Kellersberger's engineering skill that constructed this. Under the cement walk were layers of gravel and charcoal through which the water flowed for cleaning as it shed from the rooftop into the cistern. Before the rainwater was let into the cistern, the rain had to fall for a certain length of time in order to first wash the roof clean of dust. The well on our place had very cold water that was wonderful for tub-bathing but it did not have a good taste.

22

A white picket fence encircled the yard of the homestead. To the west was our vegetable garden, quite large, running parallel to our cowpen. In the back yard was a huge elm tree where three guinea fowl always roosted, indispensable alarmists at the slightest occasion, awakening everyone.

My father, who was educated in Baden, Switzerland, was quite an athlete. He had constructed a horizontal bar with three different heights, also a six-foot high double-bars for somersaults, handstands, etc. Almost every evening he would exercise, we children watching him with open mouths at the impossible feats of physical stamina that we saw him accomplish.*

THE FAMILY CIRCLE

Helen Kellersberger had the most difficult of all of her seven deliveries with Eugene. In later years she wrote of this harrowing childbirth experience:

> I was in labor for forty-eight hours and was convinced toward the end that he was dead. Every time the labor pains came, he crawled back under my heart and I prayed, "If this child is ever born, he must be used of God for a special purpose!"

When Mrs. Holman, the midwife, saw that Helene was unable to deliver, she ordered Julius to send someone on horseback immediately to call Dr. Christian. Upon his arrival several hours later, the doctor bound towels about the mother's body to push the baby down into position and force the labor. It was none too soon, for Helene's strength was completely spent. She could not have lasted much longer. Both mother and baby came perilously close to dying.

The baby boy that finally saw the light of day on August 6, 1888, was named for Julius' beloved Swiss schoolmate, Eugen Jeuch. The name given the baby, spelled in German without the final "e," pronounced "Oi-gain," was also that of one of the greatest of German heroes. *Prinz Eugen,* Prince Eugene of Savoy, lived from 1663 to 1736. He ranks among the

---

* Used by permission.

most brilliant generals of all time for his winning of the Battle of Blenheim in Austria in 1704, during the War of the Spanish Succession. He was also famous as Governor of the Austrian Netherlands, now called Belgium, and for his defeat of the Turks in 1716.

Little Eugene's middle name was also that of a prince. *Roland*, the Emperor Charlemagne's nephew, died holding the rear guard against The Saracens at the Pass of Roncesvalles in the Pyrenees in 778. Throughout his life Eugene Roland Kellersberger treasured the memory of his mother's eyes, glowing with pride and love, and the touch of her hand on his cheek as she addressed him in her gentle voice: "Prince Eugene — my noble knight"!

She had the strong, intuitive feeling that this child was destined to be a knight of a different sort who would do battle in another kind of war, against an enemy more than human. Her implicit faith in his destiny was communicated to him as a child and she lived to see her intuition become a reality.

Eugene's position in the family was squarely in the middle of the seven children, with three siblings on either side, two brothers and a sister older than he and two sisters and a brother younger. Oddly enough, his brothers and sisters, both older and younger, looked upon him as the arbitrator of their disputes. He never entered into any of their quarrels himself. Whatever his judgment of their differences, it was accepted unquestioningly by the others. An example of his peacemaking role is the time that two of his brothers could not agree and came to him for a settlement. His response was, "You two will never agree, so both of you race around that tree yonder and whoever gets back here first is the winner," a decision which settled the matter to the satisfaction of both.

THE CIRCLE BROKEN

Already evident in the drama of Cypress Mill is the dark, tragic role played by typhoid fever, carried so innocently by the beautiful, clear water. Helene's own father, Carl Matern, working at the mill, had died of typhoid at the age of forty-eight. In those days there were only unscreened houses, open

The Kellersberger Family in 1897
Left to right: Hermann, Ulrika, Julius, Annie, Eugene (standing between his parents), Helene, holding Julia, Arnold. Cypress Mill, Texas.

outdoor toilets and school water buckets filled unsuspectingly from a contaminated spring.

In the spring of 1897, a teacher friend of Helene's became ill and asked to be nursed in the Kellersberger home. Helene cared for her patient for two weeks until an aunt came from San Antonio to take her home, where her illness was diagnosed as typhoid. The blanket from the victim's bed was aired and sunned and then placed on the bed shared by Hermann and Eugene.

In September Hermann became pale, yellow and weak. Obviously more frail each day, the eleven-year-old sat listlessly in a small chair placed in a sunny spot beside the porch. On March 7, 1898, Dr. Harwood came to visit the child, now confined to his bed. He said to Hermann, "Sit up. I want to give you some medicine." Obediently, with great effort he sat up and then fell back dead.

Throughout that cold, windy March night, nine-year-old Eugene lay wrapped in a blanket on the bare boards of his and his brother Hermann's bed. The mattress had been removed to be destroyed. From that night on, his lonely sleeping place was a narrow cot placed in a small room at the very back of the house, used up until that time only for storage. It had one single, narrow window, one pane of glass wide.

Sickly and frail herself, in the early stage of pregnancy with her youngest son, Hilmar, the grief-stricken Helene planted an oleander bush on the spot where Hermann's chair had been placed in the sunshine each day. Every Saturday morning she fashioned a wreath of fresh cedar boughs and sent the children to lay it on Hermann's grave. Each Easter thereafter she prepared seven Easter baskets, six for the living children and one for the missing son.

Hermann's death had a crucial effect on the relationship of Eugene to his sister, Annie, eighteen months younger than he. As the three middle children had always been a natural family unit, the loss of one of that number drew the remaining two together in an inexplicable bond of understanding.

It occurred to the sibling pair that a living cedar tree would be a far better symbol of undying love than wreaths that withered and died and had to be replaced each week. They searched until they found just the right size of tree in the pasture. Eugene dug it up, carried it home and carefully wrapped the roots in an old tow sack. Eight-year-old Annie lugged the tree to the graveyard while Eugene carried the hoe for digging the hole and a big jug of water for settling the sapling into its new home. Long years afterward Annie's memories of this experience were penned in a letter:

> The loss of our brother Hermann welded Eugene and me into a wonderful understanding, both of us being great lovers of nature. We understood each other without talking. We were both born with "seeing eyes," communing with one another in silence. We planted a cedar tree beside Hermann's grave, bare-footing it up the trail to the graveyard, Eugene carrying the heavy jug of water and the hoe. I had to carry the little tree that had oh! so many prickles! But I always adjusted myself to Eugene's advice and did whatever he said . . .
>
> His strong, bony hands come to me! What strength, as

a little girl by his side, to feel him clasp my hand! Sincerity, confidence and love were all intertwined in his grasp. No wonder over the years God had a plan for those hands, motivated to serve with compassion and understanding! He was truly an open book to his little sister, trudging along by his side in utter confidence in his God-given wisdom!

The two, made inseparable by their brother's death, waded in the creek together, bare feet deliciously chilled by the limpid water. Sometimes they sat on a particular ledge below the mill, letting the water from the sluice pour over their outstretched hands. A huge cypress tree washed down in a spring flood had become securely lodged between trees on either bank, forming a perfect bridge from which to watch the darting fish and spastic frogs. Another favorite spot was a velvet carpet of warm moss cradled in the fork of the two branching arms of the creek. There they would lie for hours, watching the minnows, polliwogs and waterbugs, the wary reptiles and the delicate acquatic plantlife that shared the watery microcosm swirling about the knobby knees and mammoth trunks of the venerable cypresses. From the oriole nests in the branches overhead came the wistful little birdsong that fitted in so perfectly with the fresh, woodsy odors of the stream. All unknown, the future biology and botany assistant was being trained, for Eugene's best-loved pastime was examining the structure and anatomy of the various insects, counting the number of their legs and discussing with Annie the marvelous variety of the formation of their bodies.

The pair had many an adventure together. Once they both mounted "Old Pony" and rode way up the creek, Eugene with the lines and hooks in his pockets and Annie holding the can of worms. That time they caught sixty-seven perch, which they were required to bring home already cleaned, leaving the fishheads in the pasture for the cows to eat. Another adventure was killing a seven-foot-long rattlesnake. Eugene sent Annie back the next day on horseback with a long trot-line to hook about the snake's head and pull it to where he and his friends were camping beside the Pedernales. "Old Pony" did not like that arrangement one little bit! She danced all the way there, snorting resentfully to show her

dislike of the ugly, slithering noise she was having to drag behind her!

HUNGRY MOUTHS AND GROWING BODIES

Keeping the large family fed was a tremendous task. Helene baked four loaves of fresh bread every day. Julius always
built the fire in the kitchen stove for breakfast, stirred up the
morning cornbread and put it into the oven to bake while he
went to the post office to get the daily mail ready to go. Helene
then completed the breakfast preparations with ham, bacon or
sausage, eggs and hot coffee, to start her family off for the day.

Cheese was another part of the family menu. It was made
with the aid of rennet, obtained from the dried stomach of a
young deer. A little rennet added to milk made it curdle. The
curds were placed in a cheesecloth bag and hung up to drip in
order to remove the whey. When the curds were no longer
dripping, they were placed under weights for a number of
days to age. The curd cakes, when dry, crumbly and blue,
were cooked into a paste, making what was called *schmierkase*,
or cooked cheese.

This was one of Eugene's favorite foods which he continued to make for himself even after he became a medical missionary in the Belgian Congo. He always smacked his lips as
he spread his German *schmierkase* on his Congo-baked bread
and reminisced about his childhood. In his African home he
kept the aging cake of curds pressed between two boards with
a heavy rock on top, right in the middle of his office day bed!
It was beside this day bed that the family knelt each morning
for family prayers, with that mellowing cake of cheese just
inches from their noses!

Summer time at Cypress Mill was canning time when all
hands were put to gathering, picking, peeling or chopping.
Wild peaches were spread on the rooftop to dry in the hot
summer sun. Threat of rain always brought the loud cry, "To
the roof! Save the peaches!" And a general scramble followed.
Pickled peaches were stored in ceramic jars covered with
tightly-tied brown paper coated with egg white for sealing
purposes. Each year the children gathered wild plums as well

as different kinds of wild grapes which were made into succu-
lent jellies. Eight large fig trees grew along the creek bed by
the water-race, the source of many a bowl of delicious fig preserves. Watermelon rinds were carefully collected after every
feast and made into preserves, while the cucumbers grown in
the garden ended up either in brine or in hot, spicy syrup for
pickles.

The onset of cool weather always meant butchering and
the preparation of meats for the smokehouse. The cuttings of
meat were liberally salted and peppered before they were
pierced through and a string inserted by which the cut was
hung from a hook dangling from the smokehouse ceiling.
Bacon and hams were cured in this way over a slow, smoky
fire, as was beef jerky, hard and crusty on the outside but delicious on the inside.

The art of sausage-making, unknown to Anglo-Ameri-
cans, has always been a German-American specialty. The
Kellersbergers usually butchered two hogs and one beef at a
time. With all the family working together, they were able to
complete the butchering in one day but the sausage-making
process went on into the wee small hours of the morning. A
whole "wurst" was the usual serving for a man at any meal-
time, so an abundance of sausage was needed to supply the
family. During the winter the children came home from school
at noon to a hearty meal of savory hot dried lima beans, homemade fried sausage and steaming corn bread, running with
melted butter from the rich milk of their own cows. Churning
the butter was one household task that Eugene consistently
disdained; he left that to his sisters!

One of Helene's hardest jobs was sewing for her growing
family. Eugene had a pair of pants that had somehow been
put together incorrectly so that one pants leg hung down
much lower than the other. It was the cause of much teasing
from his brothers and sisters until the offending garment finally wore out.

All of the children went barefoot most of the time, though
they had shoes for winter wear and for special, dress-up occasions.

PARENTAL DISCIPLINE

A weekly schedule of daily family work was strictly followed. Monday was washday, when the boiling of clothes in
big iron kettles out in the yard and vigorous scrubbing on
washboards began at seven in the morning and continued
until around five in the evening. It was a job for strong arms,
the boys carrying the water to the tubs, the girls doing the
scrubbing. The homemade soap, a combination of cracklings,
tallow and lye, never lathered in the hard water from the well.
Soft rain-water from the cistern was used only for the final
rinsing. Tuesday was ironing day when the old-fashioned
"sad irons" took turns sitting on top of the stove till they were
hot enough to make an impression. Wednesday was sewing-
mending-darning-patching day, while Thursday saw the garden carefully weeded under Clem's supervision. Every Friday
all the furniture in the house was moved and the wooden
floors first swept then thoroughly scoured.

The disciplined life style that Helene had experienced in
the home of her grandparents, Adolf and Luise Fuchs, prepared her well to be the life-partner of Julius, also the product
of a carefully-guided childhood. Together they were a pair of
exceptionally wise and loving parents, always in firm control
of their household. With a spirit of adaptability, ingenuity and
camaraderie they managed to instill into their children the
significance of the family group and the importance of each
individual to the whole. Every child grew up feeling specifically needed, necessary to the smooth functioning of the
household, with a bounden duty to perform each day. Paddling with a shingle was used as physical punishment only
during the earliest years when the children were small. After
that it was no longer necessary, for, as the children all said,
"Mother ruled us with her eyes"!

Helene's firm determination to control the formation of
her children's lives grew out of her desire to guard them from
the bad influences and rowdy language heard at the store.
These undesirable impressions from without were in direct
conflict with the example she personally wished to set before
them. While they were still small, their play area was required

to be just outside her kitchen window, where she could oversee and hear all that went on. She would join the children in their laughter, singing and chanting game-rhymes, chiding them when she heard them repeating some bit of vicious gossip or "swear words" picked up at the store.

THE DAILY CHORES

Each child knew exactly the tasks for which he or she was responsible. Eugene's chore from the time he was only a youngster was to keep the woodbox in the kitchen filled with firewood chopped by Clem. The family's "middle son" also ploughed, using the mules, Pete and Jim, to pull the heavy implement. All of the boys chopped cane whenever that crop was ready for cutting. Each year Julius planted a large cotton field in which the children were allowed to pick cotton, being paid ten cents for every hundred pounds they picked.

The family cows were milked both morning and evening, at which time they were given a supplemental feeding of hay and grain. The Kellersbergers' pasture was unique in that a large portion of the United States Navy grazed there. Eugene named all the cows for various battleships and their calves for cruisers. While the calves of the "Main," "Texas" and "Indiana" were completing the milking process in their own manner, the children practiced sling-shooting at a target and then turned the satisfied calves back into their stall. Each evening a big sugar barrel was filled with ears of shucked corn for the mules to eat. The shucks were stuffed into a second barrel which was rolled merrily down the hill into the big pasture. As it bumped along, it obligingly scattered the shucks in all directions for the cows to enjoy. Next the children raised the slats of the cottonseed shed, allowing the seed to roll down into the trough. Then they had to scramble for their lives to get over the gate before the bulls came roaring into the enclosure to eat their favorite food.

Clem's main jobs were keeping the mill dam in repair and the family well supplied with chopped firewood. He also made all the wagon trips to Austin. An ever-recurring task for the daughters of the family was the preparation of Clem's "camp box" that he took whenever he made the three-day journey, camping beside the road both going and returning. One of Annie's regular jobs (of which she was not too fond) was killing the bedbugs that Clem brought back from the wagon yards in Austin, whenever he took a load of cotton bales over and came back with goods for the general store. She became quite adept at "murdering" the pests by means of kerosene and boiling water!

The Kellersberger children, as they grew up, contributed a great deal to the smooth operation of their father's successful business enterprise. On Saturdays, especially, when they were all busy helping either in the store or in the mill, it was never necessary at meal time to ask which ones had been working at the mill — *they* were completely worn out and covered with a floury coating of cornmeal. The children were also responsible for keeping the cotton gin free of the wasps that regularly built their nests under the eaves.

Two duties connected with the store were considered privileges. Whenever Julius suspected that a robbery attempt was about to be made, which was not uncommon, he would yell to Helene through the south window in German: "Rifle here"! and one of the children, considered the truly lucky one, would go dashing over with it. Thievery of another sort occurred when the store had several customers at a time who had children with them. Little heads had a way of ducking behind the counter in the general vicinity of the big candy buckets so temptingly displayed. Julius' call to the house would bring a competent "watchdog" or two to the scene in the shape of some of his children. Their solemn, watchful presence near the sweets was all that was needed to prevent any surreptitious snitching.

When the first telephone line was run through Cypress Mill connecting Round Mountain with Austin forty miles away, a new task was added for the Kellersberger children. Whenever there was a phone call for one of the neighboring farmers, one of them, usually Hermann or Eugene, was sent to call him. Many times they had to scurry through the back pasture where the bulls stayed, in order to reach a nearby farm.

FREEDOM TO PLAY

Life for the children was not all work. One of their favorite pastimes was watching Quinones, the Mexican blacksmith, working at his forge down the hill. The blacksmith shop had two wide double doors facing each other and a huge fireplace with a hand-operated bellows nearby. Annie commented that "the owner was a kindly man and he seemed to enjoy having us children watch him at work, for we kept our distance and were never meddlesome." Sometimes he even permitted the Kellersberger offspring to pump the forge bellows for him.

As they grew older there were certain hours in which they were permitted to roam, fish, swim, hunt or play as they pleased. Helene often warned the children when they went fishing to remove the worm from the hook if it was not in the water, for it could prove to be a too-tempting morsel for a foraging chicken. One day while Julia and Annie were fishing, this very thing did happen — but not to a chicken! It was the family cat with a fishhook caught in its upper lip, that went racing about the yard pulling the pole and line after it. Julia finally sat on the cat while Annie ran to the house for a paring knife to release the hook from the cat's lip.

Tree-climbing was a pastime as much enjoyed as fishing. The children were squirrels and loved nothing better than swinging out over the water on wild grapevines. One of their favorite trees to climb was a huge sycamore that stood beside the road where the stream flowed over it. Hidden high in the leafy branches they would drop sycamore balls or wild grapes down on the heads of unsuspecting horseback riders passing beneath them, or better still, on the heads of a whole wagon-load of people directly in their line of fire.

The neighborhood boys had a series of whistles by which they communicated with each other, signalling their gathering at the Cypress Mill swimming hole. Eugene, when he was nine years old, placed a thick cypress plank between two of the trees to form a bench on which the swimmers could sit and rest. That board is still there, now completely a part of the two cypresses on either side of it. Still another silent witness to those long-gone hours filled with splashing and laughter is the giant old cypress with initials carved into its trunk — those of "E.R.K." and his swimming companions!

As a boy, Eugene was a habitual sleepwalker. One of the earliest sleepwalking experiences that he remembered was waking up one night, standing in the far corner of the hayloft, with his hands entangled in a mass of cobwebs near the rafters. Another night his mother heard him groaning as if in pain. She hurried to his bedside only to discover that he had taken the pillowcase off the pillow and, thinking that it was his nightshirt, had pulled it over his head. His cries of frustration were heard as he desperately sought the armholes through which he was struggling to put his arms. Whenever the Kellersberger boys and their friends camped overnight at Pack Saddle Mountain on the Colorado or beside the Pedernales, Eugene's big toe was always firmly tied with a strong piece of string to the big toe of another boy, so that both would be awakened by the tugging, in case the sleepwalker started in the direction of the water.

THE HEART OF THE HOME

The northeast fireplace room, used as a sitting room, was the center of Kellersberger family life. On one of the walls hung Julius' many medals won in various gymnastic competitions all over Europe, mounted in a large frame. From Helene's straight chair in the corner, as from a throne, she ruled her family's activities with gentle strength and queenly grace. After the noon meal each day, while she sewed, each of the children was required to do some writing both in English and German for an hour. Then they returned to the schoolhouse for the afternoon session, which was in German. The morning sessions were conducted in English. The first school the Kellersberger children attended was held in the community hall beside the Pedernales. Later a schoolhouse was built less than a mile from the Cypress Mill Store and Post Office.

Every night after supper the entire family gathered about the round walnut table in the center of which was a big kerosene lamp with a green shade and a round burner. Papa Julius always kept it scrupulously cleaned and trimmed and burned only special, refined kerosene in it, so that it gave a warm, bright light to the whole room. Whenever he brought his account books home from the store to work on, each child read or studied, occupying himself with some quiet activity, until the big books were slammed shut. That was the signal for conversation to start and for taking turns reading aloud with expression, from both an English and a German classic. As a family they read together many of the works of Charles Dickens and George Eliot. In German they read *Grimm's Fairy Tales* and the German sagas, such as the *Nibelungenlied* and the works of Goethe.

Especially happy were the times around the family hearth when Julius gave his offspring accounts of their own Swiss family tradition, of his Uncle Rudolf and the California gold rush days, or his father's adventures in the Civil War and in Mexico. He often made up homey riddles for them to guess.

Music played an important role in the Kellersberger home for there was a piano and Helene played it well. Grandfather Fuchs had been her teacher. All of the children were taught to sing, but Annie and Julia were given special courses. When they both suffered injuries at the same time, one with a broken arm and the other with a broken collarbone, Helene's way of restricting their activity was to sit them down and teach them to harmonize, singing alto and soprano together.

The approach of Christmas at Cypress Mill was signalled by the spicy odor of hot baked molasses cookies that Helene made for her children each year, using her mother, Ulrika's old family recipe from Germany. Papa Julius planted plenty of cane in order to have an abundance of molasses for the holiday baking. Long after the children were asleep, Helene was shaping plump little figures, radiant stars and swinging bells from molasses cookie dough, baking them and carefully decorating each with icing.

Pecan halves were often pressed into the center of a cookie for decoration. Both walnuts and pecans from trees on the homestead were gathered and cracked by the whole family each fall. One particular pecan tree that yielded fat, squatty pecans was a favorite of Grandfather Getulius. Every year, as

long as he lived in Switzerland, the entire crop of that one special tree was gathered and packed in a big barrel for shipment
to Baden.

EARLY INFLUENCES

Eugene eagerly attached himself to the Mac Alexander
family whenever they came to make purchases or have their
corn ground at Cypress Mill. Knowing that Mr. Alexander
was a professing Christian, Eugene sensed in him a source of
information on subjects not ordinarily discussed in his own
home. It was this quiet Baptist who first told him what a missionary was, in conversation which led the boy gravely and
shyly to ask, "How can I get started learning how to help people in need?"

The first impact made upon Eugene for interest in the
medical profession was Dr. Harwood, the Kellersbergers'
family physician who served Cypress Mill and surrounding
hill country communities as a trusted, old-fashioned general
practitioner. He was a Scot, a brilliant graduate of the University of Edinburgh, who had all the gracious, polished qualities
of the British elite. Emigrating to the United States as a young
physician, he deliberately chose to practice his profession in
the raw, isolated setting of Central Texas rather than accept
the ease and lucrative offers of the safe, settled cities of his native Scotland.

He had a lightweight surrey drawn by two very fast
horses in which he dashed along the rutted country roads in
answer to calls. His large gentle hands closed the eyes of Eugene's brother, Hermann, when he died of typhoid fever. He
treated and soundly scolded Eugene when he almost killed
himself during a boyhood game of water tag, diving into what
he thought was a deep pool, only to strike against a projecting
ledge of submerged rock. Most certainly the lad's neck would
have been broken had he not taken a long, shallow, running
dive instead of his usual arrow-like plunge. Dr. Harwood was
still living at the time of Helene's death in 1933 and ministered to her in her final illness. During a difficult delivery, the
sheer strain of muscular exertion caused a vertebra in the doc-

tor's back to slip, but he continued to care for his patient in spite of the agonizing torture he himself was enduring. Two years before his death, having just recently undergone surgery, he tore open his still-fresh incision when he lifted an overturned automobile off a dying girl. In Dr. Harwood, Eugene saw epitomized, even before he was conscious of it, his ideal of the medical profession, a perfect gentleman and skilled practitioner who served any who suffered, whether indigent or wealthy, with selfless compassion and dedication.

In one of his very first letters to his future second wife, written in 1924, Eugene Kellersberger penned an interesting summary of his own boyhood:

> During all the days of my boyhood till I was eighteen years old, my father had a general store, post office, gristmill and cotton gin, as well as a farm — in fact all of this *was* Cypress Mill.
>
> As a whole my boyhood was a happy one and never full of hard labor as I saw many other boys have to do. My life was more varied, the store and the post office being the center of a large community. It was a German-American community, mixed with Americans. There were no churches within ten to fifteen miles and there was no active religious life there, though my father, raised a Catholic, and my sweet mother were honest, truth-loving, wonderful people. I never saw the interior of a church or Sunday School till I was fifteen years old, or even heard the blessing said at the table.
>
> As a boy I had a horse, a gun and swimming and fishing, especially on Sundays. I loved to read and in my time I read much German and English literature, George Eliot being my favorite author. I learned to speak both languages equally well. I always had a hunger for education and often begged my father to send me away to Austin. I was always ahead in the little country school and never quite fitted in. In the summers, aside from fishing, swimming, riding and shooting, I also picked cotton and helped in the store and the cotton gin.
>
> At fifteen years I finally succeeded in pursuading my father to let me go away to school in Austin. There I went, a green country boy who had never before ridden on a train,

who put on long pants and shoes together for the first time
the day he left! I was traveling alone and dropped my baggage check behind the radiator in all the excitement of the
seventy-five mile trip. I arrived in the city of Austin, awed
and timid. There at the Whitis Academy I had three very
important years of my life. It took that time to change me
from an awkward country boy into something else. It took
me that long to get away from some of the influences of the
area where I had grown up and to gain for the first time a
religious consciousness.

PREPARATION FOR THE UNIVERSITY

The Whitis Academy, a small, highly-geared institution,
was from its beginning closely associated with the All Saints
Episcopal Church of Austin. Since a Whitis certificate admitted students to The University of Texas without examination,
a great majority of the students were from small towns and
rural areas of the state where schools were not able to qualify
their graduates for higher education. Though the student
body rarely numbered more than a hundred, it had, nevertheless, an unusually well-equipped boarding department for
girls.

The original Whitis family residence, called "Main
House" or "The Home Building," was a large stone structure
used for classrooms. All of the day-student and primary-level
classes were held on the ground floor, while the upper-level
classes for the boarding students occupied the second-floor
rooms. Florence Hall was the girls' dormitory; Senior Hall
served as the dining hall and also housed the Music Department. Since the school had no playground or auditorium, the
student body joined in all the Episcopal Parish House activities and attended the Episcopal Church services throughout
the school year. Any Whitis girls who would carry a tune automatically became members of the All Saints Choir!

The Austin Institute for the Blind, with its spacious facilities, was the location of the important Whitis annual school
social events. Entertainments put on by the school were always well produced, drawing a large crowd of enthusiastic
Austin citizens as an audience.

The Whitis faculty was entirely female. Miss Mary Whitis, called "Miss Mollie" by her pupils, was the principal of the school, a strict disciplinarian and its excellent, scholarly teacher of English and Literature. Miss Gertrude, her sister, more gentle and less authoritarian, taught the mathematics classes.

Miss Mollie had a remarkable influence over her pupils. She was one of those gifted teachers who have a natural aptitude for inspiring young people to do their best. Her special gift was the ability to impart the basic techniques of how to study and learn. She was a perfectionist, never one for leniency or compromises. Her high standards were directly and openly held. When her pupils made mistakes, she frankly and emphatically pointed them out before the whole class.

An incident typical of Miss Mollie occurred in her classroom during Eugene Kellersberger's first year at Whitis. He had been seated in the same double desk with a mischievous Mexican-American lad who, whenever Miss Mollie's back was turned, took the greatest delight in tormenting him in every imaginable way. He would administer a rough shove, a quick kick in the shins, a sly poke in the ribs or snatch away something essential to class activity in the wink of an eye, all the while wearing the most angelic of expressions. But Miss Mollie's sharp eyes detected the continuous barrage of assaults to which the shy newcomer from the country was so docilely submitting. Finally one day, when Eugene's assailant had slipped his bookstrap around his neck and was choking him, Miss Mollie whirled about and shouted: "Eugene! You MILK-SOP! Why don't you *hit* him?" And with the greatest satisfaction, he energetically followed Miss Mollie's suggestion!

The first two years that he attended Whitis, the boy from Cypress Mill boarded with a Mrs. Poindexter whose nephew was enrolled in the same school. He milked three cows twice a day and cared for the buggy horse in exchange for his room and board.

A good Episcopalian, Mrs. Poindexter, saw to it that her two charges were in attendance whenever the doors of All Saints were open. This religious exercise was Eugene's first

experience with formal worship, other than the rare time as a
child, when he heard a Methodist circuit-riding preacher,
passing through Cypress Mill. He went unwillingly and managed to tune out most of the service, deliberately occupying
his mind by thinking of other things.

Entries Eugene Kellersberger made in his Whitis school-
days diary reveal much about his boyhood character and personality:

January 22, 1905, Whitis Academy, Austin, Texas
Well, Congress Avenue is being paved with bricks. I
declare! Austin is getting a move on itself! The next thing
will be rebuilding the dam. That is the one thing I want
them to do. The Texas legislature is in session. Good for
them! I'm going to get a job next Saturday. I don't care
what comes of it — I need the money! The gym class I am
taking is surely making me strong and hearty.

January 26th My brother Arnold is going to The University of Texas. He is staying in the same room with me. I am
surely glad, for we get along fine together.

January 29th Went to see *Macbeth* but I did not like it
much. The players were not much good so I nearly went to
sleep. The only good thing was the sword fight and the
armor. Had a dandy time at Christmas. I danced "like the
Dickens" and had a fine time all round!

February 2nd No school today because Mrs. Whitis is
very sick with pneumonia. The doctors have given up all
hope. We are all very sorry.

February 6th Mrs. Whitis died on February 2nd at 7:30
p.m. and was buried on Monday. We will have no school till
Thursday. We all give our warm regrets to "Miss Mollie"
and "Miss Gertrude." We feel for them. The ground is covered with ice. I sure like this kind of weather! You can skate
and have other fun.

February 25th I have the "grip!" Grippe means influenza. I went to school and got sore eyes so now I must wear
spects. I sure do look funny! I have missed three days of
school.

March 1st My brother is away and he has left the whole
room full of eating stuff and it is very hard for me to keep
from eating things while he is gone. But I have to do it. I am
sorry that I had to miss that Masquerade Ball back home

but I could not help it. Life does not wholly consist of pleasure. Do you know that? The north wind is still blowing down to Austin. For the past week I have been having a cough that nearly killed me. It sometimes kept me jumping for hours. Tonight we are all going to the University of Texas Auditorium to hear the annual Oratorical Contest. The prize is $75 which is worth having!

March 2nd. Today is a holiday because of Texas Independence Day. We will likely be going to Barton Springs for an outing. Later: We went and had a fine time.

March 8th A "norther" with rain came up last night. I hope it will not freeze. That would bring a great deal of damage. My brother Arnold has joined our English class. He will learn a lot. I am sure I heard "Miss Mollie" say that he is "poetical!"

March 21st Our Uncle Hermann Matern was here. We had a fine time. He took us to eat down at the Sutor Hotel with him!

March 23rd Well! I have made up my mind to go to Annapolis. I will try hard to pass exams for college. Later: Changed my mind to become an electrical engineer.

March 25th Stood all my exams — I *guess* I did! We are having fine weather now. This morning I learned to ride a bicycle. I rode way out to Hyde Park. Had a *fine time*! The Director of the Blind Institute gave a "hop" in honor of "Miss Mollie's" dormitory girls. I was invited, too. I took Miss Naomi Peacock. There were about eight couples. We had a beauty of a hall, very large and slick as everything! It was the first dance that I have been to since Christmas. I hope we'll have another one soon.

April 6th President Roosevelt was here. He is surely a fine fellow! He made a splendid speech. He surely did have a fine train. I never did see such a big engine!

April 15th Theo, Arnold and I went camping on Barton Creek last Saturday night. We camped all night and on Sunday morning we took a stroll in the creek. It is one of the most pretty creeks I have ever seen. We walked about fifteen miles that day and I enjoyed it thoroughly.

Eugene's third year at Whitis was without doubt his most interesting one. Not only did he find his school subjects more absorbing than ever — there was also a "new" girl in his class!

The name of Edna Helena Bosché was a welcome addition to the roster of the senior class of 1906, after her two years away at school in Washington, D.C. She had been a Whitis student from 1901 to 1903 during the first three years of the school's existence, so she was no stranger to many in the student body. Eugene knew, of course, how much his sister, Ulrika, had treasured her friendship with Edna and how lovingly this schoolmate of hers had tried to comfort the Cypress Mill girl in her homesickness. The fact that this merry, outgoing lass, so pretty with the big pink bow in her dark hair, shared his same birthday, gave him a warm, personal pride and joy in her presence.

Shortly after classes began in the fall of 1905, Eugene's friend, Seth Hastings, persuaded him to attend for the first time Dr. Dan Penick's Sunday School Class for young men at the Highland Presbyterian Church. He was so impressed by what he heard and saw that very first Sunday that he joined the class on the spot, rarely missing a Sunday after that. This was also the church of which Edna Bosché and her family were members, her father having given the original lots on the corner of Twenty-second Street and San Antonio, on which part of the sanctuary was built.

Near the end of Eugene's little Whitis diary is one page on which is painstakingly designed a large heart pierced by two arrows. Beneath the heart is the one word "*IT*" underlined three times. Below that is a strange combination of letters: "*Nugks.*" with a small "plus" sign beneath the "n," three dashes beneath the three middle letters and another "plus" sign below the "s." Whatever the meaning of this hieroglyph, it may be assumed that it records the first mutual agreement of sweethearts. To the right of the secret symbolism is written: "Realized April 8, 1906."

On that date Eugene Kellersberger and Edna Bosché told their families that they "had an understanding." Over the next six years their budding friendship grew naturally and quietly, leaving ample room for enriching experiences and wide companionships with many other friends, as well as between themselves. The kind of love into which they were growing together never "mushroomed" out of control, shutting out others and the real world. It grew strong, pure, and vital through involvement together in the same school, the same church and later, in the same home, until their marriage in 1912.

On June 6th, 1906, at the age of seventeen, Eugene was baptized in the Highland Presbyterian Church by Dr. Robert F. Kirkpatrick. He joined the church against his parents' wishes, for they were disturbed about his decision, being uncertain as to what "being a Presbyterian" meant.

But Eugene was filled with a glad assurance that what he was doing was absolutely right for him. He wrote on that date:
"Now I belong to *God*!"

[3]

Beloved Edna

Eugene's sweetheart was a maiden created to love and to be loved. Indeed, in later years, her discerning native friends in central Africa would give her the Bantu language name of "Munanga," "The Beloved." So apparent was the warm, winning love that spontaneously flowed from her to others!

Edna Helena Bosché shared with Eugene his birthdate, August 6, 1888, but her birthplace was very different — Cincinnati, Ohio. As her family name was obviously French, so her physical features and her personality bore clearly recognizable signs of her French heritage. She had a smooth, olive complexion, very dark brown, almost black, softly-waving hair and unusually wide-set hazel green eyes. She was somewhat slight and wiry in build, very alert and given to action. Her natural grace, an innate air of cultured refinement and a well-bred flair for quiet elegance in dress set her apart in any crowd. But this somewhat aristocratic impression by no means meant that she was cool or aloof. She was, rather, quite warm and outgoing, remembered by others for her friendly smile and unaffected manner. Even as a very small girl, she was known for her merry, infectious, delightfully "bubbly" laugh. Sincerity, openness and directness of approach were conveyed in a soft, clearly ennunciating, purposeful voice. Above all, she had a winsome, quietly-glowing quality that inspired confidence and revealed a deep, inner strength. By nature, by breeding and by God's own special touch upon a dedicated character, Edna was a beautiful, vibrantly spiritual young woman.

THE ALSATIAN PROVIDER

The family name of *Bosché*, with its proud French accent on the final "e," deliberately and distinctively differentiating it from the German "*Bosch*," originated in an area of France which is Germanic in both language and culture. Alsace has been a battleground of chronic rivalries for over two thousand years. Situated between ancient Gaul and Germany, loved by Charlemagne, this province knew Roman domination, the ravages of the Huns and occupying armies of numerous wars of European history. But the people who mingled and fused and became Alsatians calmly continued to till the rich soil of their fertile plain lying between the Vosges Mountains and the Black Forest, and to tend their fruitful vineyards. Above all, they patiently continued to build their magnificent cathedrals, such as Strasbourg, with its single soaring spire, the most delicate and ethereal of all ogival art. Alsatians became a hardy race of industrious, financially canny builders and entrepreneurs.

Edna's grandfather, Henri Bosché, was born in Phalsburg, Province of Alsace, France, on April 18, 1819. According to Edna's father, Henri's mother was high-born, a titled lady of aristocratic French extraction who succumbed to the dashing, seductive charms of a handsome commoner. She eloped with Henri's father, thus forfeiting her family position and inheritance.

After finishing his education, Henri moved to Kichheim, Palatinate Bavaria, from where he emigrated to the United States in 1843, settling in Buffalo, New York. Three years after arriving in America, Henri married Barbara Foose, who was born on March 13, 1829, in Wattenheim, Germany, where there is a record of her baptism. Her father died when she was only two and her mother, when she was twelve. In 1844, at the age of fifteen she came to the United States with her older sister, Anna Maria Foose. She was seventeen years old when she married the young Alsatian in 1846.

From Buffalo the young couple moved to Cincinnati, Ohio. There, Edna's father, Philip Bosché, was born September 27, 1855. When he was four, the family moved to New Ulm, Minnesota, where they hoped to acquire a farm of their own on land recently ceded by the Dakota Indians to the United States. With the outbreak of the Civil War in 1861, Henri joined the Minnesota Militia and served as a baker in the Union Army.

The state of Minnesota was then only four years old and the Civil War was draining its raw energies and limited new manpower. Tribal pressure from the Chippewa had drawn the Dakotas from their ancestral occupation of the northern lakes and forests down into the prairies of the Minnesota Valley, where they first encountered white man.

The causes of the Sioux Uprising of 1862 were complex and of long standing. The real name of this native American nation was *Dakota*, which means "friends" or "allies." The name *Sioux* was given them by their traditional enemies, the Chippewa. It is a contraction of the derogatory term, *Natouessioux*, meaning "Snakelike Enemy."

By a series of treaties, the Dakotas ceded almost 24,000,000 acres of rich, agricultural lands, which were opened to settlers only three years later. The Indians were left with merely two small reservations. They deeply resented the location of these reservations and rightfully felt that they had been deceived and cheated. The major Indian War resulting from this dissatisfaction began at Acton Township in Meekes County in August 1862, over a minor incident of some eggs stolen by a young Indian brave from a settler. It actually came to an end only in 1890 with the Battle of Wounded Knee in South Dakota.

At the time of the uprising, New Ulm was the largest settlement near the Dakota Indian reservation. It had been founded in 1854 by members of a German colonization society from Chicago and Cincinnati. Its population in 1860 was 635, which had increased to almost 900 by the time of the uprising. Young braves on the nearby reservations knew that many of the men had gone to war and that the remaining settlers had few guns and little ammunition. They also knew that the town was spread over several terraces descending to the banks of the Minnesota River, making attack from the different levels an easy matter.

The citizens of New Ulm had the good fortune of the leadership of two men with some idea of military defense strategy, Sheriff Charles Roos and Jacob Nix. They armed those who had no guns with pitchforks and other crude farm implements and barricaded all the citizens within a three-block area in the center of the town, which had brick buildings that could be defended. New Ulm thus withstood two Indian attacks, the first comparatively light, on August 19, at 3 P.M., and the second, a very heavy one, a few days later on August 23, at 8:30 A.M. Only the buildings within the barricade were spared the total destruction that the Dakotas administered during this second concerted assault.

This ended the sieges of the settlement itself, but occasional bands of marauders continued to attack isolated settlers in the area for the next several years. Some forts of the state were garrisoned until 1866, when the Indian raids gradually came to a halt and settlers filtered again back over the countryside.

It was in one of these later, sporadic attacks that Henri Bosché was killed on May 18, 1863, as he was working in his field near his New Ulm homestead. He was scalped as his seven-year-old son, Philip, looked on. Momentarily ignored, Philip hid behind the overturned wagon and so escaped the notice of his father's slayers. Some time later, after the departure of the raiding party, Philip was discovered by another settler passing by on horseback, and taken to his mother. His vocal cords were so paralyzed by fright that he was unable to relate what had happened, but there was little need for that, for everyone knew.

Speech was difficult for Edna's father for the rest of his life. The hesitancy and peculiar sort of lisp with which he spoke he always attributed to his childhood trauma. His father, Henri, was one of the estimated eight hundred settlers and soldiers killed during the years of the Sioux uprising.

Not long after this, Philip's mother, Barbara, married an Englishman by the name of Stocker, who had lost his wife in the same fashion. The only child of this second marriage that lived was Robert, Philip's half-brother, who was to graduate first in his class of 1887 at Annapolis, become a Rear Admiral, Acting Chief of Naval Construction during World War I, and be awarded the Navy Cross for his designing of the "Eagle" class of vessels. Widowed a third time, Barbara married a man named Veikinger and lived till her death in New Ulm, where she is buried.

When Philip was grown he went to Buffalo, New York, where he supported himself for several years as a carriage-painter. Later, he returned to his birthplace, Cincinnati. Edna's father during all his young manhood was a faithful, practicing Roman Catholic. He was a true Alsatian, canny with money and with a cool head for finances. A product of the proverbial school of "hard knocks," he developed into a successful businessman, able to deal and bargain. As the years passed, he prospered more and more in both his commercial and real estate ventures. Energetic and very stubborn, he was a hardheaded, hard-working, dutiful head of his family. His somewhat gruff, demanding outward image nevertheless cloaked an extremely generous and sympathetic heart.

A SHIPBOARD ROMANCE

Early in December 1883, when she was thirty-three years old, Miss Cornelia Blickensderfer, of the Moravian Community of New Philadelphia, Ohio, and a companion, boarded a Cincinnati-to-New Orleans steamboat for an excursion trip down the Ohio and Mississippi Rivers. During the course of this riverboat journey, she met a fellow passenger, twenty-six-year-old Philip Bosché of Cincinnati. On December 13, they disembarked from the paddlewheeler at Memphis, Tennessee, and were married in the Cumberland Presbyterian Church by the Reverend A. H. Jones. A carefully-preserved clipping from the Memphis newspaper lists their wedding along with others of that same date.

In many ways, it was a very unlikely marriage, surprising for its unexpected suddenness. It was probably quite a shock to Cornelia's widowed mother. The Catholic-Protestant barrier between them was tremendous, as were their divergent family backgrounds. Cornelia had a heritage of a disciplined, communal life-style, wealth and recognized position. Philip came from an impoverished pioneer setting that encouraged individualism and a dogged, driving ambition. Cornelia was always painfully and acutely aware that she was five and a half years older than her husband.

Shortly after their marriage, settled in Cincinnati, Cornelia became dangerously ill and was not expected to live. During this crisis, Philip made the solemn vow that if she recovered, he would leave the Roman Catholic church and become a Protestant. Miraculously, she did recover and he kept his promise. When she was well, he began attending church with her and continued faithfully to do so during his long life, even throughout the lonely twenty-eight years that he outlived her.

Two daughters were born while the Boschés still resided in Ohio. Winifred Mae was born on May 4, 1886, and Edna Helena, on August 6, 1888. The two girls were quite small when Philip made the decision to leave Cincinnati. He had carefully and deliberately considered all manner of business ventures in which he could successfully invest Cornelia's family inheritance. He finally settled on a young and brand new industry, that of commercial steam laundering, called the "Troy Laundry" business, for the method invented by the detachable collar industry of Troy, New York. An opportunity to learn about power-laundry management opened up for him in Charlottesville, Virginia. The family of four journeyed there by train and remained long enough for Philip to familiarize himself thoroughly with the various steps of the new process and the operation of the sophisticated new equipment being manufactured by the Troy Laundry Machinery Company. "Troy Laundries" had already begun to appear up and down the east coast of the United States.

The Bosché Family in 1892
Left to right: Edna, Cornelia, Philip and Winifred. Cincinnati, Ohio.

THE BOSCHE LAUNDRY

Philip took his family and headed west to Austin, Texas, where he had the opportunity to purchase what claimed to be the first steam laundry west of the Mississippi River. He deliberately chose a town which was the site of a large state university, for he had noted that the student body of the University of Virginia at Charlottesville provided the steadiest group of customers for the thriving Troy Laundry business there.

When Philip was comforting his daughter, Winifred, during her University years, for being refused membership in an exclusive sorority because her father was "nothing but a laundryman," he wiped away her tears and smilingly said to her, "Well, I just could not think of any *cleaner* business to go into!"

The 1899 *Cactus*, The University of Texas Yearbook, contains a full page photograph of the laundry plant, complete with horse and buggy tied at the front entrance, and a stone facade bearing the date *1897* and BOSCHE'S TROY LAUNDRY. A tall smokestack at the rear of the second building emits smoke, indicating that at this very moment this busy laundry is in op-

Pay some attention where you send your clothe.

THIS is a first-class sanitary Laundry

Phone 73   806 CONGRESS AVENUE

Advertisement in THE CACTUS, *1899, The University of Texas Yearbook. The original words of* The Eyes of Texas *were scribbled on a Bosché Laundry wrapper.*

eration. Large signs giving the name of the establishment, painted on both sides of the building, could be read up and down Congress Avenue from as far away as the capitol building. The text of the *Cactus* advertisement reads: "PAY SOME AT-TENTION WHERE YOU SEND YOUR CLOTHES! This is a first class sanitary laundry!"

The "prompt, neat, reliable laundry that always gives satisfaction" was consistently advertised in the *Austin City Directory* from 1893 until 1922. The 1918 *Directory* adds "Cleaning, Pressing, Dyeing and Scouring" as services offered to customers.

For eleven years, the top half of the outside cover of the *Austin City Telephone Directory* bore the Bosché Laundry advertisement, for two years on the front cover and nine years on the back cover. Upside or downside, the family business name, lying prominently on many an Austin desk, was one very familiar to Austin residents.

In 1904, an event took place which gave the Bosché

Laundry an unprecedented claim to fame. That year, a student at The University of Texas named Lewis Johnson was director of both the band and the glee club. He was a "militant crusader for the cause of adopting a school song for The University of Texas." A varsity minstrel program, called *Jolly Students,* produced by Johnson and presented at the Hancock Opera House, proved so popular that he and his collaborator, John Lang Sinclair, decided to write a new student lyric to the tune of the old "Levee Song," better known as *I've Been Working on the Railroad.*

The University of Texas president, Dr. William L. Prather, was a graduate of Washington College in Virginia when General Robert E. Lee was the president of that institution. One of General Lee's repeated admonitions to his students, often made in school assemblies, was: "Young men, the eyes of the South are upon you!" President Prather took the words of this same gentle encouragement with him to Texas and he, in turn, often said in assembly: "Young ladies and young gentlemen of The University, remember that the eyes of Texas are upon you!"

A photograph of the original writing of the song, given to The University by Mr. Johnson, forms the cover of a January 1959, issue of the *Alcade.* In a 1933 issue of the same periodical, The University of Texas alumni publication, he reminisced how the song came to be written:

> You will note that it is written in pencil in John Lang's diminutive characters; the mark-outs are still there, also the interlineations and substitutions. As I recall it, the old piece of yellow paper on which it was written was torn from the wrapping paper of a BOSCHE LAUNDRY bundle. You will note that "Till Gabriel blows his horn," etc., was not in the original. However, during John Lang's and my day, he changed it to the present form. I must apologize for having folded the manuscript and for not having taken care of what now probably is the most sacred piece of paper in the whole state of Texas — at least to Texas-Exes! (Page 75)

The "sacred piece of paper," a piece of Bosché Laundry wrapper on which is penciled the original writing of the famous University of Texas song, is now carefully displayed under glass in a small, lighted inset in the wall of the Alumni, or "Texas-Exes," Building on The University of Texas campus in Austin.

THE HOME ON WEST AVENUE

When the Boschés arrived in Austin in 1892, Winifred was six and Edna was three and a half. Briefly, they rented a small cottage on East Second Street, then moved a year later to 303 East Eleventh. A big step up in the economic bracket was made when Philip purchased in 1895 a new home at 1600 Rio Grande, painted white with lovely "gingerbread" decorations. The lot, extending all the way to West Avenue, provided a wild-flower-carpeted playground for the two little girls.

The same year that the old McDonald Dam two miles north of Austin washed away, flooding the city and taking twenty-three lives, Philip Bosché purchased a partially completed residence under construction at 1402 West Avenue. The imposing new home was located near the top of a hill overlooking the city of Austin, with a beautiful view of the capitol in the distance. The Boschés completed their new home and moved into it in 1901.

It was a three-story, red brick Victorian mansion set on a gently terraced site, well shaded by old live oak trees. An iron hitching post for horses and a large marble slab on which to alight from carriages welcomed guests at the street curbing. Generous galleries wrapped around two sides of the domicile provided shade and seating on both levels. The white-painted railings, columns and decorations of the balconies were examples of the wood-lathe and jig-saw artwork of that period, as were the fanciful turrets which broke the roofline. The doors of the downstairs porch facing West Avenue opened into a large, formal parlor at one end, and into a glassed-in sun porch filled with lush ferns and potted plants at the other. The formal entrance to the house was on the north side, where a curved driveway led up to an impressive doorway that opened into the long central hall, running the length of the house on the ground floor. At the far end of this hall a carved balustrade staircase with two right angle turns ascended to the second floor.

The parlor of the Bosché home, 1402 West Avenue, Austin, Texas, in 1906.

A dining room with elegant, lace-curtained bay windows opened into the main hallway on the left. Both dining room and parlor had elaborate fireplaces with carved mantelpieces and beveled glass mirrors set above them. Each room was furnished with delicate gas chandeliers in vogue at that time. The dining room opened into a sunny kitchen with three big windows. A massive range that consumed huge quantities of cut stove wood was used for the cooking, while a big ice box cooled daily with a large block of ice, provided refrigeration. The back porch had a staircase leading upstairs for private family and maid service use, as well as steps leading down into a flower-filled backyard and out to the turreted carriage house and barn at the back of the lot. The property extended all the way to Rio Grande Street on the east, overlooking Pease Park, and joined the Caswell property on the south toward Fourteenth Street.

The view of the city of Austin seen from the upstairs porch was delightfully framed through the branches of the gnarled old oak trees. A cozy upstairs sun parlor, which served as a well-lighted sewing room for Mrs. Bosché and her daughters, was often used by "Madame," a *couturiere,* who came to design and sew their suits and dresses. Four bedrooms and a large family bathroom were also on the second floor, with another staircase leading up to the third level student quarters.

Such was the home so loved and so happily lived in by the Boschés for twelve years, from 1901 until Cornelia's death in 1913. This was also the home where Eugene Kellersberger lived during the years that he was a student at The University of Texas.

The Boschés were closely associated with the Highland Presbyterian Church of Austin, which came to be known on July 13, 1910, as the University Presbyterian Church. First opened as a Sunday School in an old store building in 1889, it became a year later a "preaching point" with The University of Texas students particularly in mind. On January 31, 1982, a new congregation with twenty charter members was organized by the Presbytery of Central Texas.

It was on September 7, 1897, that Mrs. Cornelia B. Bosché transferred her membership from the Free Southern Presbyterian Church of Austin to the Highland Church. One week later a very determined little girl named Edna Bosché made her appearance before the Session of this same church, requesting to be accepted as a member. What happened in that particular Session Meeting is a treasured bit of family history, related with delight by some who were present.

When Edna, dressed in her Sunday best, came before the Session, a few of the elders had strong misgivings about her request to join the Church at such an early age. She had turned nine on August 6th, a few weeks before. Also, there she sat, happily swinging her foot and humming softly to herself a song she had just been singing in Sunday School — an attitude that some of the sterner church fathers felt betrayed an ignorance of the gravity of the step she was asking to take.

Clearing his throat, one of the elders rose and solemnly addressed her: "Miss Edna, you say that you want to become a member of this Church, like your mother who joined our membership last week. Do you really know what it means to join the Church? Can you tell me the meaning of Total De-

pravity? Do you know what it means to be *lost?*" Looking up
into the elder's stern countenance, Edna's face grew suddenly
grave as the smile on it took startled wing. Her foot stopped
swinging and she was silent. Once again, the well-meaning
elder asked in earnest tones, "Edna, can you explain to me the
meaning of Total Depravity?" Again, silence.

Then the voice of a second elder was heard gently remon-
strating with the first, "The knowledge of that will come all in
good time, my friend! Each of us must crawl before we walk,
you know!" Turning to Edna, he asked her gently, "Edna, can
you tell me just why you want to become a member of this
Church?" Instantly, the joyous smile alighted once again on
the upturned face. With a determined air, she stood up,
looked directly at the minister, surrounded by his elders and
said very confidently and distinctly, "I want to join this
Church because the Lord Jesus Christ died on the cross for
MY sins and I love Him with all my heart and I want to be a
missionary and to serve Him as long as I live."

No further questions were asked. The Session voted to accept Edna into the fellowship and communion of that congregation on that very same day.

On March 6, 1898, Philip Bosché made the final break
with the Roman Catholicism of his youth and joined his family as a member of the same church on profession of faith. For
years he had been attending with his wife but had consistently
refused to become a communing member. Reared a Catholic,
he was never one to discuss religious matters. Regular attendance with his family and the faithful giving of a tenth of his
income to his church were the visible proofs over the years of
the faith that he simply, practically and sincerely held.

During the pastorate of the Reverend T. B. Southall, the
growing congregation moved into the building in the 2200
block of Nueces Street, in which the Austin School of Theology had been located. Mr. Bosché served as a deacon for a
term along with E. D. Junkin, also as a member of the five-
member Board of Trustees of the Highland Church. In 1907,
he gave two lots at the corner of Twenty-second Street and
San Antonio, on which the present Sunday School building of
the University Presbyterian Church now stands. Some time

later, he added the gift of still another lot lying north of those already given.

THE MORAVIAN INFLUENCE

Edna's mother, Cornelia Blickensderfer, came from a family background totally different from that of her father, Philip Bosché. For six consecutive generations the Blickensderfers were an integral part of the disciplined and dedicated communal life style of the Moravian Church. This very strong and active Christian family heritage, handed on in fullest measure to Edna, was of the utmost importance in the life of Eugene Kellersberger. During the five years that he lived in the student quarters of the Bosché home, Cornelia's and Edna's enthusiasm for "Mission," that faithful compliance with Christ's final marching orders to go into all the world to teach, preach and heal in His Name, turned Eugene's life "about face" in the direction of medical missionary service.

Cornelia's family roots reached back into the historical movement from which was distilled the very first essence of Protestantism — the burning at the stake on July 6, 1415, of John Hus, the Bohemian martyr and "Reformer before the Reformation." The life of this brilliant dean of the faculty of philosophy and rector of Charles University of Prague was completely changed by the writings of the English reformer, John Wyclif. Like him, Hus fearlessly exposed the evils and corruption of the Roman Catholic Church of his day, calling for reformation from within.

In 1456, sixty years before Martin Luther nailed his theses to the door of the Wittenburg Church, a group of Hus's followers, led by Gregory of Prague, organized a fellowship called *Jednota Bratraska*, "The Communion of Brethren." This was expressed in Latin as *Unitas Fratrum*, "Unity of Brethren." Their meeting place was a secluded valley of the remote mountain fastnesses of northeast Bohemia, in the village of Kunwald on the Lititz Estate. During the next two hundred years, this Protestant communion grew strong and spread from Bohemia into Moravia and Poland. Then came the Thirty Years War which saw the deliberate, virtual wiping out of Protestantism in central Europe and the disappearance of all visible forms of its organization.

On a bitterly cold day in January 1628, Bishop John Amos Comenius, forced to flee for his life into Poland, stopped and took one long last look at his beloved homeland of Moravia. Kneeling in the snow, he prayed aloud: "Preserve here a hidden seed to glorify Thy Name!" His prayer was answered, for the concealed seed of the Word of God, buried under the darkness of frightful religious repression, germinated and matured in the hearts of faithful worshippers clustered here and there throughout central Europe.

In 1722, ten persecuted Moravian followers of John Hus found a refuge on the estate of Nicolas Louis, Count von Zinzendorf, a Saxon nobleman who was a Pietist and counselor at the royal court in Dresden. As those charter member Moravian refugees were joined by others at Berthelsdorf in Saxony, the Christian commune of *Herrnhut*, "The Lord's Watch" or "The Place that God will Guard," came to be the first fully organized Protestant Church.

The name "Moravian" became officially associated with this group of Christians on May 12, 1749, when the British Parliament issued an *Act of Recognition* of it as a valid "Protestant Episcopal Church" having doctrines differing little from those of the Church of England. Parliament made an extremely thorough investigation of the origin, doctrines and methods of this religious group, because of its active work both in colonial America and in England's West Indian island possessions. The resulting document refers to the members as "Moravians" because Moravia was for the most part, the place of their ethnic origin. This designation thus became the official name of one of the earliest Protestant denominations.

Edna's maternal ancestors, who were associated with the Moravian Church through consecutive generations, came originally from the small town of Blickensdorf near the Swiss city of Zug, where there are still citizens with her mother's family name of "Blickensderfer." They, too, might well have remained there if they had not listened to one Menno Simons, who, like John Hus, had been ordained to the Roman Catholic priesthood and had left it for the cause of reformation. Simons became the leader of those who were called "Anabaptists," or "Re-Baptizers," a label of reproach given them by their opponents. His followers, scattered over Switzerland, Holland and Germany, came to be called "Mennonites" from his given name. They were banned in Switzerland for their religious tenets of a firm outspoken daily discipleship to Jesus Christ, a "love ethic" which later came to be called "pacifism," and their strong insistence on separation of church and state.

"Anabaptist" Blickensderfer, whose real given name is not known, being forced to leave Switzerland, moved to the town of Speyer in the Palatinate of Bavaria in Germany. There, on February 12, 1716, he received permission from the Electoral Palatinate Court to purchase the Kohlacher Estate, consisting of some sixty-six *morgen* (1¹/₂ acres) of land from one Ulrich Schneider. The land titles for this transaction are in the government archives of the city of Speyer, then the capital of the Rhenish province of Bavaria. There, he lived in peace, producing a family of six sons, five of whom later immigrated to America, leaving the third son to keep the estate, which was still at last (1906) investigation, in Blickensderfer hands.

Edna's great-great-great-grandfather was the oldest of those six sons. Christian Blickensderfer (1724–1800) was born on the Kohlacher Estate and was married on January 7, 1748 to Catherine Shurger, daughter of a Mennonite preacher from Eisenbach, Zweibruecken. In 1753, at the age of twenty-nine, Christian and his wife, together with his youngest brother, eighteen-year-old Yost, crossed the Atlantic on the ship *Romand*, Arthur Trau, Master, out of Rotterdam, via Cowes, England. Both Christian and Yost had to sign the *Declaration of Allegiance to the King of England*, required at that time of all newcomers to the colonies. Their signatures are preserved in the colonial records in Harrisburg, Pennsylvania. Immediately upon arrival in Philadelphia, the Christian Blickensderfer family joined the Moravian community. A year and a half later, they acquired a small farm near Lititz, Pennsylvania.

The Moravian Church was among the very first to establish schools, libraries and printing presses in colonial America. The excellent reputation of Moravian schools for character-building was a natural result of Comenius' conviction that children belong to God and that it is every teacher's high privilege to lead them into Christian maturity. A seminary for girls founded in Bethlehem, Pennsylvania, in 1748, first opened its doors to non-Moravians in 1785. Institutions like Linden Hall in Nazareth, were attended by students such as Eleanor Lee, George Washington's grandniece, and daughters from the families of Thomas Jefferson and Chief Justice John Jay.

THE MORAVIAN INDIAN MISSIONS

Count Zinzendorf, in his later years an ordained bishop of the Moravian Church, made three trips from Bethlehem over the Allegheny Mountains. He signed a treaty of friendship with representatives of the Six Nations, whereby Moravian missionaries were welcomed throughout Iroquois territory. The first Moravian Indian congregation was formed in 1741. David Zeisberger and his Indian friend, Chief Glikkikan, began work in May 1772, with twenty-eight other Christian Indians on the construction of a village called *Schoenbrunn*, "Beautiful Springs," in the Tuscawaras Valley of Ohio. They were joined in August of that same year by more than two hundred Delaware Christians from Pennsylvania, led by missionaries Heckwelder and Ettwein.

The church they built was forty by thirty-six feet. There was also a large schoolhouse and sixty homes of hewn timber, each surrounded by a fence. Lay workers and artisans lived side by side with their Indian brothers, each ministering to the other with their individual capabilities and produce. By the time of the American Revolution, more than a hundred Indian children were enrolled in school there, being taught with textbooks written and printed for them in their own language.

During the Revolutionary War, time and again, British agents attempted to persuade the local Indians to turn against the settlers but their efforts failed. The strong Christian influence and moral courage of David Zeisberger, the Moravian missionary, did more than anything else to support these border colonies during that time of crisis, by helping the Delawares and their allied nations to maintain their neutrality.

When the United States had gained its independence and the American Revolution was over, Henry Laurens of the Continental Congress conveyed the official thanks of the government to the Indian Christians for their loyalty throughout the fighting and to the missionaries for turning back war parties, ransoming captives and warning officers of intended massacres. In appreciation, the United States Congress in 1796 gave three tracts of four thousand acres each in the Tuscawaras Valley of Ohio as a home for the Christian Indian community. It was soon apparent that the Indian congregations could occupy only a portion of the twelve thousand acres set aside for them by Congress. In 1797, the Directors of the Moravian Society for Propagating the Gospel were appointed trustees of the grant. An appeal went out for Moravian settlers to leave Pennsylvania and move over into Ohio.

The first group to respond organized the *Gnaddenhutten*, "Tents of Grace" Congregation. They built on the very same site where, on March 8, 1782, ninety Christian Indians had been forced into a cabin and without reason or explanation, were massacred by a Colonel Williamson and his company of militia. Among the twenty-nine men, twenty-seven women and thirty-four children shot and scalped that day were Zeisberger's friend and companion, Chief Glikkikan and his wife.

It was on this original Indian land grant that Edna's forefathers lived and worked for four generations, supporting their families and continuing to minister to the Indian populations of the integrated Moravian settlements. The sites of the early Indian missions were among the first to be farmed by the new settlers, for the land had once been cleared at Schoenbrunn, Gnaddenhutten, Tuscawaras, Coshocton, Lichtenau, Salem and New Philadelphia, Ohio.

Since Christian Blickensderfer (1753–1820) was born just one week after his parents landed in Philadelphia, he did not have the problem of having sworn allegiance to the King of England, as his father had. Not bound by this oath, he served in the Continental Army, in the State Militia of Pennsylvania for five years. His brother, Jacob, died of camp fever contracted while furnishing supplies to the Moravian hospital for Revolutionary War soldiers in Lititz.

In the spring of 1812, in response to the call to help occupy the concession in Ohio, Christian and his wife, Barbara,
moved with twenty members of their extended family. The
1200 acres set aside for the Blickensderfer family in Tuscawaras County were carefully apportioned among them all. On
New Year's Day, 1815, a new Moravian congregation was
formed at Sharon, Ohio, with forty-one charter members. An
article from a 1905 Ohio newspaper, written on the occasion
of the ninetieth anniversary of this church, states that "at that
time the woods in this neighborhood were full of Blickensderfers! And all were noted for their hospitality!" The home of
John, Edna's great-grandfather, particularly was noted as
"the place where the Moravian missionaries and ministers
and all the people of God in general felt at ease!"

Simon Peter Blickensderfer (1813–1880), Edna's grandfather, was known far and wide for his integrity and warm
hospitality. The same newspaper clipping states that "when it
came to this special quality, Simon was a chip off the old
block, only intensified, if that is possible! You could scarcely
go by Simon's home on a Sunday without being greeted in
stentorian tones of good cheer: 'Won't you stop? Better stop
and get dinner!' Warm and gracious hospitality was a particular trait that definitely belonged to all who bore the name of
Blickensderfer!"

Edna's grandfather was a man of considerable wealth
and a keen sense of stewardship and responsibility for his possessions. He and his wife, Mathilda Walton, welcomed into
their home a total of twelve boys and three girls, whom they
reared and educated along with their own two daughters, Cornelia and Martha. Several of these were orphaned children of
their Blickensderfer relatives. Edna's mother, Cornelia, was
born on September 13, 1850, at New Philadelphia, Ohio. She
was the first boarding student enrolled in the Hope Moravian
Seminary for Young Ladies, which opened in Hope, Bartho-
lomew County, Indiana on November 17, 1866. It offered a
three-year course for young women "after the completion of
an ordinary, common school education."

Cornelia's cousin, George Canfield Blickensderfer, just
one month younger than she, was the grandson of one of the

nephews who had thrown in his lot with the Christian Blickensderfer family when it migrated as a family unit from Lititz
over into the Tuscawaras Valley of Ohio in 1812. It was Cousin George who invented and manufactured one of the first
really successful portable typewriters. Much of Cornelia's
family wealth came from investments made by her father in
this business bearing the family name, which was launched
with the combined backing of several members of the closely
knit family group.

The high rank of this particular piece of office equipment
in the field of inventions is evidenced by the following description of the Blickensderfer Typewriter, popularly called "THE
BLICK":

> Produced in 1893, this portable wheel-type machine
> literally took the world by storm, being the first one of its
> type to embody the requirements of stability, speed and
> portability. Hundreds of thousands were sold both in Amer-
> ica and in the foreign market and serviceable "BLICKS"
> are still found everywhere. The inventor was G. C. Blick-
> ensderfer Manufacturing Company, Stamford, Connecti-
> cut. Similar in operation to the sleeve-wheel in the Cran-
> dall, the type-wheel in the BLICK moved to three levels to
> reach the required letter-line, then revolved to place the let-
> ter in position and struck downward on the platen to make
> an impression. This impression was powerful enough to
> make several carbon copies. The mechanics employed were
> the marvel of the hundreds of writing-machine types and
> the machine justly deserved the tremendous sale it en-
> joyed.*

Cornelia's girlhood home was a center of strong and active interest in the work of all Christian missionaries. Several
family members were themselves missionaries. Close kin
worked on the Delaware Indian Reservation in Franklin
County, Kansas. Another cousin was married to John H. Kill-
buck, a Delaware Indian educated at Nazareth, who was for
years superintendent of the Moravian Mission of Alaska. Cornelia's cousin, Hannah, of New Philadelphia, was the wife of

---

* *The Carl P. Dietz Collection of Typewriters*, George Herrel, page 14.

George A. Weiss of Bethlehem, missionary of the Moravian Church to St. Thomas in the West Indies. Both died there of Yellow Fever, only four days apart. Mission in obedience to Christ's command was no abstract concept to Cornelia Blick- ensderfer. It was clothed in the flesh and blood of her own Ohio kin! She herself always longed to serve overseas, but health reasons never permitted.

THE BOSCHE GIRLS

Winifred and Edna, being only two years apart, were very close. They once overheard a conversation in which the "Bosché girls" were being discussed. One of the speakers said to the other, "Which one do you mean, the *smart* one or the *pretty* one?" This question provided them with a lifelong topic of light-hearted disagreement for neither could ever agree with the other as to which one was which!

When Winifred, the older, graduated from Austin High School in 1903, Philip and Cornelia decided that the time had come for both daughters to have the experience of going away to boarding school.

Washington College in Washington, D.C., was selected because it offered both high school and junior college level courses. It had a high academic standard, was located in the stimulating cultural and political environment of the nation's capital and was near to Philip's half-brother, Captain Robert Stocker, residing at that time with his wife and two sons, in their Navy Yard residence in Norfolk, Virginia.

It was a particularly interesting time for two girls from Texas to become residents of Washington! A brisk and heady atmosphere pervaded the wide avenues and stately halls of the seat of government. A deep psychological change was taking place as "Manifest Destiny" broke its continental bounds and gave the people of the United States for the first time a new sense of diplomatic prestige and military prowess abroad. This initial world outlook was suddenly acquired as control over strategic Cuba, Puerto Rico, the Philippines, Guam, the Hawaiian Islands and Panama all came within the nation's surprised grasp as a result of the little war that lasted less than four months — The Spanish American War.

It was "Teddy" Roosevelt, the youngest man ever to accede to the office of the president, who largely effected these changes. Texans in particular had rallied around the young Assistant Secretary of the Navy, who so dramatically gave up his post to "charge up San Juan Hill." Many of the colorful volunteer regiment called "The Rough Riders" were hardy, adventuresome cowboy-spirts from the Lone Star State, where the group was formed and trained. A great many Texans, the Boschés and Eugene Kellersberger included, had a proud sense of proprietorship in the youthful, robust, and vigorous personality that now occupied the White House as a result of the assassination of President McKinley on September 14, 1901. In 1904, he would once again be inaugurated as president, this time not by default but triumphantly, on his own by right of election!

What was more, not every Washington College girl had an uncle close at hand who was directly involved in implementing Theodore Roosevelt's strong views on the influence of sea power and the creation of a brand new steel navy! The Bosché girls' Uncle Robert Stocker was, at that time, Assistant Chief of Bureau of Construction and Repair, in charge of the Design Division of that Bureau. He had graduated first in his class of forty-four students from the Naval Academy on June 10, 1887, and would in a few short years, with the rank of Rear Admiral, be awarded the Navy Cross for his designing of the "Eagle" class of vessels.

Edna Bosché's school-girl experiences during the fifteenth and sixteenth years of her young life are vividly glimpsed through the pages of her sister Winifred's Washington College diary and scrapbook. The spirited descriptions of lively dormitory life and the "shenanigans" the sisters shared in are delightful reading and bring alive the exciting events of a past era.

Room 16, assigned to the Bosché sisters, was a popular spot because of the seemingly endless supply of luscious Texas pecans continuously received from home. As in every dormitory, EATING seemed to be the most popular pastime any hour of the day and night!

The scrapbook contains many mementoes of the March

4, 1905, Roosevelt inauguration. There is a photograph of President Theodore Roosevelt and his wife and six handsome children and a large lapel-button picture of "T.R.," the "Rough Rider," tied with red, white, and blue bows. The menu of the Inaugural Ball Supper at the White House, which Edna attended, is tied with a silken cord and lists the numbers of the Promenade Concert by the Marine Band, as well as the waltzes, two-steps, polkas and promenades of the evening's dancing.

There is a much-worn *Member's Pass* to the House of Representatives, signed by Senator Burleson of Texas, dated January 7, 1904, stating: "Admit Miss Winifred Bosché and friends to the Visitors' Gallery of the 58th Congress." Calling cards pasted into the scrapbook include those of Uncle Robert's friends, Rear Admiral P. F. Harrington and Lieutenant Benjamin B. McCormick, Commanding Officer of the U.S.S. *Worden,* as well as those of naval cadets, members of a visiting Princeton baseball team, and numerous other young men callers.

There are handwritten invitations to parties in other girl's rooms and to meetings of Edna's 9-member Chocolate Club and her 8-member Whist Club. Winifred belonged to a more sedate 12-member Euchre Club. Theatre programs of plays attended by the Washington College girls included Ethel Barrymore in *Cousin Kate,* Julia Marlowe in *When Knighthood was in Flower,* Ada Rehan and Otis Skinner in *The Taming of the Shrew,* the Original London Company presenting the XV Century Morality Play, *Everyman* and A. H. Wilson in *The Watch on the Rhine.* Opera and musical programs attended by the girls included Calvé in *Carmen,* Edith Mattison in *Lohengrin,* the first English-language production of *Parsifal* and Madame Schumann-Heink in *Love's Lottery,* a comic opera that had the girls laughing until their sides ached!

Excerpts from Winifred's diary, many referring to Edna, give a light-hearted revelation of the two wonderful years the two sisters shared in their Washington boarding school. In years to come, Edna, in her mud-walled, grass-roofed home in the Belgian Congo, would recall those school days with nostalgic pleasure:

Christmas, 1904. We spent the entire Christmas holidays with Uncle Robert Stocker and Aunt Susie in their home at the Navy Yard in Norfolk, Virginia. What we didn't see in Hampton and Newport News was not worth seeing! We met young naval officers, Captain Low, Captain Dillingham, Captain Hill and Lieutenants Todd and Price. Had a glorious snowball fight with two paymasters! Admiral P. F. Harrington is very nice, even if he does tease us about Texas and General Sheridan. We chatted with Admiral Sigsbee, who was in command of the *Maine.*

January 1, 1905. Still with Uncle Robert and Aunt Susie. Edna went to church with Captain Low. In the afternoon, Uncle Robert took Edna and me and the other guests all over the U.S.S. *Mohawk* and later we took quite a long ride out on Chesapeake Bay in his private launch. Tomorrow, we pack our trunks and return to school.

January 23, 1905. Visit to Congress. Heard hot discussion between Senator from Colorado and Senator Bevridge on the "Stateshood Bill."

February 11, 1905. Went to see Forbes Robertson in *Love and the Man.* He ought to stick to classics. After the theatre, we had hot chocolate and crackers in our room.

February 25, 1905. We went to the Capitol to the unveiling of the statues of Houston and Austin. I heard so many nice things about Texas that I got positively excited! The Congressman from Missouri is really fine!

March 3, 1905. In the evening, the school presented two plays, Longfellow's *Miles Standish* and *Armgart* by George Eliot. Edna played the part of Walpurgia in the Eliot drama. She was absolutely splendid! She did just *beautifully,* was just as natural and pretty as could be. Mills Heiling, here with the Pennsylvania Militia for the Inaugural Parade tomorrow came by to see us!

March 4, 1905. This morning at a quarter to ten, we all took the streetcar for downtown. We had splendid rooms reserved for us over the National Theatre, from where we had a grand view of Pennsylvania Avenue. We had hardly gotten there when President Roosevelt and his escort went up the avenue on the way to the Capitol. We watched the crowd and ate peanuts and ginger snaps till one o'clock. Then we had a lunch of ham and cheese sandwiches and baked beans, oranges, and cupcakes, that we brought with

us. At a quarter to two promptly the parade began and
lasted until 6:15. We had to leave, however, at five. It was
such a grand place to see it all! Edna attended the Inaugural Ball. We girls who did not, crawled through the windows out onto the roof to watch the fireworks from the
White House.

March 6, 1905. Today, we attended the Inaugural Grant
Concert, in honor of the Army and Navy, at the Pension
Building, given by the United States Marine Band and the
Hayden Male Chorus of five hundred voices from Utica,
New York. Lt. General Adna R. Chaffee represented the
Army and Admiral Dewey, the Navy. At the Russian Build-
ing tonight, we met one of Mary's friends from her home
town. I wish that *Texas* were not so far away!

March 18, 1905. May and I sewed on our third corset covers
all afternoon. Played Whist and Euchre after dinner.
Teacher came down the hall and called us down twice for
being so noisy. Ate up two big boxes of candy!

April 1, Saturday. This morning for an April Fool "lark" the
whole school stole out before rising bell and ran away! Mr.
and Mrs. Menefee tried to call us back. Mrs. Menefee came
up to my room last night at midnight and warned me not to
try to go off campus and told me to warn the girls. So I obediently piled out of bed at midnight. Edna, Amelia, and I
went over to Mary's room to see what she thought about it.
We had a midnight conference and decided that she was
only trying to scare us. And after all the trouble that the
girls had gone to yesterday, to get all the girls to SIGN that
they would go and *not* back out, we did not want to give it
up! And we surely didn't! Mrs. Menefee patrolled the halls
last night until 3:00 a.m. and then got up at 4 o'clock. I
hope she enjoyed it! We all took the streetcar to Riverdale
and were walking along trying to find a dry place to eat our
breakfast when we saw the *grandest* old mansion! We asked
some of the neighbors about it and they said that it was the
Calvert Mansion, Lord Baltimore's home, and that it was in the
care of an old Negro couple that lived there. *Think* of it!
What luck! To run across a place like that! Even the doubt-
ful ones of us were glad then that we had come! So we ate
our breakfast on Lord Baltimore's steps and front porch!
Then the Negro caretakers took us through the house. We
played on Lord Baltimore's piano and danced in his recep-

tion hall. The library is the quaintest little thing. The mansion must have been a beautiful place, palatial in those times. We even saw his old carriage, so queer! Then a kind, old neighbor lady came out of her house and told us to be sure to see the river. So we went up and stood on the Twin Bridge and then walked up the riverbank, past the picturesque little dam and found a beautiful little place to sit and rest on the sand and on the rustic benches. Then with much difficulty, we gathered the girls together and came back, reaching the school at 10 o'clock in morning. And oh! It pains me to tell the rest! The teachers announced in cold, unsympathetic tones that they had returned our matinee tickets to *Hamlet* and that we were going to have SCHOOL on SATURDAY AFTERNOON! And we could not leave the campus again that day. But we had had our fun, so we submitted meekly, not without some blackening of character, however! It was not Mr. Menefee's fault. *He* was going to take it just as we meant it — as an April Fool Joke, but Mrs. Culler was simply *furious!*

May 28, Baccalaureate Sunday. I took Mama, my cousin Helen, and Edna to Christ Church in Alexandria for the morning service, where both Washington and Lee attended during their lifetimes. They liked the little church so very much! The choir was splendid and the tenor sang my favorite, *One Sweetly Solemn Thought.* Just as we were waiting for the streetcar in Alexandria to go back to school, Mama suddenly said, "O dear! I wish that I could see Mrs. Slaymaker!" There was a man standing on the street corner near us and Mama asked him if he could direct us to her home, which he did. So we decided that instead of going back to school immediately, we would stop at Mrs. Slaymaker's. She is the mother of the Presbyterian missionary who drowned in the Congo River when he went out for the first time in November 1903. The mission steamer *Lapsley* capsized and many were drowned, including Mr. Slaymaker. Our Highland Presbyterian Church back in Austin had supported him on the mission field. We had never met his mother, but our church had corresponded with her after his death and was very much interested in her because of him. We found her to be very pleasant, an entertaining old lady. She and her family all insisted that we all four stay for dinner! Edna, Helen and I were very glad that Mama ac-

cepted. It meant that we missed our Baccalaureate Sermon
that afternoon at the Vermont Avenue Christian Church,
but it was well worth it!

With graduation exercises on May 29, 1905, two years of
boarding school life ended in a tearful combination of great
sorrow and great joy. Edna and her sister always treasured the
warm memories of those exciting years lived in the nation's
capital, tasting with youthful relish "high society," the perfection of entertainment in a golden age of drama and musical
performance, and the innocent fun and frolic of a fashionable
girls' boarding school at the turn of the century.

Back home in Austin, Winifred enrolled in The University of Texas from which she graduated in 1910 with a bache-
lor's degree and a Phi Beta Kappa key. Edna Bosché returned
to her old school, the Whitis Academy, meeting for the first
time her classmate, Eugene Kellersberger, who had been a
Whitis student during the two years that she had been in
Washington. Both were now sixteen, ready for their final year
in high school, from which they graduated together in June
1906.

THE UNIVERSITY STUDENT
IN THE BOSCHE HOME

As Edna's Whitis classmate and sweetheart, and as a
member of their church, the Boschés knew Eugene Kellersberger well. They were also acquainted with his Cypress Mill
family through Ulrika, Edna's friend before Eugene entered
"Miss Mollie's" school. It was, therefore, with real affection
and anticipation that they invited him to be one of the students occupying the third floor accommodations of their home
for as long as he would be enrolled at The University of Texas.

Eugene's first residency in the Bosché home was very
short; only a few days after school started, he came down with
typhoid fever. He had no choice but to return to Cypress Mill
for a period of recuperation. Following his recovery, he took
an engineering job on the Mexican border at San Benito, near
Brownsville, Texas, and worked there in the heat, the sand
and the cactus throughout the summer of 1907. In later years,

Sweethearts, Edna Bosché and Eugene Kellersberger, Whitis Academy, Austin, Texas, 1906.

he wrote: "In that absence, I was held true to God in my young Christian life by Edna and drawn back to the university the next year." Edna's bright letters, and her mother's daily prayers for him and the fact that the offer of that room in the Bosché home still held good, were all strong factors in preventing him from becoming a "drop-out."

Once again, in the fall of 1907, Eugene enrolled for his freshman year at The University of Texas. It was his brother Arnold's senior year. Proud of their Swiss grandfather, Getulius' professional example, both boys were enrolled in the School of Engineering. Arnold graduated in 1908 with an engineering degree, but by then, his younger brother was already showing signs of a shift of interest to the fields of biology and medicine.

Very early one morning, shortly after Eugene rejoined the household, Edna came upon him hidden in the most secluded corner of the library, reading her father's *Bible*. So engrossed was he that he did not even hear her enter the room. Startled, he looked up at her from the depths of the big leather armchair, a guilty expression on his earnest, open face. He had never had a chance to read the *Bible* before. He was wondering if he could borrow this one for a little while each morning; he was curious to know what it had to say in entirety.

This incident of being caught "red-handed" with a *Bible* was the beginning of a lifetime habit for Eugene. He was given his own *Bible* and, from then on, every day for an hour before breakfast, he and Edna read and studied it together. When it was cold, they sat beside the library fireplace, with poker and coal scuttle handy. When the weather was warm, they read on the porch, surrounded by the sounds of jubilant birdcalls and cool, early morning fragrances from the dew-sprinkled lawn and flower garden. Systematically and consistently, they studied, seeking the answers to questions and finding them. If they were apart, they read the same passages that they had agreed upon, at the same hour of each day. Daily they grew in their grasp of God's tremendous plan for His whole creation through the ages, and in their radiant wonder at their own part in that same plan, being revealed in the deep affection, growing respect and pure love that they increasingly held for each other. It was in this atmosphere of warm acceptance that Eugene's faith matured and became strong and vital, undergirded by intercessory prayer and deep spiritual concern. It is little wonder that, in the years that followed, he always said, "I found Jesus Christ in the Bosché home."

Eugene's living expenses at the Boschés' were taken care of in exchange for his services to the family. On winter mornings, he brought in the coal and lit the fires in the various rooms. He milked the family cow morning and evening, curried and fed the horse and made a trip early each morning to the ice factory for a large block of ice to put inside the icebox. He polished the surrey, mowed and raked the lawn, ran errands and shopped for Mrs. Bosché as she requested. She came to love Eugene dearly and called him "her right-hand man"!

Cornelia was a gracious hostess, careful homemaker, and wise, thrifty shopper. She oversaw all her household affairs with meticulous attention and planned each meal in detail well in advance. She inherited the family trait of hospitality and regularly had as many as six or eight invited dinner guests each week. Social obligations, the amenities of reciprocal entertaining, as well as civic occasions and annual seasonal festivities were all gladly participated in. With her pretty daughters, Cornelia enjoyed both attending and being hostess for garden parties, afternoon teas and "at homes." During the peaceful, affluent years of the first Roosevelt era, such social life was at the same time, both refined and relaxed. Her greatest quality, however, was a loving heart that reached out in sincere interest and concern to everyone. At all times, she carried in her purse a copy of R. A. Torrey's *Vest Pocket Companion for Christian Workers*, a booklet containing selected scripture texts for various situations. The flyleaves were filled with names, addresses and phone numbers and a few telling remarks about some of the people with whom she talked. "Personal Work" to her was never a question of misguided zeal or a cursory, "Brother, are you saved?" She genuinely cared about each individual as a person and desired to know their circumstances and needs as discerned through sensitive, friendly conversation. Her love expressed itself in practical, useful ways as well as in the strong support of intercessory prayer for all who crossed her path. A number of ministers who were young seminary students during those years have recounted how a heart-to-heart talk and a quiet prayer time with Mrs. Bosché over a budding romance, a tangled love affair, a heartbreak or a difficult family, financial or school situation, always seemed to set invisible forces to work. She knew from experience that abiding prayer is truly answered!

Week after week, year after year, the lively, elegant home regularly opened its doors to Cornelia's first choice in visitors — ministers, bishops, lay leaders, professors and students at universities and seminaries, and above all, missionaries from the far corners of the earth. Phil Bosché, the reticent host, was keenly aware of his own, practically invisible but important role. He quietly watched his visitors with the keen satisfaction of knowing exactly who it was that made possible his wife's ready and bountiful hospitality.

Sharing gracious meals with such a variety of people, Eugene listened, learned, asked questions, absorbed and participated in the rich exchange of thought and conversation. He

came to look forward to the annual visit of one guest in particular, that of Bishop Edward Rondthaler. Reckoning from
Comenius, he was the 184th Bishop of the Moravian Church.
For fifty-three years after his consecration in 1891, he lovingly
shepherded his scattered flock throughout the Southern Province of the Moravian Church from its base in Salem, North
Carolina. The entire family enjoyed his visits, for he was a
great, warm-hearted man with a happy, friendly and deeply
sympathetic personality, particularly appreciated by children
and young people. A scholar of unusually broad and liberal
education, he had been trained in the University of Erlangen
in Germany, after completing his theological studies in the
United States. His special abilities as a teacher, his versatile
mind and his language gifts were all put to use for many years
as editor of the monthly Moravian organ, the *Wachovia Moravian,* to which the Blickensderfers and the Boschés subscribed.

It was at the Bosché dining table that Eugene also came
to know Dr. Wylie Hamilton Forsythe. A Kentucky lad
trained at the Hospital College of Medicine in Louisville, Dr.
Forsythe had served as an army doctor in the Spanish American War and had had a private practice in Lexington before
being sent to Korea as a medical missionary in 1904. Shortly
after arriving at Chungju, he was called at night by a wealthy
Korean who had been unmercifully mauled by robbers. When
he had finished dressing the numerous wounds, it was too late
to return to his post on his little Korean pony, so he was invited to remain as a guest in the home of his patient till morning. Before the night was over, the same band of vicious out-
laws returned, this time to kill the intruding foreigner who had
come to the rescue of their victim. Dr. Forsythe was brutally
attacked and his skull fractured by blows from heavy pistol
butts. The beating was brought to a halt only when his host's
wife threw herself across his body to protect him. The bandits
kicked him out of the house and off the edge of the porch, believing him dead. As a result of this frightful experience, the

doctor had to be taken back to the United States for a long term of treatment and rehabilitation.

In Dr. Forsythe, Eugene saw the shining qualities of Stephen, the first martyr, the same courage and self-forgetfulness in the face of danger. It was Dr. Forsythe who challenged the young University of Texas student to become a medical missionary.

[4]

Doctor in the Making

THE "LONGHORN" PRE-MED STUDENT

Though Eugene's room and board were provided for by being a member of the Bosché household, he still had to find various ways of earning his tuition at The University of Texas. He served as church janitor at the Highland Presbyterian Church, which gave him some remuneration throughout the year. He also supplemented his income by coaching German, an easy task for him, since it was the only language spoken in his boyhood home. One summer he worked in an architect's office, and during another summer he was the bookkeeper for the Bosché Troy Laundry. The most physically demanding of his summertime jobs was as a construction worker on the Congress Avenue Bridge, built across the Colorado River at Austin to replace the one destroyed in the flood of 1900.

In the earliest stages of its construction, when the pilings were first being located underwater, Eugene's boyhood swimming and diving experience came in handy. He spent almost as much time under water as above it, diving down repeatedly with necessary ropes and gear. It was while he was employed on this bridge construction that he had one of the narrowest escapes of his life. One day a board gave way beneath him as he was crossing the bridge falsework. He was just starting to

fall through the gap onto the rocky flats of the Colorado below
when the strong arm of a fellow worker, who later became
captain of The University of Texas football team, reached out
and grabbed him just in time, pulling him back to safety.

The same job gave him experience of another sort. Pressure for the rapid completion of the bridge was so great that
the company in charge of the construction began to operate
seven days a week. Eugene did not mind the overtime work on
Saturdays, but when he was ordered to report to work on Sunday morning, he spontaneously objected: "But that's the
Lord's Day!" Attendance at Dr. Penick's Sunday School Class
and the Highland Church had become an essential in his life.
He simply could not do without it! His boss's curt response
was, "Who cares? If you won't come back on Sunday, then
don't bother to come back on Monday!" This was the manner
in which he was "fired" from work as a bridge builder, an experience which made him surer than ever that the field of engineering and construction was not for him.

By the end of his junior year in 1910, Eugene's natural
gifts in anatomy, biology and chemistry were apparent to his
professors. He was awarded the position of student assistant
in The University of Texas Biology Department for his senior
year. One of his responsibilities was to collect and care for the
animal specimens used by students in the biology laboratory
for dissecting. He collected dozens of frogs in nearby streams,
fed the caged rats, cats and armadillos and watched over the
countless bottled insects in their various cycles of growth. It
was during this year that he carefully dissected and cured the
skin of a seven-foot-long rattlesnake he had killed near the
Pedernales. When mounted, the skin was all of a foot wide. It
was displayed on the wall of the entry to the Biology Building,
where it remained for years.

The biology laboratory that particular year was located
on the top floor of the Women's Building, some of the lower
floors of which served as a dormitory. One holiday weekend
an unknown prankster with a rare sense of humor opened the
doors of the various cages, allowing the animals awaiting laboratory use to escape. Many of them eventually managed to
slink, crawl or hop down the steps to lower floors. Eugene

never forgot the entire day he spent trying to recapture escaped animals, to the accompaniment of frantic female screams echoing from every corner of the women's dormitory.

Edna and Eugene saw little of each other during the academic sessions of 1908 to 1910, for Edna was in Chicago, a student at the Moody Bible Institute. Eugene continued to live with the Boschés, a totally accepted member of the family circle. The engaged couple kept in touch through weekly letters to one another and in their common daily *Bible* study hour, which they both continued to observe, studying the same passages at the same time, though apart.

During the summer of 1909, Eugene accompanied the Bosché family to Montreat, North Carolina, the summer conference center of the Presbyterian Church in the United States. Edna was not with them, for her program at Moody carried straight through the summer months.

Montreat is located in a quiet, wooded cove of the Blue Ridge Mountains, near Asheville. There at the World Missions Conference, sponsored by the Executive Committee of Foreign Missions of that denomination, Eugene had long talks with the famous medical missionary from Korea, Dr. Wylie Hamilton Forsythe, whom he had already known as a guest in the Bosché home in Austin.

Amid the sun-dappled rhododendron thickets, with the music of the rushing mountain stream flowing over the rocks, Dr. Forsythe put his arm around the shoulders of the young pre-med student from Texas and prayed aloud for him from an overflowing heart. It was then and there that Eugene made his own personal decision to give his life to medical missionary service in Africa.

A photograph of Eugene at work in the biology laboratory of The University of Texas in the fall of 1909 shows him totally absorbed in the job of dissecting a large cat. Across the back of the picture he scribbled at some time: "Hard on cats!" In the right background of the photograph is a large globe with the dark colored continent of Africa clearly outlined by light colored seas. Years later, when one of Eugene's daughters asked him if that picture had been deliberately arranged, with the field of the future missionary service in mind, his answer was an emphatic, "NO!" He had not even been aware of the fact that there was a geographical globe in the room where he was working. The result is a highly significant depiction of the missionary-to-be, lost in concentration on his project, unconsciously preparing for a lifetime of difficult service on that far continent, silently waiting in the background.

Following her graduation from Moody Bible Institute, Edna returned to Austin and registered at The University of Texas in Arts and Sciences, for the academic year of 1910–1911. This was Eugene's senior year as a pre-med student; marriage was to follow the first year in medical school.

During the week both were totally occupied with their courses, with weekends fuller than ever, now that Edna was trained in new aspects of teaching and approach. That precious hour of shared *Bible* study and prayer before breakfast each morning was often the only time of the day that they saw each other during that very happy, busy year. What a new perception, confidence and excitement Eugene now noted in Edna's instruction, as they studied together, following her two years of intensive *Bible* study at Moody! As never before, she was familiar with every part of *The Book* and was able to discuss with him topics of *Bible* history and experience that they had rarely touched on before. Their church, Sunday School and mission work that year was a rich, rewarding shared adventure!

The 1911 *Cactus*, The University of Texas annual, has an excellent picture of Eugene, the graduate, in his cap and gown. The single-mindness of his life style is witnessed to by the fact that the YMCA is his only student activity listed. His singleness of purpose is also evident in the "catch phrase" coined by student editors of the annual to characterize the personalities of each of the graduating seniors.

Beside Eugene's senior picture is the phrase: *From protoplasm to peripitas.* As a conscientious student who was also working his way through school, he had little time for anything other than the current "protoplasm" in the lab, or hurrying along the "peripitas," the walkway that surrounded The University of Texas campus at that time. The annual thus pays tribute to Eugene, the single-minded graduate, and four hard years of concentrated work of which he had a right to be proud.

Upon graduating from The University of Texas in June 1911, Eugene left immediately for his job as Assistant to the Director of the Chemistry Research Laboratory of The Marine Biological Laboratory at Woods Hole, Massachusetts. When he had free time from his projects, he was most happily occupied as the paid swimming instructor and waterfront companion of the children of Professor Lilly of the University of Chicago, who spent vacations at Woods Hole. After successfully completing his summer work, with an invitation to return the following year in the same capacity, Eugene proceeded in September to the Washington University School of Medicine in St. Louis, Missouri, to begin his first year of medical training.

Edna did not enroll again in The University of Texas. Her mother, always frail, was having increasingly frequent bouts with chronic bronchial infections and was often unable to leave her room. The younger daughter's days were now filled with the care of an invalid mother and tending to the household duties that the older woman could no longer handle.

THE WASHINGTON
UNIVERSITY SCHOOL OF MEDICINE

On September 27, 1911, Eugene began his studies at the Washington University School of Medicine in St. Louis, Missouri. The two oldest medical schools west of the Mississippi River were the Missouri Medical College, founded at Kemper College in 1840, and the St. Louis Medical College, founded in 1842, one of the first three schools in the United States to teach microscopic biology. The Medical Department of Washington University was created in 1891 when the St. Louis Medical College became a part of the University, joined in 1899 by the Missouri Medical College.

A total reorganization of the curriculum in 1910 established departmental heads and instructors in anatomy, physiology, biological chemistry, pathology, preventive medicine, medicine, surgery and pediatrics. Carefully selected clinical instructors were chosen from among the outstanding members of the medical profession practicing in St. Louis. Still more far-reaching was the agreement made that year with Barnes Hospital, the St. Louis Children's Hospital and the Martha Parsons Free Hospital, by which the University was to provide the medical staffs of these hospitals, while they in turn agreed to permit the Medical School to use the hospitals for teaching and research.

Just one year before Eugene Kellersberger matriculated, the Washington University Medical School moved from its former location into excellent new facilities at the corner of Kings Highway and Euclid Avenue, facing the wide, 1380-acre expanse of Forest Park, the site of the 1904 Louisiana Purchase Exposition.

Without any question, Eugene was beginning his career in medicine in one of the outstanding medical institutions of the world, with a physical plant comparable to any. The advanced and significant concepts of medical service to the total community that were built into the reorganized curriculum at that time are seen today in such institutional medical groupings as the Cornell-New York and Columbia-Presbyterian centers.

With his degree from The University of Texas, Eugene had no problem in fulfilling the entrance requirements in chemistry, physics and biology, nor with the requirement of the mastery of both English and German.

His subjects covered during the first year of Medical School, together with his final grade in each course, were the following: Embryology, 90; Histology, 90; Gross and Microscopic Neurology, 91; Dissection, 93; Organic Chemistry, 85; Biological Chemistry, 83. At the graduation ceremonies that year he was recognized as ranking first in his class and was awarded the Gill Prize in Anatomy. His bound embryology, histology and neurology notebook, including all of his examination questions and his meticulously drawn diagrams, is still a treasured family possession. There is something of the same clarity of design and style of shading in these drawings that is evident in the surveying maps so carefully executed by his grandfather, when he was a United States deputy surveyor.

Eugene supported himself during his first year in medical school by working as a YMCA secretary. Throughout his entire schooling he was faithful to his promise to himself and to his Lord that he would never work on Sunday. Once, back in Austin, working on the Colorado River bridge, that decision had cost him his job. Now, with the heaviest study schedule he had ever carried in his life, he continued to set each Sunday completely aside for rest and worship.

The sheer delight of waking up on a Sunday morning and knowing that for that entire day not a single thought or worry about school would burden his mind gave him a regular, planned break and a psychological holiday that made him a better student on the other six days. He proved many times over the fact that man, created in God's image, functions more efficiently when he follows the pattern set by the Creator Himself, Who rested after His own six days of labor. Eugene saw in the tense, nervous and exhausted students around him, who forced themselves through a seven-day grind that God never meant for them to endure, the living proof of the sheer, physical need for observing the Fourth Commandment.

BRIDE AND GROOM

On June 18, 1912, Edna Helena Bosché and Eugene Roland Kellersberger were married in a quiet ceremony in the Bosché home at 1402 West Avenue, in Austin, Texas, with only family and very close friends present. It was a joyful day for Helene and Julius Kellersberger and all of Eugene's family from Cypress Mill, as well as for Cornelia and Philip Bosché and their married daughter, Winifred Brown. Both families had lovingly watched the budding love affair from that very first Whitis school-day attraction, seeing it grow strong through long, faithful months of separation.

For their honeymoon trip they took the train from Austin straight to Chicago, spending ten happy days at the Moody Bible Institute where Edna had gone to school. It was Edna's delight to introduce her young husband to the institution that had come to mean more to her than any other. What a joy it was for him to meet the members of the faculty and staff whose warm interest in his wife and her missionary vision had so strengthened and enriched her life!

From Chicago they travelled by train to Woods Hole, Massachusetts, where Eugene was employed for his second summer at the Marine Biological Laboratory. This world-renowned institution for highly technical research in the biological sciences had its beginning in 1873 when the famous Harvard professor, Louis Agassiz, gathered a few of his students for a summer of study of natural history on the small island of Penikese.

The Marine Biological Laboratory provided a happy combination of the elements of a college campus — daily classes, serious individual research projects, dormitory life and a mess hall — together with the relaxed features of a sea resort. Bathing suits were as important as the microscope for they were the daily uniform worn when collecting specimens along the beaches and in the surf, or manning the fleet of small boats sent out to gather marine materials.

For Eugene and Edna, it was the ideal place for their extended honeymoon, a cozy little apartment overlooking restless, wave-crested Buzzard's Bay. The glow of their joy in each other is evident in every snapshot taken that summer and pasted into their photograph album. Here is a picture of a smiling Edna, her long, dark braids forming a crown around her head, wearing a middy blouse sailor dress, perched on a large buoy lying on the dock. There is a photo of Eugene reading in a hammock and another pushing a wheelbarrow loaded with a huge, toothy shark! Another shows Edna standing sedately beside the United States Revenue Cutter, *Acushnet,* while two whole pages are filled with nothing but swimming scenes, with the bride and groom dressed in their extremely modest, early 1900s bathing suits.

One of their favorite spots was the bluff overlooking Vineyard Sound where busy sea lanes from Boston, New York, Buzzard's Bay and the Cape Cod Canal, Nantucket and Long Island Sound all converge to pass through the narrows. Each ship had to stand in so close, passing only a quarter of a mile off shore through the straits, that the details of her superstructure and the activities of her sailors could be observed as if on a moving stage, during the few swift moments of passing. It was as near as they could get for a while, at least, to the large ocean liners that would some day carry them to far-off Africa.

It was during this summer that Eugene experienced the third narrow brush with death of his young manhood. His diving accident as a boy and his close call when working on the Colorado River bridge at Austin were events that had impressed upon him the fact of God's protective hand upon his life for some purpose.

One afternoon, after a hard day of work in the laboratory, Eugene and his friend, Edmund Montgomery, decided to go canoeing. In 1947 Edmund sent a copy of his own version of their harrowing ordeal to his companion:

> "We're a pair of fools!", blurted Eugene as soon as he was able.
>
> "We're a pair of *damn* fools!", I spouted in return.
>
> And neither of us meant "maybe"!
>
> My very first thought after our canoe had overturned suddenly in such dangerous, shark-infested waters had been, "And he's just gotten married, too!"
>
> Several hours before, in the afternoon of a beautiful July day, bronzed, wirey, sharp-featured, straight-shooting Eugene Kellersberger from Texas and I, slightly his junior, had paddled light-heartedly out of Little Harbor at Woods Hole in a borrowed canoe, clad only in our bathing suits, bound we knew not exactly where, but in the general direction of Naushan Island, which loomed up in the distance as a clump of green rising out of the water across the Bay.
>
> Naushan is one of the most easterly of the Elizabeth Chain and helps Penzance Peninsula, jutting out from the mainland, form Woods Hole, the narrow strait through which tidal rhythm, Vineyard Sound and Buzzard's Bay all toss their waters back and forth, following one of Nature's complicated mathematical formulas.
>
> The treacherous undercurrents of the "Hole" on our starboard bow were legendary; we would set our course carefully and avoid that danger by keeping well to the south.
>
> After an enjoyable half-hour paddle through the fairly

smooth waters of Vineyard Sound, we reached the south shore of Naushan, then owned by the Forbes family of Boston. Hidden in its depths among the trees was their summer home.

If we had started out with any intention of returning immediately to Little Harbor, that idea completely slipped our minds when we found that a little stream, almost obscured by overhanging foliage, leading back into Naushan, was entreating us to explore it. We had paddled in from the Sound for a short distance when suddenly there appeared ahead of us some most interesting-looking rapids, not too dangerous — just exciting-looking! We shot them and found that we liked them very much! We wanted more of that! Bringing the canoe ashore, we carried it back along the bank above the rapids and shot them again and again, perhaps a dozen times. Finally we realized that we must press on down the tidal river, aware of the fact but not heeding, that we were getting nearer and nearer to the "Hole" on the opposite side of the Island.

Suddenly we were at the mouth of the river with everything under control, we thought. There not far ahead we could see the rip-tide with its choppy, sharp-pointed waves ending their upward motion with a fling and a flip and then a burst of foam and spray. Then, just as unexpectedly, we found that we could not prevent our being swept into the current. We were actually trying to balance ourselves in that canoe as though we were on a tight wire. Over we went, clinging to the canoe as we drifted further out into the "Hole." We were being swept into Buzzard's Bay with that tremendous current carrying us at its maximum speed out toward New Bedford and the open Atlantic. It was getting very late in the afternoon and it looked as though it was going to be a wet night underfoot for us.

Fear of the dreaded undercurrents caused us to cling tightly to the overturned canoe. Eugene was holding onto the paddle as well, as we drifted along in the chilly water. The attempt to reach shore by swimming we knew would be foolhardy as our strength was no match for the powerful current. We resigned ourselves to our fate and faced the music of the waves and the smoke of New Bedford on the horizon. A brush buoy was out of our reach to the right as we sped past it. But half a mile ahead we could see a spar buoy. We knew that if we missed that, we would be in as hopeless a mess as could be imagined.

Kaleidoscopic, unrelated images of by-gone days and experiences of the past had been flashing through our minds concurrently with thoughts of much unfinished business ashore. But now the buoy ahead demanded our undivided attention. As we drew nearer it seemed as if we were being carried directly toward it. I'm afraid that for a few seconds I selfishly disregarded completely what my companion would do, for I cut loose from the canoe fifty feet or so from the buoy and started swimming toward it, watching it as though it were a running, dodging football player. I made a flying tackle at that buoy and held on for dear life, fearing for several moments that the speed of the current might wrest it from my grip. I hardly had time to congratulate myself when bang! along came the canoe, hitting me on the back of the neck and shoulders, almost going up over my head. And with the canoe came Kellersberger, who was able to clamber above me onto the spar, which was tilting acutely from the impact of the current. He was still holding onto the paddle. I held onto the painter rope of that dadblamed bit of tugging, borrowed property, while trying to hold myself, too, but it was rapidly taking all my strength.

"How much is a canoe worth?", I called up to Kellersberger. "I don't know — twenty dollars, I guess, maybe thirty."

"There she goes!", I called with relief and I let go the rope and watched the bobbing, rolling bottom drift rapidly out of sight.

We kept searching our limited horizon for signs of life but saw only disinterested seagulls. We had lost track of time but it was evident that the night was close. Finally a sail appeared, very small in the gathering dusk to the north of us. Kellersberger from his perch on the spar above me frantically lifted the paddle and waved and watched. We yelled for an interminable age, though surely, our voices did not carry over even a fraction of that distance. At last we saw what we thought was a favorable sign — they were lowering the sail! Tensely we watched and then shouted together, "They're headed toward us!"

"Relieved" was the name for the two stranded "upsets," watching the tiny object on the horizon grow from an almost amorphous speck into a sleek, auxiliary-powered sloop of substantial proportions. In turn, those aboard had watched us grow from what looked to them through powerful marine glasses like two clumps of seaweed caught on the buoy, till they could finally see the whites of our teeth, broadly smiling and chattering a grateful welcome. Our lips were blue from the hours spent in the chilly water, and our faces pale to our rescuers, but to us they were red with our chagrin born of having been caught in such a foolhardy escapade. In our hearts was a solemn prayer of thanks to a Divine Providence.

Eugene's paddle waving back and forth in the air spelled the difference between the rescue of two desperate people at the last possible moment before night fell, and the casual passing by at a distance of "two lumps of seaweed caught on a buoy"! As Edmund Montgomery concluded, a Protecting Providence was with them, keeping the waters free of slicing shark fins, putting an alert observer with powerful marine glasses in hand on watch, and saving them both for a purpose far greater than just drowning.

The medical student's second year in training was very different from his first. Now he was a married man and his father-in-law, Phil Bosché, had generously volunteered to help with a substantial portion of the necessary tuition for that year, as well as for the two remaining years of his son-in-law's medical education. So now, for the first time as a student, Eugene was completely free to devote himself to his studies!

He graduated among the top four in his class, winning the honorary Medical award called *Alpha Omega Alpha,* the medical equivalent of a *Phi Beta Kappa.* He wore his gold key on his watch chain across his vest, as the custom then was, a lovely shining object that his little daughter, Winifred, loved to hold whenever she sat on his lap!

On October 1, 1915, Dr. John F. Cannon, pastor of the Westminster Presbyterian Church in St. Louis, of which Edna and Eugene were members, preached a special sermon to his congregation. It was entitled, "The Importance and Sacredness of the Office of the Medical Missionary," after the sermon, Dr. Eugene Kellersberger was consecrated by the min-

*Dr. and Mrs. Eugene Kellersberger at the time of their appointment as medical
missionaries of the Presbyterian Church in the United States to the Belgian
Congo. St. Louis, Missouri, 1915.*

ister and elders of the Session of that Church for the medical
missionary ministry. It was a most impressive service that
touched the hearts of all present and brought Edna's and Eugene's St. Louis years to a fitting close. They left on the night
train for Kansas City, aware in a new and special way of the
hard life that lay ahead of them in Africa.

INTERNSHIP — KANSAS CITY GENERAL HOSPITAL

Among the many excellent professional contacts Eugene
made as a medical student and intern, one physician stands
out head and shoulders above the rest as the man who made
the deepest personal impact upon him, profoundly shaping his
attitudes, theories, methods and techniques as a medical missionary in the Belgian Congo. As a leader himself in international public health and medical practice, Dr. Kellersberger
would in later years still bear the mark of his influence.

This man was Dr. Arthur Emmanuel Hertzler, who was

on the teaching staff of Kansas City General Hospital where Eugene served his internship in 1915 and 1916.

Medical internships at that time were for only one year. Unlike present-day, highly specialized "residencies," they were "rotating internships" and covered three months each of intensive experience in the general fields of internal medicine, surgery, pediatrics and obstetrics. The ward study of patients, in which Eugene had already had experience in St. Louis hospitals, was also in operation in Kansas City hospitals. Individual patients were assigned to interns for history, examination, diagnosis and treatment.

Famous throughout the United States by his popular name, "The Horse and Buggy Doctor," Dr. Hertzler was called "Chief" by his associates, "Pa" by his students and "Grandpa" by his nurses and adoring children patients. He was a six-foot-two-inch tall, gangly Abraham Lincoln-like figure with rugged features. He divided his time between his teaching in the Kansas City medical schools and hospitals and his own hospital which he opened in Halstead, Kansas in 1902.

Dr. Hertzler's own comment on his teaching methods is noted in his statement: "My students were required to spend four hours a day in the dissecting room. I knew every student thoroughly and paired the good students together. Those who did not wish to learn I ignored and concentrated my efforts on those who were anxious to learn." (Hertzler, *The Horse and Buggy Doctor*, p. 195)

It is obvious that Eugene was among those who adored, listened to, and learned from the doctor and whom, in turn, Dr. Hertzler spotted as having professional possibilities, meriting his time and attention.

The doctor's professional contributions to Eugene became apparent with the passing years. Of supreme importance were the surgical and anaesthesiological techniques learned from Hertzler, the first doctor to introduce into the United States the use of cocaine in local anaesthesia. He even experimented with himself, operating on his arm, his leg and his neck, using cocaine. He wrote the first book on this subject in the English language, having researched the technique in

Germany. Ether had been invented in 1846, followed by chloroform in 1872. Of the two, ether was considered safer and was given by the "drop method." After reaching their field of work in the Congo, Eugene taught Edna how to give an anaesthetic. His trained Congolese male nurses also learned to do this extremely well.

What Dr. Hertzler called his "kitchen surgery" theories enabled Eugene to practice medicine and perform surgery under even more primitive conditions in the heart of Africa than any found in a Kansas farmhouse of the past century. His professor was convinced that the basic essential of "kitchen surgery" is that "only the wound matters! What goes on round about is of very little importance . . . Clean, rapid operating will do more to minimize infection than all the face masks ever inflicted on a docile profession. The biggest factor in aseptic operating is the prompt performance of the operation! This implies a minimum of trauma to the tissue." (*The Horse and Buggy Doctor*, p. 217) This priority of rapidity of action over sterility of surroundings was often proven true for Eugene, as he worked under conditions far less than ideal.

The missionary doctor also shared with his teacher a wise awareness of the importance of the psychology of the patient. As Hertzler discovered that some of his patients actually died because they were literally scared to death, so Eugene struggled in Africa with the same power of fear to kill. A curse, a witchdoctor's potion or an amulet were to be dealt with as real factors in a patient's recovery, and not lightly brushed aside as irrelevant expressions of an animistic culture.

During his internship at Kansas City General, Eugene was often the butt of horseplay and practical jokes played on him by his fellow interns because of his serious and unsuspecting nature. Urgently he was called to the emergency room one night to find one of his fellow interns groaning and writhing on the table in pain, his head bandaged and dripping with blood. Automatically feeling for the patient's pulse, as his first bit of emergency action, Eugene found it to be extraordinarily strong and regular. The "patient," unable to contain himself any longer, burst into hilarious laughter and produced the bottle of red ink which had served realistically enough to "bloody" the bandages!

Another time, during a diptheria epidemic, the interns were required to make cultures of their own throats for experimental purposes. A fellow intern slyly switched Eugene's negative throat culture for a real, positive one. A sympathetic friend, witnessing this exchange, suggested to the dismayed Eugene that there was only one good way to get even for pulling such a not-so-funny practical joke. His friend would spread the rumor that, as a result of finding himself with a positive diptheria culture, Eugene had given himself a large dose of serum that had made him immediately and dangerously ill. When this rumor did reach the ears of the trickster, it was his turn to be dismayed. Scared stiff at the presumed results of his little "joke," he hurried to Eugene's bedside, only to discover that Dr. and Mrs. Kellersberger were both out of the city on missionary deputation work!

The final event of that internship year was the Billy Sunday Campaign held in Kansas City during May and June. Mr. Sunday had a special tabernacle constructed for all of his protracted meetings. The use of sawdust and tanbark covering the ground made possible one of his main requirements — a perfectly still audience in uniform silence! The tabernacle was panic-proof, every aisle lengthwise and crosswise ending in an exit. Actually it looked like a big "turtle-backed barn of raw, unfinished lumber," but it had every mechanical device then known for amplifying the speaker's voice so that twenty-five thousand people could hear quite clearly. Adjoining the tabernacle at each campaign was a nursery for babies and small children, a battery of telephones and an up-to-date emergency hospital. Eugene, as a regular intern of the Kansas City General Hospital, was on duty in this medical emergency center certain evenings each week. On the evenings that he was free he joined the staff of personal workers who spoke after the meetings with all who had "hit the sawdust trail" that night.

[5]

Marching Orders

WARTIME JOURNEYS

Under cover of darkness on a crisp October night in 1916, the 16,000-ton French liner, *Lafayette,* quietly slipped out of New York harbor bound for Bordeaux, France. All portholes and entryways were carefully draped with thick, black cloth to prevent any chink of light from betraying the presence of the vessel to a lurking German submarine. Among the passengers were three young couples, all with the same distant African destination — the American Presbyterian Congo Mission in the heart of the Belgian Congo.

The Reverend Charles L. Crane from Georgia and his wife, Louise, were old hands for they had already served their first term, having gone to the field in 1912. The Reverend Thomas Chalmers Vinson had also served one term but his bride, Nan Wharton Vinson, was a new missionary, as were the new medical missionary couple, Edna and Eugene Kellersberger.

In anticipation of missionary service, Eugene wrote in his prayer notebook in September 1916, the following petitions:

> That Christ may live in us through us, giving us a special anointing for the Congo work.

That we may have a power-giving Quiet Hour early
every morning.

That we may practice the Presence of God always,
every moment.

That we may be glad to bear, carry, suffer any injus-
tice, any hardship, any persecution for His sake.

Then, as the first ocean voyage and travel under hazardous wartime conditions became a present, stark reality, Eugene penned these very practical petitions:

Open the way for us to go to THY work and to OUR
work in safety.

Give us a safe voyage to the Congo.

May we be able to procure money in Bordeaux.

May our baggage be kept safe and all our freight arrive
intact at our mission station.

The answer to these specific prayers was a major miracle.
The fall of 1916 was the low point of World War I. The
United States had not yet thrown its full weight on the side of
the stricken Allies. Civilian travel was almost an impossibility,
made only at risk of life on blacked-out vessels, through mined
and submarine-infested seas. The difficulties of international
communication, the transferring of necessary funds and foreign exchange were incredible under wartime conditions. Sei-
zure of baggage and loss of freight shipments in boats sunk by
mines or submarines were all too common.

One day out from Bordeaux, France, Eugene wrote:

Our cabin steward says he has not seen it this stormy
for the past five voyages. We are entering the northern part
of the Bay of Biscay. It is now about 9 p.m. We have just
had our daily prayer meeting for the three couples of us here
in our cabin. It is a fellowship that we welcome for we need
His protection on this stormy, war-torn sea. I am glad to
say that we all feel perfectly safe in His keeping! The wonderful steamer letters that we received on our departure
have been a real treasure. A church in the mountains of Virginia sent us a number of quotations from the Psalms all
bearing on "the sea." One of these, Psalm 107:23–30, is
particularly apt for it describes the storm we are weathering
at this very moment, but it concludes: *so He bringeth them to*

their desired haven! I was securely bolstered into my bunk with pillows last night so I slept well in spite of the rolling. The most important part of our daily shipboard schedule is the four hours spent in the study of Tshiluba, the language we will be speaking in the Congo. Mr. Vinson is our teacher and he is very patient with us, indeed. At noon the official notice read: "430 miles from the mouth of the Garonne," so we expect to reach our destination tomorrow noon. We will have to wait until 6 p.m. until the tide rises, to proceed the fifty miles upriver to Bordeaux. When we reach the coast, the customs officials will come aboard to inspect our luggage before we reach the city. We have no idea how long we will be in Bordeaux, but it will be some time, we are sure. It is hard to realize that we are already so far from home and yet we are not even one-third of the way to our work. More than ever now, we feel the need of your earnest and persistent prayers! This will have to end, for we must get our trunks ready now for the customs officials.

During the transatlantic voyage, Charles Crane enjoyed kidding Eugene about his long, so-obviously-Swiss-German name. He himself was of French Huguenot extraction, with the family middle name of "LaCoste," a fact that he felt sure would make things easier for him in Bordeaux. It was Eugene's turn to enjoy a bit of gentle, good-natured kidding when they arrived at Bordeaux and he, Eugene, was unceremoniously shoved through port authority procedures with a look of disdainful disgust the moment the name "Kellersberger" was glimpsed on the passport. Charles LaCoste Crane, on the other hand, was detained for several hours because a certain spy by the name of "LaCoste" was being sought!

They discovered, on visiting the office of the *Chargeurs Reunis* steamship company office, that they were to sail for the Belgian Congo on November 13, on the steamer *Afrique*. It was the oldest vessel of the line and long since had been declared unseaworthy. But so many ships had been sent to the bottom of the ocean by German raiders, that even the ricketiest and creakiest were being brought out of mothballs and once again pressed into maritime service.

For several nights out of Bordeaux the *Afrique* traveled in total darkness with lifeboats hanging out over the sides, ready for instant lowering. Several Allied vessels had been sunk by Germans just off Gibraltar the Sunday before their departure. In order to avoid enemy raiders, the captain plotted a wide, circular course westward out from Cape Finisterre, around the Canary Islands, completely bypassing the usual port stop of Teneriffe, then swinging back eastward to the French anchorage at Dakar in Senegal.

Eugene's family letter recorded:

> We have a packed boat and I have never seen so many sick people! Edna and I are absolutely the only ones that have remained vertical. As a physician I have been trying to find out why people get seasick. I have been doing a little experimenting with myself and have learned some things. Not the least of these is a positive mental attitude, eating a small amount every time food is served, staying out on deck as much as possible, walking in the fresh air and praying about it.
>
> The sea is so rough that our captain has to let us drift every now and then with power off, in order to avoid too great a strain on this old ship. Waves repeatedly crash up over the bow, flooding all the decks. It is quite a problem to eat. I don't see how the cooks and waiters manage at all! The high winds pile up regular mountains of water with precipitous valleys between. Our ship dips, rolls, wallows, twists, veers from side to side as the huge waves toss it about like an empty eggshell. The captain says that in his seven years of running this course, he has never experienced such a storm as this one. It is truly a majestic sight that demands all the faith I have to keep me in peace. Whenever possible, Edna and I have sat on deck in chairs roped into place. We have worshipped in the dark of the night with the sea roaring about us and the foaming crests of the great white caps shimmering fitfully through the gloom. We have sung every hymn that we know with a reference to the sea in it. *Bible* verses about the sea have also come to mean much more to us. We have watched its feverish restlessness and realized how utterly small and helpless we are, how completely dependent we are upon our God! This ship is only half the size of the *Lafayette*, but on the whole she seems to ride the waves much better.

The voyage of the *Afrique* from Bordeaux to the mouth of

the Congo River was a fascinating experience of almost a month's duration, with frequent stops at ports along the coast. Both Eugene and Edna had a love and feel for history. They were as enthralled with their own first exploration of the African coast as had been the captains of Prince Henry the Navigator's graceful little caravels five hundred years before! In their twin-masted ships with triangular lateen sails, copied from Arab dhows, they had rounded one by one the same headlands that marked the slow stages of discovery.

J. LEIGHTON WILSON

During their years of preparation for service in Africa, both Edna and Eugene were particularly impressed by the life and writings of the great pioneer missionary statesman, Dr. John Leighton Wilson, an uncle of President Wilson. The first missionary of the Presbyterian Church in the United States to serve in Africa, Dr. Wilson worked from 1833 to 1842 in Liberia and from 1842 to 1853 in the Gabon. He was the author of *Western Africa: Its History, Condition and Prospects,* which Dr. David Livingstone called "the best book ever written on that part of Africa."

Dr. Wilson exercised a decisive influence on the suppression of the African slave trade by preparing a monograph which encouraged the British Parliament to maintain their antislavery patrol squadron along the west African coast, just when it was about to be recalled. Ten thousand copies of this article, first published in *The Colonial Magazine* and reprinted in the *United States Service Journal* and *Blue Book,* were distributed throughout prominent English government circles. Lord Palmerston personally informed Dr. Wilson that, "after the publication of his article, all opposition in England to the retention of the African squadron ceased, so in directing the movement of the British navy, the humble missionary was on this occasion the foremost of admirals"!

As a linguist, Dr. Wilson was among the first to prepare a dictionary and grammar of the Bantu language, Mpongwe, and to write literature in this vernacular. Malcolm Guthrie of the School of Oriental and African Studies of the University of

London gives him credit for being the first western linguist to note the important role that tones play in all Bantu languages.

From 1861 to 1885 Dr. Wilson served as the first Executive Secretary of the Executive Committee of Foreign Missions of the Presbyterian Church in the United States. He initiated and encouraged work among the American Indians, and in Brazil, Greece, Mexico and China. He wisely shaped the far-visioned and effective missionary policies that would apply for his denomination for generations to come. But always he prayed and planned for the day when his church would open a mission on the continent of his first love, Africa.

With the anchoring of the *Afrique* in the estuary of the Gabon River at Libreville, the three young couples on their way to the very mission in the Belgian Congo for which Dr. Wilson had worked so hard and prayed, now had the joy of visiting Baraka, the historic pioneer mission post founded by him in 1842. The sight of this early endeavor increased their pride and anticipation in following in the footsteps of so effective an evangelist, author, linguist and statesman.

Baraka also gave them their first introduction to a tropical mission station compound with coconut palms, breadfruit, avocado and Ceylon cherry trees, all bearing fruit! They learned to recognize the Elieas oil-palm and the long white roots of the "Kassawa" or tapioca plant, with which they themselves were to become all too familiar as their main sources of daily food.

THE ZAIRE RIVER

On December 7, 1916, the *Afrique* entered the mouth of the Zaire River, that geographical oddity that crosses the equator not just once, but twice. This "double-saddle" position causes the river to be always in flood or never in flood, as your viewpoint may be. The alternating rainy seasons, one in the northern hemisphere and one in the southern, keep the annual flow of water always in balance. Eight thousand miles of navigable waterways comprise the upper Zaire river system, high on the central plateau before it makes its precipitous descent over the continental shelf down to the sea. Three

hundred miles inland from the Atlantic Ocean, the gargan-
tuan river pauses at a thousand feet above sea level and
broadens into an expansive lake fifteen miles wide in some
places, and twenty miles long. Indigenous tribes call this
river-lake *Malebo*, while Europeans call it *Stanley Pool*.

The river's final 220-mile-long drop to sea level is made
through the roaring chasms of the Crystal Mountains, over a
series of thirty-two thundering cataracts named by Henry
Morton Stanley, *Livingstone Falls*. The water power potential
of this stretch of river is more than ninety million horsepower,
the equivalent of the power potential of all the rivers of the
United States combined.

The last cataract, where the river reaches sea level one
hundred miles from the ocean, funnels into a maelstrom called
Hell's Cauldron. As it leaves this hole, racing along at a speed of
nine knots, so great is its force that a submarine canyon four
thousand feet deep has been ploughed into the ocean floor for
a hundred miles out to sea. For miles off shore the ocean
waters are stained with the dark, blood-colored clays of the
upland heart of the great continent.

Such a rare combination of geographical features created
a tremendous natural barrier to further inland exploration,
making the Zaire River historically unique. It is the only
major river of the world to be first fully explored from its
source down to the ocean! The mouth of the river was discovered and claimed in 1482 by Diego Cam, with no attempt to
explore its inland reaches. In 1485 he returned with three caravels, only to discover that the broad, inviting estuary was totally deceptive as an entryway into the African continent. At
the swirling edge of Hell's Cauldron the Portuguese explorer
was forced to turn his violently-tossing ship about and return
to sea. On his disappointed way downstream, some fifty yards
from the rocky peninsula called Fishermen's Caves, just below
the Cauldron, he inscribed the Portuguese cross, his name and
the date 1485 under a large rock projection beneath an overhanging cliff, where it still may be seen today. The exploration
of the upper Zaire beyond the great natural barrier had to
wait for another four hundred years. It was Henry Morton
Stanley who painfully traced the perverse river from its small

source on the upland plateau all the way down to the Atlantic Ocean, taking nine hundred and ninety-nine days to complete the arduous journey in 1876.

Even the naming process of this mammoth river has an interesting history. The Bakongo tribe, occupying the lands adjacent to the river's mouth, called it in their Kikongo language *Zadi*, "the river that swallows all rivers." The Portuguese discoverer, inquiring as to its name, repeated it, mispronouncing it as *Zaire*. Throughout most of modern history it has been called *The Congo*, for the Kongo tribespeople who, ethnically speaking, informed Stanley that this was the river flowing through the tribal lands of the Kongo nation.

As the *Afrique* started inland for the last lap of her long journey, Eugene spent every possible moment on deck, watching the changing scenery. He recorded his first impressions of the lower Zaire with lively interest:

> On December 7th I awoke at 5 a.m. to see the light breaking over the ten-mile-wide mouth of the great Congo River. Our ship was ploughing through chocolate, almost coffee-colored waters. Our first stop was at the port of Banana where we delivered mail. Then we started up the river, passing the point on the southern bank where Diego Cam in 1482 erected a monolith called a "padrao," bearing the coat-of-arms of Portugal surmounted by a cross, to mark his initial discovery of the mouth of the river. We glided past thick mangrove swamps, tropical forests and countless, low-lying islands, scattered in an alluvial plain spreading around us as far as the eye could see.
>
> Then in the distance we began to see a few, low hills. The hills became larger and finally there were real mountains. The immense river became narrower and narrower, walled in more and more closely on either side. As our ship ascended the wide estuary, the flow of water became swifter and swifter, beginning to boil up in many places. In spite of the fact that the lower Congo is known to have tremendous depth, it empties into the ocean about two million cubic feet of water per second!
>
> One hundred miles up the river, at the very gate of the Crystal Mountains lies Boma, capital of the Belgian Congo. Here we stopped for two hours, long enough to telegraph

Dr. Sims at Matadi of our anticipated arrival. From Boma
to Matadi the river runs through a canyon with steep green
hills and precipitous rock cliffs on both sides.

Shortly before arriving at Matadi we passed the Swedish Baptist mission station of Underhill, where the pioneer
founder of our own mission, the Reverend Samuel N. Lapsley, lies buried in a grave overlooking the river. The river
continued to flow with increasing wildness at every turn,
until just below Matadi, we came to a right-angle bend and
suddenly entered *Hell's Cauldron*. The hole which the river
has made here is estimated to be two thousand feet deep.
Small steamers dare not venture here at all. Our big ocean-
going vessel had to put on full steam to make any progress
against the vicious current and trembled all over as the
great, foaming whirlpools swerved us from side to side like a
toy. In certain places we saw giant suction-holes where the
surface of the water is several feet lower than the surrounding areas — sure death there! At this point where the river
makes a right-angle turn, it has eaten away over half of the
huge mountain.

Dr. Sims of the American Baptist Congo Mission met
our party at the Matadi dock and has made us quite comfortable in their guest house until December 11th, when we
take the train for Kinshasa. So far we have been on our way
for fifty-four days and have gone ten thousand miles. And
we still have a twenty-one day riverboat trip ahead of us!

The journey from Matadi to Kinshasa over the narrow
gauge railway required two full days and covered two
hundred and seventy miles. Again Edna and Eugene were
aware of a brooding sense of history surrounding them, as
they by-passed so easily the roaring gorges and mist-enve-
loped chasms of the river, along which Stanley struggled for
two years to clear one slender road. With wonder in his voice,
Eugene remarked to Edna, "Here is where Stanley labored in
1880 and 1881 to bring up an entire river steamer in sections
to Stanley Pool. Here many an African's life was laid down for
greedy ambitions of exploiters. Here our own early pioneer
missionaries braved fever and death for Christ's sake."

The railroad on which they traveled had been completed
in 1898 by an international syndicate formed by King Leopold

II of Belgium. It made possible his exploitation of the sovereign state created for him by Stanley, of which he alone was the personal suzerain. For every one of the transverse wooden ties that stretched across that slim roadbed, the price of a human life was paid during the construction process.

The tiny wood-burning engine rode on a single 2'2"-wide track, pulling first second, and third class cars. The third-class car in which the three couples and one baby were riding was amusingly described by "Chal" Vinson:

> The third class coach is equipped with little narrow hard-bottomed and straight-backed seats running crosswise, facing each other. The seats are so close together that the passengers opposite each other have to sit with their knees interlocked. If one desires to shift his position, all must shift in unison. The designer of this car must have drawn his inspiration from the days of the Inquisition. (*William McCutchan Morrison*, T. C. Vinson, p. 71)

The first five miles of the trip were literally breathtaking. The roadbed clung tenuously to the cliffs, twisting and turning with every convolution of the tortuous terrain. The river thundered terrifyingly close just below. Then came the impossible grades, some at an angle of twenty degrees up which the engine inched its way through the Crystal Mountains. Each laborious ascent was followed by a hair-raising, roller coaster descent with the whole train sliding downhill. A frantic brakeman located at the back of each separate car desperately struggled to throw his weight against the screeching brake lever in a tremendous effort to slow the train down. At the bottom of each hill there was always a long wait as the engine gathered steam for the next climb. During such lulls in the journey, the rumble of the giant cataracts down which the Congo was leaping to the sea could be heard in the distance. The sullen roar provided a deep bass accompaniment to the soprano sibilance of the hissing steam and the constantly shrilling whistle used to signal the brakeman.

Gradually the mountain ravines gave way to long stretches of forest, rolling hills and then spreading plains. But always in the distance were glimpses of spray-shrouded chasms or a turbulent stretch of foaming water rushing over a rocky projection. All of the area through which they were passing was ruled by the majestic presence of the river.

THE SAMUEL N. LAPSLEY

The arrival in Kinshasa, terminal for the railroad and junction with interior river transport, was on December 13. It coincided amazingly with the beginning of the next lap of their journey. The Presbyterian mission steamer, the *Samuel N. Lapsley*, coming from Luebo mission station in the Kasai to get them, had tied up at the river bank only two hours before their train had arrived! How welcome to the travel-weary group was the homey, "down-south" atmosphere and the clean, cozy cabins of the sturdy paddlewheeler, captained by the Reverend Arch McKinnon and hostessed by his gracious wife, Eva! Eugene's description of that first riverboat journey is filled with the keen awareness of initial observation:

> After taking on a big cargo, the *Lapsley* left the wide, island-dotted expanse of Stanley Pool and soon entered where the river narrows to a mile in width, flowing swiftly between beautiful, green wooded hills. For the most part it has been clear and cool. Whenever it gets hot and humid as it did this morning, the sky rapidly clouds over and we hear thunder. Then comes a hard, brief downpour. The shower passes over and all is cool and clear again.
>
> We are sleeping under mosquito nets and taking small amounts of quinine every day. This is the best way to ward off an attack of malaria, though all of us will have that disease in our systems from now on. This is one instance where "prevention is the cure."
>
> The greeting we received from the seventy-five Baluba who make up the crew of the ship was very hearty. They call me by their usual name for a witchdoctor, which is "Ngangabuka." Our learning of Tshiluba is progressing much faster since we came aboard, for Mutombo and Madimba, who work in the ship's dining room, have become our daily language assistants.
>
> Because our steamer burns wood, we do not travel at night. We tie up at dusk along the riverbank and immediately the woodsmen of the crew grab their axes and run into

the forest to chop five or six cords of wood. The remarkable thing is the way they work in the dark. Soon you hear them at a distance, chopping away in the forest. Then you see them coming into the floodlights of the steamer, carrying regular young trees on their strong shoulders. They seem to be able to see like owls! The idea that Africa is reeking with snakes, vermin and vicious terrors on all sides is simply not true! I like it very much myself and every day I am more and more agreeably surprised.

At 5 a.m. each morning the wood which has been chopped into proper length for the boiler is stowed aboard by the workmen, chanting in rhythm as they work together. I have already learned that if anyone wants to work in the tropics, he had better not make plans to sleep late! Early morning or the cool of night is the only time for hard, physical exertion. It gets too hot to do any real work later on in the day.

All up and down the river the *Lapsley* is called "God's Boat." It never travels on Sundays but remains tied to the bank throughout the day, giving all the crew a much-needed rest. Early Sunday morning we took our first long walk deep into the forest, following an old native path. The foliage is dense high overhead, with many vines hanging down and heavy undergrowth, but by no means is the whole country a "jungle," as the popular concept is!

At 10 a.m. we had our regular Sunday service with the entire crew gathered on the upper deck. Mr. Crane led and two of the crew, most of whom are Christians, led in prayer. And they sing just fine! Every morning we hear them singing a hymn as Captain McKinnon begins each day's work with a short *Bible* lesson and prayer-service. This morning we lifted anchor to the tune of the good old hymn, *At the Cross, At the Cross.*

By 9 a.m. we had arrived at Kwamouth and sighted the mouth of the Kasai River, the great southern tributary of the Congo up which we go about seven hundred miles. This is the place where our first mission steamer *Lapsley* capsized in 1903, with a loss of the lives of twenty-three Congolese members of the crew and a new missionary, Reverend Slaymaker.

As a schoolgirl in Washington, D.C., Edna had been a

guest in the Slaymaker home in Alexandria, Virginia. It was
with a deep and reverent emotion that the little band of missionaries, standing on the firm, steady deck of the "Second
Lapsley," passed over the very spot where her predecessor
had capsized with such a loss of life.

The original *Samuel N. Lapsley* was called "The Children's
Boat," for it was paid for with eighteen thousand dollars
worth of pennies given by the Sunday School children of the
Presbyterian Church in the United States. Built in Richmond,
Virginia, in 1900 by a company inexperienced in real riverboat construction, it was eighty feet long and twelve feet in the
beam. With a thirty-ton displacement, it was powered by a
seventy-horsepower motor capable of a cruising speed of ten
miles an hour. This was too long, too narrow and too slow for
the fast flow of the Congo River system. It was a miracle that
the little steamer survived even three years of transportation
service between Kinshasa and Luebo mission station. Only
the navigational abilities of Captain Lachlan C. Vass, Jr. and
his native crew kept it afloat that long!

At Kwamouth, where the main stream of the Zaire River,
as the "Congo" is officially called today, is joined by the
Kasai, its largest tributary, there are always dangerous currents and gigantic whirlpools caused by the marked diver-
gence in the seasonal flow of the two merging rivers. The
Kasai, south of the equator, is in flood stage from October
through February each year, the months that the upper Zaire,
flowing south from north of the equator, is at its low, dry season level. From March through September the opposite situation occurs. The upper Zaire is in flood while the sand banks
of the Kasai lie high and dry under a cloudless sky. The con-
fluence of these two rivers at Kwamouth is therefore always a
place of fantastic, watery turbulence as the two, mighty merging currents battle each other for control. The seasonal differences between the two rivers, alternating in source from each
side of the equator, are truly remarkable within only eight degrees of latitude.

Of the three missionaries aboard the original *Lapsley*
when it capsized, only the Reverend Slaymaker drowned.
Captain Vass and Reverend Motte Martin both escaped.

Vass, who was a strong swimmer, managed to climb onto the bottom of the overturned vessel. Motte Martin did not know how to swim, but reached the riverbank in safety, sitting in a large wicker rocking chair that he had purchased in the Madeira Islands. It floated within his reach just as he surfaced for the first time after being thrown into the water. Captain Vass was very busy for a while hauling as many of his crewmen as he could reach onto the overturned boat with him. Even as the little group of some twenty-two survivors knelt in prayer on the slippery bottom of the capsized steamer, Captain Vass' mind was already busily at work, planning the construction of a <u>real</u> paddlewheeler that would be a match for the mighty river system!

That "second *Lapsley*," on which Edna and Eugene were making their first African riverboat journey, was well able to cope with the surging waters. It was carefully designed and put together in the shipyards of Lobnitz and Company, Limited, on the Clyde River at Renfrew, Scotland. The beautiful little ship was worthy of her Scottish Presbyterian heritage! She was ninety feet in the hull, one hundred and five feet over all, with a nineteen-foot beam. She could travel at the speed of nine knots, her paddlewheels churning powerfully through the strongest of currents. After trial runs on the Clyde, she had been taken apart, crated and shipped by ocean freight to Matadi. The large crates by-passed the rapids of the Zaire River system on the same little narrow gauge railroad on which Eugene and Edna had journeyed. It was reassembled in 1906 at Stanley Pool by Captain Vass and the Scottish engineer, W. B. Scott. For over seventy years this hardy little vessel plied the waters of the Zaire and Kasai rivers. It was said by Belgian riverboat captains to be the very finest sternwheeler on the entire river system!

On the previous journey upriver the *Lapsley* had lodged on some rocks in the Lulua River, within sight of her Luebo mission station destination. Attempts to free her caused a large hole to be torn in the front steel plate of the bow. A temporary patch made her river-worthy enough for the trip to Kinshasa to meet the Cranes, Vinsons and Kellersbergers, but she was to go into dry dock at Dima for repairs on her return trip upriver. It would take the Belgian maritime company's machine shop crew at least a week to rivet a new steel plate onto the bow.

And so it happened that Edna and Eugene completed their journey up the Kasai and Lulua rivers on the tiny Belgian auxiliary steamer, *Antoinette*. On Christmas Day, 1916, the three young couples, seated on deck, sang the old familiar Christmas carols to the strange accompaniment of the steady swishing of the miniature paddlewheel and the unexpected splash of crocodiles and hippos, startled from their sunning spots on the sandbanks by the passing of the steamer. Their arrival at Luebo a few days later was not the same as it would have been, had they been aboard the *Lapsley*. The crew of the Belgian steamer had no idea that an answering hymn of response was expected from them, when the large crowd of Christians waiting at the landing sang a joyous hymn of welcome to the newcomers! But the Kellersbergers knew that they were at home at last, among the people that God had called them to serve. The glorious "hymns of Zion," sung in a strange tongue in a strange land, attested to that!

DR. W. M. MORRISON

January and February 1917 were crucial months in the lives of the new missionaries for they were spent under the inspired tutelage of Dr. William McCutchan Morrison. The acknowledged leader of the American Presbyterian Congo Mission at that time, it was he who put the final, on-the-spot touches to the long process of the young couples' preparation for service in the Belgian Congo. Dr. Morrison was a gifted teacher and a master of the fundamentals of the missionary's daily task. In addition to daily language classes, using the dictionary and grammar of the Tshiluba language that he himself had completed in 1906, the experienced missionary conducted carefully planned orientation sessions for the newcomers, designed to help them live comfortably and effectively in the midst of a culture totally different from their own.

Dr. Morrison rendered remarkable service as a member of the APCM from 1896 to 1918. (The Belgian custom of consistently calling an organization by its initials was applied to the Americam Presbyterian Congo Mission.) Like Dr. J. Leighton Wilson, he was a stalwart reformer and outstanding missionary statesman, who had the courage to bring to the attention of the British Parliament, the United States Congress and concerned groups in England and America, the brutal atrocities he witnessed taking place under the Congo Free State regime. There was a marked difference between those areas of Africa controlled by other imperial powers and that controlled by King Leopold of Belgium. As his private possession, the gain from all the tremendous natural resources of the Congo basin funneled into his hands alone, through his few, selected monopolies. Brutality, coercion, hunger and bloodshed stalked the land in his name!

Dr. Morrison's address on "The Treatment of the Native People by the Government of the Congo Independent State," made to the 13th International Peace Congress in Boston, Massachusetts, in October 1904, is a masterpiece of factual clarity. It is largely due to his efforts and those of his colleague, the Reverend William H. Sheppard, that Leopold was forced by international pressures to relinquish his personal sovereignty of the Congo. The small group of on-the-spot witnesses out in Africa was fully supported by the Executive Committee of Foreign Missions of the Presbyterian Church in the United States and the entire constituency of that denomination. Dr. S. H. Chester, the executive secretary, did not hesitate to present the critical information to President Roosevelt and his Secretary of State, Elihu Root, and to keep the State Department informed on all new developments.

On November 15, 1908, the 909,899 square mile area became the Belgian Congo, a colony of Belgium instead of the private property of its king. But the fight for the basic human rights of the people living there was not over. The first colonial charter for the Belgian Congo preserved the existing legislation of the old Independent State and upheld the legality of Leopold's concessionary companies. The very same officials were retained to administer the same objectionable laws for an oppressive rubber regime. Using his still absolute powers, Leopold forced all competing companies operating in the rich area of the rubber forests to combine into the one *Compagnie du Kasai*, a monopoly of which he owned the controlling stock.

Again, Dr. Morrison had no recourse but to condemn and publicize the monopolistic system by which the country was being ruthlessly stripped of its natural resources with the native populations receiving little in return. Stringent laws against the wanton destruction of the precious rubber vines were being blatantly ignored. Mutilation by chopping off of hands or arms for failure to bring in the required quota of raw rubber strips, flogging with the hippo-hide *chicotte*, slave-raiding under the guise of labor recruitment, pillage and arson were all common practices of that company in its wasteful, reckless search for rubber, ivory and gum copal throughout the Kasai region of the Belgian Congo.

The result of an article exposing these evil practices, published in the APCM organ, *The Kasai Herald*, was a libel suit against Dr. Morrison, brought by the Compagnie du Kasai. The judges who were to try the case had been personally appointed by King Leopold! But Dr. Morrison was so ably defended at this famous trial in September 1909 by the Belgian socialist leader, Emile Vandervelde, that he was acquitted and the cruel practices of the Compagnie du Kasai were officially condemned.

Sir Arthur Conan Doyle in England paid the missionary the tribute of saying, "Dr. Morrison on trial at Leopoldville, stood as a nobler and more perfect representative of liberty than the statue by Barthodi in the harbor of New York City!"

The orientation sessions that Eugene and Edna attended at Luebo in 1917 gave them the benefit of the long and fruitful years of Dr. Morrison's rich experience. He emphasized the importance of maintaining the best of relationships with the colonial government and gave detailed instructions regarding the writing of official correspondence in French. The Reverend Chal Vinson remarked about his colleague:

> As Dr. Morrison had so freely expressed indignation against the whole system of government as administered in the Congo, we might naturally think that he also had unbounded contempt for all the officials of the government, but such was not the case. He always conducted himself in

the most courteous manner in the presence of those in authority and never lost his self-control. Indeed, a very prominent official once stated that Dr. Morrison was one of the most remarkable men he had ever met, because he could rebuke a man in the most withering terms and then make himself a most pleasant and entertaining companion. He could do this because he pitied the official more than he blamed him and regarded him more as a victim of the "system" in vogue, rather than as one personally responsible for his course of action. He regarded the social relation of the missionary with the government staff as of prime importance. (*William McCutchan Morrison*, T. C. Vinson, pp. 134–135)

The yellowed, carefully-preserved pages of that 1917 orientation session are a gold mine of wise instruction. Dr. Morrison warned the new missionaries:

The general principle to be observed is that we are foreigners who wish to conform to the customs of the ruling people of the Congo. The Belgians appear to us to be effusive in their manner, while we probably appear to them to be abrupt and uncouth. Therefore, sociability and the amenities should be observed. When passing through or near a station, government post or trading establishment, always observe the custom of going in and paying your respects to the officials in charge. It is the Belgian custom for the newcomer to make the first call. Be very cautious about the accuracy of what you write in your official letters. All agreements amount to nothing unless in writing. Preserve a copy of all official letters sent. The regular course to be pursued in righting wrongs is through the local official first and then through the next higher officials, successively, if necessary. Make as few complaints as possible. Be absolutely certain of the facts in the case. Never carry an appeal to the American consul, except as a last resort. Keep cool, hold your temper, do not be frightened, stand firm, if you know you are in the right. The laws change often, but if you do the right thing, you will not miss the law by far.

Eugene served for many years as one of the elected legal representatives of the American Presbyterian Congo Mission, an official communicator to the Belgian government for the

Mission. Many times over he was grateful for this particular aspect of his training, received first hand from Dr. Morrison at the beginning of his medical missionary career.

Dr. Morrison also warned strongly against any missionary's becoming entangled in commercial activities or making any sort of profit in dealings with the local people. In the delicate Catholic-Protestant questions so prevalent then because Belgium was officially a Catholic nation, he advised:

> Extend to Catholic missionaries the same courtesies as to government officials. In case of difficulties, it is better to receive than to give insults. Do not let personal animosity enter into the controversy at all. We must teach our converts to be forgiving and not strike back. Never repeat gossip in the presence of the Congolese. We ought to encourage our followers always to pay their taxes. Neither request nor make use of special privileges from the government at all!

Dr. Morrison believed strongly in minimizing denominational differences because it saved the native Christians endless confusion. He himself was the first president of the Congo Protestant Council, an organization of many different agencies, cooperating in the geographical partitioning of fields of labor, the combining of literature and transportation facilities and the unquestioning, willing acceptance into the local flock of any Christian in good standing, baptized by any other member mission.

In regard to the supporting churches back in the United States, Dr. Morrison's advice to new missionaries was extremely perceptive:

> For the first year resolve that you will write no adverse criticism in your letter. Confine the first year to writing descriptions and portraying the bright side of life. Do not touch mission policies until your third year on the field! Never pose as a martyr! Be careful what you write to relatives because your letters are sometimes read in public!

The missionary leader's instructions for maintaining good health in a tropical environment are most interesting in the light of the accepted notions of that era:

> Be cheerful! Faith in God and reliance upon Him is a

physical benefit. Worry about nothing! Early in the morning put yourself in God's hands. Do not think about being
sick. When you have a fever, do not regard it too seriously;
thousands of people recover from malarial fevers! When you
are sick, begin treatment at once. Go to bed the moment the
fever is perceptible. Take care of your health automatically.
Have a regular time to take your daily dose of quinine.

Use your helmet and do not let the sun strike the back
of your neck. Wear thin wool or part wool underclothes.
Have the outer clothing as light and airy as possible. Always sleep under a mosquito net. Boil all of your drinking
water and be sure yourself that it is boiled! Our Congolese
helpers do not always understand what is involved in preparing drinking water.

Food is of prime importance. Stinting in this matter is
poor economy and may cause breakdowns. Study the preparation of tropical foods. Start a vegetable garden and plant
fruit trees at once. Use local native produce and avoid the
use of canned goods from abroad as much as possible.

You will have to take more rest in the tropics than you
did back in your temperate zone home. Keep the noon rest
hour sacred. Get a little sleep then, but not too much or you
will awaken feeling stupid. Always get your full rest at night
for that is your stock in trade for the next day.

When your work really begins to get on your nerves,
lay off working for three or four days if necessary. Keep
yourself at the highest state of efficiency. See that there is
some diversion in connection with every day's work, some
little time for your hobby or collection. Occasionally have a
party and wear your best clothes, for this will keep up some
social spirit and be restful.

Read some each day, books on missionary activities,
especially on the Congo, as well as for diversion. Keep in
touch with world movements, social questions, etc. Read
good biographies and subscribe to a few good magazines.

In regard to working with the local native population,
Dr. Morrison's attitude and policies were practical, far-
sighted and extremely sympathetic and accepting:

If we laugh at their customs, appearance or fetishes, we
destroy their confidence in us and repel them. Greet them
with a pleasant word and do not fear to shake hands with

them, even if they may appear somewhat untidy. On the other hand, you will need to maintain your dignity and repress undue familiarity or insolence. Be kind and firm but never harsh! Conform to the dignified customs of chiefs and dignitaries where no morals are involved. Be ready to receive any person without becoming impatient when you are busy. Don't ever try to HUSTLE AFRICA! It simply can't be done!

A palaver means any kind of a quarrel, dispute or contention. This is a very important and delicate subject and requires the utmost patience, tact and wisdom. Palavers offer us the opportunity of showing our interest in the people and of demonstrating the *Bible* principles of right and justice. But all of this has to be done very cautiously. Do not usurp the authority of the chief or let him get the impression that you are trying to do so. This requires diplomacy!

The approach to the people with the Gospel is a very important question. Some people seem to be unapproachable and therefore we should follow the line of greatest cleavage where the Holy Spirit has already prepared the people. This was the method our Savior used. He did not waste time on those who refused to hear, to the exclusion of those who were eager to hear!

In preaching, try to be as vivid as possible and appeal to the imagination. Use native proverbs and folk parables whenever possible for they are singularly rich in material with which to illustrate religious truth. Remember, *"Without a parable spake He not unto them"*! Give daily instruction to those who wish to know more about the plan of salvation and desire to become Christians. Teach them the simple attributes of God, the work of the Holy Spirit, the fall and our redemption through Christ, repentance, faith, the future life and prayer. Train them in life and prayer. Train them in worship, Sabbath observance, charity and generosity and sharing the Gospel with others. Remember that the church is a training school in which Christian character is developed.

Above all, in his own personal life Dr. Morrison exemplified to the new recruits the desirable qualities of all who follow Christ's marching orders. He deliberately took time every day to cultivate a frank, open, cheerful and uncritical relationship with each of his colleagues on the mission station. He spent a brief social interlude each day with them at afternoon tea, a game of tennis or croquet, a birthday party or a quiet cottage prayer meeting in the evening. With the same unique discipline of his time he always managed to leave the compound for an hour every afternoon and visited with his Congolese friends in their village homes sitting and talking in a friendly, relaxed manner. It is little wonder that they loved him as they did!

Dr. Morrison's most earnest advice to the newcomers had to do with the inevitable personality problems that arise whenever an unusually strong-willed group of individuals is in such close and frequent contact all day long, and must function as a unit. He also dealt with the disciplined effort which must be made in order to maintain the spiritual power necessary for effective missionary ministry:

> The necessity of living close together on the stations is liable to bring difficulties. We must bear toward each other all possible patience, forbearance and Christian endurance. Do the work assigned you as best you can, and at the same time, consult and have proper regard for the opinion of the majority of the Mission. Friction can usually be avoided by having open discussions in a frank and kindly spirit. Never be on the lookout for slights. On the station you will want to be cordial, social and brotherly, like a family. Don't be too sensitive! Have a sense of humor and try to make fun even of the most unpleasant things!
>
> It will cost effort to keep up your spiritual life on the Mission. You are constantly giving out to others and you must be vigilant to keep your spiritual life from declining. There will have to be agonizing, prayerful thought during the hour kept sacred each day. Do not take the rest hour at midday for this; this ought to be kept as sacred for physical rest! Take your daily Quiet Hour as early in the morning as possible, for this will give you peace, repose in God and strength for the work of the day.

ASSIGNMENT TO LUSAMBO

Dr. and Mrs. Eugene Kellersberger were the first medical missionaries assigned to Lusambo station, one of the loca-

tions selected in 1910 by Dr. and Mrs. Morrison on their survey journey to study the future possibilities of the entire area
assigned to the Presbyterians by the Congo Protestant Council. The official request from the mission to the Belgian authorities early in 1912 for a concession for this station site was
granted in July 1913. The Robert D. Bedingers and the A. C.
McKinnons opened the new work on the north bank of the
Sankuru River, two miles upriver from the riverport, government post and commercial center of Lusambo, founded by
Governor General Jannsen in 1889. For years this post served
as the joint transport base of the Plymouth Brethren, Methodist and Presbyterian Missions.

It was with real regret that Eugene and Edna left Luebo.
For eight wonderful weeks they had lived on a spiritual moun-
taintop to which they would look back with gratitude for the
rest of their lives. Now they faced their new task with eager
anticipation, fully prepared to be an active part of God's "task
force." In Dr. Morrison and his colleagues at Luebo they had
seen demonstrated the basic missionary principles of courage,
adaptability, and wise love that were to characterize their own
ministry over the years.

Eugene's obvious delight in his new surroundings is evident in his first letter written from their assigned post:

> Our good mission steamer *Lapsley*, captained on this
> trip by our Belgian Protestant missionary, Monsieur Dau-
> mery, brought us from Luebo to Lusambo. We left the
> Kasai River where it makes its great turn from the south
> and the mountains of Angola, where it has its source. For
> over three hundred miles we churned through the winding
> hills, up the swiftly-flowing Sankuru River to our destina-
> tion, located at an elevation of 1300 feet above sea level.
> What a view we have up and down the river for miles! Our
> compound covers a low hill facing the river about three
> hundred yards away. Just in front of us is a sandy stretch of
> embankment where our mission steamer ties up. Beyond
> that is the rapid flow of the current, with the steep hills
> crowding down to the very brink. Opposite the mission sta-
> tion are two great, bald cliffs making a sheer, three-
> hundred-foot plunge straight down into the deep water. It is
> delightfully cool at this season of the year. We sleep under

two blankets every night. The early morning fogs which rise
from the river are actually chillingly cold! The grounds of
our station are beautifully cleared so that we have practically no mosquitoes at all.

THE CARPENTER SHOP CLINIC

Eugene was quite sure that he was mentally prepared for
any sort of working conditions at his first place of assignment.
He was, nevertheless, somewhat taken aback when he discovered exactly where it was that he <u>was</u> going to practice medicine! He grinned in disbelief and wondered what discerning
comment Dr. Hertzler might make about working among the
heavy, hand-hewn planks, the wood shavings and the sawdust
of the station carpentry shop, with the Congolese carpenter
carrying on as usual at his very elbow! The twelve-by-twelve-
foot open shed had a grass roof and a three-by-five-foot mud-
walled enclosure at one end for the storage of drugs. For the
first five months of his medical missionary career, Eugene
used the carpenter's bench as his examination and operating
table and a five-gallon kerosene drum as his only sterilizer.

As soon as the presence of the white witchdoctor became
known, attendance at the daily clinic, conducted by Mrs. Bedinger, who was not a nurse, began to average well over a
hundred. Many patients were people of the Baluba, Basonge,
Bakuba and Batetele tribes but others began to appear who
had walked from as far away as two hundred miles.

The diseases that Eugene encountered were legion —
pneumonia, tuberculosis, leprosy, yaws, elephantiasis, malaria, dysentery, dropsy, hookworm, round worm, scabies,
ruptures, goiters, tumors and numerous tropical eye and ear
diseases. Hookworm was the most prevalent, causing many
deaths, both directly and indirectly, as was sleeping sickness,
that dread life-taker! There were innumerable cases of tropical
ulcers, often so large that Eugene despaired of even saving the
limb involved, let alone healing the ulcer! These were often
caused by the custom of wearing long rows of copper bracelets
on the forearm and ankles.

With the beginning of actual missionary life, the petitions in
the doctor's prayer notebook clearly marked the new adjust-

ments that were being made to the overwhelming pressures of
the work, as well as to the traditional "culture shock" and problems encountered in working with fellow missionaries:

> We pray that we may be much silent, much listening,
> not criticizing, but praying and learning during our first
> term on the field, especially.
>
> Give us the special gift of patience and perseverance to
> learn the language and give us His Word to these people.
>
> Reveal to us the mind of the people of the Kasai, that
> there may be a point of contact with them.
>
> Consecration is as hard, if not harder here on the field
> than back at home. God, keep us in Your very Presence at
> all times.
>
> Don't let the rush, the throng, the intense life of lead-
> ership and ceaseless activity take away spirituality, sweet-
> ness and strength. Let us never be irritable, cross or upset.
>
> May our Quiet Hour not be crowded out of the day.
>
> May our sensitivities and feelings be so deep that they
> cannot be "hurt" or touched.

Eugene's letters to his supporting churches during that
first year were filled with lively descriptions of his medical
cases and new experiences:

> We were sitting at the dinner table when one of our
> new workmen and his wife came to the door with their sick
> boy. Only one glance showed that the eight-year-old was
> near death. They lived in a village only a half a mile away,
> where we have helped many people and where their chief
> has been healed of a very bad ulcer. I asked them why they
> had waited till the child was nearly dead before they came
> to me. They denied that they had given him any native rem-
> edies but admitted that they had sacrificed a chicken to
> stop his dysentery. They told me that their forefathers in
> their graves were begging for food. These ancestral spirits
> would torture the abdomen of the child until they were fed,
> so a chicken had been killed to appease them. The remark-
> able thing is that the sacrificial blood is applied in much the
> same manner as it was done in Old Testament times.
>
> A rapid examination of my patient revealed blue lips
> and gums and a poor little heart beating so fast that it could
> hardly be heard, rapid, labored breathing and the moist

death rattle in the throat and lungs, with a suspiciously wet cough. The abdomen contained an enormous spleen filling most of the left side, seemingly a case of malignant tropical malaria caused by neglect and the practices of deeply rooted superstition. I had no strychnine, no caffeine or other stimulants available in my tiny dispensary. One hour after I saw the child, he was dead. The traditional death cry began and in the pouring rain they carried him back to their village to grieve, holding him on their laps for hours, surrounded by thronging crowds of loudly wailing mourners, both professional and otherwise.

This was Eugene's first real contact with Animism, the basic form of religious belief of the Bantu people of central Africa. He knew that they believed in a coldly-distant creator-god, totally indifferent to human need, that all natural phenomena were spirit-controlled and all inanimate objects endowed with personal life. But he had not realized the ceaseless effort that had to be made to placate or deceive the hostile spirits haunting human habitations. He was not aware of the degree to which sorcery and witchcraft attempted to manipulate helpless persons and malevolent forces. Now for the first time, the doctor was witnessing the result of efforts to bribe the ancestral spirits, causing a fatal delay in seeking needed medical attention, something he was to see many, many times over the years to follow.

Another morning, in the midst of a busy clinic a runner came in, dripping with perspiration. Mr. Wilson of the Plymouth Brethren Mission thirty miles downriver had been attacked by an African hooded buffalo. A crew of sixteen tall, muscular boatmen in a huge dugout *pirogue* had been sent to get me. In a short time I was seated in my camp chair, low down in the roomy bottom of that great, heavy canoe. It must have been sixty feet long and nearly three feet wide, carved from a magnificent forest giant! The marvelous rhythm and perfectly synchronized movement of those powerful bodies, together with the staccato voice and persistent tapping of the leader's stick on the side of the boat was fascinating! We glided swiftly past grassy banks, slipping beneath great, overhanging limbs at an unbelievably fast rate of speed. Once we frightened a big family of monkeys. As we passed beneath the towering cliffs, swarms of disturbed wild parrots raised their screeching cries above us. Now and then a lazy crocodile slithered into the water just ahead of us. All would be silent for a while except for that steady "tat, tat" of the leader's rod and his low, measured voice prompting the rowing. Now and then the entire group of oarsmen would break spontaneously into a beautiful, interwoven, harmonious refrain that echoed from bank to bank.

Mr. Wilson had followed a magnificent hooded buffalo into the tall grass. He was a good shot and had mortally wounded the big bull. The path that the beast had torn through the tall grass was so soaked with blood that Mr. Wilson felt sure that it was safe to follow him. But with a terrible bellow the dying animal turned and suddenly attacked him. Even with two more well-placed shots and a quick side-step, one of the great hooded horns pierced Mr. Wilson's arm and tore it open, throwing him and his gun to the ground. A buffalo usually stops and tramples its victim to death, but in this case the animal was so badly wounded that it kept right on charging and in a few seconds dropped dead.

It took Eugene several hours to put Mr. Wilson's arm back together again. The mangled arm with its multiple scars provided many an occasion for a spirited recital of that unforgettable hunt. The British Brethren missionary was soon back at work again, as indomitable and vigorous as ever, in spite of the souvenir the buffalo had given him.

One of the many interesting patients that Eugene had while working at Lusambo was an influential chief of that area. Tall and strongly-built to rule physically as well as by general appearance, he reminded Eugene of "a buccaneer of the James Fenimore Cooper novels, with his heavy beard, mustache and long, curly hair — a man of great dignity, with a deep, bass voice."

He first came to Eugene to have his feet rubbed, a visit made solely for the purpose of sizing up the young doctor. A month later he returned, this time to confide his real trouble, an ugly, long-standing ulcer of large dimensions in the groin.

Praying for guidance, Eugene said to the chief, "I can

cure your sickness but I will have to give you 'sleep-medicine' (chloroform).'' To his surprise, the chief immediately replied, "The white chiefs take it in their land. Why can't I?"

"So we snowed him under," relates Eugene. "He took it beautifully, though all his wives thought he was dead and raised quite a disturbance! I do believe that the Lord answered prayer in this case because the ulceration cleared up steadily following the surgery. The chief came faithfully every day for treatment. The time finally came when I discharged him cured. He said to me, 'You are a good doctor! I have been sick for a long time and no one has ever been able to help me before. I am very glad!' Then one day he came to the church for the first time. We had sent a special invitation to him to come and hear Dr. Morrison, who was visiting the station for a week."

After hearing that sermon, he began attending church regularly, bringing his retinue with him. He often sent any of his people who were sick to the clinic and enrolled some of his sons in the mission day school and Sunday school.

The new missionary's prayers written after he had been on the field for several months reflect the constant pressures of the demanding life that he and his Edna were now living:

Grant me supernatural wisdom and skill in physical healing. I will offer prayer before every single operation.

Give physical healing to my patients whenever possible, but may the way to *spiritual* healing be shown to each individual always.

Help me to control my tongue, not to talk so much and learn to keep professional secrets.

May I remain efficient and skilled as a doctor, always keeping up to date. That the medical work may ever be only the way-opener to Him and that many souls may be brought to Him by means of it.

That in all the fearful push and rush of the work I may be kept calm, sweet, unhurried, rest in Him. Even with the stress of the work day and night, may I remain kind, patient, sympathetic, understanding and long-suffering.

NEW BABY — NEW DISPENSARY

In August of 1917 two events made Edna and Eugene supremely happy. A baby daughter was born just after midnight on August 30th in the midst of the first tremendous storm heralding the commencement of the rainy season. Even the lashing of the palms in the tearing winds and the crashing thunder did not drown out the first cry of little Winifred Helena, named for Edna's only sister and Eugene's mother. Dr. Massey, a British physician serving as a Belgian state doctor, ushered the new baby into the mud-walled, grass-roofed house, assisted by Miss Sofia Karlson, a nurse from the Swedish Baptist Mission. The baby was especially welcome, for Edna had experienced numerous miscarriages and the young couple had at times despaired of ever having a living child.

On the day of Winifred's birth, Eugene surprised his wife with the gift of a cane-bottomed mahogany rocking chair for nursing, rocking and cuddling the baby. The station carpenter, trained at the Carson Industrial School at Luebo, took great delight in cooperating with Eugene in keeping the project secret from Edna. He welcomed the doctor's wife with an unusually broad grin whenever she appeared unexpectedly at the carpenter shop dispensary, hastily shoving the rough pieces of the little rocker under some boards as she approached.

On January 6, 1918, Eugene's and Edna's firstborn was baptized in the Lusambo Church, using the baby's Bantu language name. To the Congolese Christians who selected the name, *Misenga* was most appropriate for the finely-ground, delicately blond substance that was their little white baby. It means "Sands" or "Powder."

A baby boy named Tshifeta was baptized at the same time. His mother had been one of Eugene's patients a few months before, with symptoms of meningitis, following a severe blow on the back of her head. Eugene did not expect either the young mother or her unborn babe to live. But now the miraculously-well patient and her grateful husband stood with their Tshifeta beside Edna and Eugene, holding their little Misenga. The service of infant baptism was lovingly and worshipfully conducted by Pastor Musonguela.

This outstanding African pastor was one of the three ordained ministers of the American Presbyterian Congo Mission at that time. He was a wonderfully wise man, quiet and reserved in demeanor, endowed with remarkable qualities of leadership. A Muluba from the village of the paramount chief, Mutombo Katshi, he had served for years as a state soldier. During this time he had avenged the death of an uncle by killing two men and selling three others into slavery. After completing his term of military service, he had moved to Luebo where he had been employed by a European trader. For the first time he was in contact with Christians of the Mission. He had quickly come under conviction, been converted and baptized. Immediately he returned to the village where, according to custom, he had avenged his uncles' death and redeemed the three men he had sold into slavery. So fearlessly did he proclaim there his new-found faith that the young chief of the village, instead of killing him as he had vowed to do, became a Christian himself!

An entire village was changed in the first pastorate to which this pastor was assigned following his ordination. All fetishes and idols were burned and some three hundred people became Christians, including the gray-haired chief. Such was the quietly radiant, fearless and dynamic African preacher who was Eugene's and Edna's beloved spiritual mentor and advisor during the opening months of their first term of missionary service at Lusambo. How proud they always were that it was Pastor Musonguela who baptized their firstborn!

The second happy event of August 1917, was the completion by Mr. Hillhouse, Mr. Bedinger and the station workmen, of a neat little dispensary measuring thirty by sixteen feet. It had three rooms, the smaller ones serving as the pharmacy and the laboratory, with the third, larger one set aside as the operating room. A ten-foot-wide veranda surrounded three sides of the building, providing an airy waiting room for the patients. The building had a thick, grass roof, a mud floor covered with large handwoven reed mats and fresh, clean walls whitewashed with lime. Four small huts behind the clinic provided housing for post-operative cases. The operating room had the only brick and cement floor on the station!

A sanitary ceiling overhead was made possible by nailing
clean sheets to the rafters above the operating table. Eugene
was so proud of that first dispensary and his very first cement
floor that he kept on his desk till the day of his death a small
piece of that cement, with the date of the first operation performed at Lusambo written on it, December 4, 1917. Of this
experience, he wrote:

> With the prayer that the Lord might bless us in this
> first major operation on this station, we began, and found
> that it could be done! Nine more difficult cases were oper-
> ated on before that year ended and thirty-four minor oper-
> ations were also done, with forty anesthetics given.

NEW ASSIGNMENT

For only a few months longer the young couple would
continue their work at their Mission's river-transport station.
Edna's letters at this time glow with the warm, humorous details of the joyful activity created by the addition of a baby girl
to the family circle:

> I can write pages on how my seven-months-girlie lives
> in Africa, how she is beginning to drink goat's milk to the
> wonder of the black folks who look with horror on such
> food! Instead they stuff even their tiniest infants with
> "bidia," a boiled bread of cornmeal and cassava flour that
> turns out to be a tough, thick mush when finished. As a re-
> sult, babies often die and those who do survive on this diet
> have enormous, protruding, drumlike abdomens. This
> makes you think that the American child who heard a mis-
> sionary from Africa speak, was near the truth when she re-
> ported to her mother, "The people over there haven't much
> to eat and when they beat on their TUM-TUMS you can
> hear them twenty miles"!
>
> Winifred had the best time in the village this afternoon,
> laughing at the children. About fifteen little girls from four
> to eight years old followed Mrs. Bedinger and me wherever
> we went, rolling little Martha and Winifred in their car-
> riages. The whole afternoon they clapped their hand and
> sang in the rhythmical way that only these people know
> how to do. They sang, "*Mata wetu! Misenga wetu!*" That

means, "Our Martha! Our Winifred!" Sometimes their little leader would chant, "Our Martha!" and all the others
responded in perfect timing, "Our Winifred!" Sometimes
the group spontaneously divided into two sections, one
group singing to one baby and the other, to the other baby,
all simultaneously, in perfect harmony without a break!
Winifred just loved it and laughed and laughed and kept
reaching out her little hands to them. She loves the black
folks but hates it if any other person than her own mother or
father picks her up.

We have just been assigned to the new mission station
of Bibanga, among the Baluba people. Eugene is there now
with Mr. Hillhouse, building a house for us to live in! And
then there is Dr. Morrison's death. That seems to all the
Mission the biggest blow that could possibly fall and yet
there have been many blessings and beautiful things that
have happened because of it. He seemed to know that he
was going.

You must not feel in the least worried about our moving back "into the sticks." Eugene has been under such a
great strain here, with both medical and station responsibilities. You have no idea how hard he works and how great is
the pressure of all these fearfully sick patients and so little to
work with. Recently there was an awful strangulated hernia
as big as a melon to operate on and a <u>bad</u> epidemic of amoebic dysentery. But do not worry about us for we boil every
drop of our drinking water!

As I write, here comes Winifred Helena in from her
early morning ride in the borrowed old buggy that has been
such a blessing. She is all ready for her good goat's milk!
This baby has never had any medicine but her daily prophylactic dose of liquid quinine against malaria! She is a
bad little rascal, so full of life! Stands up in her buggy and
insists on kneeling in it even when she is being rolled. She is
a giggler, too, much to the delight of her Congolese friends,
who love her. Pray for us! We do for you! Love to all,

                                        Edna

[6]

Caravan on the Trail

For hundreds of years Central African rulers traveled by being transported in woven rattan hammocks or litters, borne on the strong shoulders of great, powerful runners with marvelous endurance. Dr. Kellersberger journeyed approximately 3000 miles in this fashion during his years as a medical missionary in the Belgian Congo.

The first hammock trip he made was designed by his colleague, the Reverend Bob Bedinger, to introduce him to this unique mode of travel, to the local areas and peoples, and to the work being done at that time by the American Presbyterian Congo Mission.

That initial venture lasted twenty-six days, from October 9th to November 4th, 1917. Fifty villages were visited by the small caravan consisting of Pastor Musonguela, Bob Bedinger, and the doctor, four pairs of hammock-bearers, a cook, laundryman and twelve box-men.

Most of the doctor's hammock journeys, however, were made in response to emergency medical calls. His elite team of carriers was ready at any time of the day or night to take him where he was needed. They adored him, for he always refused to be carried, except over smooth, level ground. Whenever the

124

terrain became rough, Eugene got out of his hammock and climbed up the steeps or slid down the slopes with his men. In the rugged country regions of the Lubilashi and Sankuru river valleys of the Kasai area of the Belgian Congo, there was more walking than riding to be done. Of the 330 miles covered on that first journey, Dr. Kellersberger made 275 on foot.

THE FIRST HAMMOCK TRIP

The former student assistant at the Marine Biological Laboratory at Woods Hole, Massachusetts, is highly visible in the journal he kept of this first overland adventure. His keen, scientific interest in flora and fauna of every sort is recorded in both verbal and pictorial sketches. Getulius Kellersberger would have been pleased with the many carefully-executed maps that his grandson drew to scale of the various tribal districts covered en route.

The tropical forests were a surprise and a delight to Eugene. He had expected impenetrable undergrowth in the understory but found instead, beneath the leafy ceiling high above, a windless, vaulted spaciousness filled with a dim, cathedral-like glow. Sunlight shining upon the spreading crowns of the emergent giants filtered down through the tangled mass of interwoven vines and branches that formed the main canopy. It finally flickered to the forest floor as tiny, elusive glints of light made momentarily visible by the wind, stirring the distant overhead foliage. Here and there miniature trees with large leaves and brilliant purple or scarlet flowers, graceful, rope-like stems of lianas and exotic epiphytes clinging to gray bark, added decorative touches to the starkness of soaring bole, flaring buttress and massive trunk. Five-hundred-foot-long stems of rattan vines hung in loops, suspended from the crowns of the towering trees to which they were attached by sharp, hooked tendrils. On the forest floor a moist, spongy carpet of fungi-impregnated, rotting vegetation silenced every footfall and gave off that delicately pungent, woodsy fragrance peculiar to the jungle.

Eugene quickly learned to identify the African mahogany with its ninety-foot-long, branch-free bole and the 200-foot-

Bibanga, October 23, 1919, the Kellersbergers leaving for the United States for furlough.

En route back to Bibanga, 1921. Winifred's baby sister, Cornelia, is asleep in the native market basket tied into one end of the canvas hammock.

high African oak. There is a sketch in his journal of the eight-foot-high buttresses of a big hardwood called *limba* and another of a strangling fig enveloping a support-tree victim. Having spent many hours in his carpenter shop dispensary, the doctor already appreciated the remarkable variety of colors and the exquisite, ribboned beauty of the grains of these tropical woods when polished.

Excerpts from Eugene's diary describe portions of that first overland journey made in 1917:

> On the fourth day we passed through a magnificent belt of forest that takes six hours to traverse. In one place the trail went down into a deep ravine, following the bed of a clear stream for a long, long way. Here, truly, there were no footprints left behind to tell of your passing! Here the sun is a forbidden guest. On all sides rise the giants of the forest, reaching up to the life-giving sun. One feels totally dwarfed by their grandeur and the thought of how much longer they last than our poor human bodies. But, praise our great God and Savior! Even as all these great trees have come about by the death of one tiny seed, even so through the death of our bodies, we will enter into a life of glory!
>
> *October 13, Village of Tshimbila*   Another hard journey today, with a powerful sun beating down all day long till evening. My lips are blistered. We are in the mountains now with deep ravines buried between them, filled with immense forests. One crawls and stumbles and falls down the precipitous slopes. Always at the bottom is a beautiful, clear stream in a rock or sand bed. Often you hear the sound of rushing waters at a great distance. Sometimes it proves to be a powerful torrent that is difficult to ford. The local people usually cut a large tree in such a way as to make it fall across such a river, forming a bridge.
>
> Then out of these cool, dank ravines one must go up again, up into the blinding heat, climbing a long, sandy ascent till you feel like dropping and are wringing wet with perspiration. When you get to the top you are always rewarded with a magnificent view! We saw this very village where we now are three hours before we reached it across a tremendous basin. To the west lies the deep green, winding serpent of the Lubilashi River and beyond it, along the ho-

Muamba–Kazadi, canny "kapita" of the doctor's faithful hammock-men.

The doctor's crack team of hammock-bearers, experienced carriers of their own tribal chiefs, ready for any emergency journey.

rizon, rise steep projecting mountains some twenty-five miles away. We rested at a village for an hour, then on we went in the heat of the day till 3:30, marched and marched till I am red in the face, hands, neck and ready to quit!

October 15, Village of Miketa Dibue What a staring one must endure and what comments are made about us! We have been here two hours and they are still standing at the doors, crowding the windows, cutting out all light, whispering, laughing, gesticulating and exclaiming over everything they see . . .

There are such sad sights along the road! The physical suffering we see is pitiful enough but on top of that there is a spiritual darkness and a groping that is appalling! Some of the sick I have treated have a look on their faces as if they expect me to heal them in five minutes! It is very unpleasant and gives me a feeling of my own littleness. How wonderful that Jesus went along and "healed the sick and those that were lame, halt and blind"! Why can't I do just that, too, O God? Grant that I may at least have that same loving, gentle spirit that He had!

October 16, Village of Lubanga This is a very pretty village with a really good evangelist. All the people met us at least a mile out to welcome us. Two women insisted on carrying my hammock <u>with me in it</u> for a while — and <u>they did it</u>, too! All along the trail the people came running out to shake hands and last of all came the Chief. He is a fine-looking fellow! The village lies on top of a high hill and the main street goes between beautiful rows of palms. It looks so clean and neat and shows the influence of the Gospel. The church shed, too, is large, clean and well-built. This afternoon we will have a meeting to examine the candidates for baptism.

October 17, Village of Tshinsaka Slept fine, only got so cold in the morning under two blankets that I could not sleep any more. We gave the goat that the Chief presented us with to our caravan men, keeping only the liver and the brains for ourselves. We have been given welcoming gifts of chickens, bananas, plantains, pineapples and eggs, so no danger of starving! The Chief fed our men eighteen large bowls of *bidia*, the native cassava bread, so our men are all very happy! After supper they danced around the fire, singing our praises. Each individual improvised a solo part and was

then joined by the entire group in the same intricately interwoven refrain. They are innately musical and harmonize in
the most perfect rhythm together. If you are looking for
grace and perfection in dance, then come here to Africa to
see it!

This morning we baptized three persons. Out of the
eight who applied, only three were accepted. This is a new
work and we believe in making the test of discipleship very
severe, to make them appreciate it and to be sure they <u>know</u>
what they are doing. I am so glad for these three! One was
a nice-looking young woman with a new baby and the other
two were lads. This evangelist, Tshibangu, has a good
work. He is so alive! I am pleased how the village people
like him and the wonderful way in which he influences
them for good. And sing! You should hear them! A little too
fast, perhaps, but in perfect unison. The small boys almost
yell in their enthusiasm!

October 18, Village of Mulanda   Lions! Boys, I "ain't
LYING!" We entered lion country this morning. South of
here they are numerous and very dangerous. We saw fresh
tracks where they had been last night. They move about at
night and sleep in the day. They have killed a number of
people in this area. I am also thankful that the hooded buf-
falos did not get too close to us on the trail today!

If you take your time on the trail you see many interesting things, for example a chameleon! One that I saw was
about five inches in length with a long, slim tail and clamp-
like feet, two toes on one side and three on the other. These
clasp and unclasp like pincers, providing a fine way of
grasping twigs and branches. The chameleon has a long,
fly-catching tongue, a big comb on its head and the funniest
eyes I have ever seen! They are on the extremity of revolv-
ing stalks. He can look forward with one eye and backward
with the other. He is green as grass, but put him in some
darker surroundings and he turns dark greenish-brown,
sometimes all mottled, so that you can hardly find him
again! The chromatophores or pigment cells expand and
contract like those of the ocean squid, making it possible for
him to control his camouflage system, depending upon
whether he is prey or predator!

October 25, Bena Tshitola   Today we arrived at the banks of
the Lubilashi River. Not a soul in sight, only red water,

crocodiles and hippos! At last "Old Charon of the Styx" appeared, the head boatman and his helpers, and came across in a leaky, hollowed-out log canoe to get us. They had to bail frantically and stick fresh mud plaster into the cracks of the boat to keep the water from filling it too quickly.

I have not believed everything I have heard about crocodiles, at least not until today! A huge one crossed the river three times just thirty feet above us, keeping a watchful eye out for a possible meal. The men warned us not to stand too near the bank for "crocs" attack very quickly, stunning their prey with a blow of their powerful tails. Pastor Musonguela told us that the native belief, when a crocodile eats a man, is that a *Mukishi* or evil spirit has entered it. I had a very creepy feeling as we crossed the river with such an escort! In places the swirling waters came to within an inch of the top of that old "tub" and there were twelve of us in it at the time. As we crossed we heard the loud guffaws of the hippos downriver and saw them alternately submerging, blowing spray and sticking their huge, ugly old heads out of the water.

As we made our way through the village cornfields after crossing the river, we came upon the fresh tracks of an elephant herd. We had just missed them! Tremendous holes made by their huge feet were sunk deep into the ground and all of the corn had been destroyed.

October 27, Village of Kambi wa Biselele I have rarely seen such a fantastically beautiful sight as I saw this morning. We awakened to the roar of the river and started our journey long before the sun had begun to fill the cups of the valleys with fog. First we crossed a rushing mountain stream and then slowly mounted a precipitously steep path along a great projecting spur of the high hills flanking the river canyon. Again and again we stopped just to gaze at the magnificent valley with its green carpets and ascents on all sides, with range after range of mountains appearing as a backdrop in the distance.

We began to see a rosy glow on the high cliffs and hills across the river. Fog was rapidly covering the whole valley floor. Then suddenly the big red ball of the sun itself rose behind us, transforming the fog-filled valley at our feet into a sea of shimmering gold. The river was also illumined by the sunbrightened fog, so that every detail of the current through the rapids was thrown into bold relief. Truly this striking Kasai "hill country," like my Texas "hill country," is wonderfully blest of God in its beauty and richness!

We have now spent a happy two days at Biselele, one of the finest villages, staying in our evangelist's nice house. Sixteen people have been baptized here, making us rejoice over the work of the Holy Spirit. Day after day we have worked, preaching, baptizing, strengthening, guiding. There are many joys but our hearts fail us when we see the remaining overwhelming darkness, the few, few workers and hear the insistent cry for help coming to us from every direction! But OUR GOD IS ABLE — that we know!

The time came when I had to leave Reverend Bedinger and hurry home to Lusambo, about seventy miles away. This distance I covered in three days with my own caravan of fourteen men. All of you know the "Call of Home," especially when the dear mother and sweet little bundle of a three-month-old daughter are awaiting you! My men heard it, too! They know that I like to travel at night, so they knocked on my door at 1 a.m. and under the dim light of a fog-shrouded moon we slipped away into the tall, wet grass. When we had crossed the last stream, climbed the last steep hill, there lay before us the glad sight of Lusambo mission station! Our descent and crossing of the Sankuru in the long, narrow boat was accompanied with songs of rejoicing. This was HOME — no matter if it were in America, or on the banks of the Sankuru in the heart of Africa! And if my home being here, by the grace of God, means an eternal home for some of these dear people, I am very glad that my home — is here!

STARTING FROM SCRATCH "IN THE STICKS"

Bibanga, overlooking the Lubilashi valley, was founded in December 1917, by the George T. McKees and the Sixten Edhegardes. The nearest American Presbyterian Congo Mission post was Mutoto, one hundred miles to the southeast. Eugene recorded and described the exact location of his new work in typical engineering fashion:

Longitude 23° and 54′ East of Greenwich
Latitude 6°–12′–30″ South of the Equator

To the southwest two hundred miles is the Portuguese

Angola border, about where Livingstone crossed it on his
famous journey from Victoria Falls to Loanda on the west
coast of Africa. Due south we are three hundred and fifty
miles from Northern Rhodesia and the headwaters of the
Zambezi River. To the southeast and east some two
hundred miles away flows the mighty Congo, heading due
north on its long journey of thousands of miles to the ocean.
Two hundred miles to the east of us is Lake Tanganyika.

At Bibanga Eugene did not have even the corner of a carpenter shop in which to begin his medical work. The very first
operation was performed out under the trees, with sheets tied
to the branches overhead to keep debris from falling into the
incision. Later a thirty-foot long shed was constructed, with a
partition. Here, using a small iron bed as his operating table,
Eugene removed a good-sized tumor with Nkuadi assisting
and Mrs. McKee giving the anesthetic. The very week that
this little mud-walled dispensary was completed, a cyclonic
wind and hail storm heralding the oncoming rainy season, collapsed the frail structure, covering the pitifully small supply of
drugs and medical equipment with a sticky mass of muddy
rubble.

The Kellersbergers were living in the four-room "shot-
gun-house" built for them by Mr. Hillhouse. Now, without
hesitation, they decided that one-half of their new home
should be made available for the medical work. Of this decision Eugene wrote:

> Our bedroom became the operating room and our bath
> and storage room became the dispensary. Two major oper-
> ations were performed here in October 1918, with a great
> crowd attending and much excitement and interest. I al-
> lowed the members of the families to watch and explained
> what I was doing. Distrust was considerably less each time.
> Thank God that both cases were successful!
>
> I asked the Mission for funds for a brick and cement
> floor for my operating room. Mr. Hillhouse delayed his
> long overdue furlough in order to complete what he called
> "the doctor's morgue" So now I have somewhat of a medi-
> cal plant here at Bibanga in which real work can be done.
> You would probably laugh at it but it means a great deal to

me! The Lord has put it here for me to use and I intend to
use it for His glory and the relief of pain of body and soul!

The first Christmas at Bibanga was a simple, contented
one. The little family attended the early morning "Giving
Service" in which Eugene presented a small goat as Winifred's gift to the Christ Child. Unconcerned, the two-year-old
toddled back and forth during the service between her parents
and her beloved little "guardian," Andrew Mukeba, clutching
her new pussy cat that squeaked and opened its mouth when
hit on the head. Breakfast was served on the cozy screened-in
porch, overlooking the marvelous valley. Edna had hung up a
cluster of red paper bells and arranged some bright red berries
in a copper bowl for the center of the table. Later there was a
tiny little tree at the McKee's for the two little girls of the station, a time made joyous by the strains of *While Shepherds
Watched Their Flocks By Night*, played on the hand-cranked Victrola.

The last night of the old year Edna wrote a special message of peace and contentment into her baby's journal:

December 31, 1918

Only a hurried note this quiet, last night of the bloody
old year of 1918, and yet the year that finally brought
peace! As I write, Daddy is reading the war radio-gram and
marking on a map the camps of the American and English
and French all along the German Rhine. I wish you could
see him in his boyish interest and enthusiasm and hear his
funny exclamation, "Man! Man!" You are asleep in your
little bed of mosquito wire and rough boards not five feet
away, for in our wee mud house, the bedroom and living
room are now one, since turning over two of our four rooms
for Daddy's medical work. But you are such a quiet little
sleeper, it doesn't matter and I love to have us all close together like this!

THE INFLUENZA EPIDEMIC

The pandemic of influenza reached the Belgian Congo in
November 1918. Fifty-three Europeans died at the Katanga
copper mines during that month and thousands of native mine

workers. The disease entered the country from the south and southeast, coming up the Cape-to-Cairo railway, as well as from the west, from steamers tying up at Boma and Matadi.

In January 1919 Dr. Kellersberger received an urgent call to Mutoto station. This, the main educational training center of the mission, was ordinarily manned by six couples. Now the Charles Cranes were carrying on there alone — so great was the toll of disease and wartime travel on the mission staff. Eugene described this experience in the following letter:

> We have at present only two doctors on our Mission, to cover the work of five stations! I have had to leave my wife alone so much of the time that I decided to take her and our baby along with me on this long distance medical call. The first part of the trip we really enjoyed very much. Winifred had a tiny hammock of her own and her own hammock men. This time we took along a tent, finding it much cleaner than the state rest houses to stay in. We took our time, for this is the rainy season and one cannot travel as fast as when alone.
>
> Just as we left Bibanga we heard rumors that the world-wide influenza epidemic had reached Luebo, but that it had quickly died out. We had no inkling of what we were very soon to run into. Two days' march from Mutoto, as we hurried into a small village to take shelter from a terrible rain and windstorm, we were met by a special caravan of ten men, sent by the Cranes. A brief note from Mr. Crane stated that their little two-year-old daughter was very sick with the "flu" and that the entire student body of the Training School was down, as well as a large portion of the local village. The urgent request was, "Drop everything and don't even stop to sleep on the way!"
>
> Fatigue marches are the doctor's lot. I won't even try to describe the twenty-four hours that followed, with our men already tired out and several already sick, the powerful rays of the African summer sun, the steep hills that demanded frequent stops to accumulate strength to go on, and a dry mouth with no good water to drink. Before we reached our destination, a second note reached us with the news that Mr. Crane was seriously ill and Mrs. Crane, who was pregnant, was on the verge of collapse. We pulled into Mutoto station as into a completely deserted town!

Three days after our arrival there Edna came down
with influenza and was very sick for eight days. Those were
strenuous days for me, the only well adult on the station!

Doctor, general nurse, baby nurse, chief cook, "*chargé
de station*" — it is a wonder I was never sick, not even a day
and our dear little girl to this day has been the picture of
health! Little Louise Crane is now fine.

All classes and school activities have been suspended
and all medical attention possible is being given to some
one thousand desperately ill people immediately around
me. Our death toll so far is twenty-two students. We have
much to be thankful for, for in the unprotected villages,
deaths are occurring in much larger numbers, most of them
dying from complications with pneumonia, that terrible
"choker of man's life breath." The native peoples with their
poor housing, underfed condition and general susceptibility
to respiratory infections, die in much greater numbers than
do white people. You need only read the current accounts of
death in the South African gold mines and in our Katanga
copper mines, to know the ravages of the disease.

In the last two years I have transferred twice, working
on three stations. It is such a loss to the work for me to have
to be on the go so much with these constant emergency
calls, just when I am able to settle down and begin to be
useful and efficient. Service to "make the world safe for de-
mocracy" is great, but service that leads a soul from physical degradation and spiritual darkness into physical victory
and spiritual light — this kind of service is the greatest of
all!

THE EMERGENCY CALL
TO THE METHODIST MISSION

The Kellersbergers finally returned to Bibanga on April
13th, following their extended stay at Mutoto throughout the
worst of the flu epidemic. It was delightful to be back into the
regular routine of work again! Only ten months of their term
of service remained, before they were scheduled to go on furlough in January 1920.

But that routine work for Eugene was extremely brief. On
April 18, he wrote in his journal:

Poor McKee! I was hoping to be able to settle down

and be a help. Was sterilizing for operations, some ten major ones waiting, when the news came. I have been called to Lubefu to see Mr. Reeve of the Methodist Episcopal Congo Missions. Since his attack of influenza at Brazzaville in December, when his wife nearly died, he, because of not taking care of himself and helping others to the point of exhaustion, has some weeks later developed heart trouble. They have no doctor on their entire mission now. It is hard for people back in America to realize what such a call means. It means laying down immediately all of my work, no matter how important, pressing or interesting, packing for a journey of eight to ten days on the path, with a caravan of twenty men. It means leaving my already over-burdened fellow workers with that much more to do while I am gone. It means leaving a dear wife and sweet little girl who is just beginning to talk real talk and learning something new every hour. It means throwing myself completely on God and telling yourself over and over, "It's your duty, your joy to be able to minister!"

This particular emergency trip took thirty days, twenty-four of which were spent in travelling. Twenty-one nights were spent in native villages and three in state posts of the Belgian government. In the course of this journey, Eugene crossed one hundred and nineteen streams and rivers, passing through the tribal lands of the Baluba, Basonge and Batetele. His route took him fifty-five miles northeast to Kabinda, then due north for one hundred and thirty miles into the Sankuru District to Lubefu. From there he went another fifty miles north to Wembo Nyama, headquarters of the MECM. His return trip took him to the Lomami River and the state post of Tshofa. Turning southwest for another eighty miles, he again reached Kabinda, fifty-five miles from the home mission station of Bibanga. Excerpts from the daily journal of this remarkable trip shed interesting light on Zaire history and on an area of that land rarely visited at that time by any white man:

> *April 29, 1919, Majiba, Basonge* Here at Majiba we suddenly heard frantic running through the grass. It was a man who had fled and thought we were State officials coming after him. They have been along this very path recently and have been catching people all over the valley so the en-

tire section is "dead." Houses and villages are empty, in disorder, overgrown with weeds. Just passed the black concubine of the Danish captain, the government agent who is doing all the "catching" in this district . . .

The results of the influenza epidemic are very evident in this area. Because they died like flies, they think that the spirits are angry with them and try to appease them in many ways. I have seen many market baskets set all along the path, rotting away, filled with corn, millet and beans, put there with the hope of placating the angry spirits — this instead of eating these good things and obtaining strength in their bodies to overcome the disease! It is so sad!

April 30, Kabinda This large, important state post is the capital of the Lomami District. This is where the formerly powerful chief, Lumpungu, now lives; it had an evil glory just a few years ago. The Basonge got guns and powder from the State and from traders and made tremendous raids into the great Baluba area that our mission now occupies. In 1880–1890 Lumpungu supported the Arab slavers when they very nearly overran the entire Congo. Later he shifted his allegiance to the white man. Now he is known and respected far and wide . . .

The colonial state is very strong here. There is a big military camp and at this time many soldiers are returning from the campaign in German East Africa, where the war killed so many of them. There is a constant stream of porters and box-carriers going to Kabalo to bring back loads of military goods.

The Commissaire was very lovely to me; I took both lunch and dinner with him and his wife. He is Flemish, very intelligent, while his wife is Jewish, from Luxembourg. Both are well educated, in politics "liberal." He traced out a map for me to help me in my journey north, showing the boundary of the Lomami District for a hundred kilometers north and wrote out all information regarding distances, sleeping places, food for my carriers, possible game and the nature of the countryside.

May 2, Kasonga Mule Our Lord does honor one who tries to keep His Word and tries to honor Him! I was so tempted to travel on Sunday, but decided to make a double trip on Saturday and rest on Sunday. This has brought many happy results. I was able to give my men a rest and

feed them well. I was able to make friends with and overcome the prejudice of the chief and Catholic evangelist at
Mpoi Muba. We had worship services with them morning
and evening and our men sang many hymns throughout the
day. Still another good result: When I got to the state rest
house here today, I found many people gathered. YESTER-
DAY the twenty-five-year-old son of the chief died, the heir,
sick for two months following influenza. If I had arrived
yesterday, if I had not rested on Sunday, I would have arrived just before or at the time of his death and my coming
would have been taken as a cause of the death! So I thank
the Lord for His guidance! I thank Him for the peace in my
heart and the assurance of His presence in the midst of this
huge, milling throng, with drums beating and people crying
out weird cries!

I thank Thee, O God, for my beloved wife who is back
there many weary miles over the hills in Baluba country, interceding for me with a heart full of love and concern. I
thank Thee for the child that is there with her, that token of
our oneness and a comfort to my Edna in my absence. I
thank Thee that I am among these people and I pray that I
may be Thy witness day by day. May these people know
that I love them!

As I sit here I am listening to the chief roaring out his
orders. His town crier is repeating each command right
after him, yelling as loud as possible, trying to sound as
much like him as he can! The bedlam was unbelievable
until this started. Now everyone in the entire village is sitting mouse still to listen . . .

It is now 4 p.m. The ceremonies of the official mourning for the chief's son are now going on and they are well
worth describing!

Everywhere there are those great triangular Batetele
drums made of hollowed-out logs, some three feet in length,
very heavy to carry. The drummers beat them with two
rubber-coated sticks, one on each side. All the people, men,
women and children together, march up and down the central path of the village. The women all utter a weird cry in
unison, somewhat resembling the wail of a siren. They are
painted with whitewash in the most varied designs, the
whole body or only the face, giving the eyes a terrible
expression. Every once in a while a young brave dashes the

length of the street, flourishing a battle axe. Every time he
does so, the women jump and follow him, dancing, twisting,
and catching imaginary objects in the air. And they say that
they will do this for a whole month!

May 6, Kapembue, Basongo   This has without doubt
been the very hardest day's travel we have ever made, 32
kilometers or 20 miles along a narrow trail buried under 14-
foot-high grass. The grass fallen across the path so ob-
structed our walking that our feet often got tangled in it and
we tripped and fell over and over again. I doubt if there is
even one mile of forest in this 180 miles of tortuous bush and
hot sun. When we reached the flood plain of the Lubefu
River, we crossed twenty streams in thirty miles, one of
which had a fascinating vine bridge swinging high in the
air, a real "suspension" bridge! It was truly ingenious in its
construction, very strong, with remarkably little sway as
one walks across.

May 7, Lubefu, Methodist Episcopal Congo Mission   On
the hilltop overlooking the Lubefu River valley is the Methodist mission station of Lubefu, the end of my journey. As
we came onto the compound, accompanied by the beautiful
hammock songs that my carriers were singing, I was greatly
impressed by all that has been done in so short a time by
this comparatively new Mission, founded in 1912. They
have the nicest houses I have seen in Congo, making good
use of *akodi*, the part of the palm used for making strong
hammock poles. They use these to make ceilings, floors,
fences, walls and doors!

I had a lovely reception from Reverend and Mrs.
Reeve. I found her still weak from the hard attack of influenza she had at Brazzaville in December 1918. I found him
also much fallen off and with what I had hoped NOT to
find, a heart irregularity brought on by the flu and his unwise exertions after returning to his work. As a result, he
has orders to give up all active work till he goes on furlough
at the end of the year.

Wembo Nyama station is 48 miles nearly north, somewhat east of here. Mr. Anker is not well and there is no doctor there, so it has been thought wise for me to go there, too,
to see if I can be of any help. I have been supplied with
eight of the finest hammock men I have ever had, except for
the *Batshioko* given me by the diamond mining company,

the *Forminiere*. We went sailing along, especially after the moon came out, to the accompaniment of the peculiar Batetele hammock songs, more a series of antiphonal grunts, with an occasional chant. They sang my praises as a doctor! I had operated on three cases from up in this area at Lusambo and at Bibanga, so they knew about me!

May 10, Wembo Nyama, MECM I have often wanted to see this interesting station, founded seven years ago by Bishop Lambuth and so ably built up by that splendid man of God, Dr. D. L. Mumpower. I am surprised at what they have accomplished in only these few years, pleased with their type of construction and the beautiful furniture made here by workmen out of the tropical wood that looks like walnut and takes a beautiful polish. Yesterday I had an interesting talk with old Chief Wembo Nyama. He was once the right hand man of the fearfully powerful chief, Ngongo Lutete. So I got him started on telling me some of his reminiscences.

May 12, Wembo Nyama, MECM Spent the morning at the clinic. Saw four cases I had done, two at Lusambo and two at Bibanga and was much pleased that the hernias were perfect results! The hairlip man was the happiest I have ever seen, now one of their best workers and a baptized Christian! Seven cases came and begged to be operated on TODAY — a scrotal elephantiasis, two bone infections, one uterine fibroid and a tremendous goiter. It made my heart cry out for a time when I can STAY PUT in ONE PLACE and WORK! It made me long for a real hospital and a good nurse to help me. Only one operation like this can open up a whole village to the Gospel!

May 13, Lubefu, MECM Today I start back home again, this time by a route 290 miles long. I'll be on the road two weeks — don't want to return by the way I came because of those terrible grass forests. Will leave Lubefu tomorrow with a fresh caravan and head for the Lomami River. The Reeves have been most generous in helping me stock up on supplies for my return journey, Mr. Reeve insisted on lending me his big rifle, so I am hoping to be able to shoot a big waterbuck or antelope or even a buffalo for my men. I have 22 in my caravan, ten of them powerful hammock men that can carry like fury! I must say that I will be very careful and have asked the Lord to give me wis-

dom and good judgment in using the gun for I am here in
this land for HIM and not for hunting. I also have a dear
wife and child that have a claim on me!

May 15, Kafua, Lumbilu   I had to get out of the nice big
State rest house here because of all the wasps' nests in it.
We about got into trouble, sure enough! Now I am all cozy
and comfy in my small, single tent. As I look back over my
journal, I find that in the last thirteen months, from April
1918 to May 1919 I have travelled 1,370 miles, all by foot
and hammock. I have travelled overland almost 2,000 miles
during the eighteen months that I have been a missionary!
The village women all went out very early this morning to
their millet fields and came back with great baskets loaded
with beautiful symmetry with the long, cylindrical heads of
the black grain. Batetele women traditionally do all of the
field work.

May 16, Kitenge Ngandu, Ngongo Lutete's village   I felt
very excited when I saw the Lomami River valley and realized that I am probably the first missionary of our mission
ever to come this far east. This is a very large village. The
houses are big and well-built, some a hundred or more feet
long. There are no openings of any kind facing the street,
only from the other direction. The enclosure of the chief's
fence is over two hundred feet long! The chief is sick and I
am going to visit him in the morning. He must have considerable prestige for this is the village where Ngongo Lutete
reigned in terror and power, and where the Arab domination of the Congo was given a severe check. These people
have a certain air of pride and superiority that I have not
seen elsewhere.

May 17, Kitenge Ngandu   I got up late, had breakfast
and went to see the chief. I was ushered into the court
through a long, dark passage, then led about through a
maze of houses, most of them large and connected with each
other. There were many fetishes in evidence, women galore
and a number of children. After I had waited for a short
time, I saw coming out through a beautiful, ornamented
door, very slowly, an <u>old</u> man, almost bald, with a sore eye
and a long beard, Kitenge Ngandu himself, one of the powerful old chiefs of this area, a confederate of Ngongo Lutete!
He told me that Ngongo Lutete's village was just across the
ravine and that he himself had been down into our Baluba

country on slave raids. He is probably sick just because he is so old, and probably near death. (He did die just six weeks after my visit.) I gave the chief a gift of two cups of salt and he gave me in return a dish of very fine rice.

May 21, Muefo This morning I rousted out my friend, the peanut and palm oil plantation owner and gave him two big slices of cake, one of fruit cake and one of chocolate, a glass of Lubefu sugar and a tin of sausage, all of which he gratefully accepted. He looked very yellow to me this morning, as if he has malaria.

May 22, Kabue on the Lumba River Fifteen miles at a trot! It's been an unbelievable relay race, with my hammock-carriers taking turns at spelling each other. I have never been on a finer road anywhere in the Congo, nor had better hammock service, nor heard more beautiful hammock chants sung than I heard today. Usually they do their singing only as we pass through villages, announcing the identity of the one they are transporting. But today they have kept on singing even when the villages we passed through were far behind. They sang me over mile after mile of smooth plain, along a twenty-foot wide highway, a proposed railroad bed! They cut capers, they danced! Fat little Disashi, the song-leader, has a voice that cracks badly every now and then but that doesn't stop him! These Batetele have several favorite choruses that fall in with each verse of his string of little antiphonal "songlets." At other times he leads and they all repeat, singing each of his entire stanzas. It is all done in perfect time and with unbelievable grace, in syncopated rhythmn with the rapidly padding bare feet on the ground and the quick, controlled grunts and pants of the entire caravan, running together as one man.

That giant of a man, Yamba, with his high forelock of hair and a great bunch of wild guinea feathers attached to the top of his head, is a regular clown! When it is not his turn to carry, he circles and ducks and twists in and out of the caravan, wiggling about and even running backwards right in front of my two carriers. Then all of a sudden he comes to a halt, stands at attention, then makes the finest bow you can imagine, with his eyes twinkling! Our entire caravan is having a great time with one of our men named Matamba. The hammock men all like him. He can't speak Otetela, but he still repeats everything they say in that language in such a cute way that it keeps them laughing. He is really strong and keeps up well with running caravans. They call him "Baluba Child"!

May 24, Mulemba Evening. I am sitting here in front of my tent as the night closes around me and I am homesick. I feel as if I'd been travelling all my life and I'll be so glad when I come to my sweet home, made so by that dear wife that God has given me and that darling little two-year-old girlie! Praise the Lord for my home and for her who makes it our heaven on earth! I have pitched my tent under a big tree in a former cornfield now lying fallow. I like tents! They are a sign to me that we are strangers on earth, only camping in our temporary human bodies, looking for an Eternal City! All morning a clean, fresh wind has been blowing through the tent, trying to snatch away my writing materials, even attempting to lift it! I slept from dark until daylight last night, disturbed only when the chief's cows began licking my tent. The night sentry chased them away by throwing firebrands at them.

May 25, Mulemba, Sunday Evening Again the shadows are gathering about me but in me shines the Presence of my Lord who gives a peace and assurance that is not found through human effort or will power. I have had a most quiet day. Had my *Bible* study and prayer. Read Erdman's *General Epistles* and was impressed with the statement: "Love is the deepest experience and the greatest blessing of the human soul." I have found this to be true in the blessing that has come to me in my dear wife. But I want that "deepest experience" of my life to be my love for Him who died for me, and through my love for Him, an endless outflowing of love and concern for the souls of others. How real the love for one's wife is, because the two are one. Often we do not experience the reality of our love for Christ in the same way. We have just had our little worship service, with songs and prayers led by the carriers. They all seem to understand what I am saying, even though it is a mixture of Tshiluba, Kituba and Otetele.

6 p.m. Word has just come that Chief Lumpungu has died. He has killed and eaten many a man in his day!

May 26, Kabinda The death of Chief Lumpungu has drawn thousands to Kabinda to observe the two months of official mourning ceremonies. A large company of soldiers is stationed in his village to prevent trouble. If the State were not here in power, all of his wives would be killed, according to custom, as well as many slaves. As I passed through the mourning village at dawn today, there was a terrible noise of wailing and crying, drums furiously beating, guns going off. Throughout the village there were many fires, with people around them and companies of soldiers with their arms stacked nearby, keeping watch. Where the beautiful stockade of Chief Lumpungu's house was when I came through a few weeks ago there was now only a mass of blackened, fallen walls. The people themselves burned his entire village after his death. They say that his body has been taken back to his original tribe of the Bekelebua and has been put in a house in the forest. He was a great and cruel man! How I wish that I could be allowed to observe all the rites in connection with his death!

The remaining months at Bibanga were comparatively free from emergency trips, permitting Eugene at last to make steady progress in his work. Only one more time did he have to go to Mutoto for medical reasons, visiting his good friend, Chief Muamba Kavula, on the way and sleeping one night within sound of the roaring falls of the Lubi river:

August 4, 1919, Tshintshianku on the Lubi I couldn't help but think, from my Texas boyhood, that the cottontail and Jack rabbit would do fine on these great plains and wooded, hilly sections! The market that I observed yesterday at Muamba Kavulu was truly astounding, four or five thousand people there. It was a veritable Babel with a wonderful variety of produce available. We had two hundred and five people in our evening service there. I was very much pleased indeed! There is much iron ore in this area, big hills covered with rocks and boulders. In all the villages we have passed through today we have seen smelters, cone-shaped houses with a low opening inside a place built of mud, where they melt the ore they have dug out of crude pits. The fires are kept roaring hot by the operation of bellows made of antelope hide. They fashion very good hoes, knives, axes, hatchets and spears. Today I watched a blacksmith making a hoe, a process which was indeed fascinating to watch.

August 5, Tshintshianku The sound of the Lubi River

rapids could not be heard during the daytime but as night fell, and the village grew quiet, it became more and more distinct till now it is a great, steady roar, something like the sound of breakers on the shore. It is dry season and the Lubi is rushing over its bed of rocky boulders, deep in between the hills. I do <u>love</u> to be within hearing distance of a roaring stream! It always gives me a kind of peace and soothes me. Somehow it reminds me of Him Who "rideth on the waters," Who Himself walked on them and was their Master!

THE FIRST HOME ASSIGNMENT

October 26, 1919, Tshiala Falls   Ever since I came to Bibanga I have wanted to see Tshiala Falls, only fifteen miles from our station. Many times I have looked down here from our hilltop, past the great block of a mountain sitting in the plain. And now here I am, sitting at the very foot of that mountain, *Nyemvue*! Our tent is beneath the dense shade of a great, feathery bamboo. Tomorrow we will head on to Bakwanga on our homeward journey back to the United States for our first home assignment.

Here we are within sight of the rapids and magnificent falls of the Lubilashi River. After leaping over an irregular ledge about three hundred yards long that runs at an angle across the river, the foaming water rushes along a rocky riverbed that makes two sharp turns within two miles. These falls are as picturesque as any I have ever seen, a truly remarkable series of rapids, whirlpools and rock formations! During the height of the rainy season all of this disappears completely under a mass of flood water that fills the entire riverbed. In some places the river is only a narrow trough twenty-five feet wide, with rock walls rising abruptly on either side. Every now and then it forms a cataract, over which the water pours in fury, dashing itself into flying spray, fascinating the observer with its force and beauty.

As we left our camp-site, we climbed the hills and looked down on the canyon and its cataracts thundering below us. We could follow its course, deeply carved into the earth, till it disappeared in the range of round, knobby hills to the north. To the south brooded old *Nyemvue* mountain, in all its towering strength, with the broad band of the Lubilashi River curving serenely about its base in a great "S" shape. As we entered one village through banana and plantain-lined streets, an old woman, the only Christian in that village, came tottering joyfully to greet us. There is no evangelist here so she keeps her little candle of faith in our Lord burning bravely alone!

A highly dramatic experience, described by Dr. Kellersberger, occurred on the downriver journey to Kinshasa:

November 21, 1919 We had left Luebo, bound for Stanley Pool, with other passengers going to America for furlough. Along the winding banks of the Kasai River there are scattered here and there small trading posts far removed from other white men, and in case of need, far from help. Some are traders, others are hunters of big game, others planters. They may be almost any nationality — Belgian, French, English, Portuguese, Italian, Swiss or Greek! They are usually men seeking wealth, or dissatisfied, chafing spirits seeking relief from the restraints of civilization. Some have left their countries because of an unsavory past. As a rule morals and religion are unimportant to such men, and they do not usually take the best care of themselves. They dare the climate, the powerful sun and the crafty mosquito and laugh at warnings. As a consequence, the sad end of many a mother's son far away from home has been a bed of burning fever, a wild delirium and a lonely, forgotten grave in some deserted spot of Africa's high grass.

The *Lapsley* was coming rapidly downriver around a great bend one sunny afternoon, with a far-reaching stretch of glassy water before her, when the call came. A white flag was up at the next trading post. Someone was asking us to stop at this lonely spot for some reason. With one long whistle we answered, "We are coming!" Slowly swinging around and tying up at the grassy bank, we were handed the following message, "Is there a doctor on board? There is a man here very sick with blackwater fever."

There he lay, a fine big physical specimen, on a poor bed in the darkened room of a mud and grass house. Immediately the attention was arrested by the ominous, penetrating mouse-like odor of a man sick with the viper of all tropical diseases, the dreaded blackwater fever. The telltale white eyegrounds, the pale nails, the sallow yellow-brown

skin, the rapid pulse and labored respiration, the burning
fever, the powerful wretching and vomiting, all of these together gave the picture of a dangerously sick man. There he
lay, now restless, now lucid, now talking disconnectedly or
dropping into a suspicious, stuporous sleep.

Day and night for three days the fearful struggle went
on in his powerful body, while the *Lapsley,* the "steamer of
God," waited patiently. Then Monday night at eight
o'clock, after a short struggle, this troubled soul left its
earthly house and the once powerful, tall, proud body lay
there utterly broken. Death is the great revealer of men's
hearts and thoughts. His poor wife — but no! she said,
trembling, that she wasn't his wife, only living with him.
She had cried as some of us had prayed and talked with him
during his lucid moments, begging him to accept the Only
One Who can forgive sins and give peace.

The very same day that he died, letters and pictures
came from a dear old mother and a faithful brother in far off
Belgium, pleading with him to write. He never saw those
pictures or letters but pictures of his lonely grave on the
banks of the Kasai, of his house on the hill were taken and
are being sent to his old mother, with the comforting news
that he was ministered to until the last breath with loving
hands and laid gently in the ground. The woman who lived
with him cried out to us as we left, "I never thought that
there were any people in the Congo that would do for us
what you have done! God bless you!"

Only God knows if he was saved, but in the Savior's
name and for His glory, he was ministered to till all hope
was gone. What a joy to be able to say, when the flag of distress is flying, "Yes, Lord, here we are! We have forsaken
the world for the high privilege of serving where the wandering sheep are uncared for!"

The Kellersbergers remained on board the *Lapsley* for a
week after reaching Kinshasa, awaiting the arrival of the Belgian ocean liner at Matadi. What a metropolis that city
seemed to be after the years of isolation back in the Kasai!
Edna went shopping, with Andrew Mukeba along to hang on
to lively little Winifred! A teddie bear and a toy duck were
purchased for the Christmas they would be celebrating on
board the *Anversville.* Of their departure from Kinshasa, the
doctor's wife wrote:

Poor little Mukeba! As our river-steamer sojourn drew to a close, he never left us unless he had to, and how constantly he kept his sad little eyes turned to our faces! He said nothing, but the tears came into them over and over again. The last thing that I saw from our train window, as we pulled out of Kinshasa for Thysville and Matadi, was our very favorite little Congolese lad wiping the tears away. I believe he truly loves us and how we love him!

THE MATADI TO NEW YORK VOYAGE

The sad end of the old *Afrique* is described in a letter written by Dr. Kellersberger in February 1920:

There were many sick among the passengers and crew of the *Anversville*. Very often tropical malaria breaks out with dangerous power when there is such a rapid change into a colder climate. It was solemn and sobering sight to see the corpse of a woman, racked by terrible blackwater fever, consigned to the great deep amid the ringing of ship's bells.

The Spanish Capes and the Bay of Biscay were true to form. On January 10th and 11th we were driven forward by an icy, wild sea. At 2 a.m. on Sunday how grateful we were to be off the French coast opposite La Rochelle! There we lay for 36 hours. Even though in the shelter of an island, the savage fury of the sea beyond was disquietingly felt. We heard rumors that the French liner, *Afrique,* which had left Bordeaux on the 10th for the Congo (the very same steamer that we had taken out of Bordeaux in 1916) had been driven and damaged by storm till it had lost course. Later came the terrible news that it had been thrown onto a shoal and its five hundred souls were in peril! How shall I forget it! On Monday morning our ship pulled anchor to go to their rescue. Another ship had stood by all night as the doomed vessel called for help. There were noble attempts to save lives but the furious sea, pitch dark night and finally, terrible silence finished an awful sea tragedy. Our hearts were sick as we saw empty lifeboats and rafts riding the waves. How wonderful to know at such an hour that one has a Savior Who is the Anchor of the soul! As we passed the French capes and Brest, we heard of another vessel that had gone down. The name, "Seamen's Grave," is truly a proper one for this restless body of water, the Gulf of Gascogne!

What a treat it was to awaken the next morning and realize that I was lying quietly in bed, instead of being wavetossed so much that sleep was impossible at times. I got up to find ourselves in the perfect harbor of Plymouth, England, with many other great ships, some of them warships, surrounded by a real city. Soon we heard good, plain English being spoken! A few hours later we were flying through the beautiful, garden-like countryside of southern England on the train. I fear that we and our traveling companions, Nan and Chal Vinson, behaved like little children! Fortunately, we had a whole compartment to ourselves, so we could yell and exclaim to our heart's content! Other passengers had no way of knowing how unbelievable it was to be seeing ivy-covered chapels, clipped hedges, thatched cottages, grazing sheep and cattle, quaint little hamlets with slender church spires and ruins of hoary old castles, with every inch of land in use, under intensive cultivation!

After our delightful train trip to Southampton, we boarded the American liner, *Manchuria*, just arrived from Hamburg. This was to be its maiden voyage after transporting troops during the war. It was the first American passenger liner to enter a German port after the war. There were only forty of us passengers aboard, which was delightful, one of whom was Mr. Melvin Stone, the American newspaper man whose story is now appearing in *Collier's* magazine. It was pleasant surprise to be asked by the purser to conduct a religious service on Sunday, rather than to have to fight for one, as I have experienced on other vessels. Another enjoyable feature was sure 'nough ICE CREAM and good old American cooking that we had not had for so long!

It took us twelve days to make the trans-Atlantic crossing instead of the anticipated nine days. Our ship was returning to the United States only in ballast so it was really exciting sport to see her fight the huge winter storm waves that at times would cover her nose, sending sheets of water in every direction. We passed through snow and sleet storms and winds that demanded your going along with them, unless you had a really good grip on the rail! A ship is a wonderful thing to see! It seems to be alive! I can surely see the fascination it holds for seamen.

On the morning of February 2nd we lay off famous Ambrose Lightship, near Sandy Hook in a dense fog. We heard the sound of foghorns, ships' bells and the regular, sad, siren-song of the Lightship. The pilot managed to find us and by noon we were entering the Narrows, ploughing through great fields of ice. The health and immigration authorities came aboard and soon we were greeting the Statue of Liberty! Before us loomed that marvel of cities with its great skyline. "So this is New York!", commented an English passenger near us. From no point can one see a more striking view of that wonderful city than from an incoming ship!

Home again for just a few months, to a land where the life, teachings and power of the Gospel of Jesus Christ has made us FREE! May this thought remove prejudice and lack of sympathy and enable us to minister to those less fortunate than we, born in the "land of the shadow of death" where no freedom is.

[7]

African Sleeping Sickness

NINE MONTHS OF HOME ASSIGNMENT

The Kellersbergers were rarely together during the spring of 1920. Eugene was traveling widely throughout the south, filling the numerous speaking engagements scheduled for him by the Executive Committee of Foreign Missions in Nashville, Tennessee. As he expressed it, he was "putting in heavy licks," telling people about the mission work and the tremendous need for a hospital at Bibanga.

He would tell of how he had no choice but to operate out-of-doors, beneath a sheet tied to tree branches. It was the only way of preventing bugs, twigs and leaves from falling into the open incision! His most difficult problem, however, he told his listeners, was in keeping the fascinated audience of curious observers from clambering into overhead branches or from pressing in to see what was going on. Often they crowded in so closely that surgical procedures were hindered by his arms being jostled. Sometimes the surgery was done to the accompaniment of the loud, frantic wailing of despairing relatives or the rattles and incantations of a witchdoctor, "making medicine" to aid the white doctor or to counteract any evil power he might be using. "A real hospital building for Bibanga station is an absolute necessity," Eugene would conclude emphatically, "— one with an operating room that has a door that can be shut so that privacy, cleanliness and concentration can be assured."

How the family did enjoy traveling by railroad train to the distant cities where Eugene and Edna were both scheduled to speak! The dining car had crisp, white linen tablecloths, napkins folded like snowy butterflies at each place, elegant water decanters and tasty, hot dishes that released a cloud of savory steam as the smiling waiter lifted the silverdomed cover with a flourish. How ridiculously funny it was to share a common lavatory with strangers, all washing faces and brushing teeth together, reflected by multiple mirrors, lurching about, exclaiming as the speeding train jostled, jiggled and jerked! Best of all was cuddling down under thick Pullman Company blankets, behind heavy, buttoned-up green curtains, in the cozy berth that opened up at night. One fell asleep, made drowsy by the monotonous cadence of the wheels, droning a measured, clackety song, interwoven now and then with the long, sad, crying sound of the steam-engine whistle, floating off into the night.

In Kansas City, Eugene's beloved Uncle Herman Mattern and his wife met the train. White-maned Uncle Herman made prickles go up and down Winifred's spine as he told her of how he and his brother, Ivo, and sister, Helene, after their father, Carl's death, used to help their widowed mother, Ulrika, with the sheep. He imitated the howling of wolves around their cabin at night, and the Indians, hooting like owls. As children they had grown up under the guardian roof and loving tutelage of Winifred's great-great-grandfather, Adolf Fuchs and his wife, Luise, in their home on the original San Jacinto bounty land grant in Texas. On this furlough visit, the childless Matterns urged Edna and Eugene to leave little Winifred with them, when and if they returned to their mission field in Africa.

At Marble Falls, Texas, Winifred met for the first time her gentle, snowy-haired grandmother, Helene, and grandfather Julius Kellersberger, who said very little, but whose blue eyes twinkled merrily above his mustache and puffing pipe. All the little first cousins had whooping cough, so the

Dr. Kellersberger with his daughter, Winifred. Concord, North Carolina, 1920.

missionary family were guests at Uncle Ivo's ranch on the Colorado River, just a stone's throw from the old Fuchs homestead. On a warm, sunny afternoon, everybody went for a picnic on the great, flat rocks at Marble Falls. Helene, wearing a flower-sprigged sunbonnet, held her little "African" granddaughter on her lap, and showed her how, by knocking two small stones firmly together, one can make the happy, clicking sound of a small frog croaking.

The return to Austin, Texas, was a heart-tugging one for Edna and Eugene. How strange it seemed not to go straight home to 1402 West Avenue, the house in which she had grown up and where they had been married, the house which could have been theirs, had they so chosen! Now the beautiful mansion belonged to the Gilbert family. It was the hospitable home of the George Beggs and their daughter, Edleen, that welcomed them instead.

After the Texas visit came another long train ride back east to the mountains of North Carolina, to Montreat, the summer conference grounds of the Presbyterian Church, U.S. Both Edna and Eugene were scheduled to be platform speakers during the Foreign Missions Conference the last week of June. They expected to go back to Texas as soon as the conference was over.

THE GIFT OF A HOSPITAL FOR BIBANGA

But plans changed quite unexpectedly. Dr. Kellersberger was requested to remain at Montreat throughout July and August, to serve as the conference grounds doctor. The physician expected to serve in that capacity had not been able to come. What a disappointment!

In July of 1920, Mr. and Mrs. Charles Lukens Huston of Coatesville, Pennsylvania, and their three children, including their twelve-year-old son, Charles, Jr., came to see the quiet mountain retreat so beloved of their dear, long-time friend, Dr. John Wilbur Chapman. Quakers themselves, and complete strangers, it was the only time that the great steel magnate and his family ever visited Montreat. Mr. Huston was a pioneer steelmaker, the grandson of Dr. Charles Lukens, the

very first manufacturer of boiler plate iron in the United
States. He was a contemporary of Andrew Carnegie and
Charles M. Schwab, having planned and designed the Lukens
Four High 206-inch mill in Coatesville, Pennsylvania, the
world's largest plate mill.

While the Hustons were at Montreat, Charles Jr. became
ill and Dr. Kellersberger was called to his bedside. The three
days of medical ministry to the lad that followed laid the foundation for a wonderful thirty-year-long friendship. On learning of Eugene's medical work in the Belgian Congo and of his
desperate need for a hospital building, the wealthy Hustons
gave $10,000 for the construction of the first unit of what was
later to become the Edna Kellersberger Memorial Hospital.

Of this humbling, awe-inspiring experience, in which the
exact, needed, prayed-for sum of money was given only after
their own tremendous efforts to secure it had ceased, Edna
wrote the following:

> In just a few weeks Eugene was to leave America. He
> had worked and prayed so hard for his hospital and now it
> seemed as if he was to be disappointed, for only two or three
> thousand dollars were in sight. His whole furlough had
> been spent in working for that hospital! Not a month had
> gone by but that an article was written for publicity pur-
> poses, showing the need for that hospital and the pitiful lack
> of equipment under which the missionary in the Congo
> must work. No matter how tired or busy, no invitation was
> refused to show the sterioptican slides of the poor little grass
> and mud sheds, where desperately sick were treated and the
> rough, wooden table where major operations were per-
> formed.
>
> But in all this fire of burning need, in that whirlwind of
> Eugene's energy and determination, the Lord did not seem
> to be! How gracious He is to use us just as we are, and yet
> how easily He can set us and our busy plans aside and work
> alone in His own still, quiet way!
>
> At the end of the furlough it became a necessity — not
> a <u>choice</u>, but a <u>necessity</u> — to practice medicine. Very defi-
> nitely Eugene was shown that he was quietly to follow his
> chosen lifework right there in the setting of our denomina-
> tion's summer conference grounds! No public life or eager

appeal to crowds possible now! It was a necessity rather unwillingly complied with!

But "how unsearchable are God's thoughts and His ways past finding out!" During these days in which he was too busy caring for the sick to work for his hospital, Eugene was called to see a little boy who was ill. The father of the boy was not a southerner, not even a Presbyterian, but a Quaker! The doctor and the father had a happy hour of fellowship, just talking of their Lord and His coming again. Three days later, without inquiring particularly into conditions in Africa, without seeming especially impressed with the needs there, the Quaker said, "How would you like us to build your hospital? How much do you need?" That very week five thousand dollars was given, followed almost immediately by the second five thousand!

But there is a deep little root to this wonderful story that is the best part of it all! When we first went to the mission field back in 1916, a few women in Concord, North Carolina, formed a prayer band and convenanted to pray together once a week for us and for the medical work. There was never any "program," only that quiet, definite, regular gathering just for intercession. These women were as much a part of the giving of that ten thousand as if it, too, had come directly through their hands, for they had prayed for it!

SEPARATION FOR THE SAKE OF THE WORK

Now came the hard part, a time of difficult testing, treading so closely on the heels of the joyous physical and spiritual renewal of furlough, the exhilaration of family reunion and the miraculous gift of the provision for the hospital. All during his first term in the Belgian Congo, Eugene had longed for the time when he could study at the London School of Tropical Medicine. He desperately felt the need of specialized training in this particular branch of medicine. At his special request, the Executive Committee agreed for him to go to England to take only the three-month-long Certificate Course in Tropical Medicine and Hygiene. The complete diploma course, requiring longer residence, they felt was out of the question.

Edna was now in the early stages of her second pregnancy, wanting and needing her husband's presence more than anything else during the months of waiting. Members of the family were highly critical of Eugene for leaving Edna at this time, even though they knew that she would be in good hands, and that the separation was for the purpose of further preparation for medical missionary ministry. So sure were the Kellersbergers of the primary importance of this specialized study that they were willing to sacrifice their own personal desires, knowing full well the criticism they would reap because of it. On their knees together, they made the decision to go through with the planned separation, in spite of the pregnancy. They would separate for as long as it took Eugene to complete the course offered in London during October, November and December of 1920.

Hardest of all to bear at this time was the lack of sympathy for their missionary calling that they were experiencing from members of their closest family circles. Some of Eugene's family were highly critical. Edna's father, Phil Bosché, was also one who had been quite sure that one term in Africa would be enough for his younger daughter and son-in-law. While Eugene was still in medical school, Mr. Bosché had offered him and Edna the family home at 1402 West Avenue, for their very own, along with full partnership in his thriving business. They refused his offer at that time, expressing the firm conviction that their missionary calling must come first.

Now during the summer of 1920, Phil Bosché again pled with them to give up the "missionary idea" and join him in his very successful business ventures. Their refusal again at this time sent an embittered, frustrated old man back to Texas. "You go your way and I'll go mine!" he shouted with rage, as he parted from them at Montreat. There is a sad little hint in one of Edna's letters to her mother-in-law, Helene, that after this her father's regular letters and usual monetary gifts to his daughter were missing.

CERTIFICATE IN
TROPICAL MEDICINE AND HYGIENE

Eugene sailed from New York for Southampton on the R.M.S. *Aquitania* on September 16, 1920. For six days he moved in an elegant, opulent, distinguished society aboard the 40,000 ton Cunard express liner. The *Aquitania*, "the most popular ship in the world," was unique in design, with a double rank of inside cabins lighted by ingenious six-inch clerestory windows. She was a true "sea queen," so beloved of two of her captains that they died on their final voyages of command, before turning over the helm to another. On this voyage, through the kindness of a friend, Dr. Kellersberger enjoyed a first class cabin, rather than the lower class quarters usually occupied by the missionaries. He always reveled in ocean travel, no matter what kind of vessel he traveled on, but this crossing on the *Aquitania* was a memorable one for its luxurious accommodations, record-breaking speed, and the sheer perfection of all weather conditions.

In a shipboard letter written in German to his parents, Eugene revealed what was really on his heart:

> What a "swell" boat this is! How I long for Edna and Winifred to be with me! I am never happy about my Edna's perfect unselfishness. She is willing to give up absolutely everything, to make any sacrifice, to make me a good doctor! But God has shown me my duty. I can only go forward, even if it is very hard. Always there is a tremendous pressure inside me, making me strive unceasingly to better myself in my profession.
>
> God has given me the gift of caring for unfortunate people, and sharing with them His love and power. There is no greater work in all the world than this. The world has not fallen to pieces just because here and there, there are a few people who with all their hearts, really care about other people! Edna's mother, Mrs. Bosché, was one of these. I can see this more and more as I look back since her death.
>
> I have high hopes that my three months of study in London will be a real help to my work in the Congo. Without doubt, it is an excellent school. Tomorrow I will be in the great city of London, a perfect stranger among millions. But if you are guided by a Purpose, you don't mind a little thing like that!

Excerpts from Dr. Kellersberger's 1920 diary, written during his three months of study, communicate the enthusi-

asm and excitement he realized in this exceptionally rich
learning experience:

> *October 3, 1920*   As darkness fell we slowly steamed up South-
> ampton Water and were soon in the midst of one of the busiest
> ports in the world. In the same berth with us lay the *New York.*
> Across from us was the giant White Star *Olympic,* and the
> smaller *Adriatic.* A great crowd was there to greet us, but no
> passengers were permitted off till the next morning.

> *October 8, 1920*   Westminster Abbey is a building of marvel-
> ous beauty and intense interest. Words fail for a description
> of it all — the Poets' Corner, and above all, the tomb of
> David Livingstone!
>   Here I could not help but offer up a silent prayer that I
> might be more like this man in devotion to duty and to God.
> All outgoing missionaries should spend time here before
> this grave of the man who opened up Africa, whose heart is
> still buried in that continent. May we go in the spirit in
> which David Livingstone went! May I go in that way, and if
> need be, lay down my life ministering to the needs of the
> people. It is likely that over these very stones where this fa-
> mous bronze marker lies, Livingstone himself walked or
> stood when, as a boy, he came to London to study medicine.
> The last words he wrote were: "All I can add in my solitude
> is, May heaven's rich blessing come down on everyone,
> American, English or Turk, who will help to heal this open
> sore of the world!" What wonderful last words these were!
> May God give me the grace and strength to heal what is still
> "the open sore of the world!"

> *October 10, 1920*   A full, intensely interesting week has gone
> by and I sit here in my room, trying to think it all out. How
> fine it is to sit and listen and work under the foremost doc-
> tors of this school! What a great impetus the World War has
> given to the study and knowledge of Tropical Medicine!
> How evident it is that grim necessity of circumstance has
> made men practical and sent them back to rockbottom
> basics! Many old theories have been exploded. Vast
> amounts of new material and experience with thousands of
> cases have enriched the subject and made it far more defi-
> nite.
>   And what a privilege to hear great preachers of the
> Word here in London! Last Sunday morning I heard Dr.

John Henry Jowett and that same night, Dr. F. B. Meyer, that dear, beautiful saint of God! It was such a blessing! A thoughtful woman asked if I would like to meet him and of course, I did! He talked with us several minutes. Such a fine face, getting old, but oh! so mature and so close to his Lord! As he preaches, his voice is full of harmony and sweetness. Just to be with him fills one with new longing and desire to be closer to Jesus, to be more of a power and witness!

October 16, 1920   Chilly all the time! I <u>can't</u> get warm! There are two comforts that the British are far behind in: heating and baths! There is one bathroom here, and that a poor one, for <u>three floors</u>! But the greatest joke is the announcement that "there will be hot water every Friday night and your bath time is from 7:30 to 8:00 p.m." Mind you — just <u>once a week</u>! And then it is charged to your bill: "1 bath, 6 pence." Horrors! And last night it wasn't a hot bath at all but a freezing one! What is more lovely than the bathroom of an average American house! How I miss it, and warm houses!

November 4, 1920   I am now learning the respective decorations of every mosquito, every tropical fly and their larvae and trying to store up certain crucial facts about tropical diseases, their diagnosis and treatment. Those species, genera, subfamilies, families, and classes of the female mosquito that cause malaria, yellow fever, dengue and filariasis or elephantiasis, are all beginning to take shape in my mind very definitely. Though very difficult, it is really proving to be a fascinating study.

November 6, 1920   Today there fell over London one of those "palls" — yellowish, heavy, sticky smoke, lying damp and chilly over the whole city. By noon it was impossible to examine mosquitoes for stripes or scales or breathing tubes. As I walked back to my room, I was gasping for breath and my eyes burned so that I had to keep closing them. I could see less than fifty yards ahead. At 3 p.m. it was dark and street lights were on.

   The weather here certainly does not buoy up one's spirits. On the contrary! I have come to the conclusion that the English are a sombre people <u>because</u> of their weather! I have had all I want of it! Any cheer you get must be from within. The realization of His abiding Presence is the only comfort and stay during such times of being alone, away from those I love. I have been forced to go down to the deeper source that never fails, no matter how distressing or depressing the surroundings!

December 16, 1920   Yesterday and today I have been dissecting mosquitoes for their stomachs and salivary glands, to see if they are infected with malaria. Exams will begin Monday and last through Thursday. In the course I have learned a <u>colossal</u> amount of knowledge. It has been money <u>well spent</u>!

The sailing of the *Saxonia* for New York has been postponed five days until January 4th. This change gives me time after my examinations to make a quick trip to Switzerland. Even though I will be there only a few days, it will give me the chance to meet Eugen Jeuch, for whom I am named, and to see my father's home city of Baden and to visit my grandfather, Getulius' grave. I can get a round trip ticket for just 12 pounds, about what it would cost me to remain here in London. It is for my father's sake especially, that I am anxious to do this!

On December 31st, 1920, Dr. Eugene Kellersberger received his certificate from the London School of Tropical Medicine and Hygiene. He graduated "with distinction," ranking second in his class of fifty doctors from all over the world. Taking advantage of the unexpected five-day postponement of the sailing of the *Saxonia*, he immediately left London for Switzerland. Of this first visit to the land of his family heritage, he wrote:

I could not have had a lovelier reception than I received at the hands of Eugén Jeuch, my father's schoolmate for whom I am named. I was royally entertained in a beautiful Swiss home in Zurich, where the eating was delightful, the featherbeds lovely and warm, the Swiss-German dialect delicious to listen to, even if not always well understood! We spent many, many hours in fascinating conversation over those marvelous Swiss meals.

And Baden! That lovely, quaint town, over a thousand years old, where the Romans used the hot sulphur baths and where the "cradle" of the Hapsburgs was, in that beautiful old ruin, Schloss Stein! I spent all day with Herr Jeuch, drinking in the beauties of the old city, seeing it from end to end, finding many connections with the past and with the history of my family.

I saw the school my father attended with Herr Jeuch, the *Kapuziner Kirche,* the Catholic church in which they were confirmed, and the factory where my father worked out his apprenticeship in commerce. It was right on the banks of the Limmat River and run by its water power. We visited the hot sulphur springs adjoining the old Hotel Shiff, where, in her day, Queen Victoria was a guest, and also Empress Eugenia. This was Frau Jeuch's birthplace, for her father owned it for many years.

Herr Jeuch and I climbed all over the old Schloss Stein! The gate to this ancient fortress is still connected with the castle ruins by a great wall coming down the cliff. From the castle to the old city there is a long, steep stairway, at least five hundred yards long, and at its top is the ancient chapel. From exactly this spot, where my father explored old dungeons and underground caves, there is a magnificent view of the old city, the church and the river. In the valley beyond is the Cloister of Wettingen, and far in the distance, against the sky, the glorious Alps.

I had the thrill of sitting in the famous "Bishop's Chair," used by the Abbot of Wettingen, a Kellersberger! My grandfather Getulius, got it from the Cloister at the time that it was ordered closed. Now it is in the home of my cousin, Frau Annie Kellersberger Unger, in Zurich. I learned that our family name used to be spelled "Kellersperger" and that ours is truly an honorable history in the past!

In Baden Eugene also paid a visit to the old Kirchhof, to the grave of his grandfather, Getulius. He took several pictures of it for his father, for burial space in this old cemetery was at such a premium that after twenty-two years the law allows the graves to be dug up and replaced by new ones, if necessary.

The remaining days of Eugene's visit were filled with tours of Lucern, Rigi-Kulm and the Bernese Alps, all graciously escorted by Herr Jeuch. The never-to-be-forgotten climax to his first, brief sojourn in Switzerland came on New Year's Eve:

At 11:30 p.m. a magnificent chorus of church bells all over the city of Zurich awoke! At five minutes to twelve, they ceased. After twelve o'clock struck slowly, they were again silent until five minutes after the hour. Then once again they all joined in a wealth of harmonious reverberation until 12:30, heralding the New Year of 1921!

During those silent ten minutes I was alone in His Presence on my knees, feeling that I could enter the New Year in no fitter way than in utter dependence upon Him!

In his prayer notebook at this very hour Eugene wrote the petition: "May this new year be one of increased spiritual growth and consecration." The year 1921 was to bring a painful, trying experience that God would use to force that spiritual growth and consecration into reality.

RETURN FOR THE SECOND TERM
IN THE BELGIAN CONGO

Arriving in New York on January 21st, Eugene quickly made his way to Richmond, Virginia, where his wife and daughter were comfortably settled in an apartment at Mission Court. This roomy complex adjoining the campus of Union Theological Seminary provided a welcome haven for furloughed missionaries. Edna was under the care of one of the best of Richmond's obstetricians and arrangements had already been made for the expected baby to be born in Memorial Hospital. On March 2nd, Texas Independence Day, Cornelia Elizabeth Kellersberger was born, named for Edna's mother.

On April 7, 1921, the Kellersbergers, including the precious bundle of a one-month-old daughter, sailed from New York on the *Mauretania*. This 33,000-ton sister-ship of the ill-fated *Lusitania*, for twenty-two years (1907 to 1929) held the "Blue Riband" for the fastest Atlantic crossings. It was a long, narrow vessel, distinctive for its four slanted stacks, painted black, and that special Cunard vermillion.

In Antwerp, Belgium, the Kellersbergers joined the group of missionaries with whom they were to travel to the Belgian Congo on the S.S. *Albertville*.

On April 21st, while the docks were crowded with

thousands and the band was playing the Belgian national anthem, *La Brabanconne,* we slowly dropped down the Scheldt, put our pilot off at Flushing, and as night drew on, we floated in a quiet sea out into the Channel and the Dover Straits, now like a lamb! We followed the sea trail that leaves no tracks, past Cherbourg, past Guernsey, past Quessant, the corner of France, and then out into the Bay of Biscay. What a difference now from the other two times we have crossed it — so quiet!

Waking up on the morning of May 9th, we rejoiced to see the low-lying African shores and the great mouth of the mighty Congo, with its colored waters, glorious in the rising sun!

THE "DREAD PROBLEM OF SLEEPING SICKNESS"

For two days the Belgian Maritime Company liner, *Albertville,* lay docked at Boma, the capital of the Belgian Congo at that time. Dr. Kellersberger paid a courtesy call on Governor General Lippens, finding him to be most friendly and courteous. He also spent an interesting hour with the head doctor, the *Médecin en Chef* of the colony, who "gave much valuable information and planned for cooperation, especially in the dread problem of sleeping sickness."

This is the very first mention in all of the doctor's writings of the disease to which his early medical ministry was so totally devoted, on which he became one of the world's leading authorities, and the author of the medical textbook about it!

The term "sleeping sickness" is often confused in the popular mind. What is called *Lethargic Encephalitis,* found in Europe and America, is entirely different from African sleeping sickness, which is known by the clinical name of *Trypanosomiasis.* This disease is caused by the bite of tsetse flies, notably *Glossina palpalis* and *Glossina morsitans,* the intermediate hosts of protozoal parasites called "trypanosomes." These belong to the order of *Flagellata,* because the adults have flagella for locomotion and obtaining food.

The formerly fatal disease which causes its victims to sleep their lives away has been known for centuries. Arab slave-traders often killed captives who showed marked signs of lethargy, or who had enlarged neck glands, one of the primary symptoms of the disease. Throughout the slave-trading centuries and even into the second decade of the 1900s *Trypanosomiasis* continued to decimate the populations of Central Africa and to present a barrier to the colonial and commercial penetration of the vast tropical belt of the continent.

The disease has first, a circulatory or blood stage, then a gland stage, and finally, a central nervous system stage, all three of these stages blending into one another as regards time and symptoms. After the so-called "blood stage" and "gland stage" have passed, diagnosis is self-evident. The presence of the disease is evident in the way the patient walks or sits, and by the characteristic, dull and listless facial expression. The patient himself often says that he has *disama dia tulu*, "the sickness of sleep." As he sits outside the dispensary door, he nods, his head begins to bob up and down. Then it droops on his chest. Suddenly he falls over in a stuporous heap onto the ground and cannot be aroused. In these advanced stages, a lumbar puncture is the final procedure that really clinches the diagnosis.

Through brilliant research, effective drug weapons have been found to remove the deadly power of this scourge. The epoch-making experiments with *tryparsamide*, instigated by the Rockefeller Institute, were first applied at Leopoldville by Dr. Louise Pearce, cooperating with the Belgian colonial medical service. Those of the Bayer Company, Leverkusen, Germany, with *Bayer 205*, were studied by Drs. Kleine and Fischer in the Katanga, also in conjunction with the colonial authorities.

Dr. Kellersberger's letter describing the journey inland for the second term contains ominous references to sleeping sickness and the presence of tsetse flies along the Congo and Kasai watercourses:

> Now for several days we have been steaming on our beloved mission steamer, *Lapsley*, up the mighty Congo River and its adjunct, the Kasai. Coming back to this land for the second time, its lure and beauty are as fascinating as ever — it's gorgeous sunsets, primeval forests, grassy plains, wonderful bird life, wicked crocodiles, ugly hippos and chattering monkeys!

We have seen only a few tsetse flies today. At Mangai we will see many more. There is much sleeping sickness here in the Kwilu province now. Several white people have it. This has become one of the worst districts in all the Belgian Congo for high incidence of the disease. At the London School of Tropical Medicine I studied two cases from right here, both agents of the palm oil company, the *Huileries Congo Belge,* who contracted sleeping sickness in this very area.

Oh joy! Finally to reach Luebo and see the lights of the Kasai Company beach, and to know that our beloved mission lay just across the river and up the big hill! A few extra toots of the whistle and in no time at all, the mission side of the river came alive with torches and lanterns and shouts! Then, as we got into the long dugout canoes to make the final crossing to the other side, in a mighty swell from a thousand throats, came one glorious old hymn after another! The jubilant welcome of the Christians echoed up and down the river and far over the hills! All Luebo, including Protestant, Catholic, heathen and scoffer, heard the gospel in song that night! This experience deeply touched our hearts, filling our eyes with tears. Then came the actual welcome — it just can't be described! We were literally carried up the mission hill by hundreds of Congolese Christians, all eagerly taking turns bearing our hammocks, to express their joy at our return!

For ten days we remained at Luebo, preparing our caravan of 45 men that had come over 230 miles of trails from Bibanga to get us.

And now it is over! I say it with thankfulness. Such a trip is a harrowing experience, particularly with a newborn babe-in-arms. The heat, the tired body, the ache, the fever are all a part of it.

We will never forget what happened when we crossed the Lubilashi River on July 13th, and slowly wound up the last 600 feet of elevation, where stands Bibanga. Long before we even got near the station, our native friends were running to meet us. Soon we were completely surrounded by hundreds of familiar faces, people running in front, alongside and behind our caravan!

Now here we are at last — at home on this magnificent hilltop, with an ever-present cool wind, a view that cannot be equalled, nights when you need a blanket for cover, and a mass of work to do that puts you on your metal! In my absence, the medical work was moved into a fresh, four-roomed dirt-and-grass house. Till the first wing of our new hospital is finished, this will be my office and clinic. Difficult cases are already pouring in, many needing operations. Supplies for the buildings, roofing, cement and hardware, are already in lower Congo and will arrive soon. We hope to break ground by the beginning of the new year.

[8]

In Line of Duty

THE BELOVED FALLS VICTIM

Dr. Kellersberger's joy in his return to Bibanga and the demanding, challenging work awaiting him there was short-lived. The looseleaf notebook in which he wrote his prayer requests is the most revealing record of the increasing evidence that something was terribly wrong with Edna. At Luebo she had begun running a fever that did not respond to quinine, so malaria was not the cause of it. Intermittent fevers continued during the exhausting hammock journey from Luebo to Bibanga. On July 17th, only four days after their jubilant arrival home, Eugene penned this plea: "Lay Thy healing hand on Edna's stubborn fever." The same prayer was reiterated on August 2nd and again on August 23rd.

Then, on August 26th, Eugene, using his microscope, found trypanosomes in a thick drop of Edna's blood, confirming the diagnosis of African sleeping sickness. In the notebook, the day that the true diagnosis was known, this is the prayer that was written:

"If it is Thy will, heal Edna of this dread disease and make us to see Thy will in it all for us. May this be the opening of a great service of soul-saving for and in Thee."

169

On Sunday, August 28th, Eugene addressed the following letter to all his missionary colleagues:

> Dear Fellow Workers: It is with profound regret and an-
> guish in my heart that I have to report that the continued
> indisposition and the recurrent fevers of my wife have
> turned out to be a case of sleeping sickness. The trypano-
> somes were found yesterday in her blood in large numbers.
> This means that we must return to London, as soon as I
> have given her a series of Atoxyl and Tartar Emetic injec-
> tions, and she is able to travel . . . We are leaving most of
> our things, hoping to come back some day.
>
> Our God is able! We are not asking why He has al-
> lowed this, but we are bowing humbly to His will and are
> asking Him to lead us in the way He wants us to go. We are
> told to "give thanks always for all things, unto God and the
> Father, in the Name of our Lord Jesus Christ." Pray for us,
> and that this may be the means of sending out many doctors
> to fill our place. "Whom He loveth He chasteneth and
> scourgeth every son whom he receiveth." From this stand-
> point, it is a privilege to receive any "marks in the body,"
> for His sake.
>
> May God's richest blessing be on every one of you
> daily, is our prayer. Pray that we may be returned to the
> work. Your brother in the work,
>
> > Dr. E. R. Kellersberger

To Edna's family in the United States he wrote:

> On the way upriver Edna was bitten by a tsetse fly,
> though we did not know it at the time. Ever since then she
> has not been at all well. At first I attributed it to weakness
> from the trip and the new baby. But, as her fever kept up in
> spite of large doses of quinine, I kept making blood exami-
> nations and now have found the dread trypanosomes in her
> blood. The terrible fact is true: she has African sleeping
> sickness.
>
> There is a chance that she can get well if she leaves
> very soon and stays under treatment for three or four years.
> Very likely she can never come back here again. We would
> leave immediately, but she is too weak to travel. We have
> notified the Mission that we are leaving in a month or so for
> London, as soon as I have given her a series of Atoxyl and
> Tartar Emetic injections.

It just breaks our hearts to go and the people are <u>so
sad</u>. The pretty little four-room pharmacy was getting so
spic and span and the work already growing and so interesting, with more time to give to it than ever before! . . .

Don't feel sorry for us! We are in His work, soldiers on
the front line, and if it is our time to get hit, we are glad of it
for His sake. If only we be found in the line of duty — and
we believe that we are just <u>there</u>! Edna has a chance of
dying, of becoming a lifelong invalid, or of getting well. A
certain percentage, not very large, of the cases do get well.

Poor girl! She is so brave and good! I am the baby
nurse these days. I carried through the complete weaning of
Cornelia in three days and now she is thriving on goat's
milk diluted with water, and sugar added.

To her sister, Winifred, Edna herself wrote a letter on
August 31st. Evidently lacking the strength to get out of bed
and search for real stationery, she wrote this poignant message on two little three inch by seven- and one-half inch strips
of paper, beginning very bravely with a fountain pen:

I want you to know that since Eugene began my treatments a few days ago, I am gaining strength fast. I'll not
lose courage and am fighting with all my strength. I can ov-
erhear our Congolese helpers out in the yard saying that I
"have a sickness of death" and it is so to them. They know
of no cure, but there have been cures in London! Dear people! I cry when —

Here the ink writing abruptly stops, and the rest of the
message is written in pale pencil, in a shaky, uncertain hand.
It is obvious that Edna was overcome with tears at this point
and was no longer able to write for sobbing. When she finally
gained control of herself — who knows how much later! — a
pencil was all she could find to continue her writing:

I think that our work for their souls may be over forever, all except <u>prayer</u>. And they care! They say about my
illness and leaving them: *Maboko etu adi matekete!* "Our arms
are weak!" All night long Sunday, Mr. Savels' beautiful
words in telling the people in church about my illness, ran
through my head with such comfort and joy. I never
thought about it as he put it. The people told us that he

said: "It is for you that she is suffering this!" I never thought of that and wonder if it can be true. If so, I'm glad to have the sleeping sickness, because it would be a faint bit like following Christ. When I first came I wrote down this prayer: "That I may gladly suffer anything for the salvation of these people." And oh! if it will be their salvation, I will gladly die!

But I'm not planning to die. I'll not let Eugene tell me even the horrible later stages of the disease or anything discouraging and I'm more cheerful than usual and laugh all I can and play and rest and my dear African helpers care for me so sweetly! Dear little Andrew Mukeba comes between meals and asks, "Mama, don't you want a cup of chicken broth?" He is the one who cried when he heard I was sick. And how beautifully my helpers have run my whole household for weeks! Untold, the big clay water jar has been scrubbed and scalded inside, and filled with boiled drinking water, clothes washed twice a week, the market buyer sent out daily, my flowers watered, etc. And my splendid cook has prepared fine meals, baking good bread and even cake! It is so hard to leave them and never see them all again.

Eugene is so good. Mrs. Savels bathes the baby, whom I have had to wean, and dear old Jane McElroy cares for Winifred. They made a dear birthday party for her yesterday. How she did enjoy it!

We are coming along fine and I am full of hope. Pray for us and ask the Prayer Bands to pray, too.

With love, Edna

Instead of the three-week overland journey all the way back to Luebo and the *Lapsley*, it was decided to make the shorter eight-day hammock trip to Lusambo, where the Belgian riversteamer, *Luxembourg*, was at its Sankuru River docks. It was in his journal that Eugene poured out his heart, expressing his thoughts and reactions to the difficulties being experienced:

October 12, 1921, on board the LUXEMBOURG
Today we left Lusambo and turned our backs on the mission work. It feels too strange and awful to believe. In my journal, on page 165, are my notes written near Mangai, going up river. Mangai is the worst infected district for

sleeping sickness; it is there that Edna must have become infected. An apparently great work only begun, and I myself better prepared in every way to do it, and now it is all a dream! And yet <u>HE KNOWS</u>! We are going into the future without fear, trusting Him.

Sleeping sickness! That dread disease and name! I have treated many cases of it and began in August of this year a special camp for them at Bibanga. I never realized that at the time, my very own wife was a case of sleeping sickness herself! Thanks to the London School of Tropical Medicine and my own experience with the disease, it was diagnosed this time much earlier than usual.

It was terrible to have to leave behind all our fellow workers, especially the George McKees and the Charles Cranes. And also that fine caravan of Bibanga hammock-men, who were so faithful to us to the very end! It hurts to leave the work more this time than ever before.

The voyage downriver on the *Luxembourg* was not without excitement, as well as unexpected delays. A trophy of World War I, this beautifully built German steamer had numerous bullet holes through cabin walls as proof of the battle on German East African waters, in which she was captured by the Belgians. The captain, a hardy and unpredictable soul, amused himself the entire voyage by shutting off the engines at will, and taking potshots at basking crocodiles or hippos unwise enough to raise their heads above the water as the ship passed.

He made good use of the presence of a doctor on board, sending Eugene several patients each day, including one of his crewmen who, for six years, had a large piece of glass embedded in his foot. With the help of the Swedish nurse, Miss Karlson, also aboard, chloroform was given while Eugene incised and removed the glass only after breaking it into pieces, and breaking his forceps in the process. The passengers and crew of the *Luxembourg* were treated to first hand observation of a very large Bangala patient, seriously objected to $CHCL_3$, yelling and kicking lustily the whole time that the operation was in progress on deck.

The captain became increasingly friendly as he recognized and appreciated Eugene's remarkable spirit of service.

He was delighted whenever Edna felt strong enough to make a batch of fudge for him and his passengers in the ship's galley.

Four times during the journey through the Lower Congo, Edna's frail body was racked with the burning, intermittent fever typical of the early stage of sleeping sickness. The fourth hard bout occurred at the Baptist Missionary Society guest house in Matadi, as the family awaited the arrival of the *Anversville*. It lasted two days, leaving her weak and exhausted. But for the fresh eggs sent for her use by the Matadi missionaries, she would have had nothing that she was able to eat. Eugene kept her going on eggnogs alone during this extremely difficult part of the long journey.

Even with a very sick wife and two small children to care for, Eugene's first concern was still his medical work. During the few brief hours that the *Anversville* was docked at Boma on its way downriver, he took advantage of the opportunity to call on Governor Lippens at his residence. Accompanied by little Winifred and Dr. Anet, a well-known Belgian Protestant pastor, he proudly showed the Governor of the Belgian Congo his plans for the Bibanga hospital. The Governor responded with enthusiasm, producing in turn the official blueprints of various government hospitals in the colony, comparing them with Dr. Kellersberger's plans and making several very helpful, practical suggestions.

A comfortable, welcome haven awaited Edna in Cabin 54 of the Belgian Maritime liner. There were real beds instead of bunks and a private bathroom. The kindly ship's doctor came to call almost as soon as the family came aboard, and proved most attentive and helpful during the entire seventeen-day voyage.

As the journey drew to a close, the canny, weather-wise captain of the *Anversville* forced his ship to its highest speed, in order to get past a certain point on the coast, near Ostend, before night. He got his ship into the mouth of the Scheldt River just in time! As they made the ascent upriver to Antwerp, an absolutely impenetrable fog rolled in right after them, enveloping them in thick, damp shrouds as they docked on the evening of December 7th. Eugene and Edna had expected to go directly to Ostend by train, and from there across the English Channel to Dover. But once again circumstances beyond their control halted them in their tracks. For well over a week, incoming ocean liners were fog-bound at the coast and all regular cross-channel shipping was cancelled. In their room at the Queen's Hotel in Antwerp, the family had to wait until December 19th to make the last step of the journey for Edna across the Channel to London.

THE LONDON HOSPITAL FOR TROPICAL DISEASES

The first letter Edna wrote from the Hospital at 23 Endsleigh Gardens on Gordon Square, described their Christmas:

> This quiet Sunday afternoon in my plain, wee hospital room, with no sound but the opening and shutting of doors in the corridor, and no sight but a dirty London fog settling down over a silhouette of dingy, brick walls and countless, quaint chimney pots, I am so eager to pour out all my thoughts to you!
>
> Here I am, surrounded by love and care and comforts! Even strangers show such touching eagerness to help that my critical heart has been warmed. I have come to know that, whether Belgian or English, these foreign people are <u>kind</u>! It is a glad revelation to my suspicious nature.
>
> I wish I could tell you of the countless courtesies shown to us during the long, hard voyage here — just our little family all alone, and some of us sick and some of us troubled! And it was Christmas, knowing that my babies must go to America in just a few days! But folks just kept on being kind!
>
> The nurses sang Christmas carols all over the building on Christmas eve. All Christmas Day they ran in with cheery words or a dish of candy or a lovely tea tray filled with good things for Dr. Kellersberger and Winifred. There were packages and letters from America, too, almost 100 of them! And I was in a comfortable, clean white bed in a cozy, steam heated room with two doctors and several other specialists called in for consultation, a staff of nurses to meet every need and a devoted family to cheer me!

On January 2, 1922, Dr. Kellersberger sailed for the

United States on the White Star liner, *Baltic*, taking five-year-old Winifred and baby Cornelia with him. In his journal he wrote on this date:

> So hard! How everyone stares at me! But Edna has been so brave in the midst of it all. Six months or more she must be in the hospital. There was no place in dark, foggy London that was right for our girls, so the haven of the dear McClung family farm in the Valley of Virginia seems to be the solution. I will return immediately after settling the children there. How I hope that the wonderful new German drug for sleeping sickness, BAYER 205, will cure Edna sooner than expected! Surely prayer will be answered, as it already has so many times for us! May these times of testing be purifying for us and draw us nearer to our Lord Jesus. May nothing be too precious to us to give up for HIM!

As the *Baltic* slowly pulled away from the great Liverpool dock, a strong voice came from somewhere in the crowd standing on the shore. Through cupped hands a man's voice shouted: "He is able!" From the deck just above where Eugene was standing, a passenger's voice promptly responded: "HE IS ABLE!" Back and forth across the ever-widening expanse of water the two voices kept repeating the same words, the voice from the shore becoming fainter and fainter, until at last it could no longer be heard. But a loving Father God's message of comfort to his burdened, grief-stricken son had been tenderly spoken again and again. All the rest of his life those three words were a bulwark of strength through trials that were to prove even more grievous than the one through which he was passing at this time.

God's enabling power to Edna, alone in the London hospital, is clearly seen in the letter she wrote to her supporting churches in the United States:

> As no doubt most of you know, I am here in the Hospital for Tropical Diseases for at least six months. Last June, on my way to our station after our year's furlough, I was bitten by a tsetse fly. Two days after reaching Bibanga I became ill and continued having fever, even while taking thirty and forty grains of quinine daily. Dr. Kellersberger soon saw that my trouble was not malaria. After careful ex-

amination of a drop of blood from my finger, he found try-panosomes in my blood, indicating that I have African sleeping sickness. In my state of the disease there is only pain in the bones, soreness in the chest, constant headaches and frequent fevers. Yet even now sometimes I have trouble with a terrible all-over numbness, similar to having one's limbs go to sleep. There is also a heavier feeling, as if I simply do not have the power even to lift a finger! I have had only a little of this nightmare sensation, but enough to realize the horror of it. I did not even know that it was a symptom, and only mentioned it to the doctor incidentally. Later on I was naughty enough to crawl out of my bed and go and read my chart on the mantel. It made much of this symptom. I can see how one must suffer with it as it grows worse and worse. Thank God I am being saved from all this but I am telling you about it because I want you to realize what unknown souls in Africa are suffering today. They become stupid, emaciated, insane, unable to walk or talk and finally they die. They always die, for the disease is fatal. O! how much I have to be thankful for!

But out there on the grassy plains there are hundreds of victims of sleeping sickness lying huddled on the ground, unconscious and dying. I hesitate to write what is in my heart, fearing to tarnish things too sacredly my own and God's, but I am so in earnest to help you face your responsibility to Africa, that I MUST tell you!

When I first got back to Bibanga and realized how poorly I had worked there as a missionary before, I wrote this prayer in my prayerbook: "May Africa be my burden in some way as the world was Christ's. May I gladly suffer anything for the salvation of this people!"

I do not know. Could God in some way be working out the answer to that prayer?

On January 10th Edna wrote to her mother-in-law, Helene Matern Kellersberger in Marble Falls, Texas:

I got my cable from New York today and now know that Eugene and the girls were met there by my sister, Winifred. It is such a comfort! I am perfectly at peace about sending my babies to America. If I had the decision to make again, I would still send them. Nevertheless, there is always a deep, tugging feeling. I dream at night of hunting for them and awaken with a start, wondering where they really are.

I do not know what is ahead, but I want you to know that I am contented and happy. I am waiting for Eugene to return. As much separation as we have had, it is strange how, when he is away, I feel as if a part of my own nature is missing. I do not seem to be a whole person to myself.

It was the familiar R.M.S. *Saxonia,* on which he had sailed back to the United States the year before, that now returned Eugene to his wife. On this mid-winter crossing the Cunarder battled the elements for thirteen days. Once again she justified her reputation for being a slow, safe and steady ocean-plodder. On January 21st, still within sight of the Ambrose Lightship, after sailing from New York, Eugene wrote in his journal:

Here I am again on the sea, and this time without those two precious girlies who were with me before. Excitement has kept me going up to this point. Now I am alone with letters that make me so sad! A deep, swelling, bursting feeling of anguish tore me apart as our ship pulled away from the dock. My loved ones on both sides of the sea! And to know from letters received today that my dear big girl is crying herself to sleep every night with the words, "I want my Daddy! I want my Daddy!" And the dear little one — so sweet and dear she is!

God alone can give me strength to bear these things. His chastening surely is sweet, though now for the present, "it seemeth not joyous." I know that afterwards it will "yield the fruit of righteousness to them that are exercised thereby." How good the Lord has been to us and how brave my dear one there so far off, bearing her burden alone.

January 23rd   For five hours last night we "hove to" and lost ground as the heavy roll was breaking things up all over the ship. Looking out this morning I saw all the wireless equipment torn down — a shambles! I don't see how they will ever get it all back together again in this icy wind. At 3 a.m. a wave broke through the porthole of my poor table steward's cabin, driving out the occupants and gutting out all their possessions. All today we have been in the grip of this blizzard. I tried to walk on deck, but NO CHANCE!

January 24th   We got into Halifax at 1 p.m. and left at 4:30. I have never in all my life been so glad to leave a place —

SO COLD! This ship is a floating iceberg. The whole vessel is covered with tons and tons of ice, like giant white armor, glistening in the sun, a magnificent sight! It is reported to be 20 degrees below zero and I can well believe it. The water is even frozen in the bathtubs <u>inside</u> the ship! Everyone on board is blue with cold and shivering. According to the Halifax papers, winds have been clocked at 64 mph, and all shipping from Europe has been delayed four to five days by this terrific weather.

I am so homesick to get through it all and to see that dear one lying there all alone. I've not had one word from her since I left. Only faith keeps me up, believing that God knows best and loves and cares and guides.

O God! Give me strength from day to day to bear cheerfully the burdens You permit to come to us. May the JOY be steady and sure and may our eyes ever be on our Dear Lord! In the 3rd Psalm I have found a comforting word: "*But Thou, O Lord, art a shield for me; my glory and the lifter up of mine head.*" (Psalm 3:3)

February 3rd, 9 p.m. 6 Tavilon Street, London Dead tired but oh! so happy to see Edna and to find that on the whole she seems better. What a relief, after all these weeks of strain, stress, partings and separations! How good God is to me! Another safe voyage and now today He saw fit to have one of Miss Poulter's boarders leave for two weeks so that I could just slip back into my old boarding place for a few days. I was too tired to go anywhere else. I have just come back from Edna. We talked and talked and it was so sweet to see her again, though the empty places of our children give us both a great inner ache and pain. Surely God knows this!

On February 20, 1922, Dr. Kellersberger began a six-weeks post-graduate course in surgery at the Royal College of Physicians and Surgeons. With eager anticipation he wrote: "I will have access to fifty different hospitals in England and will be observing the best surgery by the very finest surgeons. When I have completed this course, I hope to take the full diploma course in tropical medicine and hygiene, if my wife's health permits."

Dr. Carmichael Low and Dr. Manson-Bahr, son-in-law

of the late authority on tropical diseases, Sir Patrick Manson, were the doctors in charge of Edna's case. Together with other members of the London School of Tropical Medicine staff, it was decided that she would be given a course of intravenous injections of the new German drug, BAYER 205, developed specifically for the treatment of African sleeping sickness. But instead of seven doses on seven successive days, Edna would be given one injection a week, over a period of ten weeks. This was a much longer spacing between injections than recommended by the makers of the drug and a greater number of doses than given to any case so far treated. By giving it more slowly, Dr. Low hoped to avoid in Edna's case, the deleterious effects on the kidneys that all other patients had suffered.

One doctor on the staff was highly critical of Dr. Low to Eugene, saying that he was being far too cautious in his manner of treating Edna. He warned that, given in this way, the disease would develop a tolerance to the drug. But Eugene himself was assured that Dr. Low's procedure was a good one, for all the literature in German that he had secured directly from the Bayer Company stated that no harm would result from giving the drug at a slower pace than recommended.

Excerpts from Edna's letters to her father and sister, Winifred, reveal the plucky sense of humor and the courageous faith with which she faced the ordeal of her illness and its treatment, as well as the separation from her children:

January 10, 1922 London Hospital for Tropical Diseases
I am having one of those queer spells that come with sleeping sickness. They are hard to describe, but one does feel so sick! So far, however, this time I have not had fever. As I am taking the medicine into the veins, perhaps it may be already sufficiently under control to prevent that! No doubt Eugene has written you about this strange, new arsenic-based German drug I am taking, Bayer 205. The one drawback is that it sometimes affects the kidneys. They are trying to avoid that by spacing my treatments farther apart. I get impatient, wishing they would hurry and get the disease under control!

They keep me in bed. I am not even permitted to be rolled in a wheelchair onto the fire escape, as I begged for

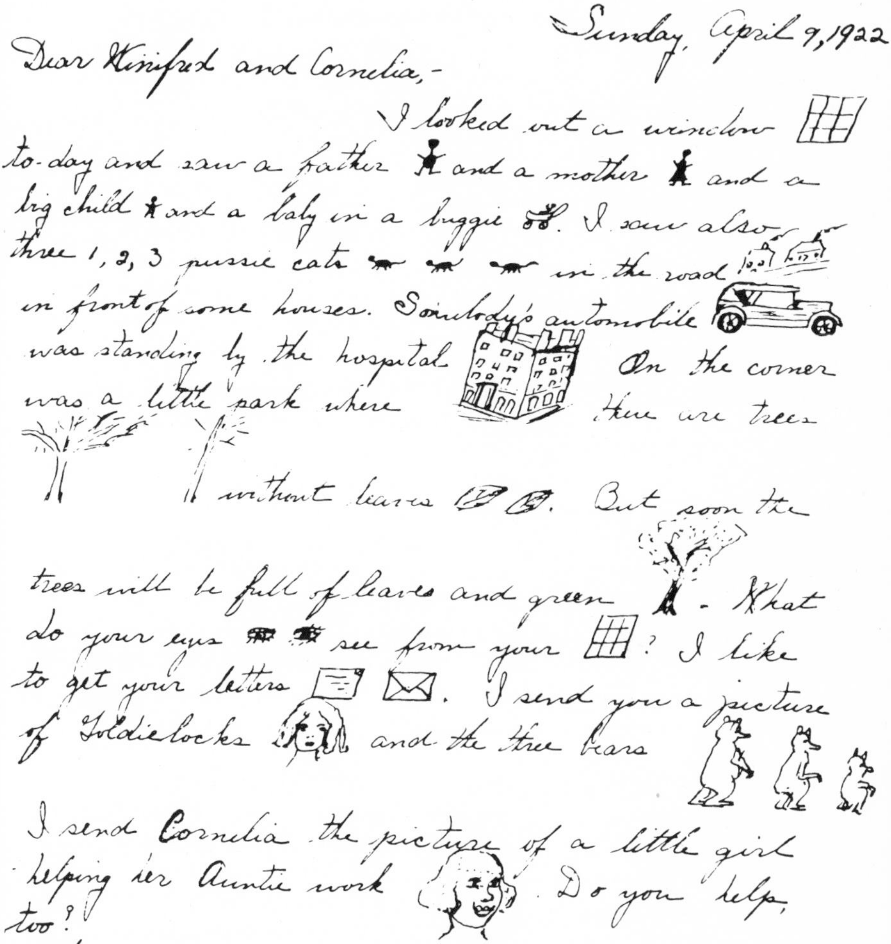

Sunday, April 9, 1922

Dear Winifred and Cornelia,-

I looked out a window to-day and saw a father and a mother and a big child and a baby in a buggie. I saw also three 1, 2, 3 pussie cats in the road in front of some houses. Somebody's automobile was standing by the hospital. On the corner was a little park where there are trees without leaves. But soon the trees will be full of leaves and green. What do your eyes see from your ? I like to get your letters. I send you a picture of Goldielocks and the three bears.

I send Cornelia the picture of a little girl helping her Auntie work. Do you help, too?

Give all the Aunties and Mother McClung my love.

With love,

Mother

Letter written by Edna Kellersberger to her children from the London hospital.

one day, but I can sit up in bed and amuse myself as I
please. I gained two pounds this week. It encourages me
today when I do not feel so well, to think of that! They feed
me six times a day here and I eat very well, too. The man
who pricks my finger and studies the drop of blood every
day to count the trypanosomes in it said yesterday that the
only other sleeping sickness patient in the hospital now
wasn't half as jolly as I am. I had to tell him that my faith
makes me willing to accept this illness, because through it,
I know that God is letting only the very best come to me.

January 20th   Even the excitement of taking a bath is taken
from me now. I have had the hardest spell since leaving the
tropics. My fever last night reached 102 and a fraction. Day
before yesterday I slept all day, could not even, with effort,
keep my eyes open. The supervising nurse, called "Sister"
here in England, said I looked "down in the dumps." My
head ached so that I just could not <u>make</u> myself be cheerful!

But I've discovered that if one looks sharp, one can
find excitements and pleasures (when GOD is ordering affairs!) even within four wee, white walls! We had a most exciting time yesterday hunting for my veins. My nurse simply could not get the needle into my vein, and had to call
the doctor. It began like a tragedy, but it ended like a romance. Oh! It's been lovely! My dear Scotch nurse, Lennie,
and Dr. Gregg are in love! I've been suspecting it for some
time. Now I <u>know</u>, even to a kissing under the mistletoe! It
is still in the uncertain, exciting stages, when things aren't
settled — the very loveliest time! I am so excited and Nurse
Lennie and I are getting over the "nurse and patient" stage.
We are becoming <u>friends</u> and can have such lovely talks —
at least when folks hush yelling "Nurse Lennie" for a second. Sometimes I just want to <u>kick</u> them!

This is not Dr. Low's regular visiting day, but in he
stalked, followed by a herd of young naval doctors. He
stood guard by my bed and shooed the silent throng over to
my fever chart and case history board on the mantel, say-
ing, "We'll discuss <u>this</u> case later. Look at <u>that</u>!' They all
turned their back on <u>me</u>, all perked up for the great occasion. While the men all "looked at <u>that</u>," Dr. Low stood by
me like a soldier at attention and made two remarks. He
said, "You are better today?" Then he took my hand and
said, "Your hand is cold. Are you warm enough in this

room?" With these remarks he shooed the docile herd back out into the hall, where it sounded as if a lecture on my case was being given.

Another excitement I have is singing hymns. When nothing else makes me behave and cheer up, that will! Last night when the fever began to go up, placing a burning hot cap on the top of my head, I was afraid that it was going up and up and up! I shut my eyes and said to myself, "I'll sing as long as I'm conscious and then maybe I'll keep on after I get unconscious!" When I had sung every hymn that I know by heart, I opened my eyes. Nothing had happened. The fever remained high for only a little bit. I began to feel cooler and when the temperature was taken again, it was only 100.2. So I stopped singing, much cheered, drank my glass of hot milk and went to sleep.

January 27th   There has been a discouraging relapse, "tryps" in my blood for three days running, fever, and feeling so sick. I have had to do an extra amount of singing and praying, to keep the faith-supply up to demand. Even in the turmoil of being admitted here, of the decision to send the children away, and while I had fever spells, no one has seen me cry about any of these things. That first day I did turn away and couldn't answer Dr. Low, when he asked me if I wanted to send my children to America. I really showed off before the "high mogul" and his crew that day!

There's always a "crew!" I often get two "pop-ins and pop-outs" during one of his visiting afternoons. From Nellie, who polishes the hearth, right up to Dr. Low and his inspection team, they all rush in and out and to all I am supposed to give the answer, "Yes, I feel better today, thank you!" "Yes, I slept well! Goodbye!" I am going to put a parrot in my bed some day and slip out and no one will be the wiser.

Dr. Low is quite thorough in spite of his odd ways. He certainly is considered "THE THING" for I can find only two doors on this whole floor that do not have his name on them. (They always fasten the doctor's name to his patients' doors, you know.) There is no doubt that he is interested in me, is almost excited over my case. He seems to be showing no great concern over this present relapse. I feel guilty of mischief when I take a small noon nap. Suppose every time you took a nap, someone would say, "You're very drowsy, aren't you?" It is only when I have fever that I am unnaturally drowsy. I slept all day, one day of this last miserable spell. It was unnatural, and I knew it and it was recorded on my history board, the only entry of its kind. My nurse said to me yesterday, "You are usually so bright. It seemed strange to have you that way."

February 19th   Well! I really believe I'm better! I have had no "tryps" or fever for a month and have passed times in the cycles when I have always had them before. Eugene is reading everything about Bayer 205 that he can get his hands on. His native German is coming in splendidly for that purpose now.

Last Thursday when Dr. Low came, quite a consultation was held over me. He brought a visiting doctor and Eugene was here and Miss O'Driscoll, and in walked Dr. Newham, who is head of the laboratory department and who has been in several times. He had with him Dr. Wenyon, who is quite famous. He is the one who has used some of my blood in his experiments with sleeping sickness in rats and guinea pigs. Dr. Low called a meeting right there in my room to decide what to do with me!

One thing for sure, if I am not cured by summer, I am going to beg to fall into the hands of the Americans! Eugene has been reading up on a new cure for sleeping sickness, called *Tryparsamide,* developed by the Rockefeller Institute. Incidentally, directly across from my window is a new building going up for this medical school, the money having been donated by the same Rockefeller Foundation, five million dollars!

I'm learning that the rest of the world is not rich like America. Eugene laughs at being allowed only one bath a week. Here in the hospital, I get my sheets changed, one, once a week. This morning one of the nurses said to me, "You Americans are far ahead of us in having and doing. But England doesn't care for such things. You Americans don't have any ancestry! I look back at our history and think of what I am because of it!"

I felt a little bit hot, but didn't argue with her. I wanted to tell her, "Well, our nation didn't just grow out of the ground, you know! Some of those with the most noble ancestry were the very ones that left Britain and went to the new world." I think they showed their superiority by making such a choice! And I didn't even tell her about or show her my own babies' ancient Swiss coat-of-arms! It really is discouraging!

March 19th They still take my temperature every four hours, feed me six times a day and give me cod liver oil, malt and an arsenic tonic three times a day. And I am being allowed out of bed every day for a bit! I have even taken some walks with Eugene, trying to gain a little strength. How thankful I am that I never reached the paralysis stage! Even if one gets better, treated with Bayer 205, the paralysis persists. I am very weak but I have perfect use of hands and legs. OH! I am so thankful! I'm not even having the tired headaches at the end of the day. Best of all, the spleen is gone!

THE LONDON ADVENTURE

Edna continued to stay on in the hospital for observation even after her series of Bayer 205 shots had been completed. Very quickly this became a highly depressing situation for her, far from conducive to a rapid return of her strength. Hospital fare, exactly the same every day, became so unpalatable that she simply was no longer able to force down a mouthful of food. The death of her former roommate, Miss Pusey, and also of the young sleeping sickness victim on the floor above, whom she had befriended, brought her real grief:

I finally got to the point where I could no longer eat hospital fare. Miss Pusey's death, among other circumstances at the hospital, indicated clearly that I was desperately in need of a change.

Eugene was a dear! One day I just was not cheerful or brave one little bit. He hunted up Dr. Low and told him that I needed to get out of that hospital! Dr. Low agreed, so now I am at Eugene's boardinghouse, just one block from the hospital.

We have a cheery room with big windows and white furniture. Every morning we have a nice breakfast downstairs with the other boarders. But I prepare our noon meal right here in our own room using a little gas burner! Yesterday we had fresh radishes, tomato sandwiches, cheese sandwiches, sardine sandwiches, cocoa and little cakes. Today we are having steaks and a fresh, green tossed salad!

Every night we take a good walk and then eat dinner somewhere in a restaurant. The evenings are delightful! It is light here until 9 p.m. We are very happy except that we want our babies. Best of all we love to ride on the top of a London bus in the evenings.

On April 23rd Eugene began the full diploma course in tropical medicine. Occupied with classes, laboratory experiments and assignments, he was no longer free to take Edna sightseeing on weekdays as before. Alone, or with a Methodist missionary friend, Edna continued her daily ventures:

June 10th London is delightful now! The climate is ideal; the days are comfortably cool, just right and sunny. The long twilights <u>are marvelous</u>! You go to bed at 10 p.m. by twilight and waken in the morning to full daylight. We are having such happy times, marred only by our constant, deep longing for our children.

I have been going by myself to visit the National Art Gallery, taking the paintings very leisurely, reading about each one as I go. I have been invited out to tea twice this week and was taken to a lovely flower show last Tuesday. To offset all these pleasant times I go to the dentist, and help Eugene prepare his plague and sprue and yellow fever outlines for his tropical disease courses. Now it is time for me joyously to dress to go to the dentist. He isn't even an interesting man — only a surprised-looking one with only one expression.

Edna's most frequent visitor during her illness was Eugene's cousin, Lili Kellersberger Goyder from Baden, Switzerland. A classic, storybook romance occurred when a young Englishman named Will Goyder, vacationing in Baden, chanced to see the lovely daughter of the aristocratic old Swiss family, and fell "madly in love" with her, courting her so persistently that her family finally consented to the marriage.

The Goyders, residents of the London suburb of Mill Hill, were the first to welcome Eugene and the convalescent Edna into their home. They were parents of three handsome, brilliant sons, one of whom, Cecil, was the first of England's youths to make and operate his own short-wave receiving and transmitting apparatus. So successful was he that the Prince

of Wales paid a personal visit to see and hear the young operator in action. Edna and Eugene were thrilled beyond measure to hear for the first time, not only Morse code, but actual
voice communication between pilots of two aircraft, a feat not
yet taken for granted back in 1922.

How fresh and fragrant was the Goyders' orchard in
bloom and their garden! How delicious their high tea, served
before an open fireplace in true British fashion! Edna reveled
in a long drive through the hedge-bordered winding lanes of
England in April in their open 1922 Willis Overland Tourer.
Her enthusiasm over stopping to pick wild anemones and vi-
olets and at seeing real Gypsies camping in their colorful wagons along the roadside gave warm satisfaction to Lili and Will.
Such adventures brought a fresh spot of color into the pale
cheeks and the first happy return of Edna's uniquely bubbly,
infectious laughter, unheard for so long. A warm and happy
relationship grew between the two couples during the time
that the Kellersbergers were in London.

Of an impressive experience of worship in London Edna
wrote:

> How I wish you could see Dr. John Henry Jowett's
> church, large, with two upper galleries. Four whole sections
> of the first gallery were filled just with Sunday School chil-
> dren and their teachers. The church was packed. People
> were even seated upon the platform. And all those MEN in
> the audience! They were a splendid-looking set! They never
> turned their eyes from Dr. Jowett's face as he preached.
> When he had finished the last word of his sermon, there
> was a great rustling sound all over the church, people relax-
> ing and settling back into their seats after listening so in-
> tently. It was wonderful! How I did enjoy it!
>
> *June 18th* We have been married ten years today! I have
> also been without fever for six months to the day! We
> bought a half-pound box of candy and went to dinner at the
> Russell Hotel to celebrate this double anniversary!
>
> We have turned "English" sure enough, and "quality"
> English at that! Eugene and I have afternoon tea even in
> our own room. When we are out we go to a tea shop. I
> dearly love China tea! It tastes like new mown hay smells.
> It is a bit more expensive, but not bad, only two shillings a

tin. When we do have tea, we eat a late evening meal. Our relaxed hours and habits here make me feel frisky, never nervous or jumpy! I sleep till 7:30 every morning. No one in England ever does anything until 10 a.m. I think it's good for your health to live this way!

My dentist says that the trouble with my mouth is my run-down condition, caused by my illness. He says that I need a long sea-voyage or a trip to the mountains. Dr. Low agrees.

On July 16, 1922, Dr. Kellersberger wrote to his parents: "You will be glad to know that in the final written examination of the London School of Tropical Medicine, I have finished "with distinction." Of the fifty-six who started this course, only forty passed the exam. Of these forty, only three received "distinction" and I was one of them. I still have one more week of very difficult oral examinations. If I pass it all, I will receive the important, coveted degree of D.T.M. and H., the "*Diploma in Tropical Medicine and Hygiene*"!

On July 20, 1922, Dr. Low and Dr. Manson-Bahr of the London Hospital for Tropical Diseases dismissed Edna as a cured case of African sleeping sickness. An article in the January 19, 1923 issue of the *London Times*, reporting on the achievements of the Royal Society of Tropical Medicine and Hygiene, refers to the seven patients "infected with *Trypanosomiasis gambiensi*, who made what appear to be rapid and complete recoveries" by being treated with Bayer 205. Beside the clipping of this article, pasted into his journal, Dr. Kellersberger wrote: "One was Edna!"

The happy couple left immediately for the long-awaited "trip to the mountains," a warm and happy visit with relatives and friends in Baden and Zurich, Switzerland. On September 12th they sailed from England for New York on the United States liner, *President Monroe*.

As they walked the decks, they said joyously in unison — over and over:

> *Bless the Lord, O my soul, and all that is within me!*
> *Bless His holy name . . .*
> *Who heals all your diseases,*
> *Who redeems your life from destruction,*
> *Who crowns you with loving kindness and tender mercies!*
> Psalm 103:1, 3, 4

[9]

The Trust of the Unexplained

TOGETHER AGAIN

October 1922, to February 1923 — four precious months together as a family of four before Dr. Kellersberger's scheduled return to the Belgian Congo! How he and Edna reveled in their joyous reunion with their two little girls! A cozy apartment was found in Concord, North Carolina, just a block from Edna's sister's house on South Union Street. For Edna, it was like playing house again. She made curtains and puffy cushions for the sofa while Eugene varnished a new dinette set and fixed shelves and screens and screws and washers. He tried to anticipate every utility and carpentry need, to be sure his little family was comfortably settled.

On January 28, 1923, Dr. Egbert Smith, the Executive Secretary of the Foreign Missions Committee of the Presbyterian Church in the United States, made a special trip from Nashville to Concord to talk with the Kellersbergers. News had come that Dr. Stixrud, the only doctor on the church's Belgian Congo mission field, had sleeping sickness.

"Eugene," said Dr. Smith, "if you feel that Edna is now well enough for you to leave, would you be willing to return to the Congo immediately?"

Together on their knees Edna and Eugene made the

painful decision that he would return alone for a two-year term, the length of time that Edna's London doctors felt she should remain in a temperate climate before attempting to return to her work in tropical Africa.

The heart-searching struggle to accept this separation, through which Edna was passing at this time, is reflected in her prayer notebook, where she wrote: "Do my prayers <u>bleed</u>? Now I am discovering the <u>real cost</u> of my intercessory prayers for Africa!" As she let her Eugene go "for Christ's sake and the gospel's," she was praying a "bleeding prayer," one of intercession <u>for</u>, and total, unequivocal committal of her loved one <u>to</u> God for His work and purposes alone.

Eugene did not want his family to see him off at the Concord railway station as he took the train for New York. He simply walked down the street, a little lopsided, for he was carrying a very heavy suitcase. Edna and her two little ones watched him go. She sat quietly in a chair, holding Cornelia on her lap, but Winifred leaned as far out over the porch railing as she could, her eyes, brimming with tears, hugging every moment that she could see even the least little bit of her beloved father. She understood clearly that he was leaving because God's call to him to heal the sick people of Africa was far more important than being together as a family.

Far down the block, just before he reached the corner, Eugene turned once and waved to the silent group on the porch down the street. It was the last time he ever saw his wife.

BACK TO THE BELGIAN CONGO

Dr. Kellersberger's third journey to the Belgian Congo was highly significant for contacts made which greatly increased his effectiveness in diagnosing and treating African sleeping sickness. For the eighth time in a little over two years, he made a transatlantic crossing, this time on the 52,000 ton Cunard liner, *Berengaria*, a British prize of war which the Germans originally constructed and sailed as the *Imperator*. Steel deck plates torn off in the violent winter storm of the previous crossing had to be replaced before the vessel could pull away from an ice-encrusted dock, make her way through the great ice-cakes blocking the Hudson River, and head eastward-bound out into the open Atlantic.

The few days that Dr. Kellersberger spent in London were medically exciting. He had lunch with Dr. Manson-Bahr and visited Dr. Carmichael Low at the Hospital for Tropical Diseases, learning there were now six more cured cases of sleeping sickness, treated with BAYER 205!

From London Dr. Kellersberger went to Germany, where he spent a week in the laboratories of FARBEN FABRIKEN in Leverkusen, a suburb of Cologne. He carefully studied the actual manufacturing process of Bayer 205, the drug which had cured Edna.

In Brussels he had an important conference with the Belgian *Medicin en Chef*, Dr. A. Broden, obtaining from him various health certificate forms and personal letters of introduction to the Belgian medical service personnel in Elisabethville. He was also given a letter from the Colonial Minister to the Governor of Katanga Province, granting him permission to spend a month in the hospitals and laboratories of Elisabethville, doing research on African sleeping sickness.

On March 9, 1923, Dr., Kellersberger sailed from Southampton, England, on the 12,500 ton *Walmer Castle* of the Union Castle fleet. On each of the eighteen days of the voyage to Cape Town he wrote a long letter by hand on ship's stationery to his wife, pouring out his loneliness and longing for her in touching, poignant words.

On March 31st Edna received a cable from Cape Town informing her of her husband's safe arrival. It was weeks later that she received his letters describing the voyage and his first impressions of South Africa.

The extended journey by train from Cape Town to the Belgian Congo over the southern portion of the Cape-to-Cairo, was a unique experience. Steadily northward the train pushed through the Drakensbergs, up onto the Great Karroo plateau, and out over the High Veldt, with its vast stretches of grass-covered savannah.

Each morning long before dawn the doctor quietly dressed and slipped out of his compartment, leaving his fel-

low-traveler, Judge Salkin, still sleeping. Out onto the platform at the rear of the coach he went to spend a happy hour of
solitude in prayer and worship, inhaling the crisp, frosty air
and glorying in the spreading radiance of a fiery sunrise over
the ever-changing African scene.

From Victoria Falls Eugene wrote to his wife:

April 1, 1923, Easter Sunday I have never spent an Easter
morning like this before, nor ever will again, I suppose! Do
you remember when, once long ago, you pinned a sweet
Easter message to my pillow at 1402 West Avenue, with the
following words: "HE IS RISEN!", and a lovely lily you
painted yourself? As you receive this letter, remember that
on Easter Sunday this year I was at Victoria Falls, watching that stupendous mass of water plunge down into that
immense, roaring, misty chasm! I thought to myself as I
watched it: "Edna's and my love is just like that, endlessly,
everlastingly flowing with mighty power!" My prayer is
that it may always be an overwhelming flood that engulfs
us completely! Above all, may this majestic "smoke that
thunders" be an emblem to us both of the limitless power of
a resurrected life! "HE IS RISEN!" and we are risen with
Him to live above sordid care and troubles.

April 3, 1923 Tuesday
We entered the Belgian territory at 2 a.m. at mile post
number 2,147 from Cape Town! Eight miles later we
reached Sakania, which we left at 3:30 a.m. for the final lap
of our journey. We are now only 242 kilometers from Elisabethville.

CERTIFICATION FOR
COLONIAL MEDICAL SERVICE

The crucial weeks which Dr. Kellersberger spent in Elisabethville in 1923 turned his medical service sharply in the direction of public health ministry. As a result of the important
contacts made at that time, the research he did on tsetse fly
distribution, and the experience gained in the government and
mining company hospitals, he was given the full status of a
MEDICIN AGREE, an officially recognized Belgian colonial
medical service doctor.

In order to cut living expenses to a minimum, the doctor slept in a small, empty room at one end of the Methodist church, using his own camping equipment. His only light was a candle by which he wrote his daily letter to Edna. He rode his newly purchased bicycle to the *Hotel de Bruxelles* a few blocks away for all his meals.

Mornings were spent in the laboratories of the various Congolese and European hospitals. Using his own personal microscope and textbooks, he examined tsetse flies, dissected mosquitoes for malaria, did blood examinations on several hundred school children for malaria, examined smears and made differentials for diagnosis. In the afternoons he visited patients and observed X-ray work and surgical procedures, particularly on hernias and tropical ulcers. He assisted in a series of autopsies to determine the reactions of African patients to grippe and pneumonia. Of 638 entries into the Elisabethville government hospital for Congolese in three months' time, there had been 124 deaths, many from a type of influenza, prompting the autopsy studies.

With free access to government documents and maps, Dr. Kellersberger made his own contribution by doing a special study of the tsetse fly distribution over the Lomami District of the Belgian Congo, his assigned place of work.

He was particularly impressed with the *Union Miniere* company's hospital for its native employees. It was built on the unit system with covered connecting walkways, "surely the most feasible system here in the tropics," wrote Eugene. He especially liked the construction of the ward units, built without windows, but having walls open above five feet, screened all the way around. Large, overhanging eaves kept out the rain and wind, providing an airy, protected interior, well suited to a tropical climate.

From Elisabethville, the doctor wrote his wife:

> As you know, our friend, Mr. Heenan, the former commissaire of the district of Kabinda, is now the acting governor of the Katanga. My letter to him from the Colonial Minister in Brussels gave me immediate access to him. He then sent me directly to the home of Dr. Volke, the *Médicin en Chef*. Both have been most cordial to me.

I believe, too, that God is very definitely using me with my four Belgian friends with whom I travelled. Last night Judge Salkin said to me, "I believe you are as pure a man as I have ever met. One can see it in your face!" Now wasn't that a compliment! And he asked me to pray for him, too.

As I walked back from supper at the hotel last night, beneath a brilliant field of stars, I saw the Southern Cross far up in the sky, the way we used to see it back at Bibanga. I could smell, too, the familiar smell of the smoke of the native village cooking fires. It made me so homesick for you! I always have a feeling of incompleteness and lack of satisfaction. How can it be otherwise when we two have been one for so many sweet years? It's like bleeding all the time, but it's for Jesus' sake and that must give us joy.

On April 24th Dr. Kellersberger received his official papers of *Médicin Agrée* of the Belgian Congo:

I am now an officially recognized government doctor and will have the entire Lubilashi Valley as my territory. I now have the right to practice medicine and to charge as well as treat government personnel at a fixed price. I have the power to summon the native population for public health purposes when necessary, to examine them or give preventive measures. I have been given supplies of smallpox and typhoid vaccine, as well as a brand new microscope and the other drugs that I requested, with the promise of more as I need them. From the *Comité Spécial du Katanga* I have secured excellent brochures on the flora and fauna of the Congo, plus a good supply of useful maps.

Quite a large party gathered at the Elisabethville railroad station to see the doctor off for Bukama. The staff of the Methodist Mission was there and a group of Bibanga friends drawn to the mining establishment for jobs. The *Médecin en Chef*, Dr. Volke, and Dr. Walravens, whose association in the laboratories Eugene had especially enjoyed, both came, as well as the head doctors of the other Elisabethville hospitals. Also there were his Belgian shipboard companions of the *Walmer Castle*, with whom he had had such lively discussions on the real meaning of faith and missionary service, the young lawyer and his wife, Mr. and Mrs. DeClerkx, and Mr. Delcroix, the wealthy Belgian wool spinner from Brazil. Most obviously touched by his departure was Judge Salkin, whose book *Etudes Africaines*, and acquaintance Eugene had enjoyed during the voyage and train trip. The high-ranking legal official seemed oddly distressed and in need of reassurance. Every few minutes, as he had opportunity in the crowd, he slipped close to his missionary friend and whispered in his ear: "You won't forget me, will you? You <u>will</u> remember to pray for me, won't you?"

A letter mailed to Edna from Bukama the next day detailed the providential timing of that departure:

April 25th, Bukama I believe you must have been praying for me especially when I left Elisabethville this morning. I went to the station, having had no confirmation whatsoever that McKee had received my wireless from Cape Town requesting that a caravan be sent there to meet me and take me overland back to Bibanga. Through these days of waiting and uncertainty, I have felt at peace and sure of God's guidance. I went ahead and bought my ticket and checked my baggage through, even though Judge Salkin repeatedly and strongly urged me <u>not</u> to leave until I heard that my carriers had arrived. But I told him, "No, it is time for me to go! Somehow I have a deep faith that it is all being prepared for me."

And lo! it was !!! Only twenty minutes before the train pulled out, Hartzler came running with a letter from McKee, dated April 11th. It said: "Dear 'Kelly,' Your radiogram from the Cape, dated March 27th, just received here. Words cannot express our joy at your coming! We are sending tomorrow to Bukama 26 caravan men and Lukuma, your cook, to get you!" With triumph I showed the letter to Judge Salkin and all the others. Without exception they all seemed to be deeply affected and said, "THAT is PROVIDENCE!"

The week that Dr. Kellersberger spent in Bukama with Dr. Kleine of the German Sleeping Sickness Commission was a climactic conclusion to the return journey to the mission field, filled with experiences designed to increase the doctor's knowledge of sleeping sickness. For several weeks that Commission had been experimenting with the effect of Bayer 205

on cattle. In cooperation with Vice-Governor Heenan, different herds of cattle had been driven to Bukama through districts heavily infected with sleeping sickness. In every case the
herds that had been given prophylactic shots of Bayer 205 beforehand came through infested areas without contracting the
disease. The control groups that were not given this preventive measure were already obviously sick on arrival.

Vice-Governor Heenan's letter of introduction to Dr.
Kleine opened the door for Eugene to an interesting, increasingly friendly relationship, as recorded in his journal:

April 25th, Bukama   I'm sure I'll never forget Bukama,
though I have been here only 48 hours. It is a deadly sort of
place, very monotonous. I knew I was really back "in the
bush" last night when the big rats had dances all night long
over the mats tied to the ceiling of my room.

My letter from Vice-Governor Heenan broke the ice
for me and my ability to speak fluent German has done the
rest! I have had intensely interesting talks with Dr. Kleine
and his wife, having spent most of the day with them. He is
truly a great and famous man, passionately German, of
course. He is very cordial to me and has given me some important stains. He can't give me any more Bayer 205 because he is nearly out himself and can't get any more, due to
conditions in Europe. I have been of some assistance to Dr.
Kousenius, the state doctor here at Bukama. Have been in
consultation with him concerning some thirty cases of sleeping sickness that he has here in his clinic.

April 28th, Bukama   My fellowship with the German professor and his wife is an unexpectedly refreshing thing! Both
are middle-aged, quiet and very nice. She is a typical blond,
blue-eyed German, always travels with him and helps him
with his research. Some of the Belgians here have been very
rude to them, which is a shame! He is taking many risks just
to benefit this needy country and is not getting paid for it at
all. I believe that I have made real friends with him and am
so glad that I met him. He has given me some really good
suggestions for the public health aspect of my work with
sleeping sickness and promises to keep in touch. He paid me
a real compliment today when he said, "You are the best informed doctor on tropical medicine that I have seen in a
long time!"

Several of the Belgians and Portuguese at Bukama openly ridiculed the missionary for expecting his caravan to arrive. They frankly doubted that any Congolese would voluntarily walk 350 miles just to transport a white man and his baggage. Some urged the doctor to find some other way of returning to his post. But on April 30th, around 11 A.M., suddenly there they were — all twenty-seven of them! "Dear old Nzongola, faithful Lukuma, Lubilaji, Kabongo and my tried and true hammockmen! And one new caravan member is the husband of the woman whose leg I straightened!", exulted an elated Eugene.

On May 1st he tried to prepare his wife for the long break in correspondence that lay ahead. During the three weeks that he would be traveling overland through bush country, there would be no way of mailing letters:

May 1st, Bukama   Dearest, all that is left on my little folding camp table is your sweet picture. My boxes are out on the veranda, all packed. At 3 p.m. my caravan will cross the Lualaba River and go on ahead. Early tomorrow morning I will follow on my bicycle with my four men, Ndola, Muamba, Kazembe and Benda Benda, who always jog along beside me.

I can't possibly reach Bibanga overland before May 21st. When I do get there, remember that it will take yet another week for a courier to go to Lusambo with the cable. So you must not be impatient if it is the beginning of June before you receive the news of my safe arrival. I am glad my men are all lightly loaded and that I have a few extras in case any get sick. I like it that way! The four I have with me carry my camp chair, thermos, food box, drinking water and the net to catch tsetses given to me by Mr. Seidel here at Bukama.

I am making a collection of *Glossina Morsitans*, the Rhodesian type of sleeping sickness-carrying tsetse. These infect cattle and kill them, but it has not yet been proven that this particular fly can infect human beings. This is all a part of my continued research!

I will also be collecting *Ornithodorus Moubata*, the tick that causes African tick fever. Areas through which we will be passing are literally infested with what my Baluba friends call "tshimputu."

Your *Alpenstock* that you gave me in Switzerland is always with me. I have carved your name on the handle, so that I can always feel the dear letters of your name as I tramp along.

My men are dear and good! We have a nightly prayer and praise service. How beautifully they have prayed for you and me! I enjoy being with them so much more than with the godless whites that one comes across in this country.

At 10:00 A.M. on May 22nd, hours after Bibanga station became clearly visible in the distance, Dr. Kellersberger on his bicycle, followed by his trotting caravan of baggage-carriers, ascended the last long hill up to the mission station. The local population in all directions knew of his imminent arrival. The communication drums and signal whistles had been sending the message over the hills since early morning. All along the trail during the last hour of travel, crowds of jubilant villagers rushed to join the caravan, racing alongside the chanting carriers, escorting their doctor triumphantly onto the compound.

The first sign of the familiar little thatch-roofed mud house beneath the towering *diwole* tree brought a tremendous lump into Eugene's throat. Late in the evening he wrote a weary note from the home so full of memories of his family:

Bibanga, May 22, 1923

Darling Edna,

Here I am since 10:00 a.m. As I sit here in our bare dining room, I suddenly realize what this separation means. It is terrible! All I can do is bury myself in my work! I have literally been stormed all day long by all my native friends and my fellow missionaries alike. My only comfort has been opening your beautiful letter, "TO BE READ WHEN YOU GET TO OUR LITTLE BIBANGA HOME AND WE ARE NOT THERE WITH YOU." What a brave woman you are!

I am sending a runner to Lusambo tomorrow to take the cable message to you. When your receive that one word, "BIBANGA," in about a week from now, you will know that I am safely back where God wants me to be.

The dear missionary ladies put flowers in our house to

welcome me and I have our nice double bed, the one, dear, in which you lay so sick! All I can say is, "O God! Give me the strength to bear this separation for Jesus' sake!"

I, the bats, the mice and the nasty old Congo cockroaches all send you greetings from our beloved little Congo home!

EUGENE

THE NEW BIBANGA HOSPITAL

There was no time for tears or self-pity. The doctor was literally hurled into his work. The first unit of the new hospital plant, given by the Huston family in Pennsylvania, had been completed during his absence. As one in a dream that first day, he walked over the clean, white cement floor of the five-room administrative unit, indicating which room would house the clinic, which the dispensary, and the laboratory, and which was to be his own private office. In a daze, he showed where he wanted the shelves and tables made in the station carpenter shop to be placed. On May 25th a dedicatory service was held with a tremendous crowd present. The first clinic opened as soon as the service was over.

Housed for the first time in a permanent building — something other than mud-and-stick — Dr. Kellersberger's career was off to a brand new start. Letters written to his wife during those first hectic weeks after his return are a unique record of the fantastic growth of the work. Page after page in the doctor's daily journal remained blank during these few months, as he used what little time he had, dog-tired at night, to dash off a few items of news to her:

May 30 Made 16 slides today. My stains are looking fine. I am using *Giemsa* instead of *Leishmann*.

June 1 Began keeping case histories today. Saw 36 patients. A sick Belgian came in, is staying with me, sleeping on a cot in our dining room.

June 2 Our lad, Andrew Mukeba, walked in from Lusambo today! I am so happy to see him! He looks so well and strong and sweet and smiling. Has grown so tall, looks clean and fine, dressed in the khaki outfit I gave him. He has a man's deep voice now. His first words were: "Tell me about Beloved Mama and the children!"

Parts for the broken sterilizer also arrived today. At last I can sterilize under high pressure again! Am treating two more cases with Bayer 205. Many mosquitoes in the village now. Must do a thorough inspection of all the village water jars next week to find where they are breeding.

Here my thoughts were rudely interrupted when I plunged my pen into the ink bottle. I could only stare like a fool when I discovered that I had bayonetted a nasty cockroach that had drowned itself in the ink. That explains the three big blotches on this sheet of writing paper!

June 3   I am going about my work in a scientific way now, because of the training I received in London. My blood and lab work are easy now and I enjoy it. Mbuyi, Luhaka's older sister, came to me two years ago and I was never able to help her. She has been sick all this time. When I examined her "thick drop" preparation, I saw some unusual forms. I said to myself, "Now here's where you make a real smear!" I did and the Leishmann turned out very well. And guess what I found! A beautiful case of QUARTAN MA-LARIA, that rare form! I've been looking for a case like this all this time. I'll make a very close study and send many slides of this to the various medical schools I am supplying with tropical materials. I am really finding out what is the matter with people now, and don't have to treat them blindly.

June 4   Today a huge scrotal elephantiasis came in. The tumor must weigh close to a hundred pounds. I expect to take it off in two or three weeks.

June 8   The sterilizer works! Giving intravenous injections again, first since my return. Tiles are being laid on my operating room floor!

June 12   Getting along fine with the eight young Congolese men that I am now training as nurses.

June 19   Read about YOUR case of Trypanosomiasis today, reported fully in the *Royal Society Journal of Medicine*!

June 22   While I was reading your letter, a woman was carried in from the Lubilashi River where she was almost eaten by a crocodile. She had some 25 fearful wounds. The women with her pulled and the crocodile pulled. Finally one brave woman got a big stick and rammed its jaws loose. My patient has high fever and is toxic.

June 25 Have sent Dr. Wenyon in London, Dr. Broden in Brussels and the Naval Medical School specimens of ticks and tsetses. The Naval Medical School has sent me a big supply of mailing tins in which to send their materials.

The old mud-and-stick dispensary is now full of patients. I have no other place to put them. Sleeping sickness is definitely on the increase right here at Bibanga! Oh! If ONLY I could get more Bayer 205!

June 17 Vaccinated all mission employees today for smallpox. Will vaccinate all villagers later.

June 28 First operation in the tiled operating room a success!

June 30 Attendance of over 1100 during the first month that our hospital has been in operation! My acquaintance with Professor Kleine has developed into a wonderful correspondence. I sent him copies of the photographs I took of him and his wife and told him of the great increase in the number of sleeping sickness cases here. Today in the mail I received a large bottle of Bayer 205! It was mailed from Germany in a PLAIN BOTTLE WITH ALL THE LABELS REMOVED! That means that he had to get it for me secretly! I had only enough left for eight cases and had already treated three!

This is a direct answer to prayer and I am SO HAPPY about it! I will be sending him full reports of how I use every gram of it, of course. He is with the Robert Koch Institute for Infectious Diseases. How I would love to study there!

July 4 My Darling Edna, the faithful old *diwole* tree that towers over our little house almost overnight took on its new coat of leaves and looks lovely. And how it roars at night now, like the distant sea! It makes me long for you. It makes me yearn to blow out the lamp and crawl into bed, wrapped in each others' arms, listening to its pleasant sound. But sweetest of all, listening to each other's words of love, enjoying to the utmost that speechless language of love! You are just the way I want you — so wise, so generous, so understanding, so yielding, so wanting, yet always knowing what is best. My dear, dear Edna! In spirit I kiss you and have

the fullest and most sacred communion with you in body
and in spirit.

Your own EUGENE

July 12   Had a fearful operation this morning, took three
hours and the rest of the day to keep the old man from
dying. The new ward is going up beautifully. All windows,
doors and fireplace are finished and walls two-thirds up.
Another Belgian patient here; I suspect syphilis. He is
sleeping in our dining room. Ten new operative cases are
waiting for me now. Am doing many new things I've never
done before. But God is with me — no one has died yet!

July 19   Today our drying kiln full of valuable *Nsanga* (African Oak) boards caught on fire and nearly burned the
whole carpenter shed down. Hundreds of villagers came
running to the rescue and saved the day AND the new hospital!

July 27   Wish you could see my little operating room, fitted
up so nicely! And soon I will have a brand new ward. I believe God is answering your prayers for my usefulness here.
I don't worry over my patients like I used to. Daily I have
more confidence in God and in myself. He surely chose this
work for me and I am filling a crying need. I am proving
myself and throwing my whole strength into the service.

One of Dr. Kellersberger's greatest joys outside his medical work was his Sunday school class of some thirty young
Baluba men, which he taught on his front porch every Sunday
afternoon. Every three weeks he had a social hour on a Saturday evening, playing the Victrola, showing his stereopticon
slides and playing games. Letters to Edna often included descriptions of the fun the young men had, throwing peanuts
into a bucket when blindfolded, or, also blindfolded, drawing
an eye for a pig sketched on a blackboard. Once Eugene
greeted his surprised guests with a jack-o-lantern he had made
from a large papaya, with a candle inside. He delighted in giving useful little prizes to the winners, a washcloth, cakes of
soap, candles or matches. In later years it was remarkable to
note how many outstanding leaders of the African church had
been members of that lovingly-taught, much prayed-over
class of young men, of which Andrew Mukeba was the elected
president.

In August 1923 tragic events occurred at Luebo station. Mrs. Savels, the wife of the ex-Father Superior of the Lusambo Catholic Mission, who had become a Protestant and joined the American Presbyterian Congo Mission, died of blackwater fever and pneumonia. In a matter of only a few weeks, seven members of the oldest station of the mission were lost, one by death and three couples by illness. Eugene was urgently called to help out in this crisis, making the trip in only two days, riding on the back of a motorcycle, driven by another missionary. While at Luebo he responded to a second emergency call from the diamond mines near Tshikapa, then still a third call from Mutoto station. He was now the only doctor of a mission serving an area of approximately 80,000 square miles of south central Belgian Congo. To Edna he wrote:

> Dearest Angel, Think of it! If I had not come out, the whole mission would be without a doctor now. With Dr. Stixrud gone because of a sleeping sickness, Miss Farmer and I are the only medical units on the entire mission! Aren't you PROUD that our courage and self-denial has now been made the mainstay of our whole mission until help comes? Your illness and the training I received because of it has made it possible for me alone to have a supply of Bayer 205 on hand! Only through your suffering has help come to Mrs. Vinson and Dr. Stixrud, as I was able to provide them both with enough medicine for a course of treatment. Isn't that wonderful? I KNOW I am in the place God wants me to be NOW! Every day recently something has happened to show me this.
>
> I am willing to forgo for a time those things that are dearest to any man on earth, loved ones and home, when I realize that four lives have been saved by my instrumental deliveries during the last few days. It is worth it when I see my sleeping sickness cases under treatment with Bayer 205. It is worth it when I welcome a mother carrying her little girl from miles away, with a great sore on her knee that threatens to ruin the child's capacity to walk forever. It is worth it when an anxious young mother comes with her little baby in her arms, a bundle of fever and rapid respiration. The blood examination shows a very heavy infection of

tropical malaria — ring forms. A rapid injection of quinine brings it under control! I am the only possible help for these unfortunates.

Oh! Do be brave, Darling! I am well and taking care of myself. I am busy every waking moment and having happy times over some of the operative cases already cured.

Your boy, EUGENE

A PERSONAL GETHSEMANE

Back in the United States Edna was busy caring for her two small daughters. In a letter to Eugene's parents she described one of the things she was doing:

You should see what a splendid record I have kept of my youngsters' lives! Each girlie has her own baby diary. I find great pleasure in doing this for them. I clip out what people say or write about them. Now and then I have something I want to tell them, so I write in their diaries directly to them. If I die, they will know what I wanted them to do and be. And if I live, it will be a good way to "preach" to them, and they will enjoy their books in later years. I will begin a third one soon for both children. I keep only things that pertain to their lives, not ours. Winifred's little letters to me in the London hospital, her first drawings and sayings, etc. are all in it and we have a wonderful collection of photos.

To her husband she wrote:

Tonight is Good Friday. I read Winifred John's account of the Crucifixion. She listened well. For some reason, I hope she will always remember this reading. Then I prayed with her, for her to love Him Who bore this suffering for her and for me.

This afternoon I kept feeling the shortness of life and uselessness of centering our time and energy on anything but Christ and Heaven. I am so glad that we are saved by grace, for nothing but undeserved Love could save me! I long so to be of use to Him! I gathered my babies to me in the big rocker and had a little prayer and quiet time with them, praying for them to be His workers.

I feel so lonely without you. At times I still feel that I

just can't keep on without you, and I pity my little babies so much! Do you know that sometimes I get frightened because I find myself almost wishing to be an invalid, so you could not leave me! But of course I do not want you held to me by such a chain. I want your life to develop in the very best way and I want only to help and not to think of myself. But I do so want my babies to know their dear Daddie! You are so unusually sweet that it would mean so much to them! Oh, I am so hungry for your fellowship! It is strange how hard some things in life are to bear. I love you, dear, I love you! I am sure we will keep our love sweet and pure and strong for one another, no one else! Good night, dear! I can count another month off of your stay before very long! Good night!

EDNA

MURDER ON THE BRAZOS

In the fall of 1921, Edna's father, Philip Bosché had married one of the tenants living on his Austin, Texas, property. Eight lonely years as a widower, the bitterness harbored over his son-in-law's rejection of his offer of a thriving business partnership, and his daughter's return to the mission field, only to come down with a "horrible disease," combined to lead him to a rash decision. "You go your way and I'll go mine!" he had shouted when he parted with his daughter at Montreat that summer of 1921. And that is just what he did, when, against the advice of family, friends and even his own better judgment, he married again.

When Eugene went to Texas to bid farewell to his parents, he visited his father-in-law and new wife at their recently purchased ranch pocketed in the giant loop of the Brazos River known as Kimball's Bend. The crumbling stone walls of the pioneer town of Kimball still mark the stretch of riverbank where the famous Chisholm Trail once crossed. The bend was notorious for being the hideout of World War I draft dodgers and for a strange house, locally known as "My Darling's Love Nest," built into a precipitous bluff overlooking the spreading, water-encircled scene.

Mr. Bosché's 2,590-acre farm in Bosque County, fifteen

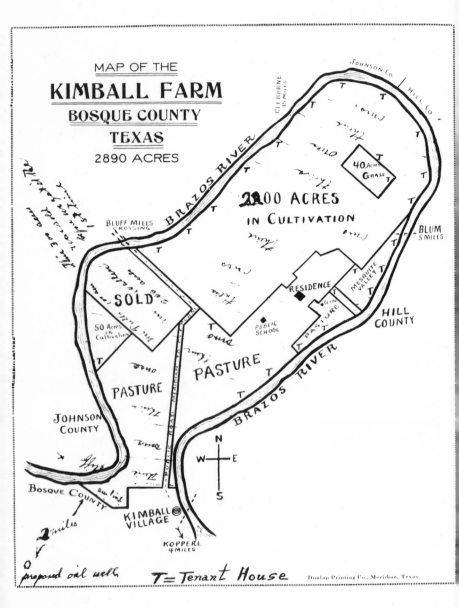

Mr. Bosché's Property in Kimball's Bend of the Brazos River, Texas.

miles southwest of Cleburne, Texas, was almost an island, fifteen miles in circumference. The only road leading onto the property threaded across the narrow neck of land three-quarters of a mile wide, where the river nearly managed to meet itself again. Atop the highest knoll was the central ranchhouse, built of native rock. Sixteen tenant houses with their adjacent fields were ranged around the perimeter of the peninsula, close to the river.

To her father, Philip Bosché, Edna wrote:

> I hope someday to have an opportunity to make friends with your wife. I can't help but believe that we can get along and that maybe she will like the children. If only we could meet some place for part of the summer! You could come in the car, perhaps.
>
> I have never had an enemy before in my life and feel that things just can't keep on this way. I shall write a letter to her some day, when you allow me, to try to bring about a better relationship. Just ignoring a situation does not keep it from existing. I MUST write about this situation that is, as I think and pray about it! But don't be troubled! I'm only searching for the right path, which only you can help me find. I never dreamed that I would feel towards her as I do — really sorry for her and <u>wishing</u> to be friends!

Early in July Edna's father, returned unexpectedly to his ranchhouse one night to find that he had ample reason for divorce. Old frontiersman that he was, he blasted his double-barreled shotgun into the bedroom near his wife and her visitor, in such a way as to send them both to the Cleburne hospital for minor repairs, proof enough to the whole surrounding community of what had been going on. Mr. Bosché's letters to Edna reveal the sad tangle of events that followed:

> *July 4, Kopperl, Texas*   It's rather lonesome and awkward to manage alone again. We are quit for good and I have filed suit for divorce, but it won't be complete till September. You know I don't believe in divorce, but I had to do it.
>
> *July 31*   She always blamed you girls for our troubles, es-<u>pecially</u> <u>you</u>, but now in this last letter, she does not mention you at all. We would have gotten along all right if she had not taken the stand she did against you girls, demand-

ing ALL my property. There is where all the trouble came
from. But she couldn't turn me against you two, not in a
1000 years! So she would fuss and fuss and I never answered a word, which made it worse, I suppose.

September 30   I see no reason why you should not come just
as soon as you can get ready, unless you are afraid of her. I
certainly am not a bit, but if you are, you will not be comfortable or happy here. There is of course no more danger
now than there would be after the divorce is granted. Do
just as you want to do. If you decide to come, get ready as
soon as you can and express some of the lighter things to
Kopperl. Take the Santa Fe from St. Louis to Kopperl.

For weeks during the summer of 1923, Edna, in her own
private Gethsemane, agonized in prayer over the question of
whether or not she should move to Texas to be with her father.
Into this sacred garden of tortuous indecision, not even Eugene could enter. She knew that her life would be in danger if
she went. Threatening letters from her father's estranged wife
made it clear to her that if she set foot in the state of Texas, she
would have no one but herself to blame for the consequences.
But even such a fear could not deter her, if she was convinced
that that was where God wanted her to be.

No one will ever know the inner agony of the decision she
made. The most important factor to her was her father's desperate need of her loving acceptance, cheerful presence and
supportive faith. During the empty years that still lay ahead
without Eugene, perhaps God would allow her to be useful in
making a pleasant, comfortable home for her father on the
ranch. She knew that the presence of his two little grandchildren, one named for his beloved first wife and one for his other
daughter, would bring him joy of a measure and quality he
had not known before. Edna also had a persistent, secret hope
that the presence of the children might somehow soften the
bitter feelings directed especially against her and even possibly provide a basis for friendship with her estranged stepmother.

The discouraged, hopeless tone of Phil Bosché's letters to
Edna, written that summer changed first to a tenuous hope,
and then to evident, surprised pleasure at her willingness to

join him. Finally, delighted, excited anticipation glowed on every page as he planned for the glad entrance of his cherished younger daughter and her two little girls into his lonely life and home.

Sheer foolhardy, unwise love some later called it, but love it was and love alone that made Edna close up the safe little Concord nest and turn her face to a barren, isolated ranchhouse to make a home for a disillusioned old man. Well she knew the danger she faced, but she trusted implicitly that her life and times rested in the hands of a loving God, whose wise, <u>permissive</u> decrees are in perfect accord with His sovereign will.

It didn't take long for the written threats to become stark reality.

Edna and the little girls had been residents of the Kimball Bend ranchhouse ten days when she wrote her final letters to Eugene:

Sunday, October 21st

Dearest, We went to Kopperl to the Methodist church today. A little theological student spoke, but he gave a very sincere gospel message and we liked it, Papa especially! Then we came home and I cooked a late dinner. The children had their nap while Papa showed me all the letters from his wife and we talked about her frankly.

The more I hear of her, the more I pity her and am afraid of her, too. Did you know her legs are crippled? She was married the first time when she was only fourteen. She was divorced and that first husband is still living.

She is working in a photography gallery in Dallas now. Papa is going there on business this week, but he says he will not see her. He will be gone only one night. Papa's brother, Uncle Mat, will be here with us.

Your letters will be more irregular, now that we are out in the country and it is not easy to mail them. I don't like this being in a new country without you. I am so afraid that people will not understand that we really do love each other, even if we are separated. I haven't heard from you in some time, but believe it is because of my trip here.

We are all going for a walk now, down to the river, perhaps. Oh! If only you were just here to take it with us, dearest! No one <u>knows</u> how hard it is without you!

With love, EDNA

October 22, Monday night

Dearest, Papa is in Dallas at the state fair. His younger brother, Mathias, "Uncle Mat," is here with us but I must confess that I feel very lonely and not very happy. This being knocked about here and there without you is not what I would choose, but I will remember that nothing happens by chance, that a wise, loving Hand guides all our changes, and I am willing for Him to choose for me, even if it is not what I like.

The children are most precious. Everywhere people speak of their loveliness. A man at church yesterday said, "Those are splendid looking children!" Another man said Saturday, "Your children look so healthy!" I am very grateful to God and find it one source of real comfort in being away from you, that they are well. When they get sick while you are away, it just tears me all to pieces. Everything is harder to bear with you away.

Eugene, my father <u>needs me</u>. I don't know what is ahead of me but I am deeply concerned about my children.

Winifred says she is tired. She did not have a nap today so I must get her to bed. Oh! How I love you and miss you and want you! With love,

EDNA

On Tuesday morning, October 23rd, Edna was standing at the kitchen stove, stirring oatmeal. Cornelia, two and one-half years old, sat in her highchair, banging her spoon on the wooden tray in front of her. Six-year-old Winifred was sitting on a kitchen chair, pulling on the first sock. The other sock and both shoes were on the floor beside her.

Suddenly the back door was flung open. A stark, stiff figure, one hand extended, holding an automatic pistol, strode with a marked limp across the kitchen floor. Steel-cold, venomous words spat out with every step: "You know what you've done! I'm going to kill you!" Edna, still holding the oatmeal spoon, said in a gentle, pleading voice, "I've been wanting to see you and explain . . ." An explosion rocked the kitchen as a bullet tore through Edna's hand. The figure strode out into the hall: "I told you no one could come between him and me!" Edna followed into the hall, repeating, "Let me explain . . ."

Edna Kellersberger with Winifred and Cornelia. Taken in Concord, North Carolina, shortly before she moved to Texas to be with her father, Philip Bosché.

A second explosion shattered her words into silence. Winifred, peering through the kitchen door into the hallway, saw the now silent figure take her grandfather's shotgun from behind the bedroom door and walk out the front door, slamming it violently behind her.

Edna lay in a spreading pool of blood in the middle of the hall. Bending over her, Winifred could barely catch the gasping words, "Uncle Mat! Go find Uncle Mat!"

One sock still clinging to one foot, Winifred ran out the back door to the barn, where Uncle Mat had gone to do the morning milking. She called as loudly as she could, "Uncle Mat! Uncle Mat!" No answer. She banged on the heavy door and tried to push it open. He must have gone to the pasture in search of the cows. She looked in all directions but there was no one in sight. Desperate, she raced to the nearest tenant house, but found it empty. Finally, she saw someone come out of one of the tenant houses down by the river. The sock came off as she raced barefooted over rocks and nettles down the long hill. Panting for breath, she told the tenant's wife that someone had hurt her mother. The woman called her husband to the door, saying, "Maybe you'd better go up to the ranchhouse and see what's the matter."

Winifred started to follow the man but he motioned for her to stay. She never again laid eyes on her mother's face. Neither was she allowed to attend her mother's funeral in Concord a few days later. Often over the years she wished that she had been allowed to see her mother in her coffin. The memory of her dying agony might then have been somewhat erased in the quiet peace of death.

When the tenant pushed the front door of the ranchhouse open, he found little Cornelia bending over her mother, trying to lift her, saying, "Mutter, get up! Get up!" She had climbed down from her highchair to see what was the matter. Immediately she was carried down to the tenant's house to join her big sister. There the two girls remained until the next day, sleeping together on a narrow cot in the same room with the tenant and his numerous family. Several times during the night Cornelia awoke crying. Her sister comforted her as best she could but never cried herself. She knew that she was responsible now and that meant not crying or asking questions.

Midmorning of the day of the murder, Sheriff Will Wright of Meridian received a shocking phone call from Kimball. A woman's voice coldly and proudly boasted of what she had done and arrogantly requested that she be taken into custody. After the doctor from Kopperl had pronounced Mrs. Kellersberger dead, her body was taken to a mortuary in Cleburne, Texas, from where it was shipped to Concord, North Carolina. The county attorney, who was the first to get to the scene of the crime, said that he did not remember ever having seen Mrs. Kellersberger, but that "he had never seen a face that gave him a better idea of what an angel might be, than that one, and that it would do any mortal man a world of good to go much out of his way, just to get to glance upon her."

Philip Bosché learned of his daughter's death only on the following day in Dallas, when a friend handed him the *Dallas Morning News* for October 24, 1923, with front page headlines that read:

WOMAN IS KILLED; STEPMOTHER HELD
Wife of Missionary Shot to Death
Near Kopperl in Bosque County

Breakfast in the tenant's house the next morning was a fried egg, cooked by the unkempt, barefooted wife with a baby astride her hip. It was served on the one china plate she owned. After Winifred and Cornelia had each finished eating their egg, she wiped the plate with her fingers licking them with relish. Then she cooked an egg for each of her stair-step children, cleaning the plate in the same manner after each one had finished. Wide-eyed at this odd way of eating, indeed, at the whole shiftless, untidy house in which they were staying, Winifred nevertheless was grateful for the kindhearted, unsuspecting guardian angel who willingly fried eggs for the hungry little children in her care.

Other "guardian angels" appeared later that day, "Uncle Frank" McElroy, fellow-missionary back at Bibanga, now on furlough, Miss Edleen Begg, Edna's girlhood friend, and her cousin, Mrs. Bolm, all from Austin, Texas. It was

"Miss Edleen" who, along with Mr. Bosché, took the two children back to Concord.

Edna was buried beside her mother, Cornelia Blickensderfer Bosché, in the Bosché family plot in Concord, North Carolina, on Sunday, October 28 at four o'clock in the afternoon. The next morning Winifred Brown took her namesake out to her mother's grave, covered with more than a hundred floral offerings. Wrote Mrs. Brown to Eugene's mother in Marble Falls: "Your lovely cedar wreaths came in good condition. Little Winifred and I took them out and put them on her mother's grave. The flowers were quite a comfort to Winifred. She said "Oh! My mother's grave does look so pretty?!" That night she said, "I wish I could see my mother! I want her always to be my mother, even in other worlds."

"GOD MUST LOVE ME, TO DO ALL THIS TO ME!"

The cable informing Eugene of Edna's death did not reach him until November 5th. Unaware of the truth, Eugene continued for two weeks to write daily letters to his wife. He described with tremendous excitement the difficult elephantiasis operation, for which he had so long been preparing!

> I am like a rag! A fearful, all-day affair! But your prayers and my dogged perseverance and swimming in blood till I was soaked to the skin, did it! Think of it! Four hours of anaesthesia, together with 1/4 Morphine and 1/100 Atrofine! It took 40 minutes to get him under! Lubilaji gave the ether and Ntambue and Tshidibi were my assistants. At first, when there was so much bleeding, I thought, "He'll die before I can ever finish!" But I just kept on and on and got there! It was the most dangerous and difficult operation I have ever done — a fearful fight, with bleeding, cutting and tying on and on for four hours straight. The tumor weighed 85 pounds! It took two men to carry it out and weigh it after I cut it off! I believe that the success of this case is a direct answer to your prayers!"

Perhaps this operation was the greater success because, unknown to Eugene, Edna was interceding for him in Heaven. She was one with him in spirit through those sweating, blood-soaked hours in a way she could never have been, still in the body, half way round the world on a Texas ranch.

Eugene was in the middle of a hot tennis match with his missionary colleagues when the runner from Lusambo walked onto the tennis court with the cable in his hand. It was Hershey Longenecker who took it, saw whom it was for, and handed it to the doctor:

REGRET TO REPORT THE SUDDEN DEATH OF MRS. KELLERS-
BERGER OCTOBER 23. ADVISE KELLERSBERGER REMAIN ON
THE FIELD. CHILDREN WITH MRS. BROWN.
                    Executive Committee of Foreign Missions

That night Andrew Mukeba brought his sleeping mat and blanket and lay on the floor beside Eugene's bed. Each night until the doctor left for the United States, Mukeba was right there, weeping with him through the long, dark hours of those first nights of shocked anguish, uncontrollable grief and the mad frustration of knowing absolutely no details. The suffering thus shared by the two men bound them together into a sacred friendship which lasted the rest of their lives.

The very same night that the news of Edna's death was received, Eugene wrote the following in his prayer notebook:

Anew I dedicate my life, my all to Christ. The loveliest, sweetest thing on earth He has taken away. She wanted me to be a LIVING SACRIFICE for Christ in Africa. O Christ! I dedicate myself anew to Africa! The fellowship of His sufferings is now so very real to me. I am being made conformable to His death for Whom I have suffered the loss of all things. Oh God! Help me to bear the pain, the ache of her being gone! All life was so full of her — nothing I did without her! And now she is GONE! Such emptiness! Fill it with THYSELF! Replace what I have lost with THYSELF, Dear Lord! *Though He slay me, yet will I trust Him!* Let Self be crucified and Christ enthroned in my life because of this experience.

To his parents Dr. Kellersberger wrote in Swiss-German on November 7th: "My heart is broken and I don't know what to do because of the pain. I am powerless to stand it. God must love me to permit all this! "Whom the Lord LOVES He

chastens!" She was too good for this earth. She gave her life
for her father and he was not worthy of it! God be merciful to
me! My heart is bleeding. Pray for me. EUGENE"

On November 11th Eugene wrote one last letter to the
"one who saved me by sharing her Savior with me, loved me
better than herself, was my only sweetheart and for eleven
years, my soul and body."

> To my dear one gone to Heaven:
> It is so very lonely without you here. The sweet times
> of pouring out my heart to you in writing are gone. My
> heart lies so heavy, and when I think of your beauty and
> sweetness and when I see your sweet face, a great, terrible
> pain sweeps over me and I feel sick and weak and miserable
> beyond all conception.
> The joy of your presence is gone. The one great help
> was to know that some day I would take you into my arms
> again, and to know your dear prayers were upholding me in
> power every day. Now your dear heart is still, and that
> sweet mouth no longer speaks, and those beautiful eyes
> can't look at me with all that depth of love. Oh! How I miss
> you and how fearfully lonely I am! God only knows, and
> only to Him can I flee for comfort in this time of irreparable
> loss.
> No man ever had more beautiful, loving companion,
> nor sweeter wife, nor more loving helpmeet. You made 16
> years of my life a heaven on earth. O why did I have to lose
> you? You went in a wave of glory! You did not consider self
> but gave your life for another, doing your duty. You fol-
> lowed in the footsteps of your Savior — you died, the good
> for the unworthy. I am the fearful loser, and those two
> beautiful little girls whom you loved so, and who are so
> much like you. I thank you for giving them to me as a sweet
> remembrance of yourself. No children could have had a
> sweeter mother and they will be worthy of you, I know!
> The pain will not go away. The tears will come. A
> heavy heart lies in my breast.

Believing that Dr. Kellersberger's "best consolation in
his overwhelming bereavement lay in his work," and wishing
to spare him heart-rending weeks of lonely ocean travel, the
Executive Committee advised him to remain at his post. A

week after receiving the cable, still completely unaware of how Edna's death occurred, Eugene began the overland hammock trip to the riverport, the riverboat journey to the lower Congo, and the ocean voyage back to the United States. He returned against the advice of the Committee, but with the full consent of all his fellow missionaries on the field, feeling compelled to see his children and arrange personally for their future.

Traveling with Eugene were Julia and Bob Bedinger, with whom the Kellersbergers had worked at Lusambo. Also aboard the *Thysville,* when it sailed from Matadi on December 1st, was a Mrs. Leona B. Brookman, a wealthy American passenger from Denver, Colorado, who was returning to the United States after visiting a station of the Africa Inland Mission which she personally supported.

At Grand Bassam on the Ivory Coast, the *Thysville* met the outcoming Belgian Maritime Company steamer with mail for Eugene, addressed care of the Bedingers, containing the full account of Edna's murder. Dr. Kellersberger recalled this experience in later years:

> Bedinger hesitated to show me the letters. But Mrs. Brookman insisted, "He has to know! Let him read them!" And thus I finally learned on December 19th the truth of how my Edna died on October 23rd. I lay in my bunk in my cabin, literally sick from the shock of it all. Mrs. Brookman came down to my cabin with Bob Bedinger and while I was sobbing and crying out in agony, she put her arms about me and kissed me and called me her boy. When I was calmer, she prayed with me. She was a real mother to me then and I'll never forget it. I thank God for her, for she made that terrible trip home more bearable, with her constant comfort and attentions. God sent her to help me in time of need. He so often does this for us.

On January 3rd the *Thysville* reached Antwerp, Belgium. Five days later Eugene and the Bedingers sailed for New York on the S.S. *Belgenland.* On January 28, 1928, he reached Concord, North Carolina, carrying an African Gray parrot in a cage, a gift for his two little girls brought all the way from the Belgian Congo. Winifred never forgot the sight of that shivering, hunched-over bird in its battered cage, its bedraggled red tail the only bit of brave brightness in a room dark with grief. Her father's total devastation, the lines of sorrow etched into his face, made his daughter's heart ache for her daddy. She climbed onto his lap and patted his face and hugged him, trying her best to comfort him. He was a new daddy that she had never seen before, so quiet and burdened, so exhausted after the long, draining weeks of travel and acute emotional strain.

But already one of the answers to the "WHY?" of the whole chain of tragic events was on its way. A letter arrived from Mr. Charles Lukens Huston, the steel magnate from Coatesville, Pennsylvania, who had given the first ten thousand dollars for building the hospital at Bibanga. It was his desire that the hospital he had given be henceforth called:

THE EDNA KELLERSBERGER MEMORIAL HOSPITAL

Like the sun's rays breaking through the dark clouds of a departing storm, a wonderful smile broke over Dr. Kellersberger's face. Edna, "being dead" would "yet speak" on and on down through the years in the place of compassionate healing bearing her name. Deep in the heart of Africa there would always be her special place of loving ministry, given in the name of the Lord Jesus Christ whom she loved and followed to the end.

There to Bibanga he would return as soon as possible, to throw all his gifts and energies into serving together with her, seeking to eradicate the scourge of sleeping sickness, for as many years as the Lord would permit him to do so.

The bronze marker to "Beloved Mama" set into the brick wall of the original unit of the Bibanga hospital in Zaire quotes John 15:13 in Tshiluba and in French: "*Greater love has no one than this, than to lay down one's life for his friends.*"

The grass-roofed combination residence and dispensary, beneath the big diwole tree on Bibanga mission station hilltop.

Edna Kellersberger Memorial Hospital, Bibanga, Belgian Congo. Ward patients in the sunshine.

Kellersberger Memorial Hospital

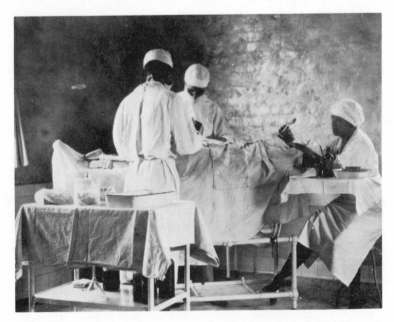

Dr. Kellersberger performing major surgery, assisted by Samuel Lubilaji, whom he trained, and Miss Ruby Rogers, R.N., giving the anesthesia.

[10]

The Acid Test

The years 1924 through 1929 were for Dr. Kellersberger a time of brutal spiritual and physical testing. He always referred to them as his "Acid Test." His total immersion in the incredible vat of human suffering about him demanded every last ounce of all the professional skill and training he had. His physical stamina was daily strained to the limit as he faced increasingly crowded clinics, impossible surgical loads single-handed, and frantic emergency calls away from the station. He often spent a sleepless night responding to some desperate "come quick" from a high-ranking state official, a mining agent or a degenerate, loose-living "trader" out in the bush, then reported as usual to his seven A.M. clinic.

The sheer volume of the work he did in the public health field alone, as he discovered and treated a total of 10,530 new cases of African sleeping sickness, is unbelievable! Added to the physical tension and fatigue of the medical work was the psychological distress of depression and loneliness. There was no one to whom he could release the pent-up stress of a difficult surgical feat or a gruelling forced march to answer a sick call in the pouring rain.

THE FATHER AND HIS CHILDREN

Leaning against the railing of the riversteamer paddling swiftly down the rapid, flood-season current of the Kasai to Kinshasa, the widower pondered his children's future. Several homes had been offered for them. By the time that sad ocean voyage, so filled with grievous inner turmoil, was over, Eugene had decided that he would take his Winifred and Cornelia to live with the Herman Matterns in Kansas City, Missouri. Even back in 1916, when he and Edna had first sailed for the Belgian Congo, the childless Matterns had offered their home for any children that might be born out on the field. In 1920, on that first furlough, their offer was again warmly renewed. And again, even more insistently, a cable sent immediately following Edna's death, begged for the two little girls.

So generations were leaped and remarkable ties with the past were stretched to include the medical missionary's children, as they went to live with their great-uncle. He and Eugene's mother, Helene, had been the small wards of their grandparents, Pastor Adolf Fuchs and his wife, Luise, following the death of their father, Carl Matern. Bitter experiences of World War I had led Carl's son to anglicize the <u>Matern</u> name by inserting a second "t," throwing the accent onto the first syllable.

In March 1924, came the long-dreaded trial at Meridian, Texas. Both Eugene and Uncle Herman Mattern took Winifred there on the train to be the key witness for the prosecution. Grandmother Helene Kellersberger came from Marble Falls to be the little girl's constant companion during those strange, frightening days. One of several headlines in the *Kansas City Star* at that time read: CHILD'S TESTIMONY SENDS SLAYER OF MOTHER TO PRISON IN FAMOUS BOSCHE TRIAL AT MERIDIAN, TEXAS.

The jury found the defendant guilty of murder as charged in the indictment and assessed her punishment of twenty years in the penitentiary. But as many predicted, this sentence was never fully served. The defendant was later pardoned by the state governor and lived a free life until her death many years later.

THE NEW PARTNER

Dr. Kellersberger had requested to be free from all speaking engagements during the few brief months that he was in the United States caring for his family's needs. Finally, however, in response to the Bob Bedingers' repeated urgings, he accepted an engagement on May 1st, at the First Presbyterian Church of Knoxville, Tennessee. Even more reluctantly, he agreed to be the keynote speaker for the Young People's Life Work Conference at the same church, the weekend of May 10th and 11th.

In between the two Knoxville engagements, the doctor returned to Kansas City for his ordination. Forty members of Upper Missouri Presbytery, meeting at the Kansas City YMCA under the leadership of Dr. Ray Dobbins, officially ordained him at that session as a minister of the Presbyterian Church in the United States.

Returning to Knoxville for the youth conference, the Reverend Doctor Kellersberger was a guest of old Mrs. Dooley and her daughter, Carrie. On the wall of their guest room, where he slept, was a picture of Miss Julia Lake Skinner, who had been for two years the Director of Christian Education for the First Presbyterian Church of Knoxville. Now in New York City, she was graduating from The Biblical Seminary the last week of May. While working in Knoxville, Miss Skinner had lived with the Dooleys, staying in the very room in which Eugene was now the guest.

The medical missionary's first casual glance at the picture on the wall overwhelmed him with the painfully startling realization of a striking resemblance to Edna. Back he kept coming to the spot where Miss Skinner's picture hung, staring in disbelief at the serene features of one whom he instinctively knew to be as loving-hearted and dedicated a woman as his own Edna had been.

Suddenly, in the midst of unpacking his suitcase, he turned, strode over to the wall and took the picture down. Kneeling beside the bed, he held the photograph in his hands, looked at the face, and prayed that God would permit him to meet her before he sailed on June 24th to return to the Belgian Congo.

On May 23rd Eugene received his first letter from twenty-six-year-old Miss Skinner, written from New York in response to a letter from him, requesting to meet her. It was agreed that they would meet in Knoxville on Sunday, June 1st. She would stay with the Dooleys, and he, with the A. P. Whites. This was the beginning of what he called "God's acid test," the day when God said to him, "Here she is, but you can't actually have her for six years!"

By the time the first meeting between Miss Skinner and Dr. Kellersberger took place on that fateful Sunday morning, the whole First Presbyterian Church of Knoxville knew that their beloved young "D.C.E." and the widowed missionary were meant for each other. Everyone was agog, excitedly wondering who in the congregation would actually have the honor of introducing them to each other.

Dr. Samuel McPheeters Glasgow in his sermon that morning preached from the text, *Weeping may endure for a night, but joy comes in the morning.* (Psalm 30:5 N.E.B.) This message, heard by Eugene on this special day, clearly indicated the setting aside of the precious "Edna Chapters" of his life, with all their memories of shared joys, ecstasies, grief and tears. He had had five years of the purest, happiest courtship and engagement a man could ever know and eleven years of the closest, most perfectly intimate marriage a man could ever experience. Dr. Glasgow's message signalled the breaking of a thrilling new day for the missionary, the far-reaching implications of which he was only dimly aware. After this service he was to see the face of the one who, when the six years of testing were over, would walk by his side for thirty-seven years. She would share with him not only the remaining years of his medical ministry in the Belgian Congo, but the as-yet-undreamed-of, unbelievably fruitful years of his world-wide ministry to the victims of leprosy.

It was Mrs. George McCully who was the lucky member by whom the doctor was seated by the usher. The split second the service ended, she leaned over and asked,

"Have you met Miss Julia Lake Skinner?"

"No, but I'd like to!"

"Oh! She's WONDERFUL! I'll introduce you!"

Julia Lake at the rear of the auditorium had already searched the congregation and found the tall, slender figure of the man she was soon to meet. As he turned to walk out of the pew, she saw his face. Her heart literally somersaulted at the beauty of the purity and depth of character she saw there. On the spur of that moment she prayed a very unmaidenly prayer: "O Lord! THERE HE IS! DON'T let him get away!"

A few moments later, they were being introduced, standing in front of the pulpit. Each knew with the first, direct eye-contact that they were destined for the other. Along the margin of that Sunday's church bulletin Eugene wrote: "We met in His house, on His day, before His altar, doing His work, His word in our hands! EBENEZER! JEHOVAH-JIREH! MIZPAH! HALLELUJAH!"

The reference to EBENEZER, "Thus far the Lord has helped us," from I Samuel 7:12, covered the past, the years with Edna. That to JEHOVAH-JIREH, "The Lord will provide," found in Genesis 22:14, was the promise that came true in meeting Miss Julia Lake Skinner. MIZPAH, "May the Lord watch between me and you, when we are absent, one from the other," (Genesis 31:49) referred to their extended parting. HALLELUJAH! was a shout of praise!

THE JULIA LAKE SKINNER STORY

The young woman who was to be Dr. Eugene Kellersberger's second wife was born at Linden, Morengo County, Alabama, on November 23, 1897, a healthy nine-pound baby. For the first six months of her life she was called Mary Josephine Skinner. Suddenly, one day, when she was six months old, her frail, ailing father announced to his wife, "I want one of our children to be named for you! Today we are changing Mary Josephine's name to JULIA LAKE SKINNER!"

The baby's mother, nee Julia Lake Woolf, was a direct descendant of General James Woolf, the courageous young British general killed at the age of thirty-two in the 1759 siege of Quebec. She was named for a much loved Alabama teacher, a Miss Julia Lake, principal of well-known female academy in Mobile. There were a number of Miss Julia

Lake's namesakes scattered over the state of Alabama, all of whom carefully preserved the double name.

When little Julia Lake was only eight months old, her father, James Lister Skinner, judge of the probate court, a highly respected citizen, died of acute appendicitis at the age of forty-two. His wife was left with five children to care for. Judge Skinner came from the same family as that of the famous actor, Otis Skinner, and his equally famous actress daughter, Cornelia Otis Skinner. A strong personality trait of the Skinner family has always been a dramatic flair for forceful speech and the ability "to tell a good story," holding an audience completely enthralled. Baby Julia Lake was destined to grow up and demonstrate this unusual gift for public speaking to an amazing degree, to thousands of spellbound listeners, first as the official representative of the Board of Christian Education of the Presbyterian Church in the United States, and in later years, as the wife of the General Secretary of the American Leprosy Missions.

Ill with malaria and worn with nursing both her sister and invalid husband, Mrs. Skinner was never physically able to nurse or care properly for her youngest child. At the age of eight months the baby weighed less than she did at birth. She was allergic to cow's milk, the only infant food-substitute available on the plantation, so was fed only boiled rice water. She cried constantly from hunger, quieting down only after a big dose of Mrs. Winslow's Soothing Syrup, which contained a potent sedative.

Mrs. Skinner was so ashamed of her scrawny, starving waif that she swaddled her in layers of clothes whenever guests came, so that no one could see the pitiful, malnourished skeleton of a little body. She often despaired of her daughter's life, but was greatly assured by an elderly minister who visited her home. He said to Mrs. Skinner, "Your child is not going to die. Her lungs are too strong! Remember that every life is immortal till that life's work is done!"

It was little Julia Lake's black nurse, Ruth, who quietly took matters into her own hands. Without a word to the baby's mother, she began taking the wee, wasted one to the kitchen. There Clora May Keziah Smith Ravizee, the plantation cook, daily baked huge pans of cornbread which were fed to the Judge's renowned pack of thirty prized bird dogs. Secretly Ruth began to feed Julia Lake chunks of hot cornbread soaked in "pot-likker," the juice of collard greens cooked with slabs of sow-belly bacon. Suddenly the baby girl began to thrive, greedily sucking up the soupy bits of cornbread from a spoon. Again, when she almost died of smallpox, it was the kindly ministrations of her black plantation friends, as well as her mother's, that God used to save this threatened little life for His great, long-range purpose.

The Skinner family moved several times as the strong-willed, courageous widow utilized the most acceptable way of providing for and educating her children — running a boardinghouse for the students of the institutions her own sons were attending. The move to Augusta, Georgia, was for Julia Lake's sake, so that she might be enrolled in Tubman, an excellent high school for girls. Her valedictory speech from that school, on the subject, "What Georgia Owes Her Women," printed in full in the Augusta daily paper, is amazingly modern in feminist sentiment and implication!

Then came four happy years at Agnes Scott College in Decatur, Georgia, made possible by service scholarships and the sacrificial cooperation of all her family. The unexpected payment of a long-forgotten debt to her father provided for her railway ticket to go to college. In an era when "middy blouses" were the accepted uniform for college girls, Julia Lake was able to stay quite respectably clothed, even on the barest minimum of monthly allowances. She graduated in 1919, an honored member of Mortar Board, and was hired immediately to teach English at Tubman High School the following academic year.

During the summer of 1920, Miss Skinner taught a *Bible* course at Montreat, North Carolina, the summer conference grounds of the Presbyterian Church in the United States. Standing at the back of the auditorium, carefully observing the enthusiastic young woman with the radiant smile, winning personality and Skinner flair for holding an audience in the palm of her hand, was Dr. Samuel McPheeters Glasgow, pastor of the First Presbyterian Church of Knoxville, Tennessee.

In the Montreat Prayer Room, beside a rushing mountain stream hidden among the rhododendron bushes, Dr.
Glasgow offered Miss Skinner the position of Director of
Christian Education for his church. This was the very spot to
which Dr. Wylie Hamilton Forsythe, in the summer of 1909,
had led Eugene, placing his scarred arm around his shoulder
and praying that he be set aside for medical missionary service
to Africa. Dr. Glasgow prayed, after offering the job, *"Speak,
Lord, for Thy servant heareth!"* He broke the silence that followed
the prayer with the confident words: "The Lord says you are
going to Knoxville!" And she did!

It was during that same summer of 1920 that Julia Lake
Skinner, walking beside Lake Susan, was introduced briefly to
the missionary, Edna Kellersberger, and her daughter, Winifred. All unknowing, the little girl walked for a few minutes,
holding the hands of both of her mothers, her real one and the
"other mother" who would some day also be her father's help-
meet.

After two amazingly successful years at the First Presbyterian Church in Knoxville, Miss Skinner made an important
decision. All her life she had felt called to be an overseas missionary. Indeed, as a child of five years, a large gathering of
women, at the request of her Sunday School teacher, had
prayed that she be set apart for that task. She decided to prepare for missionary service by enrolling in The Biblical Seminary in New York, her chosen field — China.

The two years in New York also proved to be "a school of
faith." Julia Lake had so little money for personal expenses
that she often had no idea how her legitimate needs would be
met. Time and again her dependence upon "The God Who
Provides" was honored. Responsible for meetings on Sunday
mornings in a women's prison, she needed a dollar each week
to cover the cost of carfare to and from the prison. One Saturday morning, lacking even that necessary dollar, she prayed
for "a dollar by 6 a.m. tomorrow morning." Saturday night a
special delivery letter was slipped under her door. It was from
a Knoxville friend and in it was a dollar bill. The enclosed
note read: "I don't know WHY, but the Lord has prompted
me to send this by SPECIAL DELIVERY!" Another time she

Julia Lake Skinner, in 1904, six years old, the age at which she stated: "I am a baby missionary!"

Knoxville, Tennessee, June 1, 1924. Julia Lake Skinner when Dr. Kellersberger first met her in Knoxville, Tennessee.

received an envelope in her mail box with a desperately needed five dollar bill in it, with an anonymous note that read: "God's ravens are not dead yet!"

On the very day that Eugene first saw her picture on the wall of the Dooley's guest room, Julia Lake, preparing to leave The Biblical Seminary, was experiencing a time of deep heart-searching. Of this turning point in her life she later wrote Eugene:

> Before I met you I cried out in an agony of tears before God that He would fill my empty heart with a worthy love. Just two days after that, your first letter came to me! As soon as I read it, with a woman's divine intuition, I <u>knew</u> that God had answered my prayer, and that you had come into my life to stay.

And so it was, that a perfectly prepared Miss Skinner met her future husband on that Sunday of Sundays, June 1, 1924, to become God's carefully selected spiritual and emotional complement to His servant, Eugene. The most grueling, lonely and difficult years of his life lay just ahead of him, as he returned for a full term of service alone on the field. Bereft of his loving life-partner, his only real release was in his letter-writing. In Julia Lake Skinner he found someone to whom he could pour out his heart, as to no one else. Throughout his life he always emphatically stated that having her strong, dedicated support saved not only his professional and missionary career, but even his very sanity and life.

RETURN TO BIBANGA — 1924

The brief stay in London on the way to Europe was a blessing to the doctor, with many friendships and prayer-bonds renewed. The dedicated researcher in him was delighted with the gift of a supply of a brand new sleeping sickness drug made in Vienna. Dr. Gregg of the London School of Tropical Medicine gave it to him, to do research with as he saw fit.

As on the outgoing journey the previous year, Dr. Kellersberger visited the BAYER dye, chemical and drug factory near Cologne, Germany. This time he was not an unnoticed tourist, but a recognized scientist and collaborator in the giant task of proving the best cure for African sleeping sickness. He was met at the train station by one of the chief chemists, Dr. Henning, his assigned personal escort throughout his visit. All the different departments of that amazing establishment were courteously shown to him, as well as the magnificent old city of Cologne, from a private limousine! He was introduced to the director of the BAYER plant, one of the most influential men in all Germany, as well as to Dr. Heymann himself, the inventor of BAYER 205. The latter, a kindly gentleman, was so taken with the missionary doctor's snapshot of his little daughter, Winifred, holding a bottle of BAYER 205, that he begged to be permitted to keep the picture. Best of all, Dr. Kellersberger was allowed to purchase 100 grams of the precious drug, now sold under the brand name of *Germanine*. To his surprise he was also given a supplementary supply to use for experimental purposes, and a most generous donation of complimentary samples of all the BAYER products. The fascinating day in Cologne concluded late in the evening with a lovely tea served by Dr. Henning's British wife, under a shady arbor in the backyard of their elegant home.

The return trip to the Belgian Congo in 1924 took longer than any previously made, three and a half months! On July 22 Eugene left Antwerp, Belgium, on the 8000-ton S.S. *Thysville*, the very same vessel on which he had returned to Europe only six months before, following Edna's death. The painfully familiar surroundings were blessedly brightened by his finding in his cabin a large packet from Miss Skinner, containing forty fat steamer letters! The very last thing each night, before going to sleep, he propped the letter marked with the date of the approaching day, against his *Bible*, right beside his bunk, ready to be opened and read even before the break of dawn. This anticipation alone gave life and meaning to each new day of the journey and continued the transformation of a crushed, broken-hearted worker of the Lord into a brave, valiant warrior.

It was his close personal friends, the Alfred Stonlakes, who welcomed Eugene to the Union Mission House in Kinshasa. Unknowingly, they placed him in the same room in which he and Edna had stayed, on their way to England, when she had sleeping sickness. He dropped to his knees beside the bed where she had lain and once again dedicated himself to carrying on the medical work at what was now her own special hospital.

The first lap of the forty-day journey upriver and back to Bibanga from Kinshasa was made aboard the big double-story SONATRA riverboat, the *Yser*. At the captain's request, the doctor held a clinic at each wood-loading stop, ministering in whatever way he could to the local sick, both black and white. Like Paul on his missionary journeys, wherever he landed, the Christians soon learned that he was aboard and came running to greet him. Whenever he could, he went ashore and worshipped and prayed with whatever little "cell" of the scattered Body of Christ was in that place, encouraging them in the Lord.

It was the second lap of that river journey from Basongo to Lusambo that Eugene especially enjoyed. It was made on a paddlewheeler so tiny that it was called by its number — *Auxiliare III*. The iron decks of this miniature vessel were only three feet wide.

With fatherly affection, Eugene shared in a letter to his little daughters his delight in the strange family of pets aboard the *Auxiliare III*: two African gray parrots, a tame pigeon, a yellow cat and a five-month-old baby monkey. They all ate together out of the same dish! Youdou, the mischievous Redtail monkey (*Cercopithecus ascanius ascanius*), loved to snatch pickles off the passengers' plates when they weren't looking. He cleaned his teeth with a toothpick after meals and once tore to shreds six ten-franc paper bills that the captain had put out on a table, pay for the woodcutters at one of the riverbank wood posts. Wrote Eugene to his children:

> Like you, Youdou has no mama and sometimes he looks sad. But there is a nice old yellow mama cat who has kindly adopted him. She carries him all about the deck on her neck. Whenever he gets tired, he puts his arms around her warm body and lays his head on her soft fur for a pillow.
>
> He is very curious. One day I had the curtains to my cabin pulled down while I was taking my daily "spit bath."

All at once the curtain lifted and there were Youdou's beady little eyes looking at me over his white nose, round mouth and enormous sideburns. Such nerve!

Yesterday he got into a tin of flour. He was a sight! This morning he and the old mother cat cleaned each other up so sweetly. The monkey made a careful search all over the cat's back, removing fleas. Then the cat gave the baby monkey a thorough licking with her tongue. Just now Youdou visited me here in my cabin, leaving his dirty footprints all over the page of a letter I had just finished writing!

To his parents Dr. Kellersberger wrote from the tiny *Auxiliaire III*:

I am looking forward to my work and trying to keep myself absolutely in the Presence of God, so that my longing and homesickness does not overwhelm me, especially when these marvelous tropical moonlight nights try to "hurt my heart." I know that I am following God's will for me. My first obligation is to God and when I fulfill that, I am sure that I will also be found fulfilling my obligation to my fellow-men. All I want is to adore Him with a clean, wonderful life and give myself to the needy people of this needy land.

THE "WARRIOR" RETURNS TO THE BATTLEFIELD

Four consecutive days of tough bicycling from Lusambo, along the narrow forest trails, then, with his faithful runner, Muamba, Eugene quietly slipped unnoticed onto Bibanga station at 9:30 Friday night, September 19th. He dropped exhausted into his waiting bed in the little grass-roofed house beneath the giant *diwole* tree. Some journal entries of the remaining months of 1924 record both the heartaches and the joys of his return:

September 20, 1924 Awoke at 4 a.m. Had two quiet hours of prayer and praise before the crowd learned that I had returned. Then — SUCH a welcome! Now I am again alone in my memory-laden house. I knelt down and thanked Him for the old room where all my joys and sorrows had come and thanked Him for another safe homecoming. I have forsaken all, but I am not alone. A great big mail and glorious answers to prayer await me here.

The new hospital unit is a beauty! Tomorrow Dr. Volke, the head provincial doctor from Elisabethville, is coming to see all the work. It is so hard to welcome guests like this, the very first day of my return, with so many letters waiting to be read!

September 21st   I knelt and prayed with my dear Andrew Mukeba. I have 65 unread letters — such <u>hard mail</u> to read! My Julia Lake is going through such suffering now because of me. How it is costing her!

Am receiving many gifts of chickens and eggs to welcome me back. Lukusa, from whom I removed that 85-lb tumor, brought me a live goat! My article about his case has been printed in the *Journal of the American Medical Association*!

September 23rd   I finally forced myself to read Edna's letter written to me on September 22, 1923, which came last year after I had left Bibanga to return to the United States on account of her death. It was all about her decision to go to her father in Texas. She wrote, telling me how she had gone through her own "human Gethsemane, fasting and praying all day," before making the final decision to go.

October 23, 1924   This is the first anniversary of my Edna's terrible death. It has been <u>such a hard day</u>! I just wanted to be alone, but I HAD to work. I fasted and prayed the whole day, anyway, even while working. Am so glad I had so much to do — it got me through the day. I almost went crazy that first night when I received the news. Something in my brain just seemed to BREAK. When I got to Knoxville in May, I was just desperate! Then God intervened for me and brought me Julia Lake.

November 19th   I am trying to work out a good system for indexing some two thousand medical histories. They got badly mixed up during the six months that I was gone.

Just had a sweet "talk" with my dear savior-lady, 10,000 miles away! I keep a sheet of paper rolled into the typewriter. It makes it seem less lonely when I come home to this house, so full of memories, to be able to sit down and have a typewriter chat with her. I received two special letters from her today. She is writing under grest difficulties because of her mother, poor girl! I have made it so hard for her.

December 31st, 1924   Last day of the old year, the most important year of crisis in my whole life — AND VICTORY! I am going to close this momentous year with a letter to Miss Skinner. I will set my alarm for 11:30 tonight, and keep a midnight watch, so that I can literally walk into the New Year on my knees. May it be the symbol of an humble and obedient walk with Him through the coming year!

In January 1925, came the letter of full acceptance that Eugene had so long prayed and waited for — "her exquisite November 16, 1924 letter in which she gave herself to me — I do believe it is the sweetest thing I possess!" Now at last she was his "Julia Lake," by her own will and choice and he was free to call her by that name.

To his mother, Dr. Kellersberger wrote of the heartache that was to grow bigger and bigger, almost to bursting, over the next three years:

Bibanga, March 29, 1925

My precious mother,

Yesterday I received two very hard and very sad letters from Julia Lake's mother. I have spent the last three hours trying to answer them. I also had a beautiful letter from Julia Lake herself. She loves me forever, but I have now promised to give her TIME. She has been through terrible things with her mother, who says that she will NEVER consent to her daughter's going to ANY foreign field, and that I have no right to love her, or she me.

So it has come to a crisis. Truly her mother has sacrificed everything for the girl and she loves her devotedly. It has about killed her, this fearful strain, and hiding my letters. After a week of prayer about it, she has asked me to do for her the thing that is the very hardest for me to do — to stop writing to her altogether.

So once again I am making a terrible sacrifice, but He is giving me the strength to do it. O God! With these three lonely years ahead out here, could there be a greater or severer test for us than this self-denying life? How many do it like this? Very few! Yes, mother, it may take years for all to work out. But I am ready for such a sacrifice again, in order to stand clear before dear, wonderful Edna! <u>God</u> sent Julia Lake to me! <u>HE</u> brought her to me as a wonderful gift to keep me from losing my mind. O pray for me, that in all of this I may be only "God's nobleman," honoring Him!

Your own Eugene

Throughout the long years of silence, the doctor never doubted for one moment the reality of Julia Lake's love for him, or that, in God's good time she would be given to him. In simple faith he continued to write a daily letter to her, never mailing it, but putting it carefully away until the time of separation would end and he could hand the accumulation of letters to her in person.

Every Sunday afternoon he sat down to his typewriter and wrote a letter, often in Swiss-German, to his parents, and another in English to his children. He found in these, at least, some measure of natural emotional release. He particularly delighted in receiving his Winifred's weekly letters giving childish accounts of music recitals, of President Coolidge's dedication of the Kansas City War Memorial; of Queen Marie of Roumania's visit; of the Hindenburg zeppelin that floated over the city one twilight evening, shortly before it met its fatal end in Bergen, New Jersey; and of the night that Lindberg hopped the Atlantic and Uncle Herman hounded the poor telephone operators every few minutes, asking "Has that young man landed yet?"

Love did build a bridge over the troubled waters and her name was Helene Matern Kellersberger. Eugene's mother faithfully relayed to him every letter that Julia Lake wrote to her, and to Julia Lake she sent all those written by Eugene to his parents in English.

The George McKees, going on furlough, were instructed by the doctor to purchase an engagement ring at Tiffany's in New York, and to have it sent directly to Miss Skinner in Wilmington, North Carolina. In token of the fact that she had received and accepted the ring, but could not yet wear it, Julia Lake cut a curl from her hair, wrapped it all about the ring and placed the double symbol of love in a small drawstring bag. When the McKees returned to Bibanga after furlough, the little bag went with them back to Eugene, with the understanding that he was to keep it until the day when he himself would place it on her finger. Every day of these intervening years, the doctor wore the little bag under his shirt, pinned to his "BVDs," directly over his heart!

OPERATION FOR A CROWN PRINCE

August 6, 1925, was a very special day for Dr. Kellersberger. Not only was it his thirty-seventh birthday, but on that day he also hosted Crown Prince Leopold of Belgium on an official visit to the Edna Kellersberger Memorial Hospital. In preparation for the royal visit, the old mud-and-stick, grass-roofed home beneath the *diwole* tree was torn down. It was the only home that Edna and Eugene had lived in together and had also served as the first clinic and dispensary. How lonely the towering tree looked without its little white-washed companion nestling beneath it! The doctor was temporarily assigned to one of the empty missionary residences, whose occupants were on furlough.

The day before the Crown Prince's scheduled visit to observe representative Protestant work, a patient named Misengayabo registered for the first time at the clinic. She was a small woman, some thirty years of age, a mere skeleton! She could not speak, for out of her mouth protruded an *epulis* of an unusually large size — a foul-smelling, ulcerating tumor as big as an orange. It spread out against each cheek, down over her chin, and pushed her nose up so that she could hardly breathe. She could open her mouth just enough to push a little food in under the mass. Slowly and surely she was starving to death.

For several years this loathsome tumor had been growing. She had tried every remedy suggested by the native witchdoctors and medicine men, to no avail. Finally she was cast out by her husband and beaten and driven from the village by her clan, for being one possessed with an incurable devil. A terrified, doomed expression hovered over what little of her face was not yet covered by the repulsive tumor. No one dared go near her, for all desperately feared her.

With a dirty little basket of cooking utensils on her head, leading her small son by the hand, the grotesque, emaciated slip of a woman tottered the weary miles that lay between her home village and Bibanga mission station, the one place where she had heard that there might be hope for her.

And so Misengayabo was one of several unusual operative cases that Crown Prince Leopold saw as he toured the hospital. Eugene was particularly glad when the prince paused in front of this pitiful, abject caricature of human flesh. He prayed inwardly that the sight of her would make an indelible impression, that the future king might be made aware of the crying needs of the people of his colony, when he came to the throne. Watching the reaction on the prince's face to the sight and smell of Misengayabo, Dr. Kellersberger thought, "God must have sent her to us precisely on this special day, just to glorify His Name!"

Crown Prince Leopold stared at Misengayabo and then turned to the doctor: "Do you mean to say that you intend to operate on this woman, to remove this tumor from her face?" he exclaimed.

"Of course! That's why I'm here, to do this in Christ's Name."

"I am on my way to Kabinda, but will come back through here day after tomorrow. When I return, I want to see this woman!"

It was almost impossible to clean and prepare Misengayabo properly for surgery on August 7th. The anesthesia was most difficult to administer because her nose was almost totally blocked by the tumor. The chloroform finally did take effect. Since the mass was attached to the upper jawbone and teeth, bone-cutting instruments had to be used and the bleeding controlled both by pressure and ligature.

When the Prince and his retinue returned to the Edna Kellersberger Memorial Hospital on schedule on August 8th, Misengayabo was waiting for him. She held in her hands the bottle that contained the osteofibroma removed the day before from her face. The bottle with its contents was presented to the Prince, who took it back to Belgium with him, a unique souvenir of his visit to Bibanga. The deep impression made upon the royal party by Dr. Kellersberger was evident in the October 15, 1925, issue of the Belgian daily paper, *Independance Belge,* in the following report of the crown Prince's trip:

> The Prince left Kabinda on August 8 to begin a circuit of more than 700 kilometers. This journey, averaging 160

kilometers a day, was completed under the most favorable conditions, the Prince himself being at the driver's wheel for most of the tour. He had occasion to visit various interesting establishments, outstanding among them the hospital of the American Presbyterian Congo Mission at Bibanga, where Dr. Kellersberger, attached to that mission, dedicates himself to his work in the true spirit of an Apostle! (Translation from the original French by the author.)

The whole hospital community at Bibanga enjoyed watching Misengayabo rediscover her face. A mirror was given to her so that she could look at herself. Her joy was pathetic! She had forgotten how to open her mouth properly, so her tongue hung out in a ridiculous manner for several days until she learned how to control it. Her first attempts at smiling were also ludicrous. By the time she was ready to return to her home village three weeks later, her joy was so overwhelming that the "smile-muscles" of her face miraculously resurrected. All she did was smile and smile and smile! Down she went onto her knees, when she came to the doctor to say goodbye. She clapped her hands in the fashion of African courtesy, repeating "Thank you! Thank you!", over and over again.

As Misengayabo walked out of the hospital grounds, tall and proud, her body already filling out, her skin already glossy with health, voices called out to her the same that Jesus said to the demon-possessed man He had healed: "Go home to your friends, and tell them what great things the Lord has done for you, and how He has had compassion on you." (Mark 5:19)

THE STAGGERING WORKLOAD
OF A MISSIONARY DOCTOR

To his colleagues in the medical profession Dr. Kellersberger wrote a most interesting letter in 1926:

I am swamped these days, with the sick coming in in hordes! The variety of the work here is infinite. A neighboring chief, as a result of seeing an operation, became interested in my work and decided that he must help me. One Saturday morning he marched in with his retinue and his police, and presented me with two of his men in chains. He said, "Ngangabuka, (Witchdoctor), I have brought you these men for you to operate on. They refused to come, so I put them in chains and here they are!" Think of it! An African chief recruiting patients for me, though I really have more than enough without his help!

The crocodiles also help to bring in practice. Several weeks ago a fine, strong young fellow was caught on the left leg in shallow water by a huge "croc." The men who were with him pulled him away. He came to me with a fearfully chewed-up leg, which we had to amputate below the knee.

I had two very hard operations last Friday, a goiter and a very large, involved fibroid uterus. I had to do a complete amputation on the latter. I have done very few of these. It is only by the grace of God that I have gone ahead. It took me nearly three hours. All the organs were grown to the big tumor, also the appendix. When I got through it all, I was pretty well done in! These operations cost me much in physical strength and endurance, but they are worthwhile.

It is to such as these that I like to minister. The bravery and stoicism of these people is marvelous. They make perfect operative patients, very rarely complaining! They will lie on their backs on a hard board bed for a week without turning or even murmuring, if you tell them to. Another striking fact is their utter faith. They submit like a child to all that is done to them, never asking a question, never doubting. They have a sublime faith that is an inspiration to me. In every service in the hospital church someone prays that God will give me *lungenyi lule,* "deep wisdom" to heal the many sick that pour in each day. Before every operation we have a little talk with the patient, pointing him to Jesus Christ, and then, with the laying on of hands, we have a prayer and commit the surgical work to God, Whose we are and Whom we serve.

To find some anodyne for his constant loneliness, the doctor literally buried himself in his work. At times the work almost buried him. During the first complete year of work at the Edna Kellersberger Memorial Hospital, he held consultations with 17,599 patients. Under his supervision 1400 blood examinations were made for malaria, sleeping sickness and tick fever. For the diagnosis of sleeping sickness, in its later stages 436 lumbar punctures and 456 gland punctures were made. To 295 cases of African sleeping sickness 2500 intravenous injections were given. One white doctor, assisted by one white nurse and fourteen Congolese aides, did ninety-three operations, all of this in a three-unit brick hospital with a thirty-bed capacity. The daily average attendance at the clinic that first year was 57.7 patients. Diseases treated most frequently included 263 cases of subtertian malaria, but only two of the very rare quartan malaria, hookworm (594), tropical ulcers (245), tick fever (20), hernias (52), schistosoma (108), plus assorted cases of meningitis, leprosy, yaws, amoebic and bacillary dysentery, smallpox, goiters and elephantiasis.

In 1926 the consultations made by one doctor increased to 23,427 with daily average attendance of 78 in the clinic. By 1927 there were 56,787 consultations, with a daily average attendance of 181 in the clinic. New patients registered in that one year numbered 6,162.

FIGHTING AFRICA'S GREATEST PLAGUE — SLEEPING SICKNESS, 1926–1928

As a licensed state doctor, Dr. Kellersberger was responsible for the entire population of the Lubilashi valley of the Kasai area of the Belgian Congo. His years of intense work for the eradication and control of African sleeping sickness are best described in his own words:

March 18, 1926 African sleeping sickness is transmitted as well as carried by only one particular family of flies, the *tsetse* flies, large aggressive, persistent bloodsuckers. These flies live only in Africa and are found along the Congo streams and watercourses in countless numbers. Fortunately, the majority of them are not infected. They are the natural host of the parasite that causes human sickness, namely, the *trypanosome*. This is a long, protozoal, single-celled parasite with an eyespot, a nucleus, a body and a backfin ending in a whiplike tail, by which it moves very quickly in the blood, lymph fluid, or brain fluids. When an infected fly bites a human being successfully, it injects one or more of these *trypanosomes* into the blood, where they multiply rapidly. In a few weeks slow, and then high, irregular

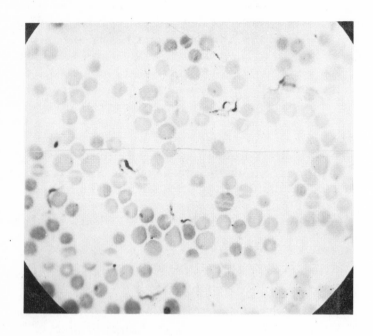

Trypanosoma gambiense. *Microphoto of trypanosomes in blood, indicating African sleeping sickness.*

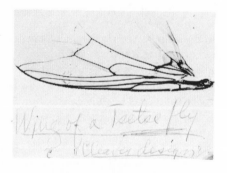

Wing of a Tsetse Fly

fevers appear. The body aches all over, there are headaches, nervousness, a rash, great weakness. After several months the glands begin to swell. The fever goes away, but gradually there are signs that the *trypanosomes* have invaded the brain, causing the poisoning, inflammation and destruction of tissue. When spinal fluid is taken, it is found to be cloudy, rather than normally clear, and the parasites are found in the fluid. Never confuse this disease with *lethargic encephalitis*, the type of "sleeping sickness" found in Europe and America. That is an entirely different disease.

Patients go to sleep on the benches. They sit up, then slowly their heads sink down. Often the whole body lies down on the knees in a stuporous sleep from which they rouse at times with a start.

It became evident that only a small percentage of the population came voluntarily to be examined. Most of the unfortunates do not even know that they have the disease until it is too late. With the efficient cooperation of Mr. Demeester, the intelligent young Sanitary Agent of the Belgian government, plans were made to visit all the surrounding tribes to examine for the disease. I spent several weeks away from the Bibanga station, examining some 17,000 men, women and children. Four hundred new cases were discovered, in all stages of advancement. Every one of these were then treated. In one tribe 25 miles south of here 110 cases were found among 4,000 people.

We have come to the conclusion that the best drug is *Tryparsamide*, developed by our Rockefeller Institute, and now widely used out here. It is especially adapted to field work, as it can be given quickly, without much pain. It is especially useful in the later cases, where the nervous system is affected. As a rule it takes only eight injections. The native patient is willing to come for this, as he sees such a marked change in his condition. The German drug, Bayer 205 (*Germanine*) has been found to be useful only in earlier cases, when the central nervous system is not yet seriously invaded. *Atoxyl* also cures in earlier cases but there is danger from blindness, and requires five months of painful intramuscular injections, which patients don't like.

May 1, 1927 I can't write much this time. I am terribly busy. The government is beginning to wake up. This month sleeping sickness cases are POURING in as a result of my

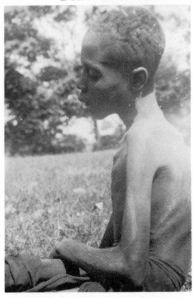

The doctor's graph of Sleeping Sickenss cases treated at the Edna Kellersberger Memorial Hospital, Bibanga, 1925–1931.

Sleeping sickness patient, sleeping his life away. Bibanga, 1927.

sending out my native nurses with the state agent. In April 303 cases came in! Yesterday we were literally swamped with a clinic of 294 people. We gave 150 injections. There are more operative cases than usual. I have a waiting list. The work is now at its best. We are crowded to overflowing in our temporary village of grass huts that we have had to construct to house the hordes of patients.

But the work at the Edna Kellersberger Memorial Hospital was not concerned only with the healing of the body. That was only the beginning of the services rendered there in Christ's name:

The hospital is organized also from an educational and a spiritual standpoint. If we send these poor people back to their heathendom and ignorance from which they came, we might just as well pack up and return to America. Christ first healed the body in order that He might later heal the mind and the soul. That is the primary purpose of the Edna Kellersberger Memorial Hospital and may it never have any purpose other than that! "In the Name of Jesus Christ, stand up and walk!"

A large grass-roofed shed has been built to house both a church and a school. A full-time evangelist and teacher work there every day, assisted by ten other teachers. The thirteen student nurses also share in the teaching load in the afternoons. Every resident in the hospital village of several hundred people attends. Many also voluntarily attend the regular Sunday morning worship services and the early morning chapel service on weekdays. They leave the hospital village knowing how to read, and with a basic concept of the fundamentals of Christianity.—

Ninety-five percent of the patients are unable to pay any fees, so there is a daily work line. Every patient who is able to do so works several hours a day under the direction of one of their own men, as foreman. I believe that a little work and exercise are conducive to better health and a quicker recovery, and it also keeps them out of trouble! They plant grass, clean the compound and are now making sundried brick for a new ward and hospital kitchen. They all seem to be happy here! At least far more come than I can possibly take care of!

1928 — JUST HANGING IN THERE

Once again, Eugene was the only doctor on the American Presbyterian Congo mission, responsible for the care of the personnel of five mission stations scattered over some 83,000 square miles of south-central Belgian Congo. The enormity of the daily pressure under which he worked is witnessed to by the fact that this period of his life is one in which his lovingly-kept daily journals went untouched for days at a time. Scrawled, sketchy entries are interspersed with blank pages. The magnitude of the medical work he organized and oversaw would have killed someone of lesser physical stamina than his.

There were also uncharacteristic breaks in his correspondence with his little daughters and his parents. Winifred haunted the mailbox beside the front steps of the Mattern home, always hoping for a letter from her Daddy. The letters that did come during 1927 and 1928 were often just scribbled notes enclosing rose petals from Edna's bush, carefully pressed for her child. Increasingly, in the letters he did write, were references to his malarial fevers, frequent colds and a deadening, numbing fatigue that would not go away. His weight at this trying time of his life stayed around 130 pounds, too little for a man lacking only a fraction of being six feet tall.

There was also the constant burden of a physical "thorn in the flesh" which Eugene, like the Apostle Paul, bore, though he fervently prayed for its removal. He called it his "Third Cross," and said of it, "I cherish it as a sign of His love for me." These years of constant nervous strain and physical depletion aggravated his disability. He would pay the price for his overexertion later.

Weekends brought no respite from his work load, only a difference in kind. He always went without breakfast on Sunday mornings in order to have time for quiet preparation of his sermon. He never forgot that he was an ordained minister as well as a physician. If he was not the designated preacher at the station church or hospital chapel, he was off on his bicycle to hold services in two or three villages away from the station. Every Sunday afternoon his cherished Sunday School class of young men gathered on his front porch for a thoughtful, prayed-over *Bible* lesson, prepared sometimes at the cost of even more sleep.

The battle with depression and fatigue is clearly evident in letters at this time:

> *March 4, 1928*   I love my mail and it sort of keeps me going. I always have the secret, nagging hope that maybe there will be a letter from my Julia Lake! It is just <u>terrible</u> to live without any real news of her. At times I just can't bear it all! I am going to quit writing for a while right now, before I begin to write really "blue" things. God knows how much we are able to bear.
>
> I'll be so glad when these four years are over. My poor children! My poor Julia Lake! My heart gets sort of numb with pain and ache at times. I guess it is getting used to it. It seems these days as if I am just too tired to get up in the morning to have my Quiet Time. The work is so insistent. These past five years have tested me to the breaking point. We are having an epidemic of bad colds and sort of a grippe. I've had a light attack of it.
>
> There are so few of us left out here on this mission field, to "hold the bag." The church at home must be blind!

They don't seem to be aware of our personnel needs and how we are suffering now for lack of funds and workers. The field force is lower this year than ever before and with the great debt this year, we have no hope for reinforcements. I can't set any date for going on furlough until there is at least one other doctor here on the field.

How long can this intolerable situation go on? I cry to God each day about it. My only consolation is that He loves us and knows what is best for us. He will solve it for us.

March 19, 1928 I am just back from the most exacting trip I have ever made, the fourth emergency journey I have had to make in three weeks. It has taken all my energy and much of my sleep. I am also sick with a bad sore throat.

I had to make a 50-mile detour in order to get within ten miles of where the young stateman was sick. I walked the last ten miles through bush and high grass and in the pouring rain by the light of a kerosene lantern. I tried to get a caravan to help me carry my medical equipment but failed. The trail was so slippery! We had to cross two big swollen rivers in the dark in native dugout canoes. I had to FORCE the boatmen to ferry me over! I hung on over those last weary miles only by prayer — thought we would NEVER get there! Got there soaking wet. They had no bed for me, so I sat in a chair, shivering until dawn, after treating my patient.

Oh! Oh! Oh! I am <u>so starved</u> for a home, a wife, my children, my friends and loved ones! I am desperate for my Julia Lake! This must be the dark before the dawn, for it has never been so long with so little real news of her. It gets to be simply intolerable at times. She was His chosen vessel to keep my bruised life from going on the rocks. Truly our prayers have been answered to the very limit, when we asked of Him that we be "those two lives that would be wholly consecrated to Him!"

One of the most fearful experiences Dr. Kellersberger had in his medical missionary career was described in a letter to his mother, written on May 27, 1928:

This has been one of the hardest weeks I have ever had. I got back last night from Kabinda, where I have been for three days. I think I wrote you about the woman who was brought in here several months ago, almost cut to pieces because she had been accused by her husband of "eating" the life of a child of another woman by witchcraft.

We worked very hard and saved her life. She was ready to go to Kabinda in a few days, when the same fiend who had tried to kill her before, came at sunset to the hospital and in a fearful, horrible way, literally chopped her head off right at the hospital door.

I got there three minutes after it was all over. A huge mob had followed the man into the tall grass to catch him. They did catch him and would have killed him if I had not prevented them, even though I wanted to kill him myself!

For two days we had an awful time. We sent for the nearest stateman. He was new, with no knowledge of the native language, so I had to do all the interpreting of the facts for him into French. We had to round up all the witnesses and send them ahead to Kabinda.

On Thursday the stateman and I left to take the murderer to Kabinda, the three of us traveling in the medical car. Half way there we had a breakdown. If a mining company truck had not come along just then, we would have had to spend the night there with that truly dangerous criminal tied down in the automobile. Thank God He sent that mine truck!

I spent three days in Kabinda, was called to testify before the judge. Now I'm back tired and worn out from the terror of it all. These are such strenuous days!

RETURN JOURNEY TO THE U.S.A. VIA EAST AFRICA

With the arrival of Dr. George Cousar at Lubondai station, Eugene was at last free to go on furlough. He left Bibanga on September 12, 1928, going to the nearest railroad point of Kabalo with George McKee in his Dodge. Ten hours and 900 miles from there by train was the Lake Tanganyika port of Albertville, where Dr. Kellersberger boarded the lakesteamer *Urundi* for the twelve-hour voyage up the long lake to Kigoma on the eastern shore. Then followed a forty-six-hour train trip across British East Africa. With a sigh of delighted relief, Eugene resumed writing in his daily journal, making such notes as:

East Africa is weird, high, dry country. I've seen great herds of baboons and roan antelope, zebra and giraffes. <u>And</u> beautiful Kilimanjaro, 21,000 feet high! The half-way point to the coast is Tabora. 800 miles of this railway, begun by the Germans in 1905, were completed by 1914. And they lost it all to the British in 1918!

On September 20th Dr. Kellersberger sailed from Dar es Salaam on the 9000-ton Peninsula and Orient-British India Steam Navigation vessel, the *Madiana*.

From the *Madiana* on September 29th, Eugene wrote in his journal:

It is very quiet on this ship for it is the "off-season." There are only 53 passengers in all and 25 of these are traveling second class.

I find that I have forgotten how to rest. That's the very reason why I decided to take this longer route back to the United States, to give myself some time to learn how to relax again. Somehow, I am now feeling the fearful strain of the past five years more than ever. I have not found any companionship aboard as yet. For once I have time to read, and am reading a novel. Maybe it will help me to quit thinking about medicine. I believe the Lord just wants me to lie down and be quiet for a while.

The remainder of that restful, interesting voyage included a stop at Port Said on the Red Sea and passage through the 112-mile long Suez Canal. On October 16th the doctor disembarked at Marseilles, France, and proceeded by train to Paris, where he spent a week with his friend, Herman Norden, author of travel books, who had been his guest at Bibanga while working on *Fresh Tracks in the Belgian Congo*. After a few days' visit with old friends in London, Eugene sailed on the 25,000 ton *Adriatic* on November 1st, arriving in New York on November 19th. "Back home!", he exulted, "Kept all these years, these journeyings, amid perils, by HIM! Truly He is a prayer-hearing and a prayer-answering God!"

On November 29th, Thanksgiving Day, Dr. Eugene Kellersberger and Miss Julia Lake Skinner met at the Westminster Presbyterian Church in St. Louis, Missouri. They had not seen each other since June 8, 1924, four and a half years. Even then, they had known each other for only a few, brief days!

When Eugene entered the quiet sanctuary, softly aglow with sunlight slanting through the stained glass windows, there seemed to be no sign at all of the one he was desperately seeking. Back and forth he paced in front of the pulpit, nervously glancing at the different entrances, anticipating her coming.

From the back of the sanctuary, hidden behind a massive pillar, Julia Lake watched him, her heart beating a tattoo so rapid she could hardly breathe. Each time his back was turned in his constant pacing, she slipped to the next pillar down the side aisle, till finally she stepped out from behind the last one. When he turned again, there she was, quietly standing right in front of him, both arms extended in welcome.

Within the next few minutes the worn little drawstring bag was pulled from Eugene's pocket. The ring, still wrapped in its soft casing of a matted curl of brown hair, tarnished with the years of waiting, was slipped by a trembling hand onto a small, steady, confident finger.

[11]

Leprosy: A New Direction

The decade, 1930–1940, broken by one furlough in 1935–1936, was a crucial period of transition in Dr. Kellersberger's career. It was during these years that his interest gradually shifted from general tropical medicine and surgery to specialization in Hansen's Disease, commonly called "leprosy." These were also pivotal years of firsthand experience in organizational administration and fund raising, a direct result of the Great Depression and its effects on the work of the American Presbyterian Congo Mission during the 1930s.

Wedding bells did not ring out immediately after that momentous reunion in Westminster Church in St. Louis on Thanksgiving Day, 1928. There remained yet another course in self-discipline and patience for the doctor to experience before he could once again know the joyous companionship of a marriage partner.

Even though Julia Lake's mother adamantly refused to meet her daughter's fiancé, a sympathetic brother, Conway Skinner, welcomed the doctor into his home on the campus of the Berry Schools, near Rome, Georgia, and gave his hearty approval of the marriage. May 12, 1929 was set as the wedding date and reservations were made on the S.S. *Arabic*, for

251

the united family to sail from New York to Belgium and the
Congo, on August 3, 1929.

Eugene did not realize how worn out he was from his
draining years of work alone in Africa. A debilitating bout of
flu further weakened him. Very unwisely, during what proved
to be a winter of record-breaking cold, he agreed to three solid
months of unremitting travel and speaking engagements in a
dozen different states. In April, the following communication
was sent to those on the doctor's mailing list:

> After months of very strenuous itinerating in the inter-
> est of the Foreign Missions Committee, Dr. Kellersberger
> felt an urgent need of rest and consulted his doctors in St.
> Louis and Nashville. To his amazement, they demanded a
> complete rest for an indefinite period of time, to be taken for
> the sake of his future work in Africa. They were strongly
> and unanimously of the opinion that, if he returned as
> planned, he would be unable to remain on the field without
> a complete nervous breakdown.
>
> The wedding has been postponed indefinitely. Miss
> Skinner will continue her work with the Christian Educa-
> tion Committee. The doctor will follow strict orders to rest,
> that he may return to the Congo at the earliest possible date
> consistent with efficient service.

To his loved ones Eugene wrote:

> I am as nervous as an old cat, really needing rest and
> quiet! The doctors tell me that I am on the verge of a nerv-
> ous breakdown. This doesn't frighten me, but I realize that
> the time has come to stop for a while, physically! The home-
> coming missionary makes a real mistake when he insists on
> taking a heavy speaking load immediately upon his return
> from the field.
>
> Now I am paying for the overwhelmingly demanding
> years alone in Africa, for my Edna's death, for that stren-
> uous schedule of speaking engagements I accepted, and a
> hard bout of flu at Christmas. I overdid it.
>
> The good side is that Julia Lake now can have more
> time with her mother. God Himself is guiding and guarding
> our love for each other. It becomes sweeter and more won-
> derful each day! When He has prepared us completely, He
> will give us to each other. He is answering many a bold

prayer for hard things that we have dared to pray in recent years. It is a tremendous relief, in a way, for we were so rushed that we didn't see how we could possibly get ready for a May wedding and then get the family packed up for an August return to the mission field.

In the meantime I am here in St. Louis in the Medical Dormitory of my alma mater, Washington University. I am truly in an atmosphere of DOCTORS, almost a stone's throw from seven hospitals, and an eighth going up. With no responsibilities, it is pure joy just to visit clinics, operating rooms, laboratories and other interesting places, as I feel up to it. I am being prepared for a greater and better work for Christ and needy Africa!

The time finally came when the two medical guardian angels, Dr. Lee D. Cady of St. Louis, and Dr. Clinton Brush of Nashville, gave Eugene and Julia Lake "the green light." On February 3, 1930, at Mt. Berry, Georgia, in the Conway Skinner home, they were quietly married by Dr. Samuel McPheeters Glasgow. Only eight persons were present. They left immediately for a month-long Gulf Coast honeymoon in Biloxi, Mississippi.

The first Sunday of their married life they hoped simply to attend worship services and then to disappear unnoticed into the crowd. At the morning service in the Presbyterian Church, the minister's wife asked their names, which they deliberately had not revealed, wishing to remain anonymous. Eugene attempted unsuccessfully to camouflage the name "Kellersberger" by slurring it indistinctly under his breath. In a loud voice the lady immediately responded. "Not THE Dr. Kellersberger from the BELGIAN CONGO? And WHO IS THIS?" A confused, red-faced Eugene finally managed to blurt out, "This is my fiancee, Miss Julia Lake Skinner!"

Attending the prayer meeting at the Methodist church on Wednesday night, they fared no better. The Biloxi postmistress, a member of that church, quickly spotted the couple that had received hundreds of pieces of mail that week, with the name, "Miss Julia Lake Skinner" crossed out, replaced with "Mrs. Eugene R. Kellersberger." "After that," ruefully confessed the doctor, "we enjoyed the privacy of a goldfish!"

How different was the sailing of the united family on July 11, 1930, on the Red Star Liner, *Lapland*, from the stricken widower's previous, sad departure in 1924 on *The City of Exeter*! Now the happy husband of a new wife and father of two daughters exulted in the presence of his loved ones. "All this and heaven, too!", he would exclaim over and over, as he reached out to touch a hand, or give a spontaneous hug or kiss to one of "his three girls." His joy in his united family was absolutely complete!

Julia Lake, experiencing her first ocean voyage, was also introduced to her first seasickness. She remained in the cabin during much of that transatlantic crossing. Thirteen-year-old Winifred jubilantly joined her daddy in his daily, energetic tramps around the ship, glorying with him in the stirring magnificence of white-cap crested waves and wind-swept seas vibrantly in motion as far as the eye could see. In perfect step, they strode along together, responding to the cries of the wheeling gulls, delighting in the taste of salt foam on their lips, and welcoming the cold sting of heavy spray dashed over them through the railing.

A brief stop in Antwerp, Belgium, was followed by the eighteen-day voyage of the Belgian Maritime company's *Thysville*, to the port of Matadi, ninety-miles up the Congo River. After getting settled in the Swedish Mission guest house, the doctor led his family on the long walk through the tall grass, to the grave of Samuel N. Lapsley, on a hilltop overlooking the river. During the empty years, the doctor had had no one with whom to share his pride and boundless enthusiasm in the great missionary heritage of all those seeking to obey Christ's last command in the Belgian Congo. In showing the site of the last resting place of the founder of the American Presbyterian Congo Mission to his beloved family, Eugene once again knew the joy of sharing his interests with his loved ones.

The train trip around the rapids of the Congo River to Kinshasa now took only fourteen and a half hours, instead of the two solid days that Edna and Eugene had once endured. An eleven-day voyage upriver on the Belgian commercial riversteamer, *Luxembourg*, brought the Kellersberger family to Port Franqui, where they were met by missionaries from

Luebo, who had driven overland by car to get them. It was the quickest journey that the doctor had ever made from New York to Bibanga — only fifty-three days!

A tumultuous welcome awaited them. Hundreds of Congolese joined the staff to greet their beloved physician. They chattered excitedly as they greeted the new "Mama," and gave rapid little cries of amazement at how the two daughters had grown since they had last been seen on Bibanga hill, as small children. Songs of salutation, sung by the throng, proclaimed the official naming of Julia Lake in the Bantu language. Her Tshiluba name was to be *Musankisha*, "The One Who Makes Happy." The local Christians selected it as the ideal name for the one who had come to comfort their lonely doctor. They were deeply sympathetic, coming in many small groups to comfort both Eugene and Julia Lake, when both of their mothers died within the first few months after their arrival at Bibanga.

THE GREAT DEPRESSION IN THE CONGO

The world-wide monetary collapse that came to be known as "The Great Depression" was experienced even in the interior of the continent of Africa. Cuts in the budget came so frequently that a percentage basis was worked out for automatically prorating them to each of the mission stations. All budget items were painstakingly categorized as either so essential to the work that they were "Irreducibles," or, regrettably, "Reducibles." The mission's wry slogan for these years came to be: "KEEP LYING DOWN TO A MINIMUM!"

In 1933 Dr. Kellersberger requested permission to withdraw the Edna Kellersberger Memorial Hospital from the working budget of American Presbyterian Congo Mission. He volunteered to operate his station's medical department entirely on receipts from the field: government subsidies, drug grants, and fees from Congolese and white patients. As a salaried *médecin agrée* of the Belgian Congo government, he received 16,200 francs a year, and was allowed to charge both colonial and company officials and their families for his professional services. Bibanga's share of the medical appropriation from the home supporting church was divided among the four other working hospitals of the mission.

On May 1, 1934, he wrote: "My department is working completely on faith now! No more money is coming to <u>this</u> hospital from the USA! Last year I received a total of $300 in all from the home church. But God is providing wonderfully. This month alone, I have taken in 12,000 francs in medical fees, about $250, at 45 francs to the dollar!"

In 1926 the contributions made by the doctor's supporting church for work on six different mission fields totalled $1,248,000. In 1934 it was only $611,763. The overseas force of the Presbyterian Church in the United States declined during that same period from 516 to 395, placing a tremendous strain on overworked staff attempting to keep essential institutions and programs in operation. Amazingly, in spite of the depletion of personnel, the devastating effect of slashed budgets, and the devaluation of the dollar, additions to the young churches on the various mission fields continued to mount through those lean years.

It was not only organizations that suffered from the depression. Human feet also suffered! An important part of the Kellersbergers' calling was the conviction that they must live within the narrow limits of their salary. In order to avoid going into debt to the mission board, the family of four agreed together to forego the luxury of ordering any shoes, clothing or canned groceries from Europe or the United States. Lack of sturdy, comfortable shoes was one of the main problems. African stores stocked only rough, open sandals or very cheap tennis shoes. The college doctor who examined Winifred's feet when she entered Agnes Scott College in the fall of 1934 was horrified at the huge calluses she found and gasped, "Heavens! Didn't your parents <u>ever</u> provide you with proper shoes?"

Instead of wearing cotton print dresses mail-ordered from the Montgomery Ward catalogue, Julia Lake's and Winifred's daily weekday "costumes" were striped probationers' uniforms provided by White Cross for the hospital. It was a legitimate use of hospital supplies, for both of them worked regularly in the storeroom, prepared daily formula for the undernourished babies, and endless trays for the doctor's many European patients.

MULTIPLE ROLES OF THE MEDICAL MISSIONARY

The ten volumes of daily diaries that Dr. Kellersberger kept during the decade of the 1930s are alive with terse references to his work as a physician: "New cases keep coming in. Happy work! Full, interesting clinic. Last month we had 7,000 consultations." "Starting a well baby clinic. Hospital overflowing. No room!" "Lots of big chiefs coming to us now as patients!" "Child with meningitis finally died." "Real flu epidemic now, followed by pneumonia." "Two children bitten by mad dog." "Cases of pulmonary tuberculosis now coming in, 100% mortality." "Many new operative cases. Glad! Need the money to support the work!" "New Year's Eve, 1932: Best year yet as far as work done. 3,000 new patients this year. 72,000 in attendance at clinic. A happy year, filled with love!"

The surgeon noted many different types of operations: "Did my first cataract operation!" "Six major operations today, goiters and hernias." "Big 40-lb. elephantiasis case and a cancer of the jaw." "Caesarean case sent me by the Catholic Mission a big success!" "Regular epidemic of sad, nasty native circumcision cases coming in." "Goiter surgery today. I am a sorry surgeon, but my patients still live!" "Did a huge tumor case and clubfoot today." "Emergency strangulated hernia—foul!" "One rotten operation on a huge ovarian cyst took <u>all morning long</u>?" "Did a hairlip operation on Mazangu today. Now he can change the name traditionally given to all with hairlip. He is elated!"

Emergency cases dealt with everything imaginable: "Called at 9 p.m. to see stateman with blackwater fever. Drove car as far as possible, then walked all day to reach him." "Up most of the night with a terrible crocodile case, amputation of the leg. Died of bleeding before I could operate. No blood banks here in the bush!" "Called to diamond mines. Truck overturned trying to avoid hitting native child. Several critically injured." "Concussion, skull fracture. Man hit on the head by his chief. My first brain operation. He did fine!"

"Did a bad fracture case today, with no X-ray to help me."
"Cotton company agent hurt in cotton gin accident." "Crocodile case, both arms badly mauled." "Amputated Belgian
man's hand, badly infected." "Kajia's wife killed by lightning
early this morning. House burned to the ground. Two children hurt but not killed." "Whole series of lion cases recently,
all badly mauled." "Amputated leg at the knee. Terrible!
Woman shot by gun-trap laid in forest path to catch wild pigs.
They let her leg rot off before bringing her to me!"

Dozens of babies, both black and white, were ushered
into the world by Dr. Kellersberger, the obstetrician: "Christmas Day, 1931: I was with a black mandonna from 10 p.m. to
1 a.m." "Three deliveries in 12 hours. Difficult forceps delivery. Tired!" "Emergency labor case. Up all night. Placenta
praevia, wife of Catholic evangelist at Bakua Tshinene." "Sad
OB case, came too late, both mother and baby dead."
"Happy! Delivered Nkoka, on whom I operated for sterility!"
"Hard labor case till 2 a.m., dead baby." "Happy result in in-
duced labor case, Chief Mukayi's wife delivered of twins, both
breech babies." "More and more babies and no white nurse to
help me!" "Emergency Caesarean section, first live baby after
eight have died. So glad!"

Administrator of his own hospital, Dr. Kellersberger carried an unending burden of correspondence necessary for running such a busy institution. Having to do all his own secre-
tarial work, his typewriter often clattered away late into the
night. Making out the necessary drug orders was a constant
chore. The ever-recurring payday was a headache, because of
so-limited resources. But there were also happy times when he
rejoiced: "Five pounds of quinine and four boxes of Tryparsamide, worth 7,700 francs, received today from the *Comité
Special du Katanga*! Thank God!"

The hospital administrator functioned as maintenance
man and contractor as well: "Went to Katanda today in the
truck for a load of cotton and lime." "Am buying up rock for
the new baby clinic." "Whitewashing all walls of hospital
with lime from the cotton company at Katanda." "Fixed up a
special ulcer porch, with its own exit for my ulcer patients.
This greatly relieves congestion in the dispensary." "Using

our donkeys to transport water for building baby clinic building." "Helping Earl King work on the ram, new water system for the station." The doctor also did his own landscaping, laying out flower beds all over the hospital compound and planting palms and acacias to shade the walkways. Periwinkles, yellow roses and Thorn-of-Christ grew along the walls of the various units. "My hospital looks so pretty!", he wrote in his diary with pride!

The director of the Bibanga Nurses' Training School had disciplinary problems: "Punished two nurses today for giving drugs without permission." "Five of my student nurses leaving today for Elisabethville, to take the state examination for certification!" "Punished a nurse for stealing. I MUST have discipline!" "Fired one of my graduate nurses today for adultery." "Shifting more responsibility onto my head nurses." "PROUD of my nurses and their work! Have regular weekly meeting with entire hospital staff, as well as daily prayers with them. Our service is well organized now." "The state sanitary agent is asking for still more of my nurses' aides. Twelve of my Christian graduate nurses are now employed in the government medical service!"

As a *médecin agrée*, a licensed, salaried colonial government doctor, Dr. Kellersberger had numerous public health responsibilities. He was in charge of the annual survey for searching out cases of sleeping sickness in his area, the long, patient process that finally brought the disease under control. He directed the giving of smallpox vaccinations in all the surrounding chieftainships. It was his duty to inspect villages for source of mosquito-breeding, and to check on the springs in the valleys from which drinking water was carried. He had to examine the village toilets, to be sure they were being built and used according to state health specifications. As a state doctor he was also called upon to perform autopsies on suspected murder victims: "Did exhumation today with stateman on suspected victim of poisoning. Dead five weeks!"

As legal representative of the American Presbyterian Congo Mission, he had "letters galore to write regarding state palavers." He was buried constantly beneath piles of what his Belgian friends called *papperasse* — multitudinous, detailed forms and questionnaires, all with rigid quarterly, semi-annual or annual deadlines to meet.

The researcher who had been trained at Woods Hole, Massachusetts, continued to collect specimens of tropical disease-bearing insects and larvae, and sent them, along with slides which he himself prepared, to medical schools in several different countries. Famous doctors came to do research at Bibanga, among them Dr. Van dem Berge, working on liver flukes (*Schistosoma*), and the Harvard Africa Expedition, led by doctors Strong, Mallingrade and Pierrepont. Eugene wrote in his diary: "Wonderful days in Dr. R. P. Strong's clinic! Did operations on blind and demonstrations of *Onochocerca* volvules, adults and larvae in skin and eye. They gave me an unbelievable trunk of drugs, a sterilizer and two excellent books on tropical medicine!"

For five years Dr. Kellersberger was the medical secretary of the Congo Protestant Council. He was also a government-appointed member of the prestigious Commission for the Protection of the Indigenous Peoples (*Commission Pour la Protection des Indigènes*).

He was constantly in the process of writing articles for religious and professional publications: "Finished 5,000 word article on 9,000 cases of sleeping sickness for medical journals in U.S.A." "Writing article on leprosy for Dr. Cochrane!" "Finished hernia article and translation of sleeping sickness materials into French!" He also rarely failed to record in his daily diary the main events of each day as it passed.

A typical letter, written to friends in the United States on July 11, 1934, speaks directly from the doctor's heart:

> As I carry on day in and day out, and often during the night, an intensive, never-ending medical and surgical work, and a leprosy colony now with over 500 inmates, besides innumerable other demands on my time, I cry out for help and yet feel His sustaining grace for added tasks. As I see the hospital buildings inadequate to hold the ever-increasing crowds, often over 500 in the morning clinic, with no lights, no running water, no sanitary system, no women's or children's wards, no isolation building, no iron beds, no mattresses, I turn again to Him and know that He <u>has</u>

blessed richly with what we <u>do</u> have and will supply our every need!

Dr. Kellersberger, the ordained minister, faithfully preached on Sundays, sometimes as many as four times! Only medical emergencies had priority over preaching! "Today preached to congregation of 105 at Bena Mpuma, then drove to the leprosarium to teach the leaders. Held an afternoon service for sleeping sickness patients at the hospital and led the service in English for the missionary staff in the evening." His real pleasure was to visit different villages, spending the night and showing his lantern slides. How the people loved to see pictures of themselves, their chiefs, or friends and relatives connected with the various phases of the mission work! This was one of the personal aspects of the doctor's contribution that greatly endeared him to the Baluba of the Bibanga region!

With his daughter, Winifred, the doctor often walked to the spot beneath the *diwole* tree where their beloved little grass-roofed dispensary-home had once stood. Together they gazed out over the miles and miles of magnificent Lubilashi River valley that nearly encircled the promontory of Bibanga hill. Winds blowing up the grassy slopes to the crest were mischievous, running cool fingers through their hair. If it was rainy season, the distant, tumbled hills were bright green velvet, with miniature crescents of dark green forest tucked into the creases enfolding the sunlit summits. The wandering river swung back and forth in a vast sea of greens and blues, its great silver curves almost succeeding in meeting, here and there in the vast valley.

If it was dry season, sloping pillars of smoke, angled sharply back to the horizon by the wind, towered up from roaring bush fires. Small, puffy pillows of smoke nestled in the hollows of the hills and all the land was a vast canvas of intermingled russet, bronze, sepia and burnt umber, surrealistically smudged together by the dry season haze.

The mission station itself was lovely, with neat paths bordered by poinsettia and lantana hedges. Bougainvillea vines draped purple and scarlet mantles over the brick walls of buildings, and erect, variegated crotons stood sentinel beside the doorways. The stately palms that crowned the hilltop wore lacy skirts of fern, delicate lichen and clinging mosses, growing out of the cups formed on the lower trunks by the fallen fronds. The mango grove beside the graveyard, halfway down the hill, had sturdy black-green foliage, decorated with bright blobs of fruit, hanging like Christmas ornaments from long, stringy stems. Graceful cassia trees perfumed the air with huge clusters of fragrant, yellow blossoms. The crew-cut acacia trees, with their feathery foliage, scrambled red-and-orange flowers, and huge, flat bean pods, were the favorite climbing trees of the station children.

THE BIBANGA LEPROSARIUM

The sequence of events which led to the establishment of the Bibanga Agricultural Colony is traceable through the minutes of the annual Mission Meetings of the American Presbyterian Congo Mission.

Under the pressure of the nation-wide scourge of sleeping sickness during the 1920s, Dr. Kellersberger simply had no time to devote to the ever-present throng of leprosy patients. It was only as he returned from his extended furlough in 1930, to find sleeping sickness well under control, that he was finally able to turn his attention to their plight.

The Executive Committee of Foreign Missions of the Presbyterian Church in the United States had at that time the policy of discouraging the establishment of leprosaria on their various mission fields. All of the doctor's first requests to begin such work were answered in the negative. The 1929 Mission Meeting of the American Presbyterian Congo Mission voted to explore the possibility of Belgian colonial aid for the establishment of a pilot leprosarium, to be operated without cost to the mission. The 1930 Mission Meeting "approved leprosy work on the condition that it be self-supporting as to feeding, housing and 50% of drugs." The breakthrough came in 1931, when the following actions were taken and a great red "A" for "ANSWERED!" was written across pages of the doctor's prayer notebook:

Minutes 31–500 Bibanga Camp approved, with dispensary, dormitory unit, church, school and workshop.

Minute 31–700 The Executive Committee approves the application to the American Mission to Lepers, for support of leprosy work, Bibanga to be the pilot station for this work. $10,000 is to be requested from the American Mission to Lepers.

By 1937 there were leprosaria on each of the major stations of the American Presbyterian Congo Mission. A lively personal account of the growth of the Bibanga colony is found in the doctor's diaries:

November 4, 1930 First road into Leprosarium completed.

November 24 Leprosarium coming along fine. Wrote a letter to Mr. Danner, General Secretary of the American Mission to Lepers about our work. Rode the three miles out to the camp on my "wheel" in 25 minutes. Forty houses going up, one house for resident nurse, pharmacy and lazaret!

January 1, 1931 Leprosarium almost finished!

January 6 122 patients waiting to enter.

January 9 Happy day! Leprosarium officially opened! 65 cases allowed to enter. Joy to see these fingerless, toeless ones come in. HAPPY IN OUR BIG WORK!

January 11 First official service at the Camp. Sixty gathered under the palms, "God's arches," seated on logs. I preached to them from Luke 5:12–13 on their "*Touching Jesus.*" They are a happy lot! Church building is going up.

January 13 All houses at Camp full.

February 8 Dedication of new Leprosarium Church. Camp visited today by League of Nations representatives, Goodall and Schaslalear.

February 9 Big Chief Kabengele Dibue visited Camp in his car. Says he will build houses for all his people who have leprosy.

April 24 To Camp tonight in the bright moonlight with our victrola, to play records for them.

May 5 Belgian government official LaDame impressed with leprosy work. Gave 5,000 francs as a gift to help!

July 16 Earl King killed a hippo, MEAT for the camp!

August 29   Chief Kabengele Dibue sent me four patients, two goats and 100 francs. 193 now in Camp. All have their own fields. Are doing fine. So <u>happy</u> in this work!

October 9   Planting chaulmoogra oil trees at the Camp.

November 16   State has given us 54 more hectares of land at Camp for agricultural rights. JOY in the Leprosarium! Happy work!

January 16, 1932   Transplanted 125 young chaulmoogra oil trees today.

January 18   Classifying all leprosy patients into four categories: *neural, cutaneous, tuberculoid,* and *lepramotous,* grouping them by tissue stains.

April 14   Laid out road into new concession at Camp. Set up chaulmoogra oil press to make our own medicine for injections. Adjusting boundary line of camp.

July 4   Making sundried brick at Leprosarium now. Patients building their own new houses and being paid for it! Happy!

September 21   Gave out new blankets at Camp today. Great joy!

Christmas Day   444 in the Leprosarium Church today for Christmas service! Sent one back home for six months, discipline for fighting. Work there is getting more complicated.

May 7   First communion service at Camp. 50 baptized Christians took communion!

May 22   Broke ground for new rock dispensary today.

By 1933 there were so many residents in the Bibanga leprosarium that the Belgian colonial government stepped in and ordered Dr. Kellersberger: "You now have more than you can handle! For the next six months you are not permitted to accept any more leprosy patients!"

Three times during these months when no new cases were being admitted, a man named Musensa came begging to enter the camp, but had to be refused. Three times he turned and sadly limped back the fifty miles to his home village, fifty tortuous miles over a hot, rocky road on his ulcerous feet, back to his father, who spit on him, cursed him and the womb that had given him birth, and refused him entrance to the house. Reaching a breaking point, Musensa did something practically unknown in African culture. He picked up a spear and killed his own father. The colonial government imprisoned him as a murderer. When it was discovered that he had leprosy, the state official sent Musensa to Bibanga with a letter: *"Le voici! Votre lepreux a tué son père!"* "Here he is! Your leprosy patient has killed his father!"

Incensed, the doctor wrote back, pointing out the restrictions which had kept him from accepting Musensa each time he came seeking admittance: "Why do you call him "my" leprosy patient? I was not permitted to take him in. He had to kill in order to get into the colony! JUST WHO IS THE MURDERER?"

In 1939 Dr. Kellersberger wrote of his now completed institution:

> As a result of the recent visit of Dr. Ernest Muir, Secretary-Treasurer of the International Leprosy Association, the number of leprosy patients has been reduced from over 500 to about 325. The simple and clear way in which he classified the cases, and the common sense interpretation of their conditions, was a revelation to me and gave me a new conception of how to deal with them. We were able to tell a large number that their disease was arrested, or quiescent, or inactive, or cured. We also learned the great importance of segregating the lepromotous cases in their own part of the village. We learned about the importance of separating children from their infected parents and the great importance of the improvement of their general condition.
>
> Dr. Muir found that the type of leprosy here is milder than in the Orient, with less open cases and fewer mutilations. It may be that this is due to less overcrowding of population, therefore less contact, and more balanced diet, making the disease less powerful.
>
> We get the best results with the fresh, whole chaulmoogra oil, with 5% creosote added, two injections given weekly, from 1 up to 10 c.c. per injection. A special feature of our colony is our thriving 1200-tree plantation of chaulmoogra oil trees (*hydnocarpus anthelmintica*). The trees are now nine years old and have been bearing for four years.

We have made about five gallons of the fresh oil ourselves in
our press, and are getting even better results than with the
oil shipped from Siam. This is the only producing plantation in the Belgian Congo. We have shared some 30,000
seeds with others, the government recently becoming quite
interested in our effort, for we have demonstrated that the
trees and the oil can easily be produced here.

We believe that leprosy can be cured, can be aborted,
can be arrested and made inactive. One of the best methods
is by an agricultural colony, which combines healthy,
wholesome, loving influences with careful, detailed scientific study and management. We need to give the loving
human touch that makes life worth living again to these, the
most despised and feared of all on earth!

THE LAST TERM IN THE BELGIAN CONGO

The last four years of Dr. Kellersberger's missionary career were traumatic. The work was greater than ever, but
there were fewer than ever to do it. Rarely were there more
than six assigned workers at Bibanga, where before there had
been at least thirteen. Often the doctor was the only man on
the station, responsible not only for his regular medical work,
but covering the tasks of those out itinerating or on furlough.
For seven years not a single new missionary was added to the
staff of the entire mission. Forces depleted by the depression
were crumpled still more by nine emergency health furloughs
in one year. One of the diary entries made at this time reads:
"We have every reason to thank God on bended knee (which
we do) for all He has so graciously done for us, in keeping us
going when so many others are falling in their tracks." Growing problems of restriction on travel, due to the approach of
World War II, were making it harder and harder for those on
furlough to get back to the field.

Of the deaths in personnel that occurred during this
term, the most shocking was at Bibanga — the suicide of the
young nurse just arrived from the States. On the last page of
her diary she had written: "O! Those dark wards! Those dark
wards!" Coming from the gleaming brightness of training in
America, she was overwhelmed by the conditions under which

she had to work — wards lit only by smoking kerosene lamps or simply wicks set into old Crisco cans, filled with palm oil. There was just too much to do, and too little to do it with! She simply could not take it!

Two other heartbreaking deaths at Bibanga added to the burden of responsibility, so hard for Eugene to bear. Any death in the compact, closely-knit community of a mission station is the emotional equivalent of a death in an immediate family, a shocking experience that takes its toll in the physical and spiritual reserves of the entire staff of that post.

But there were joyous and exciting events, too!

Two welcome weeks of solitude and rest were unexpectedly given to the doctor in 1937, when he had to be quarantined for a very light case of smallpox, contracted nursing one of the student nurses who had an unusually virulent case of it!

The visit to Bibanga of Methodist Bishop Moore and Billy Sunday's famous songleader, Homer Rodeheaver, created a sensation among the local populace. The singer's cornet, his beautiful rendition of American Negro Spirituals, and his clever sleight of hand tricks were wonderingly discussed years after this visit!

In August 1938, Dr. Emory Ross, General Secretary of the American Mission to Lepers, came to visit the Bibanga Agricultural Colony, and seemed to be really impressed! With him were Ray and Virginia Garner, sent by the Harmon Foundation and the American Mission to Lepers, to make a thirty-minute documentary film about the Bibanga leprosy work. Julia Lake set to work to write the scenario. Bibanga station was turned into a film studio and the leprosarium became a lively movie set, with several hundred excited "actors" ready for every scene! The resulting film, called *Song After Sorrow*, was widely used for many years as one of the most effective publicity and teaching tools of the American Mission to Lepers.

The outstanding event of Dr. Kellersberger's last term in the Belgian Congo was his attending the First International Leprosy Congress in Cairo, Egypt, in March 1938. Secretary of State, Cordell Hull's personally signed invitation to represent the United States officially, included both Julia Lake and

Eugene. The APCM, still on a very restricted budget, did grant the doctor leave of absence for two months, to go to Cairo, but only on condition that his trip be without expense to the mission.

Urged by Julia Lake, Eugene finally decided to cash the only life insurance policy that he had, one that he had taken out while a student at The University of Texas. Cashing the $1000 policy, he received $800, enough to buy one round-trip air fare to Cairo from Bibanga. It was money well spent, for it opened the door to the unbelievable worldwide ministry that lay ahead of them.

Throughout February 1938, the doctor had suffered with an extremely serious eye infection, caused by the strain of compiling statistics of all the Protestant medical work of the Belgian Congo, as medical Secretary of the Congo Protestant Council. His only illumination for the long hours of tedious, detailed night work was a kerosene oil lamp. For six weeks before his departure, he had been unable to use his eyes for reading, writing or operating. One of the great blessings of this trip, was that he was able to consult an excellent opthalmologist while in Cairo, a city where there is an unusual concentration of skilled eye doctors, due to the frequency of eye diseases there.

Of his interesting experiences in Cairo, Egypt, Dr. Kellersberger wrote:

> Fifty-five nations sent 500 delegates to the greatest Congress to study the disease of leprosy that has ever met! For me, it was "from bush to palace," for on the first day, the conference was opened in the royal palace by the young King Farouk I, and his cabinet. Over a thousand people — diplomats, delegates and their wives, and government officials, were given a brilliant reception at the famous Abdine Palace. I was proud to be among the eighteen official delegates from the dear old USA! Our American ambassador, Mr. Fish, and America's most famous doctor, Dr. Victor Heiser, author of *An American Doctor's Odyssey*, and President of the International Leprosy Association, introduced us. No one could enter the king's presence without a princely robe, so I borrowed a "Prince Albert" from my friends at the

United Presbyterian Mission in Cairo! Never before in my life have I seen such dressed up and decorated men and women, such display of wealth and pomp, such brilliant lights, such royal food and prodigal hospitality! It was an Arabian Night's scene in a fairy palace!

The fairy palace soon turned into the Tower of Babel! At the Royal Opera House, greetings were given in Arabic, English, French, German, Spanish and Italian. The main business of the conference was conducted in both French and English and I was privileged to be one of the official interpreters.

I was indeed gratified that, among delegates representing great organized bodies, such as the League of Nations, the Rockefeller Institute, the British Empire Leprosy Relief Association, the American Mission to Lepers, the British Mission to Lepers, etc. a goodly number of medical missionaries were present from all parts of the world and took part on the program and in the discussions that followed.

I made a special effort on this trip to see as much of the work of other societies as possible. I visited fourteen missions in all and learned enough to fill a book! I confess that when I saw modern hospitals, with a whole staff of missionary doctors and nurses, where the need was so great, but no greater than it is here, but where there was sufficient personnel to do a really lasting piece of work, my heart grew heavy as I faced home, knowing I would once again be working alone, without even one American nurse to help me!

1939–1940 — "THE DOUBLE YEAR"

There were only two doctors on the field during the final months that the Kellersbergers worked in the Belgian Congo. they always referred to this year as their "DOUBLE YEAR," because they were asked to live on two stations at once, alternating two weeks at a time, running the hospitals both at Lubondai and at Bibanga. It was the most harried, uprooted, unpredictable period of their lives. Drugs were no longer available from Europe, threatened by the German invasion. The colonial medical service had forbidden all surgery, except for the most urgent emergencies. International financial relations were suspended; Congo francs could no longer be ex-

*Left: Dr. Kellersberger with a leprosy patient at the Egyptian Gov-
ernment Leprosarium in Cairo, and Right: with one of his own patients at the Bibanga Agricultural Colony in the Belgian Congo.*

*First International Leprosy Congress, Cairo, Egypt, April 1938. Dr.
Kellersberger is seated next to Dr. H. W. Wade of Culion, Philippine Islands, and Dr. Hazeltine of Carville, Louisiana.*

changed for other currency. The crumbling health situation of members of the mission was cause for grave concern. The doctor's 1940 diary provides insight into his last months of work in Africa and shows God's perfect timing in opening wide the "new door" to a world-wide ministry to the victims of Hansen's Disease:

Bibanga, January 6, 1940 Wading into statistics! They seem to get more complicated all the time. We have to make out for the state a personal history of every one of our leprosy patients, their family history, state of health, tribe, etc. It is a terrible task which has to be done every three months! I have no secretary, and this alone requires a full week of work. It is just a question of dogged, hard constant work and keeping after things.

Lubondai, February 18 Back from emergency trip to Luebo. Had to cross Katende ferry at night. Hard time with driver ants and swift current of rain-swollen river. Road bad, lost my way, drove off into a field. GLAD to reach Julia Lake and home! Always something to be thankful for!

Lubondai, April 20 Hard to believe! Wonderful letter from Emory Ross! OPENING OF NEW WORK FOR ME! I have been asked to become THE GENERAL SECRE-TARY OF THE AMERICAN MISSION TO LEPERS! Mr. Ross has been called to head up another organization. They are eager to have us. The Board of Directors has voted unanimously in the affirmative!

Lubondai, April 22 Went to Luisa to get Miss Sawyer's passport and *Immatriculation* Card. Got stuck in 100 feet of overflowed road. Worked in water above knees for hours. Hard time getting out! Took thirty men to turn the ferry about in the swift current. Dangerous! Again, God's providential care of me!

Bibanga, May 20 WAR! At 3 a.m. Germany entered Belgium, Holland and Luxembourg.

Lubondai, May 21 Belgium almost completely occupied. All contacts with her colony broken. All guns owned by missionaries confiscated today and taken to Dibaya statepost.

Lubondai, May 24 All radio transmitters confiscated. Everyone must have a *Permit de Circuler*! Left at 9 a.m. for

Bibanga. Big 2¹/₂-ton truck upside down across road near diamond mines. Driver drunk.

Bibanga, May 28   Poor Belgium finished! Wholesale destruction! Hectic time at hospital after two weeks' absence. No end to work! King Leopold has surrendered unconditionally to Germany. Situation grave at Dunkirk and Calais.

Bibanga, May 30   Over a thousand people here for annual evangelistic conference. Have taken out 600 *Filaria Volvoulus Cysts* in five days of work. Allies being driven into sea at Dunkirk and Calais.

Bibanga, June 4   No more radio calls from other stations! All sending apparatus confiscated. No statemen in sight these days. All uncannily quiet. Leaves me in peace for a while! Did Caesarean Section on a dwarf of a woman. Had to dismember her child to remove it, when she came to me a few years ago. Child born today and mother ALL OK! Places for only eleven more operations in my old Operating Record Book! IT'S TIME FOR ME TO GO HOME!

July 29   Unusual over-full day, sick of all kinds. Rotten diseases, sad histories of rape and rotten marriage customs and ruining of women for motherhood! WHITE CROSS supplies from our supporting church arrived today. HURRAH! Never more needed! Came direct from New York to Matadi. So grateful that ship was not sunk by a German raider!

September 10   Cable received from USA today: DR. POOLE SAILING NEW YORK-CAPE TOWN, OCTOBER 5TH. We are free to leave the Congo! We knew it would all work out! God has been so good to us, and all our fellow-workers!

September 15   Last Sunday at the Camp. very happy and touching time. Met us with flowers and songs. Church full to overflowing. Fine attention. No one wanted to leave after service. Kept sitting! Opportunity to bring real message: "*Christ is the same forever!*" (Hebrews 13:8) They must forget me, the transient human worker and depend on the never-changing, eternal Head of all the work! Hate to leave these friends more than all others! Some of the old women cried, "You are not afraid to touch us! Will others do as you have done????"

September 20 LAST DAY ON THE MISSION!   My last day at the hospital. Gave two diplomas to graduate nurses,

Ngandu and Tshibamba. Wonderful surprise and tribute by the State today! Seventeen government officials and their wives came to say goodbye, and all the Medal Chiefs of this area, with all their followers! All Bibanga school children, all the hospital staff and 30 representatives from the Colony! In all, about 3,000 people! Addresses were given in French by the Commissaire, M. LeDuc, and Doctor Neles. Talks in Tshiluba were given by Chiefs Mbuyi Kasenga and Kahumba Nomba and our Pastor, Andrew Mukeba! All wore their decorations. (I, too!) So tired and <u>happy</u>!

September 30 GOODBYE TO BIBANGA! At early morning worship service at the church, talks were made by Head Nurse, Lubilaji, and others, as well as Julia Lake and myself. Our final goodbye! As car pulled out 9 a.m., great crowd came to see us off, all the hospital staff, school children, with flowers and songs. Stopped at the Leprosarium on way to Luputa. What a send-off! Very touching! Flowers and bouquets piled high all over the car. <u>I did hate to leave them most of all</u>!

[12]

The Leprosy Missions Executive

JOURNEY TO THE NEW JOB

Four full months intervened between the close of the Belgian Congo medical career and the opening of the busy administrative years with the American Mission to Lepers, Incorporated. It took Eugene and Julia Lake from September 19, 1940, when they left Bibanga, to January 18, 1941, to complete the 17,000 mile journey back to their homeland. Fifty days spent on the high seas early in World War II were as hazardous as that first outgoing voyage made by Eugene and Edna in 1916 on the unseaworthy old *Afrique*.

A brief layover in Elisabethville on the way to South Africa turned out to be a triumphal farewell. Many of the doctor's graduate nurses, trained at the Bibanga hospital, now employed in government and company hospitals, came to the Hotel Albert to say goodbye. On September 25, 1940, the Elisabethville daily newspaper, *Essor du Congo*, carried an article of warm praise for the work of a Protestant doctor, unprecedented in an officially Catholic country: "We could never estimate the immensity of the medical work he has accomplished, but we can emphatically state the beauty of his character, which makes him beloved of all who have ever worked with him, the solid friend of all who know him well."

274

That same day, Governor-General Liesnard, in a public radio address, paid high tribute to Dr. Kellersberger, voicing the deep appreciation of the colonial government for all he had done for the people of the Belgian Congo, both as a missionary and as an official state doctor.

Characteristically, the doctor and his wife spent the seven-week interval in Durban, South Africa, awaiting boat passage to the United States, in the happy pastime of making new friends. Some they met on the beach while "shelling," others, at the daily YMCA lunch hour. Eugene made one very grateful friend by rescuing her from a treacherous undertow very early one morning when no lifeguard was on the beach. While in Durban, they dined with — among many others — the director of the Bank of South Africa, the American Consul, the president of Adams College, doctors of the McCord Zulu Hospital, and Mahalil Ghandi, son of the Mahatma in India.

The most deeply satisfying event of all for the doctor was welcoming the storm-battered *Swardenhondt* on October 17th, with his daughter, Winifred, and her husband aboard. Theirs had been a dangerous seventy-day voyage from New York through the Panama Canal and across the Pacific and Indian Oceans, dodging German raiders and submarines. One week later, Eugene wrote in his diary: "Today, we saw the Vasses off on the train for the Belgian Congo! I have handed on my torch of service for Christ in Africa to Winifred and Lachlan!"

On November 23rd, the 5000-ton *Bontekoe* of the Royal Dutch line quietly slipped away from Durban during the night for ports unknown. Dr. Kellersberger's journal of that voyage records mostly names, addresses and facts about the people they met. A vivid account of the urgency and uncertainty experienced is captured in selected summaries of daily events:

> *November 23, 1940.* We sailed on Julia Lake's 43rd birthday! Blackout conditions, all portholes closed and covered. All Chinese crew, waiters and stewards. Bad night, rough sea, broken dishes, overturned chairs! Only 30 passengers, mostly Dutch.
> *December 1 — Somewhere on the Indian Ocean.* No charts, no maps posted. Have no idea where we are or where we are going! Captain says we are sailing under orders from the British Navy.

December 2. Marvelous blue, molten glass sea! Shoals of flying fish and schools of dolphin. Zig-zagged during the night. We shift course constantly. In the daytime, we go south by east, at night, north by east.

December 5. Asked by ship's doctor to visit the sick with him. Grateful for cautious going, clean boat and good food.

December 8. Held up in mid-ocean by British auxiliary cruiser. Guns, flags, signals! Young officers came aboard, checked all passports. Surprised to find United States citizens aboard!

December 15. World famous Singapore! Had no idea we were coming here! Saw masts of Norwegian ship recently sunk by a mine in 79 feet of water. Not allowed to get off or even to send mail.

December 17 — Batavia, Java. We waited seven weeks in Durban, South Africa, for passage on the *Bontekoe*. Had only three hours in Batavia to transfer to the Rotterdam Lloyd vessel, *Jagersfontein*, 10,000-ton oil burner. What a change! Real beds, lovely cabins, food delightful! Only 20 passengers! We go via Celebes, Borneo, the Philippines and Hawaii to Portland, Oregon.

December 23. Due north now, between Borneo and the Celebes. Crossed the equator for the third time on the voyage! At noon, two dark green Dutch bombers circled our ship at terrific speed. Captain says we passed right through the vicinity of German raiders in the Indian Ocean — the reason for all those zig-zags!

Christmas Day. Now in the Sulu Sea, near the Philippine Island of Culion, where there are 6,000 victims of leprosy! How I'd love to stop and see it as we pass by! The sea here is black-blue, the deepest depth of the ocean anywhere on earth — seven miles!

December 26. Dawn over vast Manila Bay. Beautiful! The Gibralter of the East! Corregidor fortified. Great city of half a million.

December 27 — Manila, Philippines. Visited the Skin Clinic with Dr. Rodriquez. He is asking for a car, a new chapel and money for two additional workers at new leprosy work sites in Manila. It is exciting to be accepting my first official requests for financial help from our Mission!

January 1, 1941. In the vast Pacific Ocean. Safe in

Him! We are sailing together into a <u>new work</u> and a <u>new year</u>!

January 4. News today gave information on a British ship sunk by a German raider in this very area of the Pacific where we now are. "*He hath delivered!*"

January 9. Got up at 4:30 a.m. to see the last of our beloved constellation, The Southern Cross, low on the horizon to the south. May HIS CROSS be our salvation! Stewards asked to meet with us at 9 tonight. Fine! Later: They kept us until past midnight, asking questions, all so hungry for better things!

January 10. Honolulu, after 12 days on the great Pacific! Dawn over Oahu, volcanic masses in the morning sun. Fifteen bombers in formation did practice dive-bombing on a target near us. "Slim" Strode, my Washington University Medical School classmate, met us at the dock and took us to visit his successful surgical clinic. Proud of him!

January 16. Rougher in the night and colder. Awoke to a real winter morning. Have been at sea two months tomorrow. Thank God, Who <u>does</u> keep, <u>has</u> kept and <u>will</u> keep! Have been off the coast of Oregon for two days now, waiting for this terrific storm to abate. Winds 60–70 mph. We are quartered into the wind, going at half-speed, constantly fighting off huge seas.

January 18. The pilot finally was able to come aboard at midnight, after four days of waiting. Purser woke us with a huge pile of mail. We read till 2 a.m.! Have given away all our clothing to refugees we have traveled with who had nothing. Have only one change of garments apiece left. It took us from 5 a.m. till noon to cover the 80 miles up the glorious Columbia River to Wilamette and Portland. HOME AT LAST! THANK GOD!

THE OFFICE AT 156 FIFTH AVENUE

The Kellersbergers "hit the ground running!" The friend who welcomed them back from Africa on Saturday evening, January 18, at the Portland dock, had scheduled speaking engagements for them for Sunday morning, the 19th! The unexpected four-day delay caused by the storm left them little leeway. They were driven directly from the ship to a clothing store which their enterprising friend had persuaded to remain open after hours, so that the doctor might purchase a new suit and his wife, a new dress, in which to make their first public appearance in the United States as official representatives of the American Mission to Lepers, Inc.

They were given a rousing welcome by the Los Angeles area office of their organization, as they passed through that city on their way to visit Texas and Alabama kinfolk, before settling in New York. The celebration was complete with a special luncheon in their honor, interviews by reporters with flashbulbs popping and newspaper write-ups. Eugene had time to buy a shiny, new briefcase, marking him now as a true executive! His very first experience in dictating letters he termed "my first act as a bureaucrat." In his diary he mentions that he added personal notes by hand to the first 466 letters sent out in his name, a practice he was soon forced to abandon!

The official service of induction as General Secretary, led by Methodist Bishop, Arthur Moore, took place on March 21, 1941, at the Town Hall Club on West 43rd Street in New York City, with some 400 friends in attendance.

The unique organization of which Dr. Kellersberger was now a leading officer had its beginnings in 1874, when a group of concerned Christians in London, England, formed THE LEPROSY MISSION, to assist the victims of that disease living in India. Within a few years branches were active in Scotland, Wales and Ireland. Similar committees or auxiliaries of the original mission were organized in Canada, the United States, New Zealand, Australia, India, South Africa and Hong Kong. The AMERICAN COMMITTEE, from which the present-day, independent, but related AMERICAN LEPROSY MISSIONS, derives its origin, was formed in 1906. Introducing old friends to his new work, the doctor wrote:

> It is international, interdenominational and inter-racial. People of all nationalities and all creeds come to our office to make known their needs. The power of this Mission is that it is supported by thousands of earnest Christian people who honor the Word of God and the command of

Christ to cleanse those with leprosy, and are showing it by their actions. One cannot remain narrow-minded and indifferent in such a ministry as this! It destroys racial pride and defies prejudice and misconceptions. It does something to one's spirit and understanding of the sufferings of the whole world!

From the beginning, the new General Secretary found himself ably supported by an ideal staff. William Jay Schieffelin was President, W. Espey Albig, Treasurer, and Raymond P. Currier, the Executive Secretary. A dedicated, informed Board of Directors and Area Secretaries of seven branch district offices in New York, Boston, Philadelphia, Cleveland, Chicago, Nashville, and Los Angeles, formed the central nervous system of this actively outreaching Mission.

THE GRAMERCY PARK APARTMENT

What a change from the wide, primitive sweep of Bibanga hilltop in the heart of Africa to the prim city-within-a-city, buried deep in the towering heart of lower Manhattan! Eugene's and Julia Lake's new address — 38 Gramercy Park — was an elegant address, not so much because of affluence as reserved, highly respectable identity. Gramercy Park is a small enclave with a distinct self-awareness. The genteel, quietly sophisticated structures facing the Park have over the years housed famous intellectual, literary, and political figures — and still do! Access through the wrought iron gate into the private park with its massive elms, flower-lined walks, gracefully curved grassy plots, and park benches discreetly arranged with an eye to privacy, is indeed a privilege of high degree.

Apartment 5G was a convenient, brisk eight-minute walk from the Fifth Avenue office, eliminating the need for transportation to and from work. Being the topmost and backmost of the complex, this apartment might be termed a "maverick" among its more well-bred counterparts. Its row of five, large windows faced out directly on eye-level with the busy Third Avenue Elevated Line connecting City Hall Station in Manhattan with 149th Street in the Bronx. Such a backdoor resi-

dence, with its combination of noise and unobstructed sunlight, suited the doctor and his wife to perfection. It was
because of the adjacent "EL" support structure that there
were no close-crowding brick walls to smother the little apartment in shadow.

Julia Lake's motif for decorating their new city dwelling
was, of course, "African." A menagerie of appropriate animal
flowerpots marched along the sunny windowsills, bearing
burdens of cacti, ivy and philodendron. The lampshade was a
map of the world, with the beloved African continent glow-
ingly outlined by the light behind it. Elephant-shaped book-
ends and candleholders matched with raffia baskets and
ebony and ivory carvings brought from the Congo home.
Their china had a different tropical animal on each plate;
drinking glasses sported designs of monkeys swinging through
the trees.

A large, open rooftop up just one short flight of stairs provided a fresh air vantage point for observing activities in
nearby penthouse gardens, or the daily antics of rooftop dove-
cote owners, waving poles in the air to force-fly their pigeons
in tight circles for exercise. A rooftop view of the Chrysler
Building, East River and the Borough of Queens was always
elegantly framed by gently flapping clotheslines filled with
laundry. In the deepest hours of the night, there was even a
glimpse of the stars from this quiet, cool retreat.

Eugene read in the *New York Times* about a wealthy man
who had his entire house turned about on his property, just so
that the morning sun would stream through the dining room
windows into his first cup of coffee. A constant theme of the
New York diaries is Dr. Kellersberger's simple joy in "sunshine in my coffee cup," combined with the particularly contented song the percolator gurgled whenever his Julia Lake
was home from a speaking trip.

Mrs. Kellersberger's full-time job of Promotional Secretary for the organization of which her husband was the General Secretary, meant that the two of them were often separated. Their renewed delight in each other's presence after
such intervals of being apart glows in one daily diary entry
after another. On departure, she always left him a love note or

some memento of her presence. He always welcomed her back with two red roses in the same slender vase, placed in the center of the table.

One of the ways in which the doctor passed his after-work hours at home was in cleaning all 172 of the window panes of their apartment. The dust and smoke of the inner city waged constant battle with detergent, sponge and a willing elbow. The windows were the metal rimmed type, with a latch, opening out, so both sides could easily be reached for cleaning purposes. Eugene's pride of accomplishment in having polished up 344 sides of glass panes always warranted a special notation on his current diary page. If he was too rushed to do this cleaning, he would leave "I Love You!" messages scrawled with his fingertip on the dusty surface.

One outstanding advantage of Apartment 5G was proximity to Dr. and Mrs. Emory Ross, who had found this apartment for them. Dr. Kellersberger's immediate predecessor with the Mission, Dr. Ross had also been his colleague from the Disciples of Christ Congo Mission back in the Belgian Congo. It was really good to have "the voice of experience" so close at hand. Nearness to his friend, serving with the Foreign Mission Conference of North America, also meant many interesting contacts. Dr. Albert Schweitzer, on the occasion of his only visit to the United States, was the guest of the Rosses. Eugene always looked back on his adventure of being the French and German interpreter for this great man, as being one of the most interesting events of his life. He never mentioned that he himself was referred to by newspaper reporters as "a second Schweitzer" or "The Schweitzer of the Congo."

As the missionary and his wife became known by local residents, they were often asked such questions as, "Are you the people who live in the apartment where there are so many coming and going all the time!" or "Are you the lady who lives where all the happy laughter and noise come from?" 38 Gramercy Park was as much the center of the Kellersbergers' ministry as the office a few blocks over on Fifth Avenue. Countless numbers of times they vacated it in order to make room for guests. It might be an incoming missionary family with small children, freshly arrived from overseas, or an outgoing one, booked to sail in a few days, grateful for Julia Lake's famous expertise in last-minute New York shopping. It might be a young couple on their honeymoon, or a person looking for a job, needing temporary shelter, or old friends come to see the sights of the big city. For any and all of them, "The Kelleys" cheerfully made room.

Sometimes the doctor arrived home from a speaking tour to find Julia Lake gone and strangers occupying his home. This never upset him. He just took his suitcase over to the Irving Hotel, where they always went whenever they turned their home over to others. The manager had become such a good friend, that he had a special suite he usually gave them whenever they needed it. In 1949, Dr. Kellersberger recorded that they had, since their arrival in New York in 1941, entertained in their "little sanctuary" more than three thousand visitors from fifty-five different countries.

Typical of the fun-filled shenanigans that overflowed their premises and spilled out onto neighboring residents was the time that a young Korean who had been in a Japanese concentration camp was among their guests. He related how he had asked the guard if, instead of _his_ awakening the prisoners so roughly at dawn each morning, _he_ might be allowed to wake them up by crowing like a rooster, barking like a dog, or roaring like a lion. Surprisingly, this permission was granted. So every morning, he cleverly imitated some animal, beginning, at least, the long, unhappy day with a small measure of unusual lightheartedness. Julia Lake commanded this guest to go to the open window and demonstrate exactly how he had served as the prison community's animal alarm clock. How the local populace must have wondered about the activities in Apartment 5G on THAT particular evening!

A telling instance of Dr. Kellersberger's typical concern and care for others occurred during Dr. Paul Brand's first visit to New York City. A Rockefeller Foundation grant made it possible for this brilliant son of British missionaries to India to visit the United States for research and consultation purposes. For seven years he had worked at the Vellore Christian Medical College in Vellore, India, specializing in nerve damage, seeking to understand the causes of paralysis and loss of sensation in leprosy. His own renowned surgical technique of Tendon Free Grafting had already placed him in the top rank of the few orthopedic surgeons in the world experienced in the difficult, unexplored field of reconstructive surgery in leprosy.

Dr. Brand attended a board meeting of the American Leprosy Missions, even though he was feeling quite unwell and had a bad headache at the time. He was welcomed as an honored guest, then left for the small, inexpensive rooming house where he was staying. Riding back on the subway, he became very ill with a suddenly worsening attack of influenza, and collapsed to the floor. His account of what happened, given at the 75th Anniversary Celebration of the Leprosy Missions on May 16, 1981 is a classic:

> The subway was full. People were standing; I was standing. But suddenly, I felt everything go totally blank, and I fell to the floor of the subway train. I lay there, I suppose, for about four or five stops, nobody — not one soul — moved or spoke a word. They just turned the other way and read their newspapers. People left at the subway stations. They stepped over me. I must say this about New York — they didn't step ON me! I might as well have been a corpse!
>
> Finally, when my stop came along, I crawled out and just sat on a bench and waited until the dizziness had passed and I felt able to go back to my little hotel. And there I lay until about five days later. Each morning, I sent the bellboy to the store to get orange juice, milk and aspirin and that is what I lived on. By that time, I had become depressed; I felt lonely and totally rejected in New York City. The utter indifference of the people in the subway, who just stepped over me, oppressed me and defeated my will to get well.
>
> A few days after the ALM board meeting, Eugene Kellersberger said to his wife, "You know, I'm bothered about that fellow, Brand! He came, and went, he talked to us, but he didn't look at all well. I'm just not happy about it!"
>
> No one seemed to know where Brand was, so Eugene Kellersberger took the New York telephone directory and telephoned every hotel in New York City. He started with "A" and went through "Z." And when he finished all the hotels, he started on the third rate places. I don't know how

long it took him — one day, two or three. He just sat there
with the telephone book. The memory of it makes me kind
of emotional, but finally he called the place where I was
and they said, "Yes, there's a fellow here named Brand, but
he doesn't come out of his room. He takes orange juice and
milk."

That day, Eugene Kellersberger turned up in the room
of my hotel. He said, "I found you! I found you!" His arms
were loaded with all kinds of good things for me to eat. His
radiant smile transformed my world! To me, he has always
remained as my picture of an angel of God!

Typically, there is no reference at all in Dr. Kellersberger's diaries to this unusual search for his friend. There are
only happy notations such as: "Dr. Paul Brand is tops, absolutely TOPS!" and "At last he is getting the recognition that
he deserves!"

DECISIONS OF A GENERAL SECRETARY, 1941–1953

The new executive who had for twenty-five years been on
the firing line in a remote corner of the world never became a
near-sighted, ingrown bureaucrat. Throughout his administration, he retained to an amazing degree the freshness of insight and consecrated drive of the strong, active Christian ide-
alist that he was. All of his decisions and policies bore the
mark of his dedicated medical professionalism and firsthand
overseas experience. He had the inimitable gift of breaking
down barriers erected around a heart, and stepping, uninvited
into a life with such a simple, childlike spirit that he was seldom rejected. His sincere interest and evident concern for a
person endeared him to even the most reserved personalities.
He really cared about people, no matter what they were like
— and they sensed it! To him, the important events of each
day were not the big meetings, the critical discussions, but the
PEOPLE involved in them. As an executive, he was able to
work harmoniously with even the most thorny and resistant of
nature!

During his administration, the American Mission to Lepers, Incorporated, acquired a new name. On June 1, 1943, the
doctor proposed that, in their title, the NAME OF THE DIS-

EASE be substituted for the word referring to a PERSON HAVING THAT DISEASE. Agreement on this touchy issue, requiring a change in the corporation constitution, was very slow in coming. Some progress was reported in a 1945 board meeting minute which read: "This Mission has taken its stand in eliminating the unhappy and stigmatizing word 'leper' from its title."

Finally, to Dr. Kellersberger's great satisfaction, a January 20, 1949 minute stated: "The name of this corporation is changed from 'The American Mission to Lepers' to 'The American Leprosy Missions, Incorporated,' this amendment effective January 1, 1950." Dr. Kellersberger made it clear why "Hansen's Disease" was not optional instead of "leprosy" in the title: "Any substitution for the word 'leprosy' will not eradicate the social stigma attached to the disease. Only a changed attitude of society and a real knowledge of the disease can do that."

The year 1941, in which the new general secretary took office, was a crucial year in leprosy drug research. Up to that time, no adequate, specific treatment for the disease was known. Chalmoogra oil, the successful use of which the doctor had demonstrated at his Bibanga colony, was beneficial, but did not arrest it. Experiments made during the 1930s in the effect of diptheria toxoid on leprosy were disappointing. In 1941, experimentation with the *sulfones* of the sulfa drug group began to prove effective in limiting the progress of Hansen's Disease.

The powerful drug *diamino-diphenyl sulfone*, DDS, was synthesized for the first time in 1908 by German chemists, but clinical tests were promptly abandoned because the substance was considered too toxic for the human body to tolerate. Experiments carried out at the United States Public Health Hospital at Carville, Louisiana from 1941 to 1943 showed that toleration of the proprietary sulfone, *promin*, was not only possible but advantageous in treating leprosy. Because it had to be given by injection, *promin* had to be administered only by trained personnel, over an extended period of time. Like the relentless disease itself, the slowest of all in developing, the sulfones act very, very slowly!

Once *promin* proved effective, other sulfones based on the more simple parent substance, DDS, appeared on the market. These new drugs, called "Dapsone" and "Diasone," were also slow to cure, but they led a revolution. Because they could be taken by mouth in the form of a tablet, it was possible for the first time to launch mass treatment projects both in Africa and India.

As a result of the effectiveness of DDS in treating leprosy, a dramatic new approach to its management emerged. No longer infectious after three months of treatment, those taking the drug did not need to be segregated as before. Designated as "discharged cases," they could lead normal lives in their own homes, securing the needed medication at a local clinic or hospital. As "arrested cases," clinically negative for at least a year, they must continue to report every six months for a check-up while continuing to take one-half the adult dose.

But early expectations of a "cure" proved to be a little too optimistic. The treatment often needs to be continued for years in order to avoid the danger of relapse. Many patients find it very hard to keep taking pills for ten years!

Now the organization with a new name, promoting the use of the potent new sulfones, resulting in a new system of control and management, found that it still had a very old human problem — prejudiced, fearful reluctance to learn a new way to THINK about leprosy! Throughout the world, it is still inordinately feared and secretly hidden. World Health Organization statistics show that it is not decreasing, but may be even more prevalent today than ever before! From twelve to fifteen million people living today are estimated to have leprosy, only twenty percent of those receiving any regular treatment for it!

Existence of an effective drug for treating a disease does not automatically halt its spread, if there is still ignorance concerning it and a traditional refusal to bring it out into the open. Even a miracle drug cannot restore useless limbs and marred visages of those already mutilated by years of infection. Only skilled orthopedic surgery, such as that done by Dr. Paul Brand, can do that! Nor does the existence of Dapsone identify the thousands of children living with infected parents.

Some eighty percent of all Hansen's Disease patients contract it in childhood, from close, family contact. Early detection is, therefore, of the utmost importance, indicating the new strategy needed for battling this ancient enemy of man.

Under Dr. Kellersberger's leadership, an aggressive new professional and investigative stance began to characterize the decisions taken by the Board. A vigorous program of public education about the facts of leprosy was further enlarged, designed to dispel unreasonable fear and encourage local acceptance, without discrimination against discharged patients sent back to live in their home communities. Innovative "preventive programs" were begun after World War II in eight different countries, massive public health drives to identify cases, especially where children were involved. Still more emphasis was placed on the support of ongoing research at such centers as the American Leprosy Missions LEPROSY ATELIER at the University of Hawaii School of Medicine, and the Schieffelin Leprosy Research Center in Karigiri, India.

Dr. Kellersberger's determination to evaluate real needs first hand led to his making two extended journeys of personal investigation of the known leprosy facilities of the world. One survey journey in 1946 covered Central and South America, Africa and Western Europe. A second one in 1947 and 1948 studied points of work with Hansen's Disease in Hawaii, the Philippines, the East Indies, China and India. The doctor and his wife together made the first trip. For the second, the General Secretary of the British Leprosy Mission, Donald Miller, was Eugene's traveling companion.

TWO INDEFATIGABLE SPEAKERS

Several times a year, the General Secretary and his Promotional Secretary made a publicity tour together. They often represented the leprosy work as a husband-and-wife team at summer conferences and large conventions. Most of the time, however, they worked on entirely different schedules. Some indication of the variety and multiplicity of the audiences addressed by Dr. and Mrs. Kellersberger is given by a New England tour which the doctor made in the late fall of 1944. Be-

tween November 5th and 10th, he spoke in the Community
Church of Salem, Massachusetts; to two different groups at
the University of New Hampshire Medical School in Durham;
at the Boston University School of Theology; to the Gordon
School of Missions, both morning and evening classes, and the
Providence Bible Institute. He gave a two-hour lecture at the
Yale Medical School; addressed the Episcopal denomination's
Berkeley Divinity School; lectured to Dr. Kenneth Scott La-
tourette's class in Missions at the Yale School of Divinity, and
held an audience of 250 girls at Lawson Junior College spellbound during a morning chapel hour!

During an eleven-day tour of the north central states in
1948, he held twenty-eight meetings, addressing some 4,000
people in sixteen different cities. In 1949, on another trip, he
traveled approximately 8,000 miles through Tennessee, Georgia, North and South Carolina, Mississippi, Alabama, Louisiana, Arkansas, Texas, Oklahoma and New Mexico. Within
a month's time, he addressed sixty-three audiences in forty-
three cities scattered over these eleven states.

A diary entry made on April 7, 1950 reads: "Just completed a strenuous southern and central tour. Gone 38 days,
traveled over 10,000 miles: by air, 2,000; by rail, 80; by car,
6,800. Held 74 meetings in 35 cities, in 12 states to an estimated 15,000 people!" On a 1951 West coast tour in March
and April, he gave 119 messages in 33 cities of California, Oregon and Washington.

Home from a forty-four-day speaking schedule, he listed
twenty-five types of meetings he had held: "6 morning church
services, 2 vesper services, 3 industrial groups, 3 young people's groups, 2 *Bible* classes, 1 men's club, 4 college lectures, 5
medical schools, 1 army medical group, 1 army camp, 1
forum, 1 high school, 2 county medical societies, 15 missionary conferences addresses, 3 radio interviews, 1 Easter Sunrise
Service, 1 leprosy missions auxiliary, 1 service at the Carville
Leprosarium, 1 Presbytery meeting, 2 Negro college chapels,
1 missionary society, 4 interdenominational women's groups
and 1 memorial service."

Always budget-conscious, trying to keep his travel expenses to a strict minimum, the doctor did most of his travel-

ing by train, using a Clergy Permit, since he was an ordained minister as well as physician. A good night's sleep in a Pullman car berth gave him the rest he needed between demanding engagements. Travelers on day coaches, in spite of themselves, became captive audiences, as the warm strength of his personality and obvious commitment to a unique cause gripped those seated about him.

Typical of his straightforward approach is an incident recorded in a February 4, 1944 journal entry: "Rode on a train today along the beautiful Ohio River from Cincinnati to Bluefield, West Virginia. Met many soldiers. One said to me, "I've seen it all!" I said to him, "No you haven't! Here's something you've never seen!" And I pulled out my photos of my elephantiasis and tumor cases. He couldn't believe it! Made him sick!"

A deep impression was always made on the crowds that clustered about him after such a deliberately shocking introduction. His diaries are crammed with names and addresses of thousands of people met during his travels in just this manner. Taking down addresses was no mere form; letters about the work of the American Leprosy Missions always followed those initial contacts, however brief.

THE UNITED STATES PUBLIC HEALTH HOSPITAL AT CARVILLE, LOUISIANA

The relationship of the American Leprosy Missions to the Carville Hospital has from the beginning been a close one. It was William M. Danner, the first General Secretary, who was largely responsible for the establishment of the United States national leprosarium. Much loved "Uncle Will," as he was called, brought to the attention of Senator Ransdell of Louisiana the sad plight of victims of Hansen's Disease in the United States, some of them soldiers infected while on military duty in the Philippines. As a result of Mr. Danner's urgings, the Committee on Public Health and National Quarantine's famous Report #306 was presented by Senator Ransdell to the United States on March 25, 1916, as a "bill to provide for the care and treatment of persons afflicted with leprosy and to prevent the spread of leprosy in the United States."

Old Indian Camp Plantation in Iberville Parish, tucked away in a bend of the Mississippi River, had served as the Louisiana lazeretto since 1894. The first eight patients were towed on a coal barge to the isolated cove and unceremoniously dumped on the shore. The Daughters of Charity of St. Vincent de Paul have from the beginning provided the necessary nursing service for this institution. In 1921, the Stars and Stripes were raised over the site, acquired by the United States Public Health Service as a national leprosarium.

For many years, the American Leprosy Missions, Inc. has sponsored and underwritten the cost of two annual, week-long seminars at Carville, designed to expose those in attendance from all over the world to an intensive review of all aspects of leprosy management. These seminars have come to be regarded as one of the most outstanding yearly events in this sphere of medicine.

Some of the happiest of all Dr. Kellersberger's journal entries are the ones relating to his Carville visits. He dearly loved the institution, its fine staff and the resident patients!

> *October 16, 1941.* The Reverend Clifton E. Rash has been invited to be the new Protestant Chaplain at Carville. He is pastor of a Christian Church in Salina, Kansas and a member of the Executive Committee of the Christian and Missionary Alliance. Housing for him is provided by the American Leprosy Missions on government property. His utilities, meals and uniforms are all at government expense.
>
> *December 7, 1941.* Pearl Harbor Day at Carville, Louisiana! We listened to the President's message. Then showed the film of our Bibanga work, "Song After Sorrow," to entire staff and personnel, including twenty Catholic sisters. We gave each one a gift of a woven palmfiber mat from the Congo.
>
> *April 16, 1943.* Fine reception by Carville staff! Very good hour's conference with Chief of Staff regarding admittance of cases recently referred to us. Full day! Rich experience!
>
> *February 14, 1949.* Visit to Carville, to the office of the *Star*, the institution's official periodical. Had happy visit and prayer with each of my good friends.
>
> *March 16, 1951.* Important meeting with Carville

staff. Full and happy day. Visited all my patient friends, read Scripture and prayed with them. Visited the Catholic sisters and the Chaplain.

February 10, 1952. Full day at Carville. Meals in government dining hall. Lovely! Visited with all the cases transferred here last year from the Virgin Islands. One is a Christian from the Moravian Mission there!

MORE THAN AN ADMINISTRATOR

One of Dr. Kellersberger's most remarkable professional contributions was made during World War II, in the field of medical education. On May 26, 1942, the Board of Directors acceded to requests from the United States Department of Health that their General Secretary be allowed time to serve on an eight-man team delegated to lecture nationwide on Tropical Medicine. With American G.I.'s fighting in the jungles and swamps of tropical areas of the world, army, navy and civilian doctors were coming face-to-face with diseases unfamiliar to them. From 1942 to 1945, the doctor managed to add to his regular work schedule this added responsibility of assisting official United States medical personnel in identification of the tropical diseases with which he was so familiar. He lectured in thirty-eight of the sixty-five four-year medical schools then in existence, some of them several times. He addressed the staffs of great hospitals and various army camps all over the nation, as well as widely assorted medical organizations. The reaction of these audiences is recorded in the diaries in words such as these:

December 12, 1941. Great experience! Guest of Dr. E. C. Faust, Dean of Tulane Medical School. Spent one hour in auditorium with juniors, seniors, post-grads and faculty. Demonstrated *trypanosomes* in brain tissue. Showed 15 slides on sleeping sickness movie and "Song After Sorrow." One full hour of rapt attention, then prolonged applause. Dr. Faust said, "This is a hard-boiled bunch. They don't usually stay or clap — just get up and leave."

November 24, 1942 Camp Kilmer, New Brunswick, New Jersey. Spoke to 75 M.D.'s and 50 nurses on Tropical Medicine. Fine response. Camp Kilmer is the clearing point for

outgoing forces to Europe. Some leaving today. All most
courteous to me.

Dr. Kellersberger made another important contribution to
medical knowledge in his professional writings. Following the
publication in the *American Medical Journal* of his article on 9,000
cases of African Sleeping Sickness, he was asked to collaborate
on *The Clinical Manual on Tropical Medicine*. This handbook was
published in 1942 for the use of Army and Navy doctors.

In March 1942, he was called to Washington to consult
with the Secretary of War about the formulation of a special
directive regarding sleeping sickness, necessary because of
troop movements in infected countries.

A diary entry of November 13, 1942 reads: "To Washington today, War Department. Fine Conference with Lt. Col.
Dr. Whayne, Surgeon General of Navy, Rear Admiral Ross
McIntire, Dr. Fred Wample, Professor of Preventive and Industrial Medicine at Medical College of Virginia, and Army
and Navy Intelligence Staff." He was called to Washington
again in 1945 to confer with Public Health authorities regarding malaria control in war areas.

His article, *Leprosy Today*, printed in Volume II, No. 4 of
Clinics, was reviewed in the January 3, 1943 issue of *Newsweek*.

On October 27, 1949, he was interviewed by *Life* Magazine and a selection of his photographs of tropical diseases
used to illustrate an article on Tropical Medicine.

The article, however, which won him the highest acclaim
was his *Social Stigma of Leprosy*, presented in person on November 10, 1950, to the New York Academy of Sciences Conference on Leprosy. It was printed in the *Annals* of that society in
March of the following year, and was reprinted numerous
times by popular request. The doctor minced no words in at-
tacking "the stupid ignorance about leprosy right here in the
U.S.A.!"

THE MINISTRY OF ACCEPTANCE

The true story of Dr. and Mrs. Kellersberger's courageous ministry to many individuals afflicted with Hansen's
Disease will never be fully known. A very few of the diary en-

tries referring to this difficult part of their work suffice to show the depths of human suffering plumbed:

June 9, 1943. Brazilian referred to me today for leprosy diagnosis by Bellevue Hospital. Studied their case histories. Some from Bermuda and Puerto Rico not diagnosed or treated for three years!

December 31, 1943. Found another case of Lepromatous leprosy today on 23rd Street. Nobody knows or cares!

June 1, 1947. Another Greek in my office today to get Dapsone for his brother who has leprosy in Greece, and cannot get the drug.

June 13, 1948. Consultation at Presbyterian Medical Center on missionary flown in from Gold Coast. Six missionaries now under treatment!

August 23, 1949. Case of leprosy undiagnosed for ten years came to me today for consultation. Out most of the day with this tragic case.

December 8, 1950. Called to see leprosy case by Director of Public Health, Philadelphia. Native of St. Croix with disease unrecognized for 25 years. Taken into custody by police squad. *Cruel and stupid!* He cried! I prayed with him, his wife and child. Got back home at 1:30 a.m.

May 27, 1952. Jesuit priest from Philippines here to see me regarding case of leprosy. Sad! Young Filipino here for only three weeks. Will probably be deported.

November 28, 1952. Sad arrested case today. Worked 20 years for Post Office department. Now refused job. Good example of social stigma of leprosy. All day with Civil Service Commission in Federal Building. Another legal battle to fight. Perhaps I am making some progress, but it is SLOW AS MUD!

November 29, 1953. Again to Legal Aid Society regarding my latest case for *Affidavits!*

The Kellersberger's apartment home was often the refuge for some arrested case officially released after a series of negative tests. Theirs was a ministry of fearless, loving acceptance, calculated to offset in every way possible the total rejection their friends met from every other quarter. This story among the hundreds that could be told illustrates Eugene's compassion in dealing with just one of the cases that he discovered. He called this experience, "An Outcast in an American City":

> It was hard to find where she lived. In the vicinity of her address there seemed to be only factories, empty lots and delapidated shacks. The correct number I finally found on what I first thought was an abandoned saloon. On closer investigation I saw printed in worn letters above the battered door: *Chapel of Our Immaculate Lady*. It was an abandoned Catholic chapel!
>
> Through an empty lot, inches deep in slush and melting snow, I worked my way into two small rooms on the damp, ground level. I knocked, and the door was opened by the victim of leprosy whom I was seeking. There was no doubt about the diagnosis. She was a middle-aged Mexican woman with badly disfigured face and hands. In the cold, bare room I talked with her. Though she spoke English fairly well, her husband, also present, could not speak a word of it.
>
> "Have you had any visitors?", I asked her.
>
> "No one has come for months now," she replied. "I just sit here all day long. I am afraid to go out for fear that people will run away from me. My husband takes care of me. He used to work in a meat-packing plant and I was a maid in a large hotel. Our only daughter supports us both."
>
> Then she told me that she did not have long to live and that she preferred to remain with her husband in her last years, and to die on that bleak back street. She did not want to go to the government leprosarium, where she could certainly be helped, though her case was too advanced and had lasted too many years to be cured. I realized that none of the million people living around her realized that in their midst was a poor, outcast victim of leprosy. Had they known, perhaps a very few would have cared enough to see that she be removed as far away from them as possible.
>
> "Has anyone ever prayed with you?", I asked.
>
> She gave me a searching, almost frightened look. I realized that she hardly knew what I meant. It didn't matter now that I was a Protestant, and she, a Roman Catholic. I told her that Christ had died for her on the Cross, and that He, the Great Physician, was the only one able to help her both physically and spiritually.

Then I placed my hands upon her head in blessing, as Christ taught us to do, and I prayed earnestly for her, feeling the tragedy and the seriousness of this stark, realistic situation. Those sad, heartsearching words from Psalm 142:4 came to mind: "No man cared for my soul!" As I continued to pray, kneeling beside her on the bare, damp floor, I felt her body begin to tremble. Suddenly she broke into a torrent of tears. Finally, she gained control of her emotions and said in broken English: "Doctor, no money on earth can ever pay you for what you have done for me today!" As I prepared to leave, a radiant smile came across her swollen, scarred face, and she said, "Doctor, I am going to pray for you, too!"

THE ALL AFRICA LEPROSY
REHABILITATION TRAINING CENTER

One of the most successful, long-term results of Dr. Kellersberger's years of work with the American Leprosy Missions is A.L.E.R.T., the All Africa Leprosy Rehabilitation Training Center, in Addis Ababa, Ethiopia.

From the outset of his administration, he envisioned for his beloved continent a special medical center which would combine the best hospital, rehabilitation, and research facilities with a strong program of basic training in every aspect of the care, treatment, prevention and control of leprosy. India had the highly successful Schieffelin Leprosy Research Institute at Karigiri, but nowhere in all of Africa was there a training institution for dealing with a leprosy problem of tremendous, continent-wide magnitude. Africa is estimated to have close to 3.5 million people with Hansen's Disease, twenty percent of these suffering with some form of disability!

On November 8, 1932, Emperor Haile Selassie I had laid the cornerstone of the Princess Zenebe Wroq Leprosy sanatorium, honoring his daughter, trained as a nurse. The construction and maintenance of this hospital was financed by the American Leprosy Missions and staffed by the Sudan Interior Mission.

When Dr. Kellersberger came to office, the only existing leprosaria in Ethiopia were government operated, on an un-

satisfactory compulsory basis, the sad result of the Italian occupation of that country from 1935 to 1941.

One of the very first efforts made by the doctor as an administrator was to re-establish the Sudan Interior Mission
leprosy work. A letter written to the Emperor of Ethiopia on
August 9, 1941, offered financial aid for this purpose. Another
letter written to the American Embassy in Ethiopia in 1944
states:

> A considerable fund will soon be raised of which ap-
> proximately $20,000 can be assigned toward the develop-
> ment of an adequate anti-leprosy program for Ethiopia . . .
> It appears to us that the institution in Addis Ababa might
> well become not only a central leprosy colony and hospital
> for the country, but also a training center where various
> Ethiopian workers, such as doctors, nurses, teachers, public
> health workers and religious leaders might receive special
> training in the social and clinical aspects of leprosy. This
> would make them able to deal with leprosy cases in one way
> or another, wherever they find them in the country. In such
> a program of training, our Mission will be particularly in-
> terested!

The years of planning, effort and intercessory prayer that
finally brought the All Africa Leprosy Rehabilitation Center
into being may be traced through the doctor's diaries:

> *May 15, 1945.*   The government of Ethiopia is open to
> a cooperative project! In our Post-War Program, we set
> aside a sum for a possible Ethiopian project, an initial grant
> for equipment, after that, funds for maintenance and per-
> sonnel.
>
> *July 19, 1945.*   Have requested Dr. Glenn Reed of the
> Presbyterian Mission in Egyptian Sudan to go to Ethiopia
> and discuss with the government the conditions under which
> cooperative leprosy work might be carried on in that country.
>
> *January 3, 1946.*   Negotiations with the government of
> Ethiopia begun. They want our Mission to provide person-
> nel for overall administration in the spheres of general pol-
> icy for leprosaria and treatment of the disease.
>
> *October 14, 1946.*   Wrote a letter to Emperor Haile Se-
> lassie today outlining our conditions for working. We will
> work in Ethiopia (1) if religious liberty is guaranteed; (2) if

an adequate legal grant of land is given by the government, enough for the economic security of the patients, free from taxation; (3) if there is a signed agreement between the Ethiopian government and the Missions involved, and (4) if drugs are admitted free of customs! As a Christian organization, we reserve the right to preach the Gospel of Jesus Christ, because of Whom this colony will exist.

February 12, 1947. To Washington, D.C. to visit Ethiopian Embassy. Our entire conferences was in French with His Excellency, Irnu, all regarding the starting of leprosy work there.

August 12, 1948. Sent Ethiopian administrators a copy of our "Leprosy Colony Policies."

On December 11, 1965, a little over a year before Dr. Kellersberger's death, the All Africa Leprosy Rehabilitation Training Center was legally established by five founding organizations. Dr. Paul Brand represented the International Society for the Rehabilitation of the Disabled. Orie O. Miller represented the American Leprosy Missions and A. D. Askew, the Leprosy Mission in London. His excellency, Abebe Reita, the Minister of Public Health, represented the Ethiopian government and His Excellency, Liji Kasse Weldemarian, represented the Haile Selassie I University in Addis Ababa.

Today, A.L.E.R.T. has a modern 120-bed hospital with dormitory accommodations for additional patients. There is a large student hostel and academic buildings for the training center. Working in cooperation with the hospital and teaching units, is the Armauer Hansen Research Institute, named for the original Norwegian discoverer of leprosy bacillus, and financed by the SAVE THE CHILDREN organization of Sweden and Norway. Skilled orthopedic surgery and physical therapy are available for all types of disability. A.L.E.R.T. is unique in its integration of leprosy treatment with general medicine and its special effort to draw patients with deformities caused by diseases other than leprosy. Excellent workshop training is also offered in the making of protective and corrective shoes and other prosthetic devices. To make the institution complete, vocational training equips patients to achieve economic status and independence after dismissal.

Trainees from all over Africa and even from other continents come to take the sixteen-week course in the supervising
of rural leprosy surveys and treatment units. After the doctor's
death on January 18, 1966, the Kellersberger Memorial Foundation was created to provide the salaries of certain positions
on the staff. In 1974, the American Leprosy Missions began
sponsoring an annual lectureship at A.L.E.R.T., called "The
Kellersberger Memorial Lecture," to advance the greater
knowledge of leprosy and its ultimate solution.

[13]

Horizons Unlimited

A VOICE FROM THE PAST

Dr. Kellersberger's attendance at the First International Leprosy Congress in Cairo, Egypt, in 1938 brought him into professional contact with significant medical figures from all over the world. Another expanding experience was the wartime journey made in 1941 from South Africa back to the United States. On this 17,000-mile voyage the homeward-bound couple touched briefly at Singapore, Indonesia, Borneo, the Philippines and Hawaii and were given an important introduction to leprosy work in Manila.

The full scope of the world-wide ministry that lay ahead became apparent in 1946, on a six-and-a-half month tour of Central and South America, the West Indies, Africa and western Europe. Between March 16 and October 2, the General Secretary and his wife journeyed approximately 45,000 miles, nearly the equivalent of twice around the globe! They crossed the equator eight times and traveled on five continents. In the course of this one journey, they flew over the Atlantic, Pacific and Indian Oceans, the Caribbean, Mediterranean and Red Seas, and the Mississippi, Amazon, Congo, Nile, Niger, Rhone and Thames Rivers. They set foot in forty different countries, visited sixty-five leprosy establishments in thirty-

299

LaGuardia Field, New York, March 15, 1946, the Kellersbergers' departure for a six- and one-half month tour of leprosy facilities of Central and South America, Africa and Europe.

five countries, and saw more than 35,000 people with Hansen's Disease. The organization they represented supported in whole or in part, forty-two of the sixty-five leprosaria visited.

A detailed account of this odyssey, combined with that of the doctor's thorough investigation of leprosy facilities of the Pacific and Far East in 1948, is recorded in the book, *Doctor of the Happy Landings*, published by John Knox Press. The title of this book originated with a Pan American stewardess, who, on learning of her passenger's extensive travels, commented: "You are a doctor of many happy landings!"

Wartime restrictions were still in force in March 1946. In a shaken world just beginning to pick up the pieces after global struggle, it was a major problem to secure passports and visas for both eastern and western hemisphere nations. The date of departure was almost at hand; neither the doctor nor his wife had passports. In a final desperate attempt to break the red tape deadlock that threatened to cancel the entire trip, Dr. Kellersberger put in a long distance call to Washington, D.C., asking to be connected with the very top official in the government department involved. When the telephone connection was complete, this is the conversation that took place:

"Repeat your name, sir!"

"Kellersberger! K-E-L-L-E-R-S-B-E-R-G-E-R!"

"Are you EUGENE Kellersberger?"

"Yes, I am!"

"Do you remember the capsizing of a canoe on Buzzard's Bay, near Woods Hole, Massachusetts in the summer of 1912?"

"Do I! Edmund Montgomery and I were in the canoe when it turned over. We clung for hours to a spar buoy until we were finally picked up just at dusk by an auxiliary powered sloop that took us back to Woods Hole! I have not heard from Ed in thirty-four years!"

"This is Edmund Montgomery speaking to you!"

The necessary passports arrived in two days.

Eugene barely had time to secure the sixteen visas required for the first portion of the trip.

Before her departure, Julia Lake determined to do a very "Julia Lakish" thing. Included in her fifty-five-pound baggage weight limit was an empty bottle into which she planned to put a bit of soil from every single country on which they set foot. This private little project was successfully carried out, to the consternation of airport authorities in some of the countries where they stopped. Flight attendants did not know what to make of the unpredictable lady who said, "Wait a minute!" and dashed to the edge of the runway to scoop up a handful of dirt, which she carefully poured into a bottle. Back in New York City, the contents of that bottle were vigorously shaken, then divided into dozens of small containers, each labeled, DIRT FROM 40 COUNTRIES. Family members and special friends are still the proud possessors of this unique, typically "Julia Lakish" souvenir.

TOUR OF LEPROSY WORK IN CENTRAL AND SOUTH AMERICA AND THE CARIBBEAN

Each of the institutions visited by the Kellersbergers on their entire journey was unique, demonstrating every different sort of leprosy management policy. The doctor, however, did not make the trip for observation purposes only. He also hoped to share his own rich professional experience with other leprologists and to evaluate at first hand new projects and critical needs which might be underwritten by his organization. Julia Lake wrote to the family:

> Eugene is spending much time with medical and colonial officials. In many places visited, he has public meetings in order to educate the populace concerning the leprosy problems of their respective countries. Many ask highly intelligent questions and manifest marked interest during the formal discussions. He is learning much and also giving out much. Many new avenues of service for our Missions are opening up!

Of the numerous leprosaria visited, a special few made indelible impressions on the visitors. There was some particular occasion, some unusually pathetic circumstance that was absolutely unforgettable. More often, it was individual residents they met, who had dealt with their illness in such a courageous, triumphant manner that just being in their presence was a blessing and an humbling benediction!

The *Asilo Jose de Lopez*, thirty miles outside Mexico City, did not give the impression of imprisonment, for thick-foliaged trees hid the tall fence that surrounded the premises. Here, the visitors met choice souls whose lives and faces glowed with incredible power, even though disfigured by disease. One such was a pretty, spirited girl who had come in a deplorable condition from an impoverished home. Love awaited her, for when her own case was pronounced arrested, she was married to one of the young men patients who had only a slight infection. Another outstanding personality was a brilliant, highly educated lawyer from a prominent Spanish family, who had probably contracted Hansen's Disease in childhood from his Indian nurse. Still another unforgettable character at the

Mexican national leprosarium was a carpenter who had lost all his fingers, but who daily tied his tools to the palms that were left and continued to supply other residents with small, useful items of furniture.

The experience at the *Asilo de Piedad* in Guatamala was in marked contrast to Mexico. The "Asylum of Pity" was surrounded by stark, high walls. Eugene and Julia Lake were required to put on gowns, masks and gloves before they were allowed to enter. With the lonely patients at this isolated hospital, they shared the small gifts of costume jewelry, handkerchiefs, soap, lace, ribbons, and ties which they had stuffed into the corners of their suitcase for just such recipients. The last thing they heard as they drove away was a song of happy thanksgiving, sung in chorus by hoarse throats. The last thing they saw was dozens of crippled hands, waving goodbye to them through the bars of a locked gate.

From a hilltop in Colombia, South America, a party of seventeen doctors and one Julia Lake looked down upon "the largest city of sick in the world." A small steel bridge across the Bogota River provided the only access into the *Aqua de Dios* Valley. The bridge was called *Puente de los Suspiros*, "The Bridge of Sighs," because it led into the vale of tears. Spread out over this secluded valley, the party on the hilltop could see nine separate hospitals clustered around the soaring tower of a Catholic cathedral in the center.

The only way to visit such a huge, sprawling establishment was on horseback. Eugene, the Hill Country Texan, was delighted at this prospect right out of his boyhood, but Julia Lake had never in all her life worn pants or ridden a horse! While her husband was being escorted to each of the hospitals by his hosts, she spent a never-to-be-forgotten day, sitting quietly on that hilltop, looking out over the "Water of God" Valley below and praying that every single soul down there might drink of the true Water of Life.

The tiny, cramped asylum of Chacachacare was memorable for being located in such a totally forbidding, isolated setting. Tucked into several tiny coves, backed by steep cliffs, on an island six miles off the coast of South America, it was completely dependent on mainland sources for food and drinking water. At this remote encampment, reached only by boat from the sea, there were other heroic personalities that the Kellersbergers never forgot. There was a Syrian artist who had for years continued to paint exquisite pictures with his disabled hands. There was the attractive, obviously cultured woman whom they saw, sitting, wholly engrossed in reading her *Bible*, and there were sixteen plucky young Boy Scouts, who proudly formed an honor guard through which the doctor and his wife walked into the brightly decorated church.

Children at the Paramaribo, Dutch Guiana colony, run by the Moravian Evangelical Church of Holland, were allowed to have as many pets as they liked. There were canaries, monkeys, ducks, chickens and a brightly-colored macaw, whom the children sympathetically showed to Julia Lake. "He's sick, too, like we are!", they told her. Sure enough! The bird had only one leg, so the little group of patients had welcomed him into their fellowship of suffering.

Of all the nations visited on the tour of South America leprosy facilities, Brazil made the best impression on the Kellersbergers because of its enlightened approach to the problem of the disease. In the chapel of the Pirapitingui Leprosarium, in the State of Sao Paulo, Eugene gave his message in German, which was interpreted by the Danish pastor into Portuguese.

TOUR OF LEPROSY FACILITIES
OF SEVENTEEN COUNTRIES

A giant Pan American Clipper took the Kellersbergers across the South Atlantic, from Natal, Brazil to Fisherman's Lake, in Liberia, West Africa. There were no reliable travel connections between Liberia and the British colonies farther down the coast at that time. Travelers were forced to resort to slow, coastwise native longboats, in order to reach connecting points with inland cities. Several days' delay due to such uncertainty would play havoc with the tightly coordinated schedule of the leprosy missions representatives. Unexpected accommodations and transportation were graciously provided when the director of the Firestone Rubber Company's plan-

tations near Fisherman's Lake learned that a member of the
the United States Health Department's Advisory Committee
on Leprosy was stranded there. He invited the doctor and his
wife to be his personal guests for the night and arranged the
next day for priority places on a United States Army plane
flying from Roberts Field, Liberia, to Accra, on the Gold
Coast. From there, regular connections by British Overseas
Airways took the Kellersbergers to their first destination in
Nigeria.

Dr. Francis Akanu Ibiam was the doctor in charge of the
colony of 4,000 patients run by the Church of Scotland at Itu
mission station in Nigeria. Knighted by Queen Elizabeth for
outstanding service, this man later served both as president of
the University College of Ibadan, and as the first governor of
the Eastern Province of independent Nigeria. Of their memorable visit to Itu, Dr. Kellersberger wrote:

> It was an inspiration to see this large community of
> sick growing their own food, raising their own cattle, distill-
> ing their own medicines, pressing their own oil, making
> their own soap, and forming for themselves, even with phys-
> ical handicaps, an independent community. It was encour-
> aging to find as their medical advisor, during the absence of
> their regular superintendent, a physician of their own race,
> a distinguished graduate of Edinburgh University. He had
> refused a responsible position offered him by the British
> government. "I am a product of this Mission," he ex-
> plained. "What I am, I owe to Christ and His people, so I
> am morally obligated to service in this place!"

We were privileged to have dinner in the attractive home
of this Nigerian doctor and his talented wife, who is a registered nurse with the blue blood of an African princess in her
veins. Their spacious residence overlooked the historic Cala-
bar River, on whose banks once stood slave blocks, and from
whence once flowed to America a stream of broken life which
had been ruthlessly caught in the terrible whirlpool of human
greed. This African man and woman, emancipated both physically and spiritually, represented to us an indigenous Christian leadership for whom Mary Slessor and those upon whom
her mantle had fallen, had given their lives.

Not far from Itu, we visited unique itinerant clinics where native chiefs had voluntarily isolated those of their tribe who were found with leprosy. These communities are periodically visited by British doctors and nurses, whom we accompanied on one such medical call. (*Doctor of the Happy Landings*, pages 110–111.)

Dr. Kellersberger's diary entries give some idea of the exertions of overland travel and the great variety of leprosy work observed as they made their way across central Africa:

May 11, 1946. Drove 425 miles in 23 1/2 hours to Garkida, in northern Nigeria, in an old Ford pickup. Bad tires, flats, rains. Crossed vast tree-lined plains. Stopped for four hours of sleep in state guesthouse. Dead tired. Saw gazelles, baboons, hartebeest. Stopped at Sudan Interior Mission for tea. They had no water for the tea!

May 12. At unique station of Garkida. Segregation of leprosy cases of the right kind here! Held service in leprosy colony church. Fine singing by 496 inmates! Dr. Bosler is fine organizer, practical, enthusiastic. Well run, well managed colony. Two "clean" native helpers, the head nurse and the lab technician. 1000 fertile acres of land. Best mission colony seen so far on entire trip! All have fields, do their own work. Have fruit trees, granaries. Our Mission built all the buildings here!

May 13. Back to Jos, Nigeria, in pickup driven by D. D. Heckman. Had two blowouts in first 50 miles. Slept in road. All night trip of 425 miles in 17 hours. Hard and tiring!

May 14. Jos. Conferences with doctors, mission heads, government officials. Open meeting tonight on leprosy for all Sudan Interior missionaries.

June 13. By Portuguese steamer 300 miles to Lobito, Angola.

June 14. Met by Leslie Biers. Drove 300 miles to Elende, 7,000 feet high over Bihe Plateau.

June 16. To Camundongo, Canadian Mission. Leprosy asylum only 300 yards from station. 500 inmates, 100 infected. Not enough food. Need help. Tragic!

June 17. To Chissamba, station of Canadian United Mission. Saw outstation dispensary with 40 leprosy patients.

One of best mission hospitals I have seen, run by Dr. Strangeway.

June 18. Real bush driving, 250 miles to Boma, Belgian Congo. Stopped to visit leprosy village of 60. Fine, small piece of Christian work. Drove over continental divide into area drained by our Kasai River, along old slave trail followed by Livingstone. Sandy roads. No water, no villages for miles! Saw 9 mission stations in Angola, 7 leprosy colonies. Have traveled approximately 30,450 miles so far in Africa!

The highlight of the Africa part of the entire trip was, of course, the Kellersbergers' return to the Belgian Congo. From June 18th to August 12th, they were in the land of their own former mission field, visiting points of leprosy work already familiar to them on the upper and lower reaches of the Congo River, and in the Katanga and the Kivu.

The few, brief days back at Bibanga on the American Presbyterian Congo Mission, after an absence of six years, were unbelievably and joyously hectic! Thousands of former patients and mission employees came to greet their beloved "Doctor NOT AFRAID" (Ngangabuke Bukitu) and "Mama-Who-Makes-Happy" (Mamu Musankisha). Many brought welcoming gifts of eggs and live chickens or goats.

During Eugene's years of work at Bibanga, a capable woman named Mua Mbiya had been responsible for the care of the orphans brought to the Edna Kellersberger Memorial Hospital. She had also been Julia Lake's faithful prayer partner, coming each week on market day morning to kneel with her in a secluded, natural prayer room created by the overhanging branches of an old mango tree. When the couple had left Bibanga in 1941 to take up their leprosy missions career, Mua Mbiya promised to pray for them every single day by name without fail. When they parted, she had emphatically stated: "I will see you again. I will not die till these eyes have looked upon your faces once again!"

Frail, sick and old, she had now lain for months at death's door. No one thought that she had even the slightest chance of living to see her beloved friends again. But survive she did, seemingly by sheer will power! When the doctor and his wife drove onto the station to a tumultuous welcome, the very first place they went was to Mua Mbiya's bedside at the hospital, for a quiet, praise-filled reunion. Two days later, a peaceful, satisfied Mua Mbiya slipped away, having gazed once again on the faces of the two for whom she had so faithfully prayed for so many years.

More than to any other factor, Dr. and Mrs. Kellersberger always attributed the success of their work to the intercessory prayers of two very special people. One was an old Texas schoolmate, Miss Mattie Hayes, and the other — Mua Mbiya! These two women, like the Apostle Paul's friend, Epaphras, "labored fervently in prayer" for their dear friends in leprosy work. Their unseen, unsuspected supporting ministry of <u>enablement</u> was as necessary as the more dramatic, out-front activities of those for whom they never failed to pray.

The journey overland across central Africa continued through Uganda, Tanganyika, Kenya, Sudan and Ethiopia, during August and September of 1946:

> *August 14.* To Shinyanga, Africa Inland Mission, Tanganyika Territory. Visited general hospital, five units well spread out. Leprosy colony one-third mile away in a shallow valley. Nice houses and dispensary. Clean, well-organized, 250 patients, but no separation according to types. Small fields. Needs money for chapel, childrens' home and playground.
>
> *August 15.* To Kiomboi, Swedish Free Mission. Unusually hard trip through black dirt swamps, vast baobab and thornbush forests, over the great Wembere Steppe, down dangerous escarpments. Got lost on the Steppe, went 15 miles out of our way over sandy riverbeds, no road in sight. Kiomboi colony is agricultural type with 240 residents.
>
> *August 24.* Flew from Nairobi, Kenya to Khartoum, Sudan, on 12-seater Lockheed. Glorious sunrise and exquisite view of Kilimanjaro from 10,000 feet! Passed over vast flood plains of both the Blue and White Nile. Visited the Church Missionary Society asylum in Omdurman, Sudan.
>
> *September 2 Addis Ababa, Ethiopia.* Had official conference regarding future leprosy work with representatives of all four protestant missions working here. Full, frank discussions!

September 3, Addis Ababa. First official conference with His Excellency, Ababa Retta, Ethiopian Vice-Minister of Health. Made important proposals for leprosy work. Had tea with United States Consul. Laying groundwork for future cooperative work, to be supported by our Mission. My gold watch was stolen!

Five happy days in Cairo, Egypt, with old friends brought to a close, the African part of the extended journey. The next lap was by British Overseas Airways to Tripoli, Malta, and Marseilles, France, with London the final destination.

One final institution remained to be visited, a European one — La Chartreuse de Valbonne, in southern France. An asylum is known to have existed on this site since 1003 A.D. The Carthusian Monastery built to house it in 1201 was confiscated by the French government following World War I. The organization represented by the Kellersbergers purchased this property at that time and gave it to the Protestant Church of France for use as a leprosarium. Set among clustered cedars, spreading vineyards and manicured olive groves, it has a graveyard adjoining, where many who died with leprosy are buried beside the monks who cared for them. Much damage was done to the property by World War II troops stationed there, necessitating a special, large grant from the American Leprosy Missions for renovation and repairs.

At the time of the Kellersbergers' visit in 1946, 150 German prisoners of war were billeted in the cells once occupied by the monks, assigned to the work of reconstructing the old monastery. Eugene held services in German for these workers both morning and evening. The response was truly touching. At Valbonne, the bitterness of being a prisoner of war was overcome and forgotten in the loving atmosphere of Christian forgiveness, acceptance and trust found there. The captain of the German group, one of several who had made a profession of faith in Christ, said to Eugene, "I had to be made a prisoner of war in order to come to know my Savior!"

Plane reservations had been made months beforehand for the General Secretary and his wife to fly from London to New York on September 29th. The doctor needed time to prepare

The Monks' Walk of the Carthusian Monastery in Valbonne, France, was photographed by Dr. Kellersberger. A leprosarium has existed on this site since A.D. 1003, the present one supported by the American Leprosy Missions.

the main address, reporting on the entire trip, for the Fortieth Anniversary Celebration and Annual Meeting of the American Leprosy Missions, Inc., on October 4th.

But one of the unforeseen aftermaths of World War II was a tremendous backlog in plane bookings at that very time. EVERYBODY was trying to get back to the "good old U.S.A." in the fall of 1946! The *New York Times* of October 4th reported that a total of 12,000 Pan American bookings from London to New York were being worked off at only 1,700 per week! The doctor and his wife were told that their passages had been cancelled, that they should keep in touch for some possible booking at an indefinite time in the future!

"ME keep in touch with YOU!", exclaimed Eugene to the agent in the London office of Pan American. "No way! YOU keep in touch with ME!"

He promptly placed a trans-Atlantic phone call to New York City to his secretary, a close personal friend of the president of Pan American, Juan Trippe.

On October 2nd, with only one hour's notice, a frenzied phone call ordered the doctor to report to Heathrow Airport immediately.

"It's your affair to get yourself here," he was told, "and only you will be permitted on this flight. Your wife cannot go."

Donald Miller of the British Leprosy Mission drove them to the airport, Julia Lake going, too, prepared to take off, in spite of the discouraging words of the agent. A nerve-wracking delay was caused by Mr. Miller's car running out of gasoline on the way. They arrived to find all other passengers already boarded and themselves being frantically paged.

"Both of you board immediately!", they were told at the gate. Special instructions had been phoned long-distance from New York at the very last minute! A weary but triumphant Eugene addressed the large audience of the Fortieth Anniversary Annual Meeting on schedule, having landed at two A.M., on October 3rd, after an eighteen-hour flight.

*The General and Promotional Secretaries, American Leprosy Missions, Inc.,
1950, Eugene and Julia Lake Kellersberger.*

*Fortieth Anniversary Celebration and Annual meeting of the American Leprosy
Missions, Inc., October 4, 1946. Dr. Kellersberger arrived in New York from
London just the day before, following his 45,000-mile leprosy-fact-finding jour-
ney through Central and South America, Africa and Europe.*

RESEARCH JOURNEY OF LEPROSY FACILITIES OF THE ORIENT

Between October 23, 1947 and March 13, 1948, Dr. Kellersberger made a five-month-long encirclement of the globe. On this 42,000 mile journey, he visited fifty different camps, colonies and hospitals and addressed more than 300 different audiences regarding the problems of Hansen's Disease control.

The first lap of this flight, twenty-two hours long, covered one-third the circumference of the earth. Leaving LaGuardia at one A.M. on Pan American Flight One, he arrived in Honolulu at eight o'clock the same day. Once again, his Washington University School of Medicine classmate, "Slim" Strode, met him and extended the hospitality of his beautiful home facing Diamond Head.

HAWAII

The leprosy mission executive was greatly impressed with what he termed the "vigorous, intelligent policy of Hawaii" in dealing with the disease. In a group of seven islands where it had been almost epidemic, a common sense, realistic approach now provided a small, unobtrusive building in the poorer section of Honolulu, where those who suspected they had the disease might quietly go for a diagnosis. In case of a positive finding, patients were taken to the Kalihi Receiving Station for further observation. The old idea that every case of leprosy automatically went to Molokai no longer held! Because of this new availability of trustworthy diagnosis, new cases were being contacted within six months of the appearance of active clinical symptoms, whereas before, it had taken years to identify many, just because of the secret fear of detection.

In order to reach the Molokai colony, made famous by the writings of Robert Louis Stevenson, Dr. Kellersberger had to fly through storm and rain in a tiny, two-passenger plane. The present site at Kaluapapa is on the north side of the island, on a tongue of land comprising some 10,000 acres, thrusting far out into the ocean. The old, deserted colony of

Kalawao, where Father Damien came in 1873 and died in 1889, is two miles away, crowded in under a towering cliff hung with waterfalls, with magnificent breakers creaming in over the dark, volcanic rocks. How deeply the doctor was touched by his visit to Molokai is revealed in his letters:

> This was once a terrible place, where hopeless, forgotten creatures came to await death. In 1890, there were 1,200 on Molokai. Now there are only 292 — thank God!
>
> While I was there, I witnessed once again the tragedy of released cases. A patient had been allowed to leave the colony, his disease arrested by taking *Diasone*. He was forced to return to Kaluapapa that very same day, after trying in vain to be accepted once again by his family, and to find work to support himself.
>
> I was so stirred by his plight, that when I spoke at the Kahului Union Church on the neighboring island of Maui that same evening, I challenged my audience to have the Christian courage and compassion to offer this young man a home and a job! I discovered that not a single one of my audience had ever dared to visit nearby Molokai!

THE PHILIPPINES

Of the 5,000 mile flight from Honolulu to Manila, by way of Guam and Wake Islands, Dr. Kellersberger wrote:

> I am writing quickly now because it is 6 p.m. on Tuesday, November 2nd, 1947, but in a few minutes it will be 6 p.m. Wednesday, the 3rd, for we are now crossing the International Date Line. There is not a single woman passenger on board this plane. There are 30 of us in all and we are very famous! We are traveling with Prince Bernadotte of Sweden and five of his compatriots, members of a trade delegation going to Manila.
>
> About an hour after we had breakfast on Guam, the co-pilot asked me to come into the cockpit. For a full hour I watched the intricate working by four skilled "supermen" of this vast flying mechanism, most appropriately named "The Southern Cross"! It was a marvelous experience! The navigator's map and weather chart showed devastating Typhoon Flora approaching from the South Philippines. We were running away from her as fast as we could! Using the

tailwinds between the high and low pressure areas, we flew
into Manila half an hour ahead of schedule!

On September 5, 1947, Dr. Kellersberger had written a
carefully worded, much-prayed-over letter to Fleet Admiral
Chester W. Nimitz. He informed him of the multiple, world-
wide aspects of the leprosy work and told him of his own approaching tour of the major facilities for controlling the disease in Hawaii, the Philippines, China, Siam and India. He
requested the Admiral's assistance enabling him to fly to one
of the most important points of Hansen's Disease management and research in the entire world — the government leprosarium of Culion, in the Philippines.

With only twelve days allowed for the Philippine part of
the tour, it would be impossible to visit other places of leprosy
work in Manila, on the islands of Luzon, Leyte, and Panay,
and visit Culion, too. Interisland steamship service to the isolated Calamian Group was slow and infrequent, necessitating
at least ten days of travel by ship. The only possible way for
the American Leprosy Missions executive to visit Culion
would be by air with the help of the United States Navy!

In closing his letter, Dr. Kellersberger referred incidentally to the treasured German-American heritage that he and
Admiral Nimitz had in common, deep in the Texas Hill Country. The Admiral's hometown of Fredericksburg was just over
the hills and down the road a piece from the doctor's birthplace of Cypress Mill.

The gracious reply, personally signed by "C. W. Nimitz,
Fleet Admiral, United States Navy," was a letter authorizing
naval air transportation for a civilian group from Manila to
the government leprosarium in the Calamians and back. The
Commander of the Naval Forces of the Philippines had orders
to arrange details of the flight from his headquarters at Sangley Point, Cavite.

Two weeks before leaving New York, Dr. Kellersberger
was informed that a Catalina Flying Boat would take him and
twelve others to Culion. It was the same plane that had flown
scientists to the Bikini atoll to study the atomic bomb explosion. Letters of invitation from the doctor to be the guests of

In reply refer to Initials
and No.

NAVY DEPARTMENT

OFFICE OF THE CHIEF OF NAVAL OPERATIONS

WASHINGTON 25, D. C.

SEP 16 1947

A2-14(2)
Serial 1129P55F

15 SEP 1947

Dear Dr. Kellersberger:

  Thank you for your letter of September 5, 1947,
which arrived while I was away from Washington on a trip
to New England. It was with keen interest that I learned
of your Texas background and of your medical work throughout
the world.

  Upon my return to the office, I have been informed
that in connection with your request for air transportation
from Manila to the Culion leper colony and return, the
Commander, Naval Forces Philippines, will be in a position
to assist you. I suggest that you contact him at his
headquarters, Naval Air Station, Sangley Point, and arrange
a mutually satisfactory schedule for the flight.

  May I extend my best wishes for a highly successful tour. With kindest regards, I am

       Sincerely,

       C. W. NIMITZ
     Fleet Admiral, U. S. Navy

Dr. Eugene R. Kellersberger,
American Mission to Lepers, Inc.,
156 Fifth Avenue,
New York 10, N.Y.

the United States Navy on this special flight were mailed to national Philippine leaders, including all the members of the Philippine Leprosy Committee.

In 1947, the 17,000-island nation had a population of approximately 17,000,000. The "Jewel of the Pacific" has been historically heavily infected with leprosy, even long before the Spanish arrived. The first official governmental care of patients was begun at Culion by the famous Governor-General of the Philippines, Dr. Leonard Wood. The prize-winning novel by Dr. Perry Burgess, *Who Walk Alone,* brought this leprosarium the sympathy and attention of the whole world.

At dawn on November 10th, 1947, Dr. Kellersberger led his select group of guests to the Catalina Flying Boat at Sangley Point in Manila Bay. Truly, she was an amazing ship, with land wheels that folded in under and pontoons that folded up or down on the ends of both of the great wings. Later, in describing the flight, the doctor exulted: "She landed like a lamb on the glassy sea and took off like a roaring lion, as she plowed through the waters!"

Proving again that "it's a small world," Captain Williams, in charge of the flight, was a 1924 graduate of the Richmond Academy in Augusta, Georgia. Dr. Kellersberger's wife's twin brothers, Conway and Lister Skinner, had been his professors there! Captain Williams said to Eugene: "We are not permitted to carry civilians, but this time we had orders that were different!"

For an hour and a half, the 200-mile flight at six to eight thousand feet altitude carried the special party over multitudinous, mountainous islands, rising from placid seas. Culion is in the westernmost Calamian Group which includes a number of islands scattered over 400 square miles. Before landing on the water, the plane circled several times over the great settlement and its clustered homes, hospitals, wards, dispensaries, administrative units, schools, and churches. The majestic flight and lovely downward sweep of the great flying bird over the steep hills, and skimming along the shoreline, caused the wildest excitement! There had been no way of letting the people of Culion know exactly when their guests would arrive. All who could run, walk, limp or crawl came down to the beach to greet the amphibian with shouts of joy, singing and much waving of welcoming banners. To his friends back in the United States, Dr. Kellersberger wrote:

> Those who were fortunate enough to have our experience will never be the same again. What a welcome! What a need! How patient and polite all the patients are and how beautifully they sang for us! And what they have suffered! In 1941, there were 5,600 cases here. Then came the war. When the Japanese "tornado" struck in December, many patients fled in boats. Some were killed outright and others died of malnutrition and starvation. By April of 1942, there were only 1,400 cases left. Now there are 1,850.

> Everywhere we see the deterioration of material, equipment and personnel. Our visit to the hospitals, where there are some 300 advanced cases, still shows the sad effects of the war years' lack of food, medical care, drugs and, general care.

To Admiral Nimitz, Dr. Kellersberger wrote:

> It would have been impossible without your gracious and most generous offer! You made it possible for me to take to isolated Culion twelve important leaders who had never been there before. It was a revelation to them and has already born fruit. It gives me new pride in my country! I am humbly grateful that you were willing to entrust me with this mission. I want to be worthy of it!

> Captain Williams was a perfect host. He, together with his crew of six real Americans, were very kind to us, and truly upheld the tradition of the Navy. They handled that great flying boat like a mother would her baby. Hats off to them! I only pray that I may do my great task of ridding the world of leprosy as well as they do theirs, and you, yours, in your great leadership!

CHINA

On November 12th, the Pan American Clipper *Westward Ho* took the General Secretary of the American Leprosy Missions from Manila to Hong Kong. The flight was delayed eighteen hours, for the plane had limped in on three engines the day before. The verse in the little *Daily Light* for that date reassured the doctor once more that "our STOPS as well as our STEPS are in His good Hands!" It was Psalm 78:53: *He led them on safely.*

Dr. Kellersberger's traveling companion for his two months' tour of China was Mr. A. Donald Miller, his counterpart in the British Leprosy Mission. The two General Secretaries arrived in Hong Kong within one hour of each other, one from the West, the other from the East. They were joined by Dr. N. D. Fraser, a medical missionary of the English Presbyterian Church in Swatow, China, who was serving as the Medical Secretary for China, for both the British and American organizations. The two Britishers and one American were joined by their official Chinese escort and interpreter, Dr. S. T. Yang, of the Epidemological Department of the Chinese National Health Administration in Nanching.

The time of this visit was one of deepening crisis for the Nationalist Government of China. During December and November of 1947, Communist fighting activities became more and more ominously aggressive. Areas well distant from the fighting when the leprosy representatives arrived on November 12th, were deeply involved by the time they left on January 12th. Even at such a critical time, on the eve of the total taking over of the entire country by the Communist regime, the highest national officials showed a lively interest and gracious goodwill to their distinguished guests.

Kuangchou (Canton) on the southern coast, in Kwantung Province, the one with the highest incidence of leprosy in all China, was the first stop. From there, the party of four flew northeast to Fuchou, Fukien Province, then north by air to Shanghai, Kiangsu Province, on the eastern coast. The round trip southwest across Chekiang Province to Hangchou and back to Shanghai was made by train.

From this point on, the group itinerary turned out quite differently from what was originally planned. Dr. Kellersberger's passport and camera were stolen from the upstairs bedroom of the home of Presbyterian missionary friends with whom he was staying in Shanghai. He was forced to drop out and wait for an emergency replacement from his friend, Edmund Montgomery, in Washington. Sadly, he watched Don-

ald Miller, Dr. Fraser and Dr. Yang take off without him for
Lanchou and the far northern provinces of Kansu and Tshin-
ghai.

Thanks to Edmund Montgomery's expert assistance
back in Washington, the new passport arrived in only four
days! An unscheduled five-day visit to Nanching, the capital
city, enabled Dr. Kellersberger not only to procure his visas
for Siam and India, but also gave him memorable hours with
the United States Ambassador to China, Dr. J. Leighton
Stuart, and the privilege of lecturing on leprosy to the Nanching Rotary Club, and both the Central Government and
Union University Hospitals. Another Chinese physician, Dr.
K. C. Hu, was assigned to him as escort by the Nanching authorities. Together they journeyed to Chungch'ing and
Chengtu, in the far western province of Szechwan.

Returning to Nanching, Dr. Kellersberger was rejoined
by his friends who had been miserably stranded in Chinese
Tibet by freezing weather for eighteen days! Their flight north
was made in an unheated plane with "portholes," most of
which had lost their covers. The result was a penetratingly
bone-chilling flight which gave Mr. Miller a flare-up of malaria, combined with a deep bronchial cold. The reunited
group flew north together into Communist territory to Tsinan, in Shantung Province. Their final flight carried them
800 miles south from Tsinan, back to Shanghai, and then to
Hong Kong.

Dr. Kellersberger's faithful recordings of his momentous
China itinerary indicate that the stealing of the passport
turned out to be an unexpected blessing!

> *November 14, Tungkun.* My first day in China! Took a
> taxi from the airport, then a ferry to the mainland. Next
> came a train, then a boat, then a two-mile walk through rice
> fields, then another boat for a five-mile downriver ride to
> the 100-year-old Rhenish Lutheran Leprosarium at Tung-
> kun. Work here would have come to a halt during World
> War II, while cut off from the mother church in Germany,
> if our Mission had not helped with personnel and funds.
>
> The whole place is covered with streamers, confetti,
> and bunting. Long strings of firecrackers hang from all the

trees and houses. The noisy welcome has lasted the whole time that we've been here!

The finest pottery shop I have ever seen supports the 250 patients. All kinds of beautiful ware go out from here all over China. The floors are laid with lovely tiles made by the patients. Best occupational therapy ever! EVERYONE has something to do!

Two years ago, at Yeung Kong just south of here, the commander of a troop of soldiers lined up over 100 people with leprosy on Easter morning and, after making them dig their own graves, shot them all dead. The missionary said to us, "When I came here, those with leprosy were living among the graves, begging for food during the day." The beautiful church was <u>filled</u> with people, with such joy on the faces of all the sick as I have never seen! They have come from a GRAVE TO GOD! How marvelous!

November 22, Fuchou. "The Lacquer City" is fascinating! I have fallen in love with it! Last night twenty-four of us were invited to an official dinner by the Governor of Fukien Province. Nine doctors were present, all six of the Chinese Methodist bishops here for the Methodist Centennial Celebration, the mayor of this city of 400,000 people, the Provincial Medical Commissioner, representatives of the Fuchou branch of the Chinese Medical Association and of other groups. Grace was asked before the meal and no wine was served! The Chinese are truly courteous people! They drank our health with a <u>glass of water</u> — something that very likely would not have happened in the U.S.A.!

November 30, Hangchou. We have found in this city a tremendously strong Christian community. We are guests of the Church of England's "Church Missionary Society." Dr. Sturton's hospital is one of the greatest missionary hospitals in the world. It is the main teaching one for the Provincial Medical College.. It includes a Tuberculosis Hospital and a well conducted home for leprosy patients which has been in operation for 60 years, one of the fine projects of our Mission in London. There are signs all over the place: WELCOME OUR FRIENDS WHO HELP US TO SELF-SUPPORT! YOUR COMING IS ONE OF THE HAPPIEST DAYS IN OUR LIVES! WE WANT BETTER MEDICINE!

As Dr. Sturton took us through his hospital, I saw a

Dr. Kellersberger's photograph of this old camelback bridge between Hangchou and Nanking, China, taken in January 1948, was the prize-winner at the Hobby Exhibit of the 1949 Annual Meeting of the American Medical Association in Atlantic City, New Jersey.

room marked "No Visitors." In it was the five-year-old son of the Governor of Chekiang Province whom Dr. Sturton had saved from sure death from tubercular meningitis by streptomycin injections. No wonder he was appreciative! There is no end to the opportunities opened up here by the hospital and the leprosarium, the only one in the whole province of Chekiang, with 22 million people!

December 20th, 1949, Chungch'ing, Szechwan Province. This was the wartime capital of China and the northern end of the famous Burma Road. The Lord's Hand was surely in it when He prevented my going to Lanchou. Yesterday no plane returned from there. No telling how long my three partners will be stuck there! As a result, I am the only one available for studying West China Union University as a possible project for us in connection with the medical school. During the recent war, 6,000 students from eight universities fled here to "The Texas of China," to continue their studies. The first real effort to teach about leprosy has been begun here, fitting in with our plan to found a teaching center here.

In the airport station here, on an island in the Yangtse River, I sat waiting for my plane. I noticed a man with ears three times the normal size. I was amazed! Here was a case of leprosy! He was well-dressed, with nice gloves on, and would be getting on the plane soon. He went over and got a meal where Dr. Hu and I had just eaten. This is the way it is in China: open, lepromatous cases are not even diagnosed, nor taken care of in any way!

Christmas Day, Chengtu. Last night I was deeply touched when first, all the leprosy patients, and then the theological and medical students came, carrying their Chinese lanterns, singing the old, familiar Christmas carols! They gave me the gift of a beautiful, embroidered silk banner with these words down the center in Chinese: THE LOVE OF THE CROSS. A priceless keepsake of my visit to China! I shall use this as the subject of future messages!

January 1st, 1948, Tsinan, Shantung. Now we are inside the communist ring, in a city of nearly a million, with a pillbox and soldiers on every corner and barbed wire entanglements and trenches all about us. We are here by special permission, on condition that we leave quickly. Cheloo University Medical School is here and a fine small teaching leprosy colony. Yesterday, in a freezing cold room, the patients put on a very clever play they had prepared themselves, entitled THEY ALSO ARE USEFUL. When I see these brave friends, so patient and long suffering, I am humbled and realize how little I am doing. Over a million with leprosy in this great land of China, and only some 3,000 receiving any sort of care! It is STAGGERING!

THAILAND

On January 15, 1948, the Pan American "Clipper Lightfoot" had the happy task of carrying Dr. Kellersberger from Hong Kong, 1100 miles across the South China Sea into the wonderful warmth of weather and welcome of Thailand. Sitting in a bucket seat on the flight to Chengmai, with his portable typewriter propped on his lap, he wrote to his wife of the surprising reception that awaited him in Bangkok:

For the first time in my life, I have been received and

given tea by a Prime Minister. It was at his official residence — beautiful architecture, elegant furnishings, an ornate dining table with a dainty "high tea" spread out upon it, impeccable service, no forcing of "drinks" — a truly exquisite experience! I had the privilege of two long talks with the Premier, a spiritual sort of man. He was delighted when he discovered that I speak French, for he was educated in France. During our second hour together, we conversed entirely in French.

At the elaborate dinner given by the American Ambassador and his wife, I met Princess Poon, a famous member of the Siamese royal family. When she was in England, Queen Mary called her "The Pocket Venus," she is such a tiny, exquisitely refined person!

There is something different about the Siamese. Life doesn't seem to rush them. Life in Thailand is quiet, dignified and controlled, without the pressuring masses and constant surging about of the countless Chinese.

Chiengmai, a city of 25,000, is tucked away in the mountains of northwest Thailand, near the upper Burma border. The Presbyterian Mission's McCormick Hospital was founded here by Dr. James W. McKean, who began his medical work in 1899. In 1948, at the time of Dr. Kellersberger's visit, this hospital was completely self-supporting, staffed almost totally with native personnel, and averaging some 4800 patients a year, of whom fifty-six percent were being treated free.

The leprosy unit of this thriving hospital is situated on two-mile-long White Elephant Island, in the middle of the Meh Ping River. The Leprosy Mission's representative described his happy visit there to his wife:

This is one of the most beautiful places I have ever seen! The individual cottages, the normal life-style, the industries and good agricultural land, the schools and the fine spirit of cooperation make this one of the finest colonies I have visited in my whole trip! Equipment, housing, and cleanness are all in fine balance, for 1,568 residents!

For two nights, I have slept in the suite where the Crown Prince lived while interning for a year at McCormick Hospital — against the wishes of the royal family!

On Sunday morning, I had the great joy of helping to baptize 64 new converts and serve them communion. The message I gave was translated into Thai by an interpreter. The church is open, surrounded by flowers and trees — no chairs, but woven mats covering the floor. In the afternoon, the Governor of the province gave a garden party reception for me beside the river. Dr. Cort told me when I left that I had been a blessing to them all, especially to all the dear leprosy patients in this island colony! I am so grateful!

INDIA

Dr. Kellersberger's tour of India began with what we termed a personal pilgrimage. He was determined first of all to visit Chandag Heights, only fourteen miles from the Nepal border in far north India. This isolated outpost of leprosy work was founded in 1891 by Miss Mary Reed, a Methodist missionary from Lowell, Ohio, herself a victim of the disease. For fifty-two years, she superintended the asylum jointly supported by both the British and American organizations. In order to reach Chandag, the doctor took a thousand mile rail journey on the Pan-Indian Express from Calcutta to Kathgodam, at the foot of the Himalayas. Then came a hair-raising, eighty mile ride in an Indian bus to the Methodist mission station of Almora. They climbed from 1,691 feet to over 7,000 feet in altitude, around dizzy curves and escarpments crumbling away to valleys thousands of feet below! Last of all, there was a fifty-two-mile, four day mountain trek by pony and on foot to Chandag itself! At Lucknow, Dr. Kellersberger had been joined by the Reverend B. L. Gandon, representative of the British Leprosy Mission, who would make the Chandag journey with him. Their caravan consisted of a guide and two porters, two sturdy Tibetan saddle ponies, and a pack pony to carry their food, bedding and suitcases. Once again, the faithful daily diary recorded informative details of this dramatic pilgrimage:

> *January 23, 1948.* Dog tired! Traveled the last two hours by moonlight. We are doing our own cooking and sleeping in a rough guest bungalow built by the British. This is SOME PLACE Miss Reed came to! Truly inacces-

sible and off the map! Only brave souls come here! The great pines blow in the wind. The sky is azure blue, the air clean and sweet! The giant rhododendrons have flowers as big as roses. To the east, the majestic Himalayas tower, range after range, standing out as clear as crystal.

January 24. A memorable day through the breathtaking, awe-inspiring mountains. Had to walk a lot; our ponies could not climb with us on them. It's hard to breathe while climbing! We passed Drum Rock, where in centuries past, a great drum was beaten to warn of bandits and danger on the trail.

January 25, Gongoli Hat, 5,750 ft. altitude. A hard trek today, down 3,000 feet into the gorge of the Ramganga, a glacial river, blue as steel, cold as ice. Cloud shadows changed all day in the deep valleys. At night, the peaks turned rose while the base of the mountains were still in shadow.

January 26. Chandag at last! We could see it plainly at 8 a.m., but did not arrive until 6 p.m.! We were met at the final curve of the winding road by Dr. Young herself. The mantle of Mary Reed has fallen on this young Scottish doctor, a graduate of Edinburgh University and daughter of medical missionaries to China. We are the first representatives of the two supporting Missions to come here since she took over in 1944, following Miss Reed's death in 1943. She is doing a fine piece of work with faithful Indian workers to help her. Tomorrow Mr. Gandon and I will lay the cornerstone of the new Mary Reed Memorial Hospital.

January 27. At dawn, I stole out of the house, for I wanted to explore this mountain top alone. Wandering among the giant *deodhar* firs, I came upon lovely little Bethel Chapel, framed against the backdrop of the majestic mountain range, turning to rose in the first rays of the sun.

There, on the sloping hillside with "all her mountains" in view, was what I had come so far to see: the simple, white cross, marking Mary Reed's grave. Approaching slowly, I read: MARY REED, FRIEND OF SUFFERERS, 1891–1943. *I will make all my mountains a way.* (Isaiah 49:11)

As I bowed my head, I thought, "I am one of the favored few whose eyes have seen the place where she was born in Lowell, Ohio; here, the place where she worked and suffered and loved; the room in which she died, and now,

this cross, marking where her tired body was laid to rest."
Then I did what I don't often do: I knelt at the foot of that
grave and that cross and asked God to help me to follow in
her footsteps, as she did Christ's, and as her successor, Dr.
Katherine Young, is doing, too!

Excerpts from one of Miss Reed's letters, written from
Chandag in 1893, shed a glowing light on this courageous soul
and show why Dr. Kellersberger so desired to honor her work
and memory:

> Away to the north, seemingly only two or three days'
> journey away, are the eternal snows, whose grandeur and
> sublimity are indescribable. They are so pure and bright
> and peace-suggestive! At sunset and sunrise, it is easy to
> imagine them to be the visible foundations of the Eternal
> City of God, they are lighted with such a halo! . . .
>
> Yes, I am more and more satisfied with knowing that
> each moment of suffering, both mental and physical, per-
> mitted by the dear Hand of God, is working out His Will in
> and through this poor, frail instrument. I am comforted
> that not one unkind thing can be done or said but by His
> permission! My times are in His hands, whatever they may
> be! . . .
>
> Of the 59 patients now with us, all but 6 are Christians.
> Gentleness, patience and peace are now manifest in the
> lives of some who, only a year ago, were unhappy and so
> quarrelsome that I was often called several times daily to
> settle differences. I do not urge baptism. When hearts are
> new and the light of the Sun of Righteousness shines in,
> they will ask for this rite. Human kindness and love seem to
> make them realize so much more clearly our Father's love,
> that my heart is often filled with inexpressible joy because
> of the tender mercy He has shown me in permitting me in
> Jesus' Name to minister to these, my fellow-sufferers!

Dr. Kellersberger traveled approximately 7,000 miles in
India using the highly efficient railway system inherited from
the British colonial era. His itinerary stretched from Calcutta
northwest, almost to the Nepal border, southward down the
entire east coast to the southernmost tip of the subcontinent,
then turned northeastward through central India back to Calcutta. He traveled second class the entire time, finding Eng-

lish to be the one language that tied multi-lingual India together, another positive aspect of the British heritage!

Of the twenty-six institutions in India in 1948 operating
with American Leprosy Missions support, Dr. Kellersberger
was able to visit only twenty-one. One of the most exciting
was Vellore, the site of the famous Vellore Christian Medical
College founded by Dr. Ida Scudder. At this great institution,
an outstanding new program of leprosy prevention was being
launched.

> *February 11, 1948 Vadathorasalur.*   This unique work,
> begun in 1923 by Donald Miller, is now under the leader-
> ship of the nearby Danish Mission. It has a fine balance of
> uninfected children, children with an early infection, and a
> large group of adults in various stages of the disease. This
> morning a company of patients with shining, happy faces
> were seated quietly on the clean, bare floor in the lovely In-
> dian church. Behind the altar, was a beautiful, life-sized
> painting of Jesus putting His Hand on the head of the man
> with leprosy, kneeling before Him. For the first time in my
> life, I preached in my stocking feet! Everyone removed their
> shoes for it is the Indian custom to do this before entering a
> sanctuary. My subject was THE LOVE OF THE CROSS,
> using the beautiful Chinese banner given to me in Chengtu.
>
> *February 16, Chingleput.*   I have just visited the first
> Rural Leprosy Prevention Unit I have seen in India. It is
> not just an injection center. All of the cases in this area are
> KNOWN, and DIAGNOSED, and the infectious cases
> sleep away from their families! Living conditions in the vil-
> lages have been studied and improved. After eight years, it
> has been found out, where this scientific prevention pro-
> gram is carried out, the incidence of infection among chil-
> dren has decreased 50%! The Lady Willingdon Sanitarium
> here is a government hospital with 800 patients.
>
> *March 4th, Purulia.* This great work was founded by a
> German doctor in 1888 and was taken over by the Church
> Missionary Society in 1915. It is the largest colony in India,
> with 900 patients! This is where my beloved colleague and
> travel companion, Donald Miller, spent 23 years of his use-
> ful life.

The most beautiful farewell service was held for me
here today! Beneath a large tree in front of the dispensary,

some 600 patients gathered. A blessed old elder who has been an inmate here for 41 years, gave a touching message, leaning on his crutches. Another farewell address was made in perfect English by the young president of the patient-body. Then came the gifts, a hand-woven rug, other woven pieces and a beautiful book! More and more I discover that in Christ every barrier is broken. The common ties that bind us together are strong enough to last throughout Eternity!

March 14th. As we roared out of the great Calcutta airport, I watched the night out of my window. There was the sacred symbol of the Southern Cross shining brilliantly, low over the horizon to give me peace and comfort! As we lifted up over the great Atlantic, I again prayed for another "Happy Landing." The captain stopped at my seat and explained: "Coming westward, there are usually strong head-winds and it is always much more difficult. In addition, we have a heavy fog tonight!" I said to myself, "others may be sleeping. I am going to keep watch in prayer!"

As we approached Newfoundland, once again the captain approached my seat and said, "Doctor, I cannot understand it! We have made it across the ocean ahead of schedule, on a record-breaking trip of eight hours and ten minutes! Instead of bucking head winds flying west, this time we have actually had tail winds pushing us forward! This has been one of my finest crossings!"

Surely, his Goodness and Mercy have followed me all the days of my life and God's tail winds have brought me safely home again!

[14]

The Happiest Landing of All

THE FLORIDA HAVEN

Lunching with Homer Rodeheaver at Winona Lake, Indiana on July 24, 1944, the Kellersbergers asked Billy Sunday's famous song leader if he knew of any semi-civilized place in the United States where the doctor might make up for twenty-five years of lost fishing time. Much as he longed to, he never permitted himself to "go fishing" during the years of his missionary service. He had felt it his responsibility to keep well; that meant avoiding unnecessary proximity to the thick foliage of the tropical river banks infested by tsetse flies that carry sleeping sickness.

"Rody's" ready response to their question at that time was: "Come and be my neighbor on South Melbourne Beach in Florida!"

In 1946, Eugene and Julia Lake purchased for the price of $1,500, a strip of Brevard County land adjoining the Rodeheaver property. It extended from the Atlantic Ocean on the east to the Indian River on the west. A sturdy cottage built by the Ballard Milling Company stood on the ocean side of the lot. Scattered about were the remnants of slave cabins, still-flowing artesian wells, and luxurious palm and citrus groves. Clearing for construction two years later, it was evident that the acreage had also been a tribal burial ground. As bulldozers approached, Smithsonian archeologists worked frantically to preserve Seminole Indian artifacts and skeletons, buried beneath great mounds of seashells. A short distance down the beach, Spanish "pieces of eight" sometimes gleamed through the surf, near where Prince Philip of Spain's treasure galleons lay on the ocean floor.

In June of 1948, three sectionalized Camp Blanding houses were bought for $1,125 and moved onto the property on a 15-ton truck, for the fee of $100! To celebrate the completion of their first building venture, Eugene and Julia Lake staged a jubilant watermelon-cutting for the workmen who had assembled their houses.

That first "Kelly Kamp" really was just a camp! Surrounded by rows of towering, feathery Australian pines, it was hidden away in primeval wilderness reached over unpaved roads buried inches deep in ocean sand. There was no mail delivery and no electricity — only oil lamps and a kerosene stove. The long, shiny streak of the aluminum cars of the Florida East Coast passenger trains, skimming along the distant mainland across the Indian River, and the far-off wail of the engine whistle, were the only visible and audible indications of nearby civilization! Sulphur-flavored water and hoards of mosquitoes hovering in the warm air were aspects of the new Florida possession that were not too appealing. Very quickly, the new residents learned to fill jugs with the odiferous water. Allowing it to stand overnight helped somewhat to dilute the strongly medicinal flavor. And how they cheered whenever the small mosquito-control plane swooped by, leaving the air smelling of sprayed chemicals!

On March 7, 1955, the Kellersbergers moved into "HAPPY HAVEN," a home beautifully constructed for them by their good Dutch friend, Neil Spitters, on a lot farther south, facing the Indian River. Julia Lake preferred the quiet of the inland waterway to the constant restlessness of the view from an ocean lot. The doctor's diaries sparkle with gems of delighted appreciation of the setting in which he and his "B.B." (Best Beloved) now lived. They also record his excitement in being a front-seat spectator to the tremendous events

occurring at Cape Canaveral, clearly visible, jutting out into
the sea just to the north of them:

June 8, 1954. Followed tracks of a great loggerhead
turtle weighing some 400 pounds, with barnacles on her
back. Found her making a hole in the sand and laying her
eggs. Huge head moved back and forth. Flippers went
through methodical motions. She was two-thirds covered
with sand and had already laid some 20 to 30 eggs when I
found her. She didn't pay any attention to me. What a marvel! How wonderful are God's laws! Likely, very few people
have seen this.

December 22, 1954. Glorious dawn! Waning moon!
Morning star! A superb sunrise over the ocean through the
clouds! Praise God!

February 2, 1955. Amazing sight! Great schools of por-
poises chasing mullet. Dinner bell for the pelicans! Thousands of leaping fish! Glorious sunrises over the ocean and
sunsets across the Indian River, framed by our Australian
pines, palmettos and seagrapes.

July 8, 1955. Quiet, lovely morning on the river. Josephine, the white crane, and Mary Alice, our blue heron, are
stalking the banks in front of our house, looking for their
breakfast.

April 4, 1958. Up at 3 a.m.! Beautiful full moon! Julia
Lake and I walked over to the ocean just to see it. Early
each morning a little bird near our house sings to my B.B.
"You're sweet! You're sweet!"

April 23, 1958. Missile went up at 8 p.m. right in front
of our house. Awesome sight! A clear night, we were able to
watch it for thirty minutes into ascension.

December 18, 1958. Temperature 56 degrees. Up at 5
a.m. Lovely German sausage, Christmas gift from my sister, Annie, grits and coffee for breakfast. God is so GOOD
to us! Swamped with things to do. Feel so well and happy!
A 9,000 pound Satellite went off from Canaveral at 6:02 last
night.

Autumn 1960 family letter: For some reason, our God
Who does not sleep awakened us one night recently at 3
a.m. We got up and went into the living room. There we
saw our river shining strangely with indirect lighting from
beneath. There was no moon, not a single bit of light from

the sky, but an inner light was diffusing the whole surface of the water, as if a million fireflies were swimming underneath it. They were multi-billion *infusoria,* which cause phosphorescence, truly a phenomenon of Nature! We had never seen this before and probably will never see it again. We now know what the rivers of Heaven must look like!

October 15, 1962. Storm "ELLA" is in the Caribbean. The river is very high and tremendously high surf on the ocean. Feeling the effects of this hurricane far and wide, powerful beyond all our comprehension! But this is God's world, in spite of storms, atheists, murderers, and all the vile persons in it who have forsaken Him.

December 17, 1965. Today we saw the Gemini 6 men brought safely back. I'm sure they'll be glad to have a shave after some millions of miles at 17,500 mph! Oh boy! I am not itching to make a soft landing on the moon. We think we are getting smarter, but "He that sitteth in the Heavens shall laugh!"

The steady stream of guests who came to enjoy vacations in the Kellersbergers' three furnished, rent-free cottages seldom kept the doctor from enjoying his fishing. By 1957, their first Florida guest book was completely filled with 2,082 different names.

December 26, 1950. Caught a 54 1/2-lb. Salt Water Drum in my net! My picture taken with it, in the local paper. Much publicity!

March 29, 1954. On ocean front from 5 to 6 a.m. Ocean very rough. Caught two Whiting and an 8 1/2-lb. Channel Bass. A BEAUTY! Oh boy!

May 23, 1954. Showed our leprosy films, *Healing of Mvondo,* and *Song After Sorrow* to our ten house guests. None of them had ever seen them before! Used of God!

June 30, 1954. We are as busy here as in Gramercy Park! Unbelievable! Not a single day has passed since our arrival here that we have not had guests. We love it and thank God that the world still comes to our door. Nineteen young high school seniors came to spend several days with us, as their graduation gift. A new Baptist minister friend here with his family of two generations. Had a big Sunday School picnic in our backyard!

July 2, 1954. Bought a 14-foot boat, cypress with all

54¹/₂-pound Salt Water Drum caught by Dr. Kellersberger at Melbourne Beach, Florida, December 1950.

brass screws. Weighs only 150 pounds. Christened her "Lil' Ann." My dream come true! Our guests leaving today. Have been here for five weeks.

July 9, 1954. My first REAL catch: One 13-inch Trout, eleven 4-lb Snook, eight large catfish, six Whiting and three sorry "Sailor's Choice"! Fun anyway, even if NOT big ones!

October 3, 1954. Perfect dawn, a glorious day! 60 degrees. Julia Lake has taken all our guests to see Sebastien Inlet and to the groves to pick fruit. All eating lunch here. Sharing my nice fish I have caught with my guests.

October 11, 1954. Have been asked to speak to the Medical Society here on tropical medicine. Very strong east winds and heavy seas. Too rough for ocean fishing but fishing on Indian River good. Blues and Amberjacks running, and Mackeral, too! BIG ones!

January 12, 1955. Thrilling morning! I prayed before I cast. Caught five lovely fish and one magnificent 3 1/2 pound Speckled Trout. What a strike and fight out of water! He didn't get away!

March 14, 1955. Up early together. I fishing at dawn. Heaven on earth! Something exciting every day!

June 20, 1955. Since coming here a year ago, we have shown our leprosy films to our house guests forty-one times!

November 20, 1959. A glorious day! Caught 15 lovely Trout, weighing in all about 15 pounds.. Didn't lose a one! Caught them on a mirror lure 2, tripled black-back and golden sides. I enjoy giving away all my nice frozen trout fillets! Gave some to my doctor!

November 17, 1960. At 10 a.m. in my boat, I hooked a BIG one! It went around my boat, then I lost him. I felt like crying! Hard to explain. Fish are funny, like people!

December 22, 1961. Today I helped a big fish. He was on my Pfluger limper and going heavy and I fought him hard. All at once, I lost him! Had he gotten my line? No! Suddenly, I found myself holding onto a second line some 30 feet long, with a sharp hook on it, bent almost straight. He may have been carrying it around for weeks! Both of the lines and hooks were all mixed up. He was hungry, so I just set him free. He weighed four or five pounds or more!

October 19, 1962. Boy! Biggest fish I've EVER had on my line! Caught him on a Pfluger limper. Fought him more

than half an hour. Called Neil Spitters, who came in his
boat to help me! That fish ran away with my reel and brake
and pulled me all over the place! I never got near enough to
really see him, but Neil was able to grab the line and pull
him slowly to his boat. It was a huge Sea Bass weighing
some 30 to 35 pounds! As Neil maneuvered to get him, he
broke the line. Neil said he was every bit of three feet long.
What a story! If the water had not been deep. I could have
jumped in and led this big one to shore. Moral: Next time,
use a heavier reel and line. What a story!

ON-THE-GO RETIREMENT

A clear indication that Dr. Kellersberger thought of himself as a world citizen is evident in what he wrote on his identification card, pinned to his lapel at the 45th reunion of his
University of Texas, Class of 1911. He wrote: "I am Dr. Eugene R. Kellersberger, a Texas Ex, Class of 1911, of Austin,
The Belgian Congo, New York, Florida and THE WORLD!"

The Kellersbergers traveled constantly and extensively,
always the ardent ambassadors of the cause they had so long
represented. They were so accustomed to being always on the
go, that it was only natural that they continue this pattern of
"perpetual peregrination." It was the only life-style they had
ever known. The doctor and his wife literally wore out several
different automobiles, as they drove all over the south, partic-
ipating in conferences, conducting seminars, making addresses to school assemblies and civic clubs, and speaking in
churches of all denominations. They never turned down a single request to speak to any sort of audience.

To celebrate their "32nd Honeymoon" in 1951, the couple made another of the doctor's beloved trans-Atlantic crossings, spending two delightful months in Switzerland, renew-
ing relationships with beloved Swiss relatives and friends.

In 1961, they enjoyed a four-month-long voyage around
the world on the *Oranje*, of the Holland America Line. Boarding at Port Everglades, Florida, they passed through the Panama Canal, continuing westward to Papeete, Tahiti, in the
Society Islands. They were welcomed at Auckland, New Zealand, by Leprosy Missions staff and treated to a fantastic over-

land tour down to Wellington, where they again joined their steamer. A part of that memorable trip that did not turn out too well was their 2,000-mile-long transcontinental train ride across the Australian outback, in the dead of winter. They journeyed from Adelaide to Freemantle over the longest straight stretch of railroad track in the world. As a result of the prolonged, bone-chilling exposure, the doctor came down with pneumonia. The inside of *Oranje* Cabin 254 was all that he saw for much of the rest of that voyage. On reaching Amsterdam, the Kellersbergers again headed for their favorite Switzerland, this time, by leisurely riverboat passage, up the Rhine, through locks and canals to Basel.

One incident on board the *Oranje* is highly typical of the quiet, loving way in which Eugene Kellersberger reached out to people in need. Tramping briskly around the deck, he kept noticing one passenger who sat, motionless and dejected, in the same deck chair, day after day.

"There is something wrong with that man," he said to his wife. "When we pass him the next time around, I'm going to stop and speak to him and find out what it is."

As good as his word, the doctor stopped in front of the man in question and asked: "My friend, is something wrong? Are you sick? May I help you?" There was not the slightest response.

The next time around the deck, Dr. Kellersberger came to a halt before the silent figure. In French he said: "Mon ami, etes-vous malade? Puis-je vous aider?" Again, there was no reaction whatsoever.

The third time around, the doctor stopped right beside the man and said firmly in his native German: *"Mein Freund, sind Sie Krank? Kann ich Ihnen irgendwie helfen?"*

Instantly, the dejected figure was transformed. The man leaped to his feet, threw his arms about his questioner's neck and shouted back in German: "Those are the first words I have understood since I boarded this ship!" Rudolf Scheberl, of Vienna, Austria, a freshly-bereaved widower, was taking his very first ocean voyage in search of solace for a lonely, grieving heart. From that day on, he and the Kellersbergers were a 'threesome," as he joined them for meals, conversa-

tion, walks and sightseeing tours at the various port stops. In
Egypt, Eugene and Julia Lake provided their new friend with
an excursion ticket from Suez to Cairo, and back to the ship,
waiting at Port Said. At the end of the voyage, Dr. Kellersberger was of unexpected assistance to Mr. Scheberl. He successfully intervened on his behalf with European authorities,
when, because of current political and military pressures, the
Austrian was refused permission to return to his native Tyrol.

As the years passed, Julia Lake did most of the public
speaking. The doctor, because of increasing disability, occasionally showed his leprosy films, or closed a meeting with
prayer. Whenever possible, they were still included in the annual meetings of the American Leprosy Missions, flying to
Los Angeles or New York, always adding a special spark of joy
and enthusiasm whenever they were in attendance.

RECOGNITION

A unique honor was accorded Dr. Kellersberger in 1954,
when a year's series of church giving envelopes featured him
on the Sunday, January 10th envelope. Printed beside a
sketch of him, portraying him as the traditionally-helmeted
medical missionary, was the story of how his leprosy patients
named him DOCTOR-NOT-AFRAID-TO-TOUCH-US.

Almost simultaneously in February of 1957, two special
events celebrated Dr. Kellersberger most significantly. On the
20th in St. Louis, Missouri, at the 104th Anniversary of Washington University's Founders' Day, he was one of "twelve distinguished alumni selected to receive an Alumni Citation in
recognition of outstanding achievements and services reflect-
ing honor on the University." Chancellor Ethan A. H. Shep-
ley read the citation:

> Because of his contribution to the spiritual and social
> advancement of mankind while serving for 25 years as a
> medical missionary of the Presbyterian Church in the Bel-
> gian Congo, because of his effective leadership in the world-
> wide fight against leprosy, because of his creation of the
> basic textbook for the study of sleeping sickness, and be-
> cause of his inspirational and enlightening articles and

books on scientific, religious and medical subjects, this citation is awarded to Eugene Roland Kellersberger.

Baron Robert Silvercruys, the Belgian Ambassador to the United States, had already informed the doctor by telephone in January that his government was presenting him with yet a third medal of honor. In 1936 he had been made a *Chevalier de l'Ordre Royale du Lion*, followed by a *Chevalier de l'Ordre Royale de la Couronne*. Now he was to be made *Officier de l'Ordre Royale de la Couronne*. In a ceremony in Atlanta, Georgia, on February 25, 1957, Mr. Robert S. Sams, representing the Belgian Consulate, presented the doctor with the cross signifying that he was an *Officer of the Royal Order of the Crown*! New York, St. Louis, Texas, and Florida newspapers, among others, all carried articles reporting this honor on the following day.

Further recognition came to Dr. Kellersberger on June 9, 1958, when he was made an Honorary Emeritus Member of the American Society of Tropical Medicine and Hygiene.

Also, in 1958, in a letter to his personal physician, Dr. D. Lee Cady, he wrote: "My film on African Sleeping Sickness is now part of the Armed Forces Research Library in Washington, D.C. We helped lick sleeping sickness in Africa!"

He wrote in his diary on February 15, 1961: "If I had had the money, I would have flown to Austin, Texas, for our half-century class reunion. I didn't dream that they would choose me as 'the outstanding graduate of the Class of 1911!' I am very happy about it anyhow!"

In June of 1965, he went to St. Louis to attend the 50th reunion of his Washington University Medical School, Class of 1915. At the Alumni Day ceremonies he received a plaque for distinguished service for his contribution to medical science in the fields of leprosy and sleeping sickness.

The Fiftieth Anniversary Issue of the Medical Center Alumni Office contains a complete record of all of Dr. Kellersberger's professional achievements. It lists his winning of the Gill Anatomy Prize at the end of his freshman year in medical school, and his membership on graduation in the honorary medical fraternity, *Alpha Omega Alpha*. His ordination as a Presbyterian minister, and his memberships in the American

Society of Tropical Medicine and Hygiene, the New York Society of Tropical Medicine, and the International Leprosy Association are cited. The three medals of honor awarded him by the Belgian government are acknowledged, as well as his numerous publications in medical, religious and secular journals. The King of Belgium also appointed him as the very first Protestant member of the Father Damien Leprosy Foundation.

Listed as outstanding contributions to general medical education are his years of administration of the Edna Kellersberger Memorial Hospital and his conducting from 1916 to 1940 a government-recognized, three-year medical course for training African medical personnel, with an average of eleven graduates a year.

Other accomplishments recognized are his preparation of more than 2,500 microscope slides of various tropical diseases, used in many different medical schools, his motion pictures and still-life slides researching the same, and his unique production of Chaulmoogra oil for use in treating leprosy.

His success in his field is also acclaimed by his 1957 Citation for Distinguished Service from his Alma Mater, and his United States Public Health Record. As a member of the United States Advisory Committee on Leprosy, he was an officially-appointed United States delegate to three World Leprosy Congresses: in Cairo, Egypt, in 1938, in Havana, Cuba, in 1948 and in Madrid, Spain, in 1953.

The Kellersberger Memorial Lecture is a major annual event at the All Africa Leprosy Rehabilitation Center in Addis Ababa, Ethiopia. The 1984 lecture was given by none other than the Chief Medical Officer of the Leprosy Division of Communicable Diseases, World Health Organizations, Geneva, Switzerland. Sponsored by the American Leprosy Missions as a living remembrance of Dr. Kellersberger, it is now recognized as the yearly international landmark in the field of leprosy research.

He was listed in the 1943 *International Who's Who* and ensuring issues, as well as in *The Directory of Directors, Who's Important in Religion, Who's Who in America* and *Who's Who in the Western Hemisphere.*

Like the proverbial "tip of the iceberg," these human achievements are only a small indication of the immensity lying hidden beneath the surface — all that God really enabled Eugene Kellersberger to do for His eternal purposes during the span of his lifetime.

THE DEATH OF A FISHERMAN

During the last years of his life the doctor became subject to epilepsy-like seizures. He began to experience what he termed "blackouts" while still living in New York. In letters to his personal physician, he frankly refers to his illness as *petit mal*, for his periods of unconsciousness were of short duration. In a letter to his brother, Arnold, dated July 16, 1959, he says, "My doctor advises me not to drive my car any more."

Noticeable changes in the 1964 and 1965 diaries portended Dr. Kellersberger's death. The usual, spirited entries become perfunctory and erratic. More and more frequently, a clipping or picture fills a page. In the 1965 volume, sometimes for three and four days in a row, there are no entries. Only during the "crucible years" of the 1920s, are there comparable gaps in the faithfully-kept records. More and more frequently, the statement is found: "Batching it alone 'for Christ's sake and the Gospel's.' Julia Lake is away on a speaking engagement." No longer was he able to accompany his popular wife, "the woman with 10,000 best friends." But he still had his beloved fishing to while away the hours and provide him with something to share — his famous frozen fish fillets.

Looking back over the last weeks of her husband's life, Julia Lake recognized signs of his awareness that his time was short:

> He seemed to have had an intuition that we would not be together much longer. Every night for the last few weeks before God called him, he wrote special love notes to me and left them on my pillow. He always kissed my pillow. Every night I found a slight dent there where his lips had been! Here are a few of the little love notes he wrote shortly before his death on January 28th:
>
> "Thank you, Dear Lord, for Home Sweet Home and my Best Beloved!"

Melbourne Beach, Florida, 1965, Dr. Kellersberger preparing for a leprosy slide presentation. The shelf above the doctor's head shows some thirty of the volumes of daily diaries that he started keeping in 1916. He is seated in what he called his "DOG HOUSE," his desk in one corner of his small <u>bathroom</u>!

"I 'luf' my special nurse! But I have to take care of YOU! Come and rest!

"Best Beloved, more than ever you are indispensable to your Boy Blue! I love you more than words can tell!"

"God sent you to me and to my family! You are the best this side of Heaven. ALL THIS AND HEAVEN, TOO!"

"I love you and I love everybody in the world and you know why!"

Winifred and her family were in the United States on home assignment at the time of Dr. Kellersberger's death. She was in Gainesville, Florida, studying Journalism at the University of Florida, preparing to train the editorial staff of the *Zairean* periodical for which she was responsible. The Vass family spent their 1965 Christmas holidays at "Happy Haven."

Christmas morning, his face glowing, the doctor handed his daughter a package. "It is something very special that came in yesterday's mail," he said. "I want you to take it back to Africa with you!" All family festivity waited while he animatedly described his tramps around the deck on the *Oranje,* and how he had had to "cast" three times, with three different kinds of "language baits," before he could "catch" the friend who had sent this gift. It was a beautiful Austrian nativity set from Rudolf Scherberl!

On January 9th, as he did every Sunday, Dr. Kellersberger recorded in his diary the sermon text and summarized the morning's message: "We are to be CHILDLIKE always, as a little child, but never childish, even into maturity." Of no one was this more true than the man who had listened to the last sermon he would ever hear in Eastminster Presbyterian Church.

On January 11th, he wrote: "Heavy, steady rains all night. Julia Lake gone to town. I walked in the rain but did no fishing. I have promised not to go alone when everyone is gone."

From January 18th to the 24th, Eugene and Julia Lake were in Gainesville with the Vass grandchildren, while their parents were away on a speaking assignment. Before returning home to Melbourne Beach on Monday, the 24th, Dr. Kellersberger insisted on visiting the Diagnostic Clinic of the University of Florida Medical Center.

The result of this brief visit and happy contacts with Dr. Swenson and Dr. Meleney was his promise to send them right away a supply of his teaching materials, for the use of the students of tropical medicine at the University of Florida Medical School. Arriving back home that evening, he immediately went to his office and began pulling out boxes and files. By the morning of the 27th, he had stacked up on the floor beside his desk a sizable collection of his microscope slides of malaria, sleeping sickness and leprosy, made in Congo. There was also a large pile of reprints of all his published articles and monographs on tropical diseases. No one but the doctor himself could have selected this teaching material. The slides later proved to be the very last that he had to give away.

One of the happiest phoned messages that Julia Lake received after the doctor's death was an excited call from Dr. Meleney, amazed at the exquisite professional workmanship displayed in those slides, now the proud possession of the medical school. He said that they were, without doubt, the most perfectly executed microscope work that he had ever seen.

The very last entry, made on January 27th, is a simple weather report: "Colder. Snow in the Florida panhandle. Near 40 degrees here."

This is Julia Lake Kellersberger's account of the death of a fisherman, both of fish and of men:

In the early morning of January 28th, from our devotional book, *Daily Light*, Eugene read to me: *Awake, O North Wind, blow upon my garden, that the spices thereof may flow out . . . No chastening for the present seemeth to be joyous, but grievous; nevertheless, afterward, it yieldeth the peaceable, fruit of righteousness unto them which are exercised thereby . . . Though our outward man perish, yet the inward man is renewed day by day. For our light affliction which is but for a moment, worketh for us a far more exceeding and eternal weight of glory.*

The North Wind blew that day. The outward man perished, and grievous chastening came.

On the Day of the North Wind, Eugene went fishing. I was in the house, my brother next door was away from home, and my cousin, Bill Varner, came to bring some fruit. Having put it in the garage, he walked to the river just as Eugene had a heart attack, as later medically diagnosed, and fell unconscious into the water. Fortunately, he was not far from shore. Bill plunged in after him, brought him to land, and called me. We dared not move him, but covered him with blankets. The icy water had brought him back to consciousness.

On the way to Melbourne in the ambulance, we drove into the most glorious sunset I have ever seen in our twelve years of living on the Indian River! I squeezed Eugene's hand and exclaimed, "What a sunset!" That unforgettable sunset will forever be exclusively mine, for within a few hours, it was SUNRISE for him. "Our life is immortal until our life's work is done."

Two wonderful doctors and efficient nurses did all they could to save him, but Eugene's noble life's work was ended and immortality was his.

The Associated Press news release of his death was printed in newspapers all over the United States and abroad. Thousands of letters of condolence came from literally every corner of the world, from the high and the mighty, the low and the unrecognized. People of every station of life, race, and many nations, including many with leprosy, had been personally touched for God by this man.

Dr. Kellersberger is buried in his beloved Texas Hill Country, in the Cypress Mill Cemetery, a family burial plot just across the country road from his birthplace and the site of the mill once owned by his forefathers. The burial service was held in the little Episcopal chapel near Johnson City, where the original millstone, which he used to watch turn, is part of the floor, and a wooden cross, fashioned by Carl Matern, his grandfather, is set into a window. His gravestone was quarried from the familiar landmark of his boyhood, Granite Mountain at Marble Falls. Cut into the rosy, polished surface are the words:

MORE THAN CONQUERORS THROUGH HIM THAT LOVED US

World Deaths

MELBOURNE BEACH, Fla., Jan. 29. — (AP) — Dr. Eugene R. Kellersberger, a retired physician widely known for his work on tropical diseases, died Friday night in Brevard Hospital. He was 77.

Earlier Friday he fell from a fishing boat near his Indian River home. He was pulled from the river by neighbors and taken to the hospital.

Born in Cypress Mills, Texas, he was former executive secretary of the American Leprosy Mission and for 25 years served as medical missionary from the Presbyterian Church in Central Africa. He was an ordained Presbyterian minister.

A graduate of Washington University Medical School, he was cited by the Belgian Colonial Government three times for his relief work on tropical diseases.

Bibliography

ARTICLES

Bosche, Edna. "The Master-Knot of Human Fate." *The Christian Observer,* 31 January 1906, Pp. 16–17.

Bucher, Henry H., Jr. "John Leighton Wilson and the Mpongwe: The Spirit of 1776 in Mid-Nineteenth Century Africa." *Journal of Presbyterian History* 54:3 (Fall 1976).

Everhart, William C. "St. Louis: Gateway to Westward Expansion." *National Geographic Magazine,* November 1965, pp. 643–669.

Hester, Bluford. "Copyrighting 'The Eyes of Texas.'" *The Alcalde,* April 1940, pp. 150, 167

Johnson, Lewis. "Planning 'The Eyes of Texas': A New Note on the Famous Song." *The Alcalde,* January 1933, pp. 74–79.

——. "Johnson Instigated University Song." *The Alcalde,* April 1940, pp. 150, 167.

——. " :The Eyes of Texas' Comes Homes." *The Alcalde,* January 1959, Cover p. 10

Kellersherger, E. R. "*Serving Christ in the Congo.*" *The Christian Observer,* 26 March 1924, p. 6.

——. "Inasmuch As." *The Christian Observer,* 7 August 1925.

——. "The Romance of an African Hospital." *The Christian Observer,* 24 March 1926, pp. 7–8.

——. "In the Footsteps of the Great Physician." *Congo Mission News,* 27 April 1927, pp. 16–17.

347

——. "Relationship of the Evangelistic Work to the Medical Work." *The Congo Mission News*, 27 April 1927, pp. 23–25.

——. "Africa and Modern Medicine." *Virginia Medical Monthly* 71 (April 1944): 173–175.

——. "African Trypanosomiasis: A Brief Clinical Study of African Sleeping Sickness." *Medical Clinics of North America* (May 1943). New York Number.

——. "Photographs Illustrating Sleeping Sickness and Surgical Conditions Found in the Lomami District, Congo Belge." *Transactions of the Royal Society of Tropical Medicine and Hygiene.* London, January 1928.

——. "St. Louis Physician Achieves Renown in Congo." *The Asklepion*, Quarterly Journal of the Phi Beta Pi-Theta Kappa Psi Medical Fraternity, Fall Issue, 1928, pp. 292–294.

——. "Tropical Diseases: They Include Appalling Human Afflictions." *Life*, 1 May 1944, p. 60–67.

——. "Report on 100 Cases Treated with Tryparsamide." *Annales de la Societe Belge de Medicine Tropicale*, VII:3 (December 1927): 1–19.

——. "From Bush to Palace." Address given at First World Leprosy Congress. *Egyptian Annals of Medicine*, 1938.

——. "Review of 9,000 Cases of Sleeping Sickness." *American Journal of Tropical Medicine* XIII:2 (March 1933): 211–241.

——. "Sleeping Sickness in a Child Three Months Old." *Transactions of the Royal Society of Tropical Medicine and Hygiene* XIX:1 and 2 (July 1925): 81–83.

——. "Lithopedian." *Time*, 8 September 1939. (This entry is found in the "Letters" section of the issue and refers to a calcified foetus successfully removed on May 11, 1939.)

——. "Interesting Excerpts of the Kellersberger Leprosy Paper." *The Alcalde*, May 1951, p. 215.

——. "Leprosy Today." *Clinics* II:4 (1943).

——. "The Social Stigma of Leprosy." *Annals of the New York Academy of Sciences* 54:Article 1 (March 1951): 126–133.

—— and Rule, William. "Sulfoxone Sodium (Diasone) in the Treatment of Leprosy: A Summary Analysis of Field Reports." *International Journal of Leprosy* 19:3 (July–September 1951).

Kellersberger, Julia Lake. "A Sabbath Morning at Bibanga Hospital." *The Congo Mission News*, October 1940, pp. 16–18.

——. "Astronauts of Inner Space." *The Presbyterian Journal*, 11 May 1983.

——. "Better Bibanga Babies." *The Presbyterian Survey*, August 1935, pp. 491–492.

——. "Come Sing Along With Me." *The Presbyterian Journal*, 5 January 1983.

——. "Look What I've Got!" *The Presbyterian Journal*, 2 August 1967.

Shields, P. E. "A History of the Moravian Seminary for Young Ladies, Hope, Indiana." *Transactions of the Moravian Historical Society* X:Pts. II and IV (1917); 11–229.

Roberts, John Storm. "A Continent of Music." *Africa Report* 23:5 (September–October 1978): 45–49.

Studer, Jack J. "Julius Kellersberger: A Swiss Surveyor and City Planner in California, 1851–1857." *California Historical Society Quarterly* (March 1968): 3–14.

——. "The First Map of Oakland, California: An Historical Speculation as Solution to an Enigma." *California Historical Society Quarterly* (March 1969): 59–71.

Weaver, Esther Richter. "Adolf Fuchs — Pastor, Poet and Pioneer." *The Highlander* (Marble Falls, Texas, Hill Country History), 10 February 1972, pp. 2–3.

BOOKS

Acheson, Sam. *35,000 Days in Texas: A History of the Dallas News and Its Forbears.* Westport, Conn.: Greenwood Press, 1973.

American Presbyterian Congo Mission. *Minutes of Annual Mission Meeting: Lubondai, October 1–November 3, 1931.* Luebo, Congo Belge: J. Leighton Wilson Press, 1932.

Ayensu, Edward S., ed. *Jungles.* New York: Crown, 1980.

Biesele, Rudolf Leopold. *The History of the German Settlements in Texas: 1831–1861.* Austin, Texas: University of Texas, 1930.

Blickensderfer, Jacob. *History of the Blickensderfer Family in America.* Lebanon, Missouri: n.p., n.d.

Bliven, Bruce. *The Wonderful Writing Machine.* New York: Random House, 1953.

Carley, Kenneth. *The Sioux Uprising of 1862.* St. Paul, Minnesota: Minnesota Historical Society, 1976.

Coe, Edith C. *The Hertzler Heritage.* Emporia, Kansas: Irene A. Koeneke and the Hertzler Research Foundation, Emporia State Press, 1975.

Currie, Thomas White, Jr. *Austin Presbyterian Theological Seminary: A Seventy-Fifth Anniversary History.* San Antonio, Texas: Trinity University Press, 1978.

Dabney, Mary. *Light in Darkness.* (Life of Robert Dabney Bedinger). Knoxville, Tennessee: Privately printed, 301 Smokey View Road, 1971.

De Armond, Frederick. *The Laundry Industry.* New York: Harper and Brothers, 1950.

De Remer, Bernard R. *Moody Bible Institute: A Pictorial History.* Chicago: Moody Press, 1960.

The Directory of Directors. New York: 461 8th Avenue, n.d.

Du Bose, Hampden C. *Memoirs of Rev. John Leighton Wilson, D.D., Missionary to Africa and Secretary of Foreign Missions.* Richmond, Virginia: Presbyterian Committee of Publication, 1895.

Early, Eleanor. *And This is Cape Cod.* Boston: Houghton, Mifflin Co., 1936.

Ellis, William T. *Billy Sunday: The Man and His Message.* Chicago: Moody Press, 1959.

Forbath, Peter. *The River Congo: The Discovery, Exploration and Exploitation of the World's Most Dramatic River.* New York: Harper and Row, 1977.

Fries, Adelaide L., and Pfohl, J. Kenneth. *The Moravian Church Yesterday and Today.* Raleigh, North Carolina: Edwards and Broughton Co., 1926.

Gilliam, Harold. *San Francisco Bay.* Garden City, NY: Doubleday and Co., 1957.

Goeth, Ottilie Fuchs. *Memoirs of a Texas Pioneer Grandmother: 1805–1915* (Was Grosmutter Erzaehlt). Translated from the German by Irma Goeth Guenther. Austin, Texas: Eakin Press, 1982.

Gunther, John. *Inside Africa.* New York: Harper and Brothers, 1955.

Hamilton, Kenneth G. *Church Street in Old Bethlehem: An Historical Pamphlet Published in the Interest of the Bi-Centennial Celebration of the Founding of the Moravian Congregation of Bethlehem, Pennsylvania.* 1942.

Hansen, Harry, ed. *A Guide to the Lone Star State.* New York, Hastings House, 1960.

Hertzler, Arthur E. *The Horse and Buggy Doctor.* Garden City, NY: Blue Ribbon Books, 1941.

Herrl, George. *The Carl P. Dietz Collection of Typewriters.* Publications in History, No. 7. Milwaukee Public Museum, 1965.

International Who's Who. 1935 and ensuing issues. London: Europa Publications, Ltd.

Jackson, John. *In Leper-Land.* London: Marshall Brothers, n.d.

——. *Mary Reed, Missionary to Lepers.* London: Marshall Brothers, 1899.

Jordan, Terry G. *German Seed in Texas Soil: Immigrant Farmers in Nineteenth-Century Texas.* Austin: University of Texas Press, 1966.

Kellersberger, E. R. Chapter III, "Trypanosomiasis," Volume 1, Diseases Due to Protozoa; *Stitts Diagnosis, Prevention and Treatment of Tropical Diseases.* 6th Edition, Edited by Richard P. Strong, Blakiston.

Kellersberger, G. *Memoirs of an Engineer in the Confederate Army in Texas: 1861–1865* (Erlebnisse eines Schweizenschen Ingenieur in Californien, Mexico, Texas, zer Zeit des Buerger-Krieges: 1861–1865). Zurich, Schweiz, 1896. Translated into English and privately printed by Helen Schroeter Sundstrom in 1955.

Kellersberger, Julia Lake. *Betty: A Life of Wrought Gold.* Richmond, Virginia: John Knox Press, 1943.

——. *Congo Crosses: A Study of Congo Womanhood.* Boston: Central Committee on the United Study of Foreign Missions, 1936.

——. *God's Ravens: A Story of Life and Work in the Belgian Congo.* New York: Fleming H. Revell, 1941.

——. *A Life for the Congo: The Story of Althea Brown Edmiston.* New York: Fleming H. Revell, 1947.

——. *Morning Glories.* Clinton, South Carolina: Jacobs Brothers, Thornwell Orphanage, 1962.

——. *Rooted in Florida Soil.* Volume 1 in the Local History Series, Kellersberger Fund of South Brevard Historical Society. Melbourne, Florida: Florida Institute of Technology Press, 1971.

——. *The Salt Baby.* New York: Fleming H. Revell, 1945.

—— and Kellersberger, Eugene. *Doctor of the Happy Landings.* Richmond, Virginia: John Knox Press, 1949.

Lebacq, L., and Geeraerts, P. *Le Commerce des Bois Tropicaux dans le Cadre du Marche Commun.* Tervuren, Belgique: Documentation Economique No. 1, Edition 1962.

Longenecker, J. Hershey. *Memories of Congo.* Johnson City, Tennessee: Royal Publishers, 1964.

McKelvey, John J., Jr. *Man Against Tsetse: Struggle for Africa.* Ithaca, New York: Cornell University Press, 1973.

McKinnon, Arch C. *Kapitene of the Congo Steamship "Lapsley"* and McKinnon, Fannie W. *Treasures of Darkness.* Boston: The Christopher Publishing House, 1968.

Maxtone-Graham, John. *The Only Way to Cross.* New York: Collier Books, 1973.

Mead, Frank S. *Handbook of Denominations in the United States, Their History, Doctrines, Organizations, Present Status.* New York: Abingdon-Cokesbury, 1951.

Miller, A. Donald. *All My Mountains.* London: The Mission to Lepers, 7 Bloomsbury Square, n.d.

Moody Bible Institute of Chicago. *Catalogue of.* Founded in 1896 by D. L. Moody. Chicago: 1909 edition.

Moravian Church in America. *The Five Hundredth Anniversary Celebration of the Moravian Church, UNITAS FRATRUM, 1457–1957.* Bethlehem, Pennsylvania, Winston-Salem, North Carolina: Interprovincial Board of Christian Education for the Quincentennial Committee, n.d.

Penick, D. A. *Fifty Years of Student Work at the University Presbyterian Church: Austin, Texas, 1899–1949.* Mimeographed brochure. Compiled by Daniel A. Penick, Edited by DeWitt C. Reddick, n.p., n.d.

Presbyterian Church in the United States. *Report of the General Assembly in Session at Charlottesville, Virginia, May 22, 1930.* pp. 6–11.

——. *Jubilee Report of the Executive Committee of Foreign Missions, 1861–1936.* Nashville, Tennessee: Executive Committee of Foreign Missions, 1936. pp. 6, 7, 59.

Sauceau, Elaine. *Henry, The Navigator: The Story of a Great Prince and His Times.* New York: W. W. Norton and Company, 1947.

Schattscheider, Allen W. *Through Five Hundred Years: A Popular History of The Moravian Church.* Bethlehem, Pennsylvania, Comenius Press, Moravian Church of America, 1956.

Scherer, James A. B. *The Lion of the Vigilantes: William T. Coleman and the Life of Old San Francisco.* New York: The Bobbs-Merrill Company, 1939.

Schnelle, Annie. *Yesterdays: Memoirs of Annie Kellersberger Schnelle.* Privately-printed, 1974.

Shaloff, Stanley. *Reform in Leopold's Congo.* Richmond, Virginia: John Knox Press, 1970.

Stringer, Harry Roy. *The Navybook of Distinguished Service.* Washington, D.C.: Fasset Publications, 1921.

Student Volunteer Movement for Foreign Missions. *Students and the Present Missionary Crisis*. Address delivered before the Sixth International Convention of the Student Volunteer Movement for Foreign Missions, Rochester, New York, December 29 to January 2, 1910. New York: 1910.

Tourist Bureau for the Belgian Congo and Ruanda-Urundi. *Travelers' Guide to the Belgian Congo and Ruanda-Urundi*. 2nd Edition. Brussels, Belgium: IIIrd Directorate, Information and Public Relations Bureau, 1956.

U.S., Department of Agriculture. *Properties of Imported Tropical Woods*. Forest Service Research Paper FPL 125. Madison, Wisconsin: Forest Products Laboratory, March 1970.

U.S., Department of the Navy. *Dictionary of American Naval Fighting Ships*. Vol. VI. Washington, D.C., 1976. pp. 744–745.

United States Naval Academy. *Register of Alumni, 1844–1977*. Class of 1887. p. 27.

Who's Important in Religion. New York: Institute for Research in Biography, 296 Broadway, n.d.

Who's Who in America. 1943 and ensuing issues. Chicago, Illinois: A. N. Marquis Company.

Who's Who in the East, 1943 and ensuing issues. Chicago: A. N. Marquis Company.

Who's Who in the Western Hemisphere. New York: 315 5th Avenue, n.d.

Wills, Mary Motz and Irwin, Howard S. *Roadside Flowers of Texas*, Austin: University of Texas Press, 1969.

Zaire: A Country Study. Third Edition. Washington, D.C.: Foreign Area Studies, Superintendent of Documents, 1979.

INDEX

354

355

356

359

132, 172

Savels, Reverend and Mrs. Joseph, 171–172, 203

Saxonia, R.M.S., 162, 178–179

Scheberl, Rudolf, 337–338, 343

Schiefflin Leprosy Research Center, Karigiri, India, 287, 295

Schiefflin, William Jay, 279

Schloss Stein, 1, 162–163

Schnelle, Annie Kellersberger, 22, 26–28, 33, 35

Schnelle, Julia Kellersberger, 33, 35

Schoenbrunn, Ohio, 60

Schroeter, Ulrika Kellersberger, 25, 42

Schulenberg, Texas, 10

Schweitzer, Dr. Albert, 281

Scudder, Dr. Ida, 328

Sheppard, Reverend William H., 107

Sharon, Ohio, 62

Shiyanga, Tanganyika, 308

Silvercrys, Baron Robert, 339

Sims, Dr., (A.B.C.M.), 100

Sioux Uprising of 1862, 46–48

Skinner, Cornelia Otis, 226

Skinner, James Lister, 317

Skinner, Judge James Lister, 226

Skinner, Olin Conway, 251, 253, 317

Skinner, Otis, 226

Slaymaker, Reverend Henry, 69, 103–105

Smith, Dr. Egbert, 189–190

Smithsonian Institute, 12, 331

Solms-Braunfels, Prince Carl of, 12, 15, 16

"Song After Sorrow," 267, 290, 291, 333

Sonntag, Dr. August, 6

Southall, Reverend T. B., 56

Southampton, England, 150, 158, 160, 192

Southern Cross, 194, 277, 314, 329

Spanish American War, 64–66, 74

Spitters, Neil, 331, 336

Stanley, Henry Morton, 98–102

Stanley Pool (Malebo), 98, 102, 147

Steinwarder, Bark, 3, 4

Stixrud, Dr. and Mrs. T. T., 189, 203

Stocker, Rear Admiral Robert, 48, 64–68

Stonelake, Reverend and Mrs. Alfred, 231

Stuart, Dr. J. Leighton, 320

Sturton, Dr., (C.M.S.), 321

Sudan Interior Mission, 306

Sulfone, (See DDS)

Sunday, Evangelist Billy, 91, 330

Sutter's Mill, California, 4, 7

Swedish Free Mission, 308

Swiss Consulate, San Francisco, 3, 4

Swiss Genealogical Almanach, 1

Switzerland, 1–3, 9–10, 162–164, 188, 337

T

Tacitus, 1

Tehuantepec, 6

Texas Hill Country, 13–21, 132, 303, 345

Thailand, 323–325

Thirty Years War, 57–58

Thysville, Compagnie Maritime Belge, 149, 217, 231, 254

Tiger Mill, Texas, 17–20

Torrey, Dr. R. A., 73

Tshofa, Zaire, 137

Trans-Mississippi Confederate Troops, 8

Trypanosomiasis (African Sleeping Sickness), 115, 152–188, 189, 191–193, 195–197, 200–201, 241–245, 292, 339, 344

Tryparsamide, 166, 184, 243

Tshiala Falls, 146–147

Tshiluba, Bantu Vernacular, 94, 102, 106

Tubman High School, Augusta, Georgia, 227

Tuscawaras Valley, Ohio, 60–63

361

U

Underhill, Swedish Baptist Mission, 100, 254
Union Minière, 193
Unitas Fratrum, 57
United States Advisory Committee on Leprosy, 305, 340
United States Department of Health, 291–292, 340
United States Service Journal, The, 96
University of Florida Medical School, 343–344
University of London School of Oriental and African Studies, 96–97
University of Texas, The, 41, 50–53, 70–72, 76–80, 268, 336
University Presbyterian Church, Austin, Texas, 55, 56
Upper Missouri Presbytery, 223

V

Vadathorasalur, India, 328
Valparaiso, Chile, 3, 4
Vandervelde, Emile, 108
Vass, Reverend Lachlan C., Jr., 104–105
Vass, Reverend and Mrs. Lachlan C., III, 275
Vellore Christian Medical College, 282, 328
Vera Cruz, Mexico, 8, 9
Veramendi, Spanish Governor, 15
Victoria Falls, 133, 192
Vigilantes Committee, 6
Vineyard Sound, 83, 85
Vinson, Reverend and Mrs. Chalmers, 92–106, 108, 150, 203
Volke, Dr., 193–196, 234

W

Wachovia Moravian, The, 74
Walmer Castle, Union Castle Line, 191, 194–195
Washington College, Washington, D.C., 64–70
Washington University School of Medicine, 80–82, 87, 253, 277, 313, 338–341
Wegmann and Company, Baden, 10, 163
Weiner-Neustadt, Austria, 3
Weiss, George A., 64
Wembo Nyama, Chief, 141
Wembo Nyama, M.E.C.M. Station, 137, 140–141
Wenyon, Dr., 184, 201
West Avenue, Austin, Texas, 53–55
West China Union University, 322–324
Westminster Presbyterian Church, St. Louis, 87–88, 250–251
Wettingen, Cistercian Cloister of, 10, 163
Whitis Academy, Austin, Texas, 38–42, 70
Wilson, Reverend and Mrs. H., Plymouth Brethren, 117–118
Wilson, Dr. John Leighton, 96–97, 107
Wilson, President Woodrow, 96
Wood, Dr. Leonard, 317
Woods Hole, Massachusetts, 80, 83–87, 125, 301
Woolf, General James, 225
World Leprosy Congresses, 267–271, 340
Wyclif, John, 57

Y

Yang, Dr. S. T., 319–322
Yser, SONATRA, 232–233

Z

Zaire River, 97–105, 166–167
Zambezi River, 133
Zeisberger, David, 60
Zink, Nicholas, 15
Zinzendorf, Count Nicholas von, 58, 60
Zug, Switzerland, 58
Zurich, Switzerland, 162–164, 188

362